The
Cheese Lover's Cookbook
and Guide

Over 150 Recipes

with Instruction on How to Buy, Store,

and Serve All Your Favorite Cheeses

Paula Lambert

New York   London   Toronto   Sydney   Singapore

To Mother and Jim

SIMON & SCHUSTER
Rockefeller Center
1230 Avenue of the Americas
New York, NY 10020

SIMON & SCHUSTER and colophon are registered trademarks
of Simon & Schuster, Inc.

Designed by Richard Oriolo

Manufactured in the United States of America

10   9   8   7   6   5   4   3

Library of Congress Cataloging-in-Publication Data
    Lambert, Paula, date.
        The cheese lover's cookbook and guide : over 150 recipes,
    with instruction on how to buy, store, and serve all your
    favorite cheeses / Paula Lambert.
            p.   cm.
    Includes bibliographical references and index.
    1. Cookery (Cheese)   2. Cheese.   I. Title.
    TX759.5.C48 L36 2000
    641.6'73—dc21   00-058797

ISBN 0-684-86318-9

Contents

Why My Book Is Like It Is

This book has an eclectic mix of recipes. Many are creative. I just love to experiment and come up with new and different things. Others you will recognize as classic recipes, changed slightly to modernize them. Overall, my goal was to try to reproduce the delicious flavors of meals I have served myself and have been served in restaurants or by friends, at home and abroad.

Many of the recipes are traditional ones, those you wouldn't think of making without cheese. Yet there are others where the addition of cheese may surprise you, making the dish even more flavorful than before. Overall, I hope that this cookbook will spur your own creativity—adding cheese to favorite recipes of your own or teaching you about cheeses you have never tried before. While some cheeses will be more suited to one dish than others, there are no hard-and-fast rules, and the only thing that matters is what tastes good to you.

As a reflection of my life and my experiences, this book has a multitude of influences. It is Southern; it is Italian; it is Southwestern; it is Mexican; it is international; and it is homey with a touch of sophistication. When I was growing up in Fort Worth in the 1950s, it was part of the Old South. My parents were both born in Fort Worth, my father in 1899. We were as Southern as you could get, and all our meals were Southern: corn bread, biscuits, fried chicken, you name it.

In the late 1960s and early 1970s, I spent five years in Perugia as a graduate student. Italian food had a tremendous effect on me; it was so fresh and pure. The flavors were clean and direct. I began to look at food in a completely new and different way. When I returned to Texas and soon thereafter founded the Mozzarella Company, I became friends with the young chefs nearby who were using indigenous Texas and Mexican ingredients to forge a new and modern regional cuisine. They influenced me profoundly, as have my other customers, creative chefs who practice their own particular cuisine all around the country.

A further influence has been my neighbors to the south. Mexican foods have always been very popular in Texas; after all, Mexico still owned Texas just a little more than a hundred and fifty years ago. But Mexico isn't the only other country that influences my palate. I love to travel. I love to go to new places and try new foods, and then I enjoy trying to re-create them at home.

Because, for all my love of travel, I most love cooking and entertaining at home. I want my guests to feel comfortable in my home, to relax and have a good time. My favorite thing of all is to spend all day Saturday shopping and cooking for a dinner party. Inevitably I bite off more than I can chew and am seldom ready when my guests arrive, but I have understanding and cooperative friends who pitch in to help. We all have a great time, and I hope you will too.

P. L.

The Story of the Mozzarella Company

I founded the Mozzarella Company because I couldn't find fresh mozzarella in Dallas. It was as innocent as that. My goal was quite clear—I wanted to make mozzarella and tomato salad, a simple dish I'd had while living in Italy.

My dream began at Christmastime in 1981, when my husband, Jim, and I went to Italy to visit friends. Knowing my love of cheese, our Italian friends Suzanne and Enrico Bartolucci served fresh mozzarella for lunch on the day we arrived. It was there, in the Bartolucci's kitchen, that a lightbulb went on. I knew the fresh mozzarella that I loved wasn't available in Dallas. I thought, I'll create a company and make mozzarella in Dallas. Just like Mickey Rooney and Judy Garland putting on a play in a barn.

That afternoon, we all went down to the local cheese factory, and I asked the owner, Mauro Brufani, if he would teach me to make mozzarella. Fortunately, he said yes. Once the Christmas holiday ended, Jim went back to Dallas, but I stayed on in Italy. I bought a pair of rubber boots and a little white cotton cheesemaker's hat, and I went to the small cheese factory at 6 o'clock sharp each morning to learn to make fresh mozzarella. I was fascinated by the ability to start with fresh milk in the morning and have mozzarella made and ready to sell the same afternoon. Before leaving Italy, I arranged for a young Italian cheese professor to travel to Dallas, to help me refine the art of mozzarella making and instruct me on how to meet U.S. requirements once I had built my cheese factory.

Back in Dallas, I began to assemble enough information to initiate the project in earnest. I called cheese-equipment manufacturers in Wisconsin, talked to the FDA in Washington, searched for a location, and scoured the countryside for a raw milk supply. Things got easier when I found a wonderful dairy-equipment salesman, Rodney Lockhart, in nearby Fort Worth. Approaching retirement, Rodney had been involved in the dairy industry all his life. He was enchanted with my plans and soon became my major cheerleader and invaluable consultant. Along the way, I persuaded two friends to become my partners, Suzanne Bartolucci and Carole Jordan.

Despite daunting challenges, I succeeded in renovating a small vacant corner drugstore in an old warehouse district near downtown Dallas into a tiny cheese factory, just in time for the arrival of Giovanni Marchesi, the Italian cheese professor. I bought raw milk and we made fresh mozzarella the day after he arrived. We practiced day after day to perfect our cheese. Once the difficulties were worked out and I had a consistent product, I began to call shops around Dallas to tell them of my great new product—fresh mozzarella cheese.

At long last, I had delicious, moist fresh mozzarella for my favorite salad, and so would all of Dallas. My partners and I invited all our friends to see our cheese factory at an opening party. We served mozzarella and tomato salad and lasagne made with our cheese. Soon our new cheese was featured in newspaper and television stories. It was all very exciting and great fun.

As the years have passed, many new cheeses have been added to the Mozzarella Company's repertoire. I have traveled to various countries to learn their traditional cheesemaking techniques and returned home to create my own versions of these cheeses from cow's milk and goat milk. Today, the Mozzarella Company produces more than twenty kinds of cheese, many of which reflect the flavors of Texas and the Southwest. The cheeses are sold to restaurants and fine hotels across the country, as well as to gourmet and specialty food stores. Our cheeses are also available individually and in gift baskets by mail-order directly from the factory.

In retrospect, the Mozzarella Company has turned out to be more like Lucille Ball's chocolate candy factory—we are making cheese as fast as we can and shipping it out the door as soon as it's made. It's fast and crazy and lots of fun.

Mozzarella Company Cheeses

Fresh Mozzarella—including Bocconcini, Mozzarella Rolls, Burrata, Smoked Mozzarella, and Capriella (goat milk mozzarella)

Smoked Scamorza

Caciotta—including Traditional, Ancho Chile, Texas Basil, Black Pepper with Garlic, and other flavors

Crescenza

Fresh Cream Cheese

Fromage Blanc—cow's milk and goat milk

Feta—cow's milk and goat milk

Ricotta—cow's milk and goat milk

Taleggio

Crème Fraîche

Mascarpone and Mascarpone Tortas

Triple-Crème Cheese

Queso Blanco and Queso Fresco

Queso Oaxaca

Fresh Texas Goat Cheese—including plain, herbed, and wrapped in hoja santa leaves

Goat Milk Caciotta—including Traditional, Ancho Chile, and Mexican Marigold Mint

Montasio and Montasio Festivo

Sweet Cream Butter

Introduction

What Is Cheese?

CHEESE IS CONCENTRATED MILK. CHEESE is milk in a form that can be consumed immediately or preserved. It is made by coagulating milk with enzymes or acid and then draining away the resultant liquid, leaving the solids, or curds. The curds are then pressed together to form cheese. It's an amazing process. As Clifton Fadiman once said, cheese is truly "milk's leap to immortality."

Milk is mostly water. In fact, one gallon of milk, which weighs almost nine pounds, generally yields less than one pound of cheese. When cheese is made, milk is coagulated and the excess water is drained away in the form of whey. The solids in the milk become the curds that contain all the proteins and fats from the milk. Cheese is a concentrated source of milk's nutrients, including calcium, phosphorus, and magnesium, as well as vitamins and trace elements.

All cheese is made from milk. That is the commonality of cheese. I've always considered that cheese, like music, is a variation on a theme. The milk can come from any number of animals, even yaks, mares, and reindeer. Most cheese, however, is made from the milk of cows, goats, or sheep, and the particular milk influences the characteristics of the cheese. Even the breed of the cow or goat is a factor in the flavor of the milk and, eventually, the cheese. Milk is flavored by the grasses the animal eats, as well the locality, climate, topography, and even the season of the year. All are reflected in the cheese. Whether or not the milk is pasteurized also affects the cheese, as do all of the following factors: the temperature the milk is heated to; various bacteria and cultures that may be added; the size the curds are cut; how much the curds are stirred; whether or not the curds are washed; how much they are heated, if at all; the molds the curds are drained in (whether large or small, round or square); whether the curds are pressed or left to drain naturally; whether or not the exterior of the cheese is sprayed with mold spores; and whether or not the cheese is washed with whey or brine or coated with wax or wrapped in cloth. All of these factors, as well as countless others, determine the final cheese; innumerable variations can be made, and each will change the cheese in some distinguishable way. The choices are endless, and so are the varieties of cheese that exist around the world. And each begins with milk. It's just amazing!

Some cheeses are meant be consumed fresh, as soon after they are made as possible. Others, like wine, are meant to be matured or ripened to develop a richness of flavor and texture. Some cheeses are best served on their own, while others can make the most mundane recipe stellar.

The New Popularity of Cheese

Since the years following World War II, when Americans began to travel extensively overseas, an interest in foods of high quality and greater diversity has fueled the growth of the specialty food industry. Cheese is an important part of this industry. Until recent years, most cheeses in the United States were industrially manufactured in gigantic factories. Designed primarily to survive transportation across the country and months of storage in warehouses, they had little taste. They had no heart or soul. But, not too long ago, things began to change.

In recent years, there has been a renaissance of high-quality cheesemaking across the United States. Hand-crafted specialty cheeses are making their way to the marketplace in ever-increasing amounts. The public now wants new varieties of cheese, and people want cheeses that have flavor.

The number of specialty and artisanal cheesemakers has grown by leaps and bounds since the early 1980s, when there was only a handful. There are now more than two hundred small independent cheesemakers across the country. Some are farmstead cheesemakers, producing cheese exclusively from the milk of their own herds. Others are artisanal cheesemakers, producing handmade cheeses in limited quantities. Add to that the number of specialty cheesemakers who produce high-quality cheeses in somewhat larger quantities, and the number is even greater. A wide array of specialty and artisanal cheeses is now available in cities and towns across the country. Even supermarkets carry a greatly expanded selection of cheeses, and, in recent years, there has been enormous improvement in the range of offerings.

Many books have been written in the past few years detailing cheeses, their characteristics, and origins. Every time you pick up a magazine or newspaper, there seems to be an article about cheese. There are hundreds of sites on the Internet with information about cheese. New cheese shops are springing up across the country. And restaurants are using more and more cheese, in cooking as well as in cheese courses. At her restaurant Campanile in Los Angeles, Nancy Silverton sets aside one evening each month as "Grilled Cheese Sandwich Night." Her ever-changing creations use the finest cheeses from around the world, melted on crunchy hearth-baked breads from her well-known La Brea Bakery, with swanky accompaniments such as prosciutto di Parma from Italy, chutneys from England, and olives from France.

The pendulum is swinging back. The fear of fat is on the decline, and finally the public is coming to realize that fresh natural foods are healthy and that no food groups should be left out of the diet. Throughout the years, Julia Child has always been an advocate of everything in moderation—from fat to wine. Now, young and old alike, people are learning that all things are good in moderation. As nutritionists emphasize that the body needs a reasonable amount of fat to live, they are coming to realize that butter is better than margarine and that cheese is wholesome and healthy as well. Suddenly, cheese has become an *in* food.

A Little Cheese History

We really don't know when or where cheese actually originated, but archaeological surveys indicate that cheese was being made from both cow's and goat's milk in the area located between the Tigris and Euphrates Rivers that is now Iraq between 7000 and 6000 B.C. We also know that nomads had domesticated sheep and goats by 5000 B.C.

Most likely the first cheeses were made by souring, or "clabbering," milk and then draining the whey from the curds in baskets. It is also likely that some ancient traveler discovered, upon carrying milk across the desert in a bag made from a sheep or goat's stomach, that it became another substance altogether—cheese. As the milk heated in the sun, the rennet in the stomach lining of the bag caused the milk to coagulate, and the bouncing up and down as he rode caused the curds and whey to separate. Later that evening, the traveler no doubt found that the whey quenched his thirst and the curds satisfied his hunger. Voilà: Another cheesemaking method was born.

About twenty different types of cheese are described in ancient Sumerian writings from 3000 B.C. Archaeologically, the oldest known cheese was found in an earthenware pot in the Egyptian tomb of King Horaha, dating back to 2300 B.C. Amazingly, the cheese had been stored in a pot of the same type that is still used today to separate the curds for the soft Egyptian cheese called *mish*.

As years passed, cheese was made from the milk of goats, sheep, cows, mares, water buffalos, and yaks in many different regions of the world. Travelers from Asia are thought to have brought the art of cheesemaking to Europe. During Roman and Greek times, cheese was popular in the more southern countries, where milk would have spoiled quickly because of the hot climate, while butter and milk were more important components of the diet in northern European and Asian countries. Cheese is even mentioned in *The Iliad* and *The Odyssey*.

It was not until the time of the Roman Empire that cheese-ripening processes were perfected. Cheese made with skill and high standards, with various flavors and characteristics, was served on the tables of the nobility. Larger houses even had separate cheese kitchens, called caseale. Roman soldiers received rations of cheese as an integral part of their diet. As the Empire expanded, cheesemaking was introduced to the conquered regions. Soon a cheese trade flourished, and cheeses were brought back to Rome from Switzerland, France, and England, as well as other parts of the Empire.

Many of the cheeses that are still popular today originated as many as two thousand years ago in Europe. Pliny, the great naturalist historian, mentioned Sbrinz and Bleu d'Auvergne in his writings, and Charlemagne is said to have enjoyed Brie and Roquefort in the ninth century A.D. Gorgonzola can be traced back to 879 in the Po region of Italy; Roquefort is mentioned in monastery records that date to 1070; and in the fourteenth century, Boccaccio wrote of Parmigiano in his *Decameron*. During the Middle Ages, religious communities developed many cheeses that became an important part of their diets, among them Pont l'Evêque and Munster. Gruyère is said to have been made in Switzerland as early as the twelfth century, when the age and quantity of cheese in the family cellar was an indication of prosperity. Cheese was even used as currency in Switzerland and in Scandinavia. Cheddar, Stilton, and Cheshire were well known in England by the seventeenth and eighteenth centuries and were regularly shipped abroad.

During the Middle Ages, cheesemaking thrived on large estates and in monasteries, and its secrets were passed from generation to generation. As the years passed, the northern European countries became known for their harder aged cheeses, while softer cheeses with moldy or washed rinds were characteristic of France. The origins of many cheeses we enjoy today date back centuries.

In Europe, there are laws dictating that many traditional regional cheeses must be made in specific geographic regions, using specific milks and according to specific techniques. In France, this system is known as *appellation d'origine contrôlée*, which is similar to the rules controlling wine production. The same holds true for several Italian cheeses such as Parmigiano-Reggiano. The names of some cheeses, like Stilton, have even been copyrighted and have their own certification trademark. Cheese is serious business!

From the Middle Ages until the eighteenth century, much of the dairying and cheesemaking in Europe was done by women, at home and by hand. Europeans brought these traditions to the Americas in the seventeenth century. In fact, cheese was among the supplies when the Pilgrims sailed on the Mayflower in 1620. Other European emigrations resulted in the development of cheesemaking in countries from Australia and New Zealand to South Africa, because the Europeans missed their cheeses from home.

The first American cheese factory was established in the state of New York in 1850, and by 1865 there were at least five hundred cheese and butter plants in that state alone. The United States was fast on its way to becoming a cheese capital. During this period, the largest cheese market in the world was located in Little Falls, New York, where cheeses from more than two hundred factories were sold. Population expansion in the East, however, soon forced dairy farms to move westward. By the beginning of the twentieth century, Wisconsin had become the center for dairying and cheesemaking in the United States.

Originally cheese was made with natural airborne bacteria working together with the natural bacteria in the raw milk. In these early years, cheesemaking was considered an art. Accidental modifications or changes resulted in the development of different cheeses. Pasteurization, introduced in the 1850s, allowed large-scale cheese production to advance, as did economic and industrial advances in the later years of the ninteenth century. As scientific knowledge increased, cheesemaking began to move from being an art to a science, so a more uniform product could be produced. By the beginning of the twentieth century, bacterial cultures had been developed for cheesemaking. Transportation and distribution advances were also factors in increased cheese production. Today the United States is the largest producer of cheese in the world, with Cheddar and Cheddar-based cheeses accounting for the major portion of all the cheeses produced.

While cheese was a very regional product in the past, today cheese knows few national boundaries. Cheddar and Gouda are made in South Africa, Brie is made in Wisconsin, and buffalo mozzarella is produced in Venezuela. Most of the world's cheeses are produced in gigantic factories in North America, Europe, South America, Australia, and New Zealand. Although the majority of European cheeses available in markets in the United States are made in large-scale factories, special regional and handcrafted cheeses are imported on a small scale and sold in specialty stores across the country.

In recent years, we have seen a resurgence of small-scale and farmhouse cheesemaking operations in the United States. It began with the "back to nature" movement of the 1960s and 1970s. By the late 1970s and early 1980s, a handful of specialty cheesemaking operations had begun to flourish. In the 1980s, European cheese plants established branches in the United States. Because these American-made European-style cheeses were made on a larger scale and distributed more widely, they fueled the appreciation of specialty cheeses. The growth has been steady ever since, and standards of quality have risen dramatically.

Today there are hundreds of small-scale specialty cheese factories. They are located in nearly every state, as well as in Canada, England, Ireland, Argentina, Australia, and New Zealand. Most produce regional cheeses in limited quantities. Others distribute their specialty cheeses more widely. It's a cheese explosion!

I urge you to seek out locally produced artisanal cheeses wherever you live. One of the best places to begin your search is the American Cheese Society. Call them at 505-583-3783 for a cheese resource guide, or visit their website at www.cheesesociety.org.

How Cheese Is Made

Cheese is made by coagulating milk to form lactic curds. This can be done several ways: by letting milk sour and clabber, by adding bacterial cultures to the milk, or by adding an enzyme called rennet, which will speed up the coagulation. Milk can also be coagulated with extracts made from plants such as fig trees, cardoons, and thistles.

There are two basic types of cheese: unripened fresh cheeses and ripened aged cheeses that are cured and matured. Normally, aged cheeses are made with rennet (animal or vegetable) because the curd must be well coagulated in order to drain off the whey sufficiently.

The general cheesemaking process is as follows: The milk is warmed and bacterial cultures and a coagulant such as rennet are added. The milk then coagulates into one huge curd. Once firm, the curd is cut and stirred and the whey is drained away. The curds may or may not be heated and cooked, depending on the type of cheese being made. Finally, the curds are placed in molds to shape the finished cheese; the cheese may or may not be pressed. Then it is salted, and, if it is to be an aged cheese, allowed to mature.

There are minute variations at each step involving timing, temperature, stirring, draining, molding, and ripening that will determine the particular characteristics of the individual cheese. The finished cheese is affected by the type and quality of milk used, as well as by whether or not the milk is pasteurized. Microorganisms resident in each cheesemaking facility also influence the final cheese. Cheddar made in one plant day after day will never taste like that made across the road in another plant.

Cheesemaking is an art. It involves balance as well as technique. It is a dance. It is a symphony.

Cheese and Nutrition

Nutrients in Cheese

 **CHEESE IS VERY NUTRITIOUS. IT** contains almost all the protein and other nutrients of milk, such as minerals and vitamins, in concentrated form. Included are three major minerals that are important for our proper skeletal, cellular, and biochemical functioning: calcium, phosphorus, and magnesium. Cheeses are also excellent sources of complete protein and riboflavin, as well as vitamins A and D. The value of any nutrient depends on how well the body absorbs and uses it, and the nutrients derived from dairy products are particularly well absorbed by our bodies, much more readily than if taken as a supplement. This may be due to the particular combination of lactose and minerals present in milk products.

Despite their traditional images as wholesome foods, milk and dairy products have come under increasing scrutiny in recent years. While milk is still the drink of choice for children, many adults worry that the fat content of milk and dairy products may offset their benefits. However, the opposite is true: These benefits may outweigh any risks.

With phosphorus, calcium provides part of the "latticework" of bones. Bone formation starts with a protein matrix, followed by deposition of calcium, phosphate, and other additional minerals that add strength to the bone. About 99 percent of the calcium that our bodies absorb ends up in skeletal tissues, with a small portion as deposits in our teeth. The other 1 percent is taken up by soft tissues or remains a part of intracellular fluid. The science of nutrition has long accepted that calcium plays an important role in protecting the integrity of cell membrane permeability, and that it is important in the absorptive mechanism involving vitamin B_{12} in the small intestine. Calcium also plays a major role in a number of enzyme systems, including those necessary for muscle irritability or excitability (the ability of a muscle to receive and respond to a stimulus), normal nerve transmission, blood clotting factors, and glucose metabolism. And calcium is essential for preventing osteoporosis, the bone-thinning disease that affects some twenty million American women.

Health professionals agree that too many Americans (nine out of ten women) are not getting the calcium they need to help build strong bones and prevent osteoporosis. New and alarming statistics were revealed at the 2000 National Institutes of Health (NIH) conference on Osteoporosis Prevention, Diagnosis, and Therapy. Researchers stated that a staggering twenty-eight millon women are at risk for fractures as a result of osteoporosis. They further stated that "increased calcium intake helps increase bone mineral density and decrease fracture risk." They advocated that "calcium intake should be increased through dietary measures if at all possibe," asserting that "dairy products are the best choice." The 1994 National Institutes of Health Consensus Development Conference on Optimal Calcium Intake recommended a higher calcium intake for most groups and said that the preferred sources of calcium are foods rich in calcium, such as dairy products.

While you don't hear as much about it as you do calcium, phosphorus is an important constituent of nucleic acids, or the genetic material we possess. It is necessary as a chemical part of phospholipids, which are integral to each cell. Our cells use a high-energy compound, adenosine triphosphate (ATP). Phosphorus is involved in energy transfer as a part of ATP and functions as a coenzyme in numerous chemical reactions. In addition, phosphates are part of the buffer system that maintains the acid-base balance in the body.

Magnesium also functions in the reaction that transfers phosphate to make ATP. As a result, magnesium is necessary for glucose metabolism; protein, fat, and nucleic acid synthesis; and membrane transport systems. There are an estimated three hundred-plus enzyme systems identified in the body that require magnesium. Approximately 40 percent of magnesium is stored in bone, and another 15 percent is stored in muscle and soft tissue.

The recommended dietary allowances (RDA) for calcium, revised in 1997 by the Food and Nutritional Board of the National Academy of Sciences, Institute of Medicine, are listed below.

Age Group	Adequate Daily Calcium Intake
Children 4 through 8 years	800 mg
Males and Females	
9 through 18 years	1300 mg
19 through 50 years	1000 mg
51 through 70 years	1200 mg
Women during Pregnancy and Lactation	
18 or younger	1300 mg
19 through 50 years	1000 mg

Jane Brody wrote in the *New York Times* that calcium is "fast emerging as the nutrient of the decade, a substance with such diverse roles in the body that virtually no major organ system escapes its influence." Not only for bones, but for cells, hormones, digestion, metabolism, blood clotting—you name it—calcium seems to have a role. Medical research is beginning to support some of the claims for the efficacy of the *super nutrient* calcium in treating or preventing a wide variety of health conditions.

A recent study conducted at Purdue University indicates that calcium may help keep the pounds off. Over a period of two years, researchers looked at the calcium intake of women aged eighteen through thirty-one. Women who consumed less than 1900 calories per day and had at least 780 milligrams of calcium either lowered or maintained their body fat. Those who consumed less than 1900 calories per day but got less than 780 milligrams of calcium gained body fat. Further, women who got their calcium directly from dairy products experienced greater weight benefits than those who used nondairy sources or supplements.

Numerous animal and human studies have been designed to investigate the importance of calcium in lowering blood pressure. Research from Harvard links a diet high in potassium, magnesium, and fiber with reduced risk of stroke, particularly for people with high blood pressure. The Harvard authors also noted that previous research has linked higher calcium intake with a decreased risk of stroke. Further research presented at the 1999 Federation of American Societies for Experimental Biology annual conference cited a study involving older adults. More than 70 percent of those with self-reported hypertension were not meeting the national recommendations for calcium and magnesium. Other researchers recently conducted a meta-analysis of forty-two randomized control trials that examined the effect of calcium on blood pressure. One conclusion they came to was that, again, calcium-rich foods may have a greater effect on lowering blood pressure than calcium supplements.

The results of a randomized double-blind clinical trial published in the *New England Journal of Medicine* indicate that calcium may also play a role in reducing colon cancer risk—the third leading cause of cancer deaths and new cancer cases in both men and women in the United States—and, in a study published in the *Journal of the American Medical Association,* Dr. Peter Holt presented findings consistent with these results. Holt found that the addition of low-fat dairy products such as milk, yogurt, and cheese to their diet significantly reversed precancerous changes in the colons of those individuals at high risk for colon cancer.

Animal research shows that certain compounds found naturally in milk, called sphingolipids, may significantly reduce colon cancer tumors. Other dietary components of milk, such as vitamin D, conjugated linoleic acid (CLA), butyric acid, and ether lipids, may have cancer-preventive effects as well. While individual risk factors must be considered in order to make a case for the relationship between diet and disease prevention, medical experts continue to collect data to determine if there is a definite link between calcium consumption and the prevention of these diseases. So, even though no claims are being made for calcium as a miracle mineral, researchers are continuing to elucidate promising possibilities of health benefits from foods like milk and cheese.

There's no question that milk, along with cheese, is a stellar source of dietary calcium. While you can get calcium and magnesium from beans, some leafy vegetables, and other foods, you have to eat a lot of them. Milk, by contrast, is a concentrated source. Two or three servings a day of milk or another dairy product will readily meet the RDA (recommended dietary allowance) of 1,000 milligrams of calcium, and cheese provides the healthy nutrients contained in milk in an even more concentrated form. It is good to remember that hard-pressed, cooked curd cheeses such as Emmental and Gruyère contain the most nutrients per ounce, while moist fresh cheeses such as cottage cheese have the fewest nutrients per ounce because they are so high in moisture content.

Fats in Cheese

Researchers have documented that fats are an important source of human fuel. Fats are necessary for proper functioning of the nervous system and for the absorption of several vitamins and minerals. Fats also play an important role in the structural integrity of cell membranes and the retina.

The National Cholesterol Education Program recommends that no more than 30 percent of a person's calories should come from fat and that daily consumption of cholesterol should be less than 300 milligrams. For a woman whose daily caloric intake is around 2,000 calories, this would mean 67 grams of fat. There are 9 calories per gram of fat, so that would amount to approximately 600 calories from fat.

Universally, the fat in cheese is measured on a dry or solid basis. When you read on the label that a cheese is 45 percent fat (FDB—fat on a dry basis—in the United States; FDM—fat in dry matter—in England; or m.g., mat. gr., or matière grasse in France), it does not mean that 45 percent of the cheese is actually fat. Instead, it means that 45 percent of the dry matter, after all the moisture has been removed, is fat. Most cheeses are about 50 percent moisture, so if you divide the fat figure by two, you will come up with the approximate percentage of fat in a cheese, which in this particular case would be about 22.5 percent fat. Because fresh cheeses are considerably higher in moisture, you should divide their fat figure by three.

> While milk is only 4 percent protein, cheese can be from 18 to 36 percent protein. A 2-ounce piece of cheese can supply up to 20 percent of the daily protein requirement with only 10 percent (200 calories) of an average 2,000-calorie allowance. And cheese is delicious.

The following table shows the proteins and fats per ounce of certain cheeses, the percentages of dry matter, moisture (water matter), and the fat in dry matter, as well as the calories per ounce. As you can see, hard-pressed cooked curd cheeses, such as Cheddar, Emmental, and Parmigiano-Reggiano, have the highest calorie content per ounce while

Cheese	Protein per ounce	Fat per ounce	Dry Matter	Water Matter	FDB	Calories per ounce
Brie	5g	6g	43%	57%	49%	75
Blue cheese	6g	8.5g	57%	43%	52%	105
Cheddar	8g	9g	63%	37%	51%	112
Double-crème	3g	6g	33%	67%	60%	64
Emmental	8g	8g	64%	36%	46%	110
Goat, fresh	4g	5g	35%	65%	17%	63
Mozzarella, fresh	6g	6g	48%	52%	45%	82
Parmigiano-Reggiano	10g	7g	70%	30%	37%	111
Ricotta (whole milk)	3.5g	4g	22%	78%	13%	54
Cottage cheese						
Full-fat	3.5g	1.25g	20%	80%	17%	30
1% fat	3.5g	.25g	17%	83%	3%	20

moist fresh cheeses, such as cottage cheese, ricotta, and mozzarella, have the fewest calories. Normally people eat more cottage cheese than Cheddar at one time, though, so the total calorie intake is probably about the same. Parmigiano-Reggiano, however, is both high in nutrients and low in fat, since it is made from partially skimmed milk. It also has lots of taste per ounce, so less cheese is needed for flavor than with a fresh cheese. Double- and triple-crème cheeses, which contain over 60 percent or over 72 to 75 percent butterfat, respectively, have an actual fat composition of only 20 to 35 percent, because of the fact that they are usually so moist, with a water content of up to 67 percent.

The main thing to remember is that, unless cream has been added, the moister a cheese, the fewer fats and calories it contains per ounce. More strongly flavored cheeses provide more flavor with less cheese, but they generally have more calories per ounce because they are firmer and contain less moisture per ounce.

Fat gives cheese its texture and depth of flavor. That is why low-fat cheeses lack both body and texture as well as flavor. The reduced-fat versions of various cheeses typically have little or no flavor, even though they may contain half the fat. Whole-milk cheeses can be a much better choice. They have much more flavor, allowing you to use less cheese and subsequently cut down on fat and calories.

Cheese is a healthy food. It can be an important part of a nutritious and balanced diet. It is low in lactose and high in nutrients. The milk curds, which form the cheese, retain almost all of the milk's high-quality protein, vitamins, and minerals. Few other foods compare with milk products in calcium content.

Whole-milk and dairy products do, unarguably, contain significant amounts of fat. However, coupled with lifestyle choices such as exercising regularly, not smoking, following the Food Guide Pyramid, and consuming everything in moderation, cheese can add enjoyment to your entertaining and life to your everyday meals without compromising your health.

Lactose Intolerance

Much confusion exists concerning various intolerances to dairy products. One of two basic conditions is usually the culprit: milk allergy or lactose intolerance.

A true allergy to milk products involves an immune system response to the protein in milk. The immune system response may be as simple as a runny nose, dermatitis, or diarrhea, but it can be as severe and life-threatening as anaphylactic shock, involving dangerously low blood pressure, swelling of the trachea, and unconsciousness. Milk allergies are not common. They are found mainly in young children whose immune systems are immature.

A more common and widely discussed problem is lactose intolerance. Many people claim to be lactose-intolerant, but often the condition has been self-diagnosed. Minnesota researchers Suavez, Savaiano, and Levitt contend that the concept of *severe* lactose intolerance is "nurtured by innumerable articles in the news media and advertisements for lactose-digestive aids." They note that some people are quick to give up milk and milk products despite the fact that by doing so, they are depriving their bodies of a rich source of essential nutrients.

Lactose is the main carbohydrate and natural sugar contained in milk. In fact, lactose exists only in milk and milk products. It is a disaccharide and consists of two molecules, one glucose unit and one galactose unit, joined together. Lactose needs the enzyme lactase in order to be digested and broken down into its components in the small intestine before it is absorbed into the bloodstream and used by the body. If lactase is not available, then the sugar passes through the intestines without being absorbed and thus causes symptoms resulting in discomfort and distress in the intestines and colon.

It is interesting to note that there is not an appreciable difference in the lactose level of cow's milk and goat milk: 11 grams per cup for cow's milk and 9 grams per cup for goat milk. So drinking goat milk rather than cow's milk does very little, if anything, to alleviate lactose intolerance.

Cheese, yogurt, and other cultured dairy products are virtually free of lactose because their original lactose was consumed and converted into lactic acid when the milk was fermented. According to an article published in the *New England Journal of Medicine,* most ripened cheeses contain about 95 percent less lactose (0.4 to 1 gram per serving) than whole milk (9 to 12 grams per serving), and even less than Lactaid milk (3 grams per serving), a brand of milk that has most of the lactose specially removed. Therefore, most people who are lactase-deficient can tolerate cheeses, especially those cheeses made with cultured bacteria and rennet, because the cultures cause the lactose to convert into lactic acid. When the milk is coagulated and the curds are cut, the lactose is drained away with the whey. Cheeses produced with cultures and rennet contain less lactose than those produced through direct acidification, such as whole-milk ricotta and deli-made mozzarella, because the milk in these cheeses is not fermented and a lactic curd is not produced.

Yogurt and other cultured and soured dairy products made with active cultures, such as acidophilus, are easier to digest because, similarly, their lactose has been consumed and converted by the production of lactic acid. It is the lactic acid that makes these products thick.

Studies conducted in the 1960s verified that adult lactase deficiency was the rule rather than the exception throughout the world: 90 percent of Asian-Americans, 8 percent of Native Americans, 75 percent of African-Americans, 50 percent of Hispanic-Americans, and 20 percent of Caucasian Americans have varying degrees of lactose intolerance. Generally speaking, only those of northern European heritage were found to be capable of easily digesting lactose in adulthood. It is not coincidental that those same countries are where dairying and cheese production were developed centuries earlier. Lactase levels are highest immediately after birth, and in most of the world, milk consumption declines after infancy. When humans stop consuming substantial amounts of milk, their need for the lactose enzyme ceases, triggering the body to stop producing lactase. But this is not the case in the northern European countries, where dairy products have always been a part of the diet.

Lactose intolerance occurs in several forms, which vary in severity and incidence. Unlike those individuals with milk allergies, who are allergic to milk proteins and must totally avoid milk, most lactose-intolerant individuals are able to consume about a pint of milk per day without severe symptoms. Many find they experience no symptoms unless their lactose intake is very high.

Put simply, lactose intolerance is the inability to digest the sugar in milk. Symptoms may occur anywhere from fifteen minutes to several hours after consuming foods or drinks containing lactose. The severity of the symptoms depends on when and how much lactose is consumed and the amount of lactose the particular individual can tolerate. Sometimes eating smaller portions of lactose-rich foods helps alleviate the symptoms. Others find it is better to eat lactose-rich foods as part of a meal, rather than alone. It has also been substantiated that the higher the fat in the dairy product, the slower the rate of digestion and, therefore, the slower release of lactose into the intestines. So the higher the butterfat content of a cheese, the better it will be tolerated by a person with lactose intolerance.

Lactose intolerance is not an all-or-nothing situation. By trial and error and by gradually increasing the amount of lactose-containing foods in one's diet, it is possible to determine personal tolerance levels and even increase these levels. In some cases, people are able to increase their tolerance by gradually increasing the amounts of milk products they consume, thereby changing the gastrointestinal bacteria, sometimes causing the reappearance of the missing enzyme. There are also lactase enzyme supplements, available without a prescription, that can be chewed or swallowed prior to eating lactose-rich foods.

If you suspect that you might be lactose-intolerant, avoid the mistake of trying to diagnose yourself. There are well-established tests to measure lactose intolerance. The symptoms might well be caused by another condition. Aside from heredity, lactose intolerance can also be the result of certain diseases, medical conditions, surgery, and various medications. It is always best to get a diagnosis from a doctor.

Because people's tolerance to lactose varies widely, lactose-restricted diets must be highly individualized. Some people must follow lactose-free diets. This can be difficult, because lactose is found not only in milk and milk products but also in many nondairy foods, such as breads, cereals, breakfast drinks, salad dressings, and cake mixes. People on lactose-free diets need to read labels and avoid foods that include milk, milk solids, whey (milk liquid), and casein (milk protein, which may contain traces of lactose). They also need to check all drugs with their pharmacist, because many prescriptions and over-the-counter drugs contain lactose as a filler.

The World of Cheese: Cheese Types and Characteristics

THE WORLD OF CHEESE CAN be confusing, especially when it comes to classifying or categorizing cheeses by types, because often cheeses belong to several families. Many distinctions exist, and there are many considerations. For example, Gorgonzola can fall into the washed-rind category or the semi-soft or semi-hard category, depending on its age and whether it is a Gorgonzola dolce or a Gorgonzola piccante. Simultaneously, it can be classified as a blue-veined cheese or even just an aged, ripened, or cured cheese, as opposed to a fresh cheese. To add further to the confusion, it may have been made in Italy or in the United States. So there really are many possibilities.

An easy way to approach this dilemma is to group cheeses into families according to their textures: soft, semi-soft, semi-firm, hard, and extra-hard. This would seem simple. However, soon you begin to realize that cheeses change and evolve during their lives, developing completely different textures. For instance, a cheese such as a Crottin de Chavignol begins soft but eventually becomes rock-hard with age. The flavors also change as a cheese matures, moving from mild to sharp. The exterior of a cheese undergoes many changes as well. Crottins, for example, begin without a rind and in time mature to have a moldy, crusty, dry blue rind.

Another approach is to classify cheeses by ripening method, in categories such as fresh, surface-ripened, and so on. They can be classified according to taste, such as mild to strong. A completely different system is to classify cheeses by country of origin. What then do you do, though, about the different Gruyères that are produced in Switzerland, France, Germany, Australia, and even the United States? Should you just call all cheeses of this type mountain cheeses, since they all originated in mountainous regions? Similarly, there could be a category for the monastery cheeses that originated in monasteries during the Middle Ages. And yet another category might be table cheeses, cheeses that are used daily for eating and cooking. There seem to be as many methods of classification are there are cheeses.

The classification system that seems to make the most sense for me is to go by texture with subclassifications of ripening methods, veining, and other distinguishing characteristics, such as pasta filata cheeses, whey cheeses, and high butterfat cheeses. I have developed some tables (see the Cheese Tables beginning on page 349) in which cheeses are sorted according to texture, flavor, and country of origin.

SOFT FRESH CHEESES

Soft cheeses are usually mild and milky in flavor. These are fresh cheeses that are just a step away from being milk. They do not go through a ripening period or maturing process. Simple and delicate, they are often unsalted, and some are even considered bland. They are best consumed soon after they are made. Among the most popular is **Cottage Cheese,** made of skimmed-milk curds mixed with cream. **Fromage Blanc,** or **Fromage Frais,** is fresh, very soft, barely coagulated lactic curds that have been quickly drained and sometimes whipped. The Germans have a similar cheese called **Quark. Cream Cheese** is a somewhat drier fresh cheese made creamy and smooth with the addition of cream. Commercial renditions are whipped and stabilized with gums, but artisanal cream cheese can be found every now and then.

From northern Italy comes **Crescenza** or **Stracchino,** so called because it was originally made from the rich milk of cows who had just come down from a summer of mountaintop grazing. This cheese, a younger cousin of **Taleggio** and **Gorgonzola,** is quite mild and creamy. A similar cheese that also comes from northern Italy is **Robiola.**

Farmer Cheese can take several forms: It can be a crumbly cheese of curds similar to cottage cheese, without the cream. It can be drained in a basket or mold. Or it can be pressed into a cake for slicing. Mexican **Queso Fresco** or **Queso Blanco** is quite similar to farmer cheese or pot cheese, but it is pressed into a disk shape.

SEMI-SOFT CHEESES

Cheeses that fall into this category are often buttery and mild in flavor. They are good table cheeses.

Bel Paese, a popular semi-soft cheese, originated in northern Italy. *Bel paese* means "beautiful country," and the cheese is named for a book written by Antonio Stoppani; the name is a trademark of the Galbani company. Stoppani's portrait and a map of Italy are on the label of the cheese made in Italy, while the American-made version has a map of the Western hemisphere on its label. Quite similar are **Caciottas,** small cheeses that are made on farms by artisanal cheesemakers. In Italy, they are sold still fresh, usually at about ten days, when they are relatively bland. In Tuscany, small Caciottas are made from sheep milk and called **Pecorino Toscano.**

From the Low Countries comes **Havarti,** created by pioneer cheesemaker Hanne Nielsen in the mid-1800s. It has lots of tiny irregular eyes and is often flavored with herbs or spices. The original Havarti was a washed-rind cheese. It is quite similar to German **Tilsit.**

Tomme de Savoie is semi-soft when young but becomes firm with age. Many other washed-rind cheeses also fit into this category because they are usually semi-soft in texture.

SEMI-FIRM CHEESES

Most cheeses in this category are pressed to become firm. They are often mild when young, becoming more and more flavorful as they age. They also become much harder as they age, and some, like Gouda, eventually move into the extra-hard family. When young, they are very good table cheeses, which means that they are good for cooking and for eating as snacks and in sandwiches. Some of the cheeses have small irregular eyes, others do not.

From Italy come **Asiago,** a strongly flavored cheese with irregular holes; **Fontina,** a marvelous melting cheese; and **Montasio,** another good melting variety. Another interesting cheese that falls into this category is **Umbriaco,** which means "drunkard." It has been soaked in wine and matured with a coating of grape skins and seeds so that its rind is stained purple. From Holland come **Edam,** a small round cheese that is often coated with red wax, and **Gouda,** a larger and more complex cheese. **Mahón** comes from the island of Minorca. It's a very attractive cheese with a rind that has been rubbed with olive oil and paprika. **Morbier** is a French cheese that has a layer of ash running through the middle of the cheese, which traditionally separated the curds from the morning and evening milkings.

Tête de Moine, whose name means monk's head, is a semi-firm cheese from Switzerland. The cheese is eaten by scraping off layers from the top using a *girolle,* a device with a rotating blade that leaves the cheese resembling the bald spot on a monk's head. Raclette is another Swiss cheese. Traditionally it is served by placing it near a fire so that the face of the cheese softens and melts from the heat. It is then scraped off onto a plate and eaten with boiled new potatoes, pickled onions, and cornichons, tiny gherkin pickles. Morbier can also be enjoyed in this same way.

Dry Jack, also known as Dry Sonoma Jack, is a California cheese that fits into this category because it begins as a mild cheese and hardens with age to become a drier and more flavorful cheese.

CHEDDAR-STYLE HARD CHEESES

All cheeses in this family go through the cheddaring process, in which the curds are cut into pieces and stacked in the cheese vat to drain and mat together. The cheeses are firm-textured and have a clean, mellow taste when young, becoming sharp and tangy with age.

Cheeses in this family include first, of course, Cheddar. Cheddar is so named because it was originally made in the town of Cheddar in England. It is a cheese that dates back to ancient times. Although it originated in England, it is now made all over the world, from New Zealand to Canada to South Africa to the United States. The finest Cheddars are traditionally made from unpasteurized milk and bound in cloth to age. Cheddars can be aged from three months to three years, the longer, the more flavorful. Two famous farmhouse English Cheddars are Keen and Montgomery. Tillamook in Oregon makes a fine Cheddar, as do Cabot, Grafton, and Shelburne Farms in Vermont.

Colby, invented in Colby, Wisconsin, around the turn of the century, is similar to Cheddar but softer, milder, and moister, with a more open texture. Longhorn is Colby made in a long tubular shape.

Another cheese that belongs in the Cheddar family is Cheshire, which is claimed to be England's oldest cheese. Cheshire is aged for only one to two months and does not store well. It is a good cooking cheese and, in fact, was the original cheese used for Welsh rarebit. Its flavor works well with eggs, especially in soufflés. Blue Cheshire has dark green-blue veins. Stilton also falls into the Cheddar family, as does Gloucester, which is a bright orange cheese that is aged for six to nine months. There are two types: Single Gloucester, made from partially skimmed milk, which is softer and milder, and Double Gloucester, made from whole milk, which is mellow, creamy, and stronger. A striking and lovely cheese is Huntsman, Gloucester with bands of Stilton in the middle. Another English cheese that is great for melting is Lancashire, which is made from curds combined from several days of milkings. And from Wales comes **Caerphilly,** another moist, crumbly cheese that is good for melting. Caerphilly is sold quite young.

Cantal, a cheese that has been made in southern France for centuries, is also made with the cheddaring method. When young, it is very similar to a Lancashire; when aged, it is very much like a Cheddar.

HARD CHEESES WITH EYES

Most of the cheeses in this category were originally made in mountainous regions of Europe, mostly by farmers in isolated mountain houses. Their curds are all cooked and then pressed and aged, so these cheeses are more solid. Their interiors are dotted with holes (eyes) created by a gas that develops within the cheese during the ripening process. The gas is actually natural carbon dioxide that is given off with the growth of *Propionibacter shermanii* bacteria. Often these cheeses have tough, hard rinds.

Emmental is the cheese commonly called Swiss cheese. It has olive-shaped eyes that can be as large as a walnut. Law dictates that it cannot be exported until it is four months old. Some cheeses are gigantic and weigh almost three hundred pounds. The Norwegians created a similar cheese in the mid-1950s called **Jarlsberg.** It is claimed to be the most popular imported cheese in the United States.

Several cheeses fall into the Gruyère family. First and foremost is Swiss **Gruyère.** It is softer and smoother than Emmental and considered to be a better cooking cheese. The finest Gruyère has a slight dampness in its pea-sized eyes. The French cheese **Beaufort,** known as the Prince of Gruyères, is higher in butterfat than most Gruyères and has a sticky moist rind from the bacteria *linens*. **Comté,** also known as Gruyère de Comté, has been made in France since the thirteenth century. It has marble-shaped holes. Younger cheeses have a floral aroma, while older cheeses have a farmyard character. **Appenzell** is sharper than Gruyère and has an even more pungent farmyard aroma. During its aging period, it is washed with wine, spices, and salt. It has small, irregular pea-sized holes.

EXTRA-HARD CHEESES

Cheeses in this category are all of the grating variety. They are very hard and very low in moisture, and they have a brittle texture. Mellow, robust, and sweet, they sometimes become sharp and piquant with age. They have all been cooked and then pressed and aged for years so they become hard and dry. Because they are so old, they often develop crystalline bits of casein that crunch when you bite on them.

Parmigiano-Reggiano is known as the the King of Cheeses. It has been made since ancient times. Boccaccio even wrote of a mountain of Parmigiano in *The Decamaron* in the fourteenth century. Produced in a restricted geographic region in Italy from the milk of specific cows during a specific period of the year, Parmigiano is graded throughout its aging process. According to set standards, true Parmesan cheeses are sold at different ages, called *Giovane* (young) at fourteen months; *Vecchio* (old), eighteen months to two years; *Stravecchio* (extra old), two to three years; and *Stravecchione* (very old), three to four years. **Grana Padano** is made in northwestern Italy. It is made just like Parmigiano, except in a different region. It is often sold when young; however, when aged for two or three years, it is very similar in taste and texture to Parmigiano. **Pecorino Romano** is a sheep milk cheese made near Rome and also in Sardinia. It is said to be Italy's oldest cheese. It is a good table cheese when young and develops into a very hard, sharp, and piquant cheese as it ages. **Locatelli** is a brand of Pecorino Romano.

Sbrinz, the oldest of the Swiss cheeses, is a very hard cheese of which Pliny wrote. It is similar in flavor to Parmigiano and wonderful for grating. Another unique Swiss cheese that falls into this extra-hard category is **Sapsago.** It is a pressed cheese made from cow's milk. Its pale green color comes from melilot, an herb that strongly and assertively flavors the cheese. This herb, which grows only in the area where the cheese is made, is thought to have been brought back from Asia Minor by the crusaders.

BLOOMY-RIND AND SOFT-RIPENED CHEESES

Cheeses in this category have rinds covered with a thin layer of a white mold, known as a bloomy down or flowery rind. To achieve this coating, the surfaces of the cheeses have been treated with a mold called *Penicillium candidum,* which develops into a white crust. Most of these cheeses are soft. Their interiors soften as they age, becoming creamy and sometimes thick and runny. The cheeses ripen from the outer edge to the center, so you can determine if a cheese is mature by lightly touching the center of the cheese to see if it is soft. The cheeses are tangy and rich, yet delicate and luscious. Their flavors become fuller with age. The white rind is edible, but if you don't like it, just cut it off and discard it.

The most famous bloomy-rind cheeses are **Brie** and **Camembert.** The most magnificent Brie of all is **Brie de Meaux,** which is farm-made in France from unpasteurized milk, and therefore seldom found in the United States (see 47). It has a satiny and silky texture and is runny when mature. It has an impressive history. Charlemagne was quite taken with it, as, centuries later, was the French diplomat Talleyrand, who declared it "the King of Cheeses" at the Congress of Vienna in 1815. Most of the Bries imported into the United States are factory-made from pasteurized milk. They are much milder and do not mature like Brie de Meaux. Camembert is a similar cheese from Normandy, but it is smaller than Brie and has some brown mottling on the rind. Its flavor becomes more complex as it ages. Neither Brie nor Camembert should ever have an ammoniated aroma or taste. If they do, they are past their prime and you should not buy or eat them. **Coulommiers** is quite similar to Brie except that it is smaller in size and eaten at a younger age.

Most bloomy-rind cheeses have a butterfat content of 45 to 50 percent. Some, however, are triple-crèmes and have a butterfat content above 75 percent. These cheeses are exceedingly rich and luscious. They are almost like a mousse and literally melt in your mouth. They are wonderful with caviar as well as fresh fruit. The most famous of these are: **Brillat-Savarin,** named for the eighteenth-century writer and statesman who declared that "a meal that ends without cheese is like a beautiful woman with only one eye"; **Explorateur,** named for the *Explorer* satellite rocket that was fired in 1958; and **Saint André.** These cheeses are a delicious, decadent addition to any cheese tray.

BLUE-VEINED CHEESES

Blue cheeses are among the most popular of all. Their blue interior veins and marbling are actually molds that range in color from blue to blue-green to blue-black. Some of the cheeses even have small pockets of mold throughout. All have been sprayed or inoculated with mold spores of *Penicillium glaucum* or *Penicillium roqueforti.* Sometimes the mold is incorporated into the cheese curds as well. During the aging process, the cheeses are pierced with wire needles to allow aerobic mold development throughout their interiors. Normally these cheeses ripen from the center out to the crust so that when they are fully mature the veining is well developed and well distributed throughout the cheese.

Blue cheeses all have intense, strong, tangy flavors. Some have a pungent aroma. Some are semi-soft; others are semi-firm and crumbly. Others, such as **Gorgonzola,** are quite soft and creamy.

The most widely known of the blue-veined cheeses is **Roquefort,** which is made from sheep milk. It is a controlled-origin cheese that has been aged in the same limestone caves in Cambalou, near Roquefort, in southern France for over one thousand years. Charlemagne was quite enchanted with Roquefort. There are also delicious blue-veined French cheeses made with cow's milk, such as **Bleu d'Auvergne,** about which Pliny wrote in the first century, and **Fourme d'Ambert,** which has been made since the seventh century and is unusual because it has a crusty rind.

Every country has its own blue cheeses. In England, the most famous is **Stilton,** a cheese of ancient origin with a crumbly texture and a natural crust. **Colston Basset** is considered the finest and creamiest Stilton of all because it is made from unpasteurized milk. Another interesting English blue is **Shropshire Blue,** easily recognized by its intense orange color, which comes from annatto. It's sharper than Stilton and quite striking in appearance. From Ireland comes **Cashel Blue,** a cheese that is tangy and crumbly when young and softens as it ages. **Cabrales** is a powerful Spanish blue that is traditionally wrapped in sycamore leaves that impart a distinctly woody flavor. Italy's **Gorgonzola** is said to be the oldest named cheese, dating back to 879. Creamy and moist, it is made in the same way as Stracchino and Taleggio. In fact, the legend is that some Stracchino was forgotten and left in the storeroom of an inn in the town of Gorgonzola, where it developed mold. When the innkeeper served it to his guests rather than throw it away, it was such a hit that the practice of leaving the cheese to mold became a tradition.

Several blue-veined cheeses are more recent additions to the world of cheese: **Danish Blue** was developed after World War I as an imitation of Bleu d'Auvergne. **Maytag Blue,** a cow's milk cheese made in Iowa since 1941, is based upon Roquefort. And **Cambozola,** which is made in Germany, is a rich and creamy Brie-type cheese with a bloomy rind and blue interior veining—thus its name: *camb* for camembert and *zola* for Gorgonzola.

PASTA FILATA CHEESES

These are cheeses with curds that have been heated, kneaded, pulled, and strung, or stretched, repeatedly in hot water to achieve an elastic consistency. Fresh cheeses of this family have an elastic texture and are quite springy to the touch. As they age, this elasticity decreases and the cheeses become softer, depending upon their moisture content.

The best-known cheese in this family is **Mozzarella.** There are actually two types of mozzarella: high-moisture mozzarella, a cheese with more than 52 percent moisture, commonly called fresh mozzarella, and low-moisture mozzarella, a drier and firmer cheese. Fresh mozzarella is like the cow's milk mozzarella found throughout Italy that is called *fior di latte*. Usually it can be purchased salted or unsalted. It is available in Italian delis and stores with specialty foods. It has a shorter shelf life than low-moisture mozzarella, a cheese that was developed in the United States to withstand transportation and storage for long periods of time. Low-moisture mozzarella is often shredded and used for pizza. In Italy, *fior di latte* is made from cow's milk, and *mozzarella di bufala* is made from water buffalo milk, with a higher butterfat content and a gamier taste. Mozzarella can be formed into small balls that are called *bocconcini,* and it can also be smoked. A specialty of southern Italy is fresh mozzarella formed around a lump of sweet cream butter, called *burrata* or *burrino*.

It is a misconception that fresh mozzarella should always be purchased floating in its whey. Water is used in the manufacture of mozzarella, and once the cheese is strung with hot water, it is must be placed in cool water to firm and chill. Years ago, refrigeration was rare in Italy and the only way to keep the mozzarella cool was to surround it with fresh well water. Nowadays the tradition continues and often mozzarella is sold surrounded by liquid, but the longer the cheese remains in the liquid, the more whey leaches out of the cheese and into the water, thus giving it a milky appearance. Sometimes the liquid contains citric acid, which helps preserve the cheese. When fresh mozzarella is removed from the liquid and packaged, its texture and consistency will be slightly firmer, yet it has more flavor because its whey is not being continually leached out and replaced with water.

Scamorza and **Provolone** are the cheeses often hung from the rafters in Italian food shops. Scamorza is a small cheese that is firmer than fresh mozzarella. Creamy and mild, it is shaped like a pear with a little topknot. Sometimes it is smoked. Provolone is still firmer. It is usually formed into a bell or a sausage shape, some as large as eight hundred pounds, and hung to age. **Provolone Piccante** is made with kid lipase and rennet and is very sharp when aged. **Caciocavallo** is another pasta filata cheese that has been made since Roman times. Its name is said to come from the fact that two cheeses are tied together with raffia and hung over a pole to dry as if they were on horseback: *cacio* for "cheese" and *cavallo* for "horse." Similar cheeses are made in other nearby countries: **Kashkaval** in Bulgaria and Yugoslavia and **Kasseri** in Greece.

WASHED-RIND CHEESES AND CHEESES WITH PUNGENT AROMAS

The cheeses in this group are all rubbed, brushed, or washed with a liquid while curing. The liquid can be brine, whey, or wine or spirits, and it fuels the growth of surface bacteria that affect the flavor of the cheeses. These cheeses are usually cured for longer periods than bloomy-rind cheeses. Some develop thick crusts and others have sticky surfaces that encourage the development of the *linens* bacteria, which causes them to become very pungent and powerful in aroma. Despite the fact that they are so stinky, they vary in taste, some having very strong and pronounced flavors, while others are surprisingly mild. Generally, washed-rind cheeses are semi-soft in texture; however, some become very soft and runny when mature. The development of many of these cheeses can be traced back to monastic orders during the Middle Ages; therefore they are sometimes referred to as monastery cheeses. The monks spent a great deal of time and effort developing these various cheeses, which have a range of flavors from mild and luscious to gutsy and even meaty.

Among the cheeses in this category is **Brick** cheese, which originated in Wisconsin before the turn of the century, in an attempt to recreate German Limburger. It was called brick cheese both because it is shaped like a brick and because it is pressed using bricks. Another American cheese in this family is **Liederkranz,** which originated in Ohio. It was meant to replicate German Schlosskäse. It is quite pungent, but less so than Limburger.

The French developed many of the washed-rind cheeses. They range in strength from mildly flavored cheeses to the strongest imaginable, often complete with aromas of barnyards and stables. **Pont l'Evêque,** which is quite mild in flavor, is a monastery cheese; the first record of it dates to the thirteenth century. **Reblochon,** another monastery cheese, which dates back to the fifteenth century, also has a mild flavor. It was so named because it was made from milk that came from a second milking, *reblochon*, that occurred after the landlord had passed by to collect the milk that paid the rent. **Port Salut,** a mild and mellow cheese, was created by Trappist monks during the French Revolution. **Munster,** developed by the Benedictine monks in the seventh century, is mild in flavor when young but becomes very pungent—and smells like a stable—when old. **Maroilles,** created by monks in the tenth century, has a very pungent aroma but a medium-strong flavor. **Livarot,** which is strong and assertive in both flavor and aroma, is sometimes called "the colonel" because the strips of grass that encircle the cheese resemble the stripes on a colonel's uniform. The rind of **Epoisses** is washed with an eau-de-vie. It is very runny when ripe, has a pungent and barnyardy aroma, and is quite strongly flavored.

Limburger, which was originated by Trappist monks in Belgium, is a very smelly cheese with a pronounced and pungent aroma. It is strongly flavored, but it does not taste as strong as it smells. Italian **Taleggio** has a pungent aroma and is very runny when mature but is relatively mellow in taste. Among the more mildly flavored washed-rind cheeses are **Gubbeen** and **Milleens,** from Ireland.

Vacherin Mont d'Or was traditionally made at home by Swiss farmers in the winter when it was so snowy in the mountains that they couldn't deliver their milk to the cheese-making facilities. It is a very pungent, runny cheese that is contained within a thin strip of pine that encircles the cheese while aging. When mature, it has a strong, barnyardy flavor. It is best eaten in its box, by removing the top rind and scooping out the interior with a spoon.

TRIPLE-CRÈME CHEESES

All the cheeses in this group are exceedingly rich because cream is added to the milk to achieve a cheese with a butterfat content of 72 to 75 percent or more. They are all luscious, velvety and very creamy.

Some, like **Mascarpone** and **Boursin,** are meant to be consumed when fresh. Technically speaking, mascarpone is not a cheese but rather clotted cream. It comes from northern Italy, where it is used in both sweet and savory dishes. French Boursin is a fresh triple-crème cheese that is often flavored with garlic and herbs.

Other triple-crèmes are aged for about three weeks. Among this group are **Brillat-Savarin, Saint André,** and **Explorateur,** which are ripened with bloomy rinds, and the blue-veined **Cambozola.**

WHEY CHEESES

These cheeses are made from whey drained away from curds used to make another cheese and recooked to form a secondary cheese. Whey cheeses range from very soft, mild, and fresh to firm, aged, and sharp.

Typically **Ricotta** is made from whey that comes from the curds used to make mozzarella. It can be made from cow's, sheep, goat, or water buffalo whey. The whey is boiled or recooked (thus the name *ricotta*, which means "recooked" in Italian). The curds are precipitated from the whey by the addition of an acid and then ladled into baskets to drain. Ricotta can be salted, pressed, and aged to become a firm, sharp cheese called **Ricotta Salata.** In Greece, a similarly made firm cheese is called **Manouri. Mizithra,** another Greek sheep milk–whey cheese, is both eaten when young like ricotta and aged.

In Norway, **Gjetost** is made by cooking whey from cow's milk or goat milk with sugar until it caramelizes and becomes dark golden brown.

GOAT CHEESES

Chèvre is the generic name for all goat milk cheeses in France, and the name is widely used in the United States as well. There are said to be more than eighty varieties of goat cheese produced in France alone. They are made in all shapes and sizes, with various rinds and molds, and each has its own distinct characteristics and flavor. Many are rustic and home-spun in appearance, with flavors that are earthy and tangy. Goat cheeses develop wonderful, pronounced, complex flavors when they age. The French are masters at *affinage*, which means aging. Often the young cheeses are sold to shopkeepers who age and coddle them until they are ready to sell.

Montrachet, imported from France, is the most commonly found fresh goat cheese in the United States. It was named for the glorious Burgundian white wine of the same name. A soft fresh log of goat cheese, Montrachet is very mild in flavor and usually sold at an age of less than one month. Most Montrachet imported into the United States is factory-made, sometimes from dried milk or frozen curds. But there is an abundance of American-made goat cheese, and I urge you to seek out these cheeses rather than purchasing factory-made French Montrachet. The American-made cheeses are all finely made artisanal cheeses of high quality. Names you should look for are Laura Chenel, who pioneered American-made goat cheese in the 1980s; Capriole, from Kentucky; Cypress Grove, from California; Coach Farms, from New York; and Vermont Butter and Cheese Company.

Another oft-imported French goat cheese is **Bucheron,** a fat log of fresh goat cheese that has been coated with a bloomy rind and ripened. **Sainte-Maure** is a somewhat thinner log of goat cheese that is covered with ash, coated with a bloomy rind, and aged. Sainte-Maure from the Touraine is made with a long straw running inside the cheese to help hold it together. **Selles-sur-Cher** is a smaller round coated with ash. As it ages, a blue mold often grows under the ash.

Chabichou, which means "little goat," is a cylindrical cheese with a bit of mold atop its white bloomy rind. **Valençay** is also known as Pyramide because of its flattened pyramid shape. It has a bloomy rind covered with ash. **Crottin de Chavignol** is a tiny round of goat cheese that is aged to become hard as a rock. (Then it really does resemble the animal dropping for which it is named.)

Banon, named for a town in Provence, is unique in that it is first dipped in eau-de-vie and then wrapped in a chestnut leaf to cure. Banons can be made from any milk, but they are usually associated with goat milk. When made from cow's milk, they may be called **Saint-Marcellin.**

Many other cheeses are produced from goat milk, including **Arina,** a goat milk Cheddar from Holland, **Gjetost,** and **Feta,** to name only a few.

SHEEP MILK CHEESES

The generic name for all sheep milk cheeses in France is *brebis.* In Italy, the term used is *pecorino.* Since sheep milk has two to three times the butterfat of cow's milk, all sheep milk cheeses are exceedingly smooth and rich. Cheeses made from sheep milk come in a wide variety of shapes, sizes, and types and range in flavor from mild to sharp.

There are some delightful young sheep milk cheeses made in Italy, especially in Tuscany and Umbria, where they are called **Pecorino** or **Pecorino Toscano.** There are also many sheep milk cheeses in Sardinia and Sicily, which makes one of my favorites, **Pepato,** which is studded with black peppercorns. **Pecorino Romano,** which is commonly found in the United States, has been made in the countryside around Rome for the last two thousand years. When young, it is a table cheese, and when aged it is hard, sharp, and piquant and an excellent grating cheese.

Brin d'Amour can be made from sheep milk, goat milk, or a mixture of the two. It is a lovely cheese that is coated with ash and then dried herbs and aged. Originally made in Corsica, it is soft when young, then it becomes runny, and, eventually, quite firm. Brin d'Amour means "sprig of love," and it is so named for its coating of herb sprigs.

Manchego is the most famous Spanish sheep milk cheese. It is a pressed cheese and quite firm. Its rind is ridged with the pattern of the mold in which the cheese is made and often shows traces of a green-black mold that grows on the cheese during aging. **Idiazábal** is a fabulous cheese from the Basque region of Spain. Traditionally, it is lightly smoked.

The dry, rocky terrain of Greece is well adapted to goats as well as sheep. Many cheeses there are made from sheep milk, as are the cheeses of Sicily, Sardinia, and Corsica. Sheep milk was originally used to make **Feta.** (Its name comes from *fetes,* which means "large block of cheese" in Greek.) Today it is still made with sheep milk, but there is often a bit of goat milk mixed in because Greek shepherds usually have a few goats living in the midst of their herds. Others of the sheep milk cheeses that abound in Greece include **Manouri, Mizithra,** and **Kasseri.**

The popular blue-veined **Roquefort** and **Cabrales** are both sheep milk cheeses.

MILD, BLAND, AND BUTTERY CHEESES, OR TABLE CHEESES

Table cheeses are cheeses that are good for cooking as well as eating plain or in simple sandwiches. Cheeses that fall into this category have smooth, creamy textures and mild, pleasant flavors and aromas. Such cheeses as **Monterey Jack** and **Caciottas** fit into this group. Cheeses such as **Edam, Gouda,** and **Havarti** fall into this category when they are quite young, as do many others.

FLAVORED CHEESES

Flavored cheeses can be found in all countries and in all cheese catagories. Flavorings range from pungent garlic or fiery chiles to the mildest of herbs. Cheeses can be coated with herbs, studded with nuts, or coated with grape seeds. The list is endless.

In France, **Gaperon** is a well-known flavored cheese. This soft cheese is very strongly flavored with garlic and peppercorns, coated with a bloomy rind, and hung to ripen. In olden times, Gaperon was hung from kitchen rafters to age, and the number hanging was an indication of a farmer's wealth.

In Denmark, **Havarti** is often flavored with herbs or caraway seeds. In Holland, some cheeses are flavored with cumin seeds. Italian **Pecorino** can be flavored with peppercorns. In France, **Boursin** is flavored with herbs and garlic or coated with black pepper, and fresh goat cheeses are often rolled in fresh or dried herbs. England's **Derby Sage** is flavored with sage. In Switzerland, **Sapsago** is flavored with herbs. Corsican **Brin d'Amour** is completely coated in herbs.

Leaves also impart special flavors to the cheeses they wrap: **Banon** is wrapped in chestnut leaves, **Cabrales** in sycamore leaves. At the Mozzarella Company, we wrap goat cheese with hoja santa leaves, which impart a sassafras flavor.

In the United States, many cheeses are flavored, such as **Pepper Jack,** a Monterey Jack with hot chiles. At the Mozzarella Company, we flavor many of our Caciottas with herbs and chiles to regionalize them. Many cream cheeses are flavored with herbs and some with fruits and nuts.

Smoked Cheeses also fall under the category of flavored cheeses. Most are hung and smoked with natural smoke; some, however, such as mozzarella, may merely be painted with liquid smoke.

PROCESSED CHEESES

Processed cheeses are natural cheeses of varying types that are heated, pasteurized, and cooked together to blend them into a new cheese. **Velveeta** is a prime example. Processed cheeses are quite hardy, able to withstand long periods of time unrefrigerated.

You put your left index finger on your eye and your right index finger on the camembert . . . if they sort of feel the same, the cheese is ready.

–M. Tattinger

What to Look for When You're Buying Cheese

YOU SHOULD ALWAYS LOOK FOR quality when you are buying cheese, both in the store and in the cheese.

SHOP AT A STORE WITH A GOOD SELECTION

First and foremost, buy cheese from a store that sells a lot of cheese. Such stores always have the best selection. You can rest assured that their cheeses are fresh, that they have been stored and handled properly, and that the cheeses are in good condition. Ask for advice from the employees in the cheese department. In such a store, they know about their cheeses and which cheeses are at their prime, and they can guide you in making your choices. By all means, ask for tastes.

Make cheeses that are in top-notch condition your number-one priority. Let your eyes be your guide first, followed by your nose.

EXAMINE THE COLOR AND TEXTURE

The cheese should look fresh and clean. There should not be any mold that is not intended to be there on the cheese. The edges of the cheese should not be dried out, and the cheese should not have cracks or fissures. There should be no shrinkage of the cheese away from the rind; it should be plump and full within the rind. It should not be discolored with pinkish or grayish mold. Gauge the texture of the cheese with your finger; firm cheeses should feel firm, soft-ripened cheeses should feel softer and more mature.

EXAMINE THE PACKAGING

The packaging should be neat and clean. Examine it for signs of spoilage. The wrapping should never be inflated; it should be intact, not torn. The cheese should not be leaking or seeping liquid, and there shouldn't be any visible moisture under the wrapper. Keep in mind, though, that artisanal cheeses sometimes look handmade—this is in their favor.

READ THE LABEL

Read the label to see what kind of milk was used, and if it was raw or pasteurized, what the fat content of the cheese is, where it comes from, and whether it is a farmstead or a factory-made cheese. Look for the name of the producer.

TRUST YOUR SENSES

The aroma of the cheese shouldn't be overly strong, and it should never be ammoniated. If it doesn't smell good, it probably won't taste good either. There are, however, exceptions to this rule, because some cheeses, like some wines, smell of "noble rot." Some even smell like a barnyard or stable, or dirty feet. Such aromas are a particular and valued characteristic of washed-rind cheeses.

The cheese should be ripe and ready to enjoy, neither before nor past its prime. Always ask to taste the cheese if you have any doubt.

PASTEURIZED VERSUS UNPASTEURIZED MILK

Ask if the cheese is made of pasteurized or unpasteurized milk. Fresh raw milk cheeses are widely available in Europe and Latin America, but they are banned in the United States. U.S. health codes dictate that all fresh cheeses, both domestically made and imported, that are less than sixty days old must have been made with pasteurized milk. Illnessess that have been associated with fresh cheeses made from unpasteurized milk are brucellosis, listeriosis, and tuberculosis. Often doctors caution people with compromised immune systems, expectant mothers, and the elderly to steer clear of unpasteurized cheeses.

You should be aware, however, that there are two different methods of pasteurizing milk: a slow lower-heat method and a fast higher-heat method, which is also called flash pasteurization The slow method is considered superior because fewer of the milk's natural flora are destroyed, and this leaves more for the cheesemaker to work with in creating a flavorful cheese. Cheeses that are aged for more than sixty days may be made from unpasteurized milk because it is generally accepted that the milk's harmful bacteria are destroyed during the aging process.

SERVE CHEESE AS SOON AS POSSIBLE

Is it better to buy from a cheese shop or counter that cuts the cheese to order, rather than from the supermarket case? What about prepackaged cheeses? Is it true that plastic wrap kills a cheese and keeps it from breathing? Why do some shops prefer it? It's all a matter of which kind of cheese you are buying and storing, but the best general advice is to buy cheeses that are freshly and recently cut and packaged and to enjoy them as soon after you purchase them as possible. And remember to treat them well and give them a chance to breathe and come to room temperature before you serve them.

For fresh cheeses, such as goat cheese, mozzarella, and ricotta, that have delicate flavors and are meant to be consumed soon after they are purchased, it's best to buy them from a cheese counter that sells lots of cheese so that you can be assured that the cheeses are impeccably fresh and haven't taken on the odors and flavors of other cheeses in the case. They can be purchased over the counter (from a cheese or deli counter, where they are cut to order from whole and large pieces of cheese) or from a well-refrigerated case where the cheeses are individually vacuum-sealed. Cheeses packaged in this manner should be dated, so look for the freshest.

Vacuum-sealing has been a boon to the fresh cheese industry. It triples or quadruples the shelf life of a fresh, delicate, perishable cheese. Keep your cheese vacuum-sealed, for as few days as possible, until you are ready to serve it. Remove the plastic package and any interior wrapping prior to serving so that the cheese can breathe and come to room temperature (70°F.) in the open air. If it will be an extended time before you serve it, the cheese can be covered loosely with a damp dish towel or plastic wrap so that it doesn't dry out.

For aged cheeses, again, the best decision you can make is to go to a store that sells lots of cheese. Soft-ripened and washed-rind cheeses are best when still in their original perforated packaging, because it allows them to breathe. Try to buy such cheeses whole. Lacking this possibility, try to purchase cheese that is cut to order or from a cheese case that has freshly cut and packaged cheeses.

How Much Cheese to Buy

It is easy to overestimate the amount of cheese you'll need, especially when you're planning for a party. There are ways to avoid this.

If you plan to serve cheese as an hors d'oeuvre and to serve other foods as well, one to two ounces per person is sufficient. This, however, partially depends on the number of guests or the number of other hors d'oeuvres. For large parties, serve only half an ounce of cheese per person, especially if the cheese will be served on a buffet table and there will be lots of other food. The smaller the party, the more cheese you will need to serve per person.

Serving size also depends on when you are serving the cheese. If you are serving only cheese at cocktail time and you expect everyone to be hungry, you should serve up to three or four ounces per person. If you are serving cheese as a prelude to a light dessert, plan on a very small amount per person, about a half ounce to an ounce.

To determine the total amount of cheese you need to buy, multiply the ounces of cheese you plan to serve per guest by the number of guests, then divide this total by sixteen (since there are sixteen ounces in a pound). That number will tell you how many pounds of cheese to buy in all. Once you're at the store and have chosen the cheeses according to the amount you have calculated, look over the selection and see if you want to buy more so that you'll have a more abundant cheese display. Then buy the additional cheese, realizing that you will probably have great leftovers to enjoy.

How Many Different Cheeses to Buy

Generally, I recommend serving three or four different cheeses. Five is the maximum. The cheese selection should be diverse yet balanced. Try to have a variety of textures and flavors, as well as shapes. The cheeses can come from different countries. They can be made from the milk of different animals. The secret is balance and harmony.

The cheeses should reflect your preferences. Let them be an expression of your mood. There are many questions you can ask yourself that will help you determine which cheeses to buy: Do you want to have all cow's milk cheeses, or would you prefer one cow's milk, one goat milk, and one sheep milk cheese? Do you want to have all the cheeses from one particular country, or do you prefer a mixture? Do you want the cheese selection to relate to a theme or a menu? Would you like to try all new-to-you cheeses? The questions are endless, but they will help you focus on the types of cheese you want to buy.

One simple and classic approach is to choose one soft-ripened cheese (like Brie or Camembert), one mild cheese (like a locally made chèvre), one sharp and tangy blue cheese (like Roquefort or Stilton), and one mellow aged cheese (like Gruyère or Gouda).

Generally, I recommend that one cheese always be mild and plain and another be sharp. The remaining cheeses should contrast with the others. One might be a cheese flavored with herbs or a soft-ripened cheese, another might be a very rich cheese, or a blue cheese, or a stinky washed-rind cheese. It's always nice to have one farmstead or artisanal cheese. The secret here is variety and contrast. (See The Cheese Course, page 339.)

Another possibility is to serve just one fabulous, magnificent, superb cheese. Was there a particular cheese at the store that enchanted you? Then serve just that one perfect cheese and forget all the others!

Storing Cheese

In terms of storing cheese, the smartest thing you can do is purchase only the amount of cheese that you will be using within a few days. If you must store them for longer, wrap the cheeses individually and tightly in clean plastic wrap. Store them in a location where the temperature is consistent, such as the vegetable bin of the refrigerator, and use them as soon as possible.

HOW LONG WILL CHEESE LAST?

The shelf life of any cheese depends on the type of cheese. The softer the cheese, the shorter its shelf life. Very soft cheeses should be used within a few days. More substantial fresh cheeses will usually keep for one to two weeks after opening. Semi-soft cheeses will usually last for about a month. Harder cheeses will last for months; in fact, they will continue to age, albeit slowly, in your refrigerator. Extra-hard cheeses like Parmigiano-Reggiano can be kept for extended periods, even years, if properly wrapped.

REWRAPPING CHEESE

After you have served a cheese, the leftovers should be rewrapped tightly in clean plastic wrap. This is because, at room temperature, bacteria that could contaminate the cheese can quickly grow on the old wrapper. Cheeses can also be stored wrapped tightly in waxed paper, butcher paper, or aluminum foil.

Don't place unwrapped cheeses in plastic containers for storage—they will mold quickly because of lack of air circulation. If you plan on keeping a cheese for any length of time and you want it to breathe, loosely wrap it in waxed paper, parchment paper, butcher paper, or aluminum foil. You can perforate the wrapping material by punching small holes in it with a toothpick prior to wrapping. Remember that refrigeration pulls the moisture out of the air and has a drying effect, so care for your leftover cheese accordingly. For short periods of time, firm cheeses such as English Cheddars can be wrapped in a damp cloth that is remoistened daily.

MOLD ON CHEESE

Mold spores are airborne and a natural part of the environment. If cheese is left unwrapped, especially in a humid environment, it will mold quickly and naturally. If your cheese develops a bit of extra mold, don't worry, just cut it off with a clean knife. If there is a lot of mold, it is a good practice to clean your knife intermittently while cutting away the mold so that you don't reinoculate the cheese with mold as you cut. The general rule is to cut ¼ inch to ½ inch deeper than the mold, so that all the contaminated cheese is cut away and discarded.

WHERE TO STORE CHEESE?

Store cheese in the coldest section of the refrigerator, where the temperature is constant, at 35° to 40°F. The colder you keep the cheese, the longer it will last. The moisture content of the cheese also affects the length of time you can store various cheeses. The harder the cheese, the longer it will last. Soft and semi-soft cheeses will last according to their moisture content, with the most moist cheeses spoiling first. You should not keep soft fresh cheeses such as ricotta and cottage cheese for more than a week; in fact, it is better to use them even sooner. Harder cheeses like Parmigiano, with moisture content under 40 percent, will last almost forever. Grated and shredded cheeses should always be stored in an airtight container. Shredded cheeses are the most vulnerable to mold and will keep for the shortest period. It's really best not to shred more cheese than you will use.

Cheese absorbs other food odors readily, so don't store fresh delicate cheeses near cut onions or garlic. And vice versa—if you have a very strongly flavored cheese like a Limburger, it should be well wrapped and even placed inside a sealed container to prevent its odors from transferring to other foods and cheeses in the refrigerator.

Don't plan to store cheeses at room temperature and out in the open indefinitely, unless you have a cheese cellar. Cheeses left uncovered for too long will dry out and develop hard places around the edges. The ambient temperature is critical. If the room is too warm, the fat will come out of the cheese like beads of oil and soft moist cheeses will sour and spoil. Use a glass cheese dome only for short-term storage, because the cheeses inside will not be able to breathe. If you put two cheeses under a dome, molds and bacteria can jump from cheese to cheese. Soon you will have a completely new cheese.

CAN YOU FREEZE CHEESE?

Fresh cheeses such as mozzarella and goat cheese can be frozen in their original packages or rewrapped in plastic wrap, placed in a zipper plastic bag, and frozen. The wrapping should be moisture-proof and airtight. These cheeses can be frozen for up to two months. Always thaw them in the refrigerator prior to using. Mascarpone can be frozen, but it may shatter, or separate, when defrosted. To re-emulsify the cheese, whip it with a whisk while it's still very cold. Ricotta cannot be frozen.

Soft-ripened cheeses should not be frozen unless absolutely necessary. Semi-soft cheeses often become crumbly after being frozen. Hard aged cheeses need not be frozen, since they keep well and will continue to age in your refrigerator.

WHAT IF YOU WANT TO AGE CHEESE?

To age cheese, you'll need a dark, humid, well-ventilated space, like a wine cellar. The humidity should be about 90 percent; the temperature should be about 50° to 60°F. The cheeses should be laid out on clean boards, straw mats, or stainless steel racks. They should be cleaned and turned daily to keep them from deteriorating. If mold problems develop with the rind, you can brush the cheese or wash the rind clean with a piece of cloth dipped into a vinegar or brine solution.

WHAT TO DO WITH LEFTOVER CHEESE

My favorite thing to do with leftover cheese is to use it in a salad or a pasta dish. Because you can often substitute one cheese for another, you can easily incorporate different cheeses in various recipes. Try not to keep those little leftover pieces of cheese for too long, because they will develop mold and deteriorate.

The French are very thrifty with their leftover bits and pieces of cheese. They save them and make a spread called *fromage fort,* which, literally, means "strong cheese." To make it, just trim off any dried-out or moldy pieces from all those little bits and ends of cheese you have in your refrigerator. Place 8 ounces of cheese in the work bowl of a food processor fitted with a steel blade, along with 1 or 2 cloves of garlic and 1 to 2 tablespoons dry white wine, Cognac, or cream. Add freshly ground black pepper or fresh herbs, if desired. Process until smooth, transfer to a small crock, and cover the crock with a lid or plastic wrap. You can serve the cheese immediately or age it in the crock in the refrigerator. Serve on rusks of bread. The French often age fromage fort for several months, until it becomes very strong and stinky. It all depends on what you like.

The great Norman cheeses were served as well: Camembert, Pont l'Evêque, and the stinky Livarot. But my father warned: "Not for Mademoiselle Simone, the strong cheeses." He thought young girls shouldn't be allowed to pollute their mouths with smelly odors.

—Simone Beck

Cooking with Cheese: Troubleshooting

IT'S EASY TO GET INTO trouble when cooking with cheese. And it can happen in a flash, before you even know you have a problem. The most typical problems encountered are curdling, stringiness, and toughness. The secret is to cook cheese at a low temperature and not to cook it for too long.

CHEESE CAN CURDLE IF COOKED AT TOO HIGH A TEMPERATURE

Cheese is a protein food. When heated to too high a temperature, the casein, which is the protein, can curdle and separate from the fat and water in the cheese and form a tough, stringy, rubbery mass of curds in an oily puddle. Once this happens, it's beyond rescue.

The best way to avoid such a disaster is to add the cheese to a sauce at the end of cooking. Grate or shred the cheese, or crumble it into small pieces, so it will require less heat and less time to melt. It's also best to add the cheese slowly, little by little, stirring and melting each addition before adding the next one. Often cheese will melt just from the heat retained within a sauce after it has been removed from the stove. If all the cheese isn't melted sufficiently, you can return the sauce to low heat just long enough to melt the cheese and blend it into the sauce.

ADDING A STARCH CAN KEEP CHEESE FROM SEPARATING

If you plan to bake a casserole containing cheese for a long time at a high temperature, choose a sauce recipe that includes a starch. The starch will prevent the cheese from curdling while the casserole cooks.

This principle applies to fondue (see page 233) or chile con queso (see page 98) where the addition of a starch, such as flour or cornstarch, will prevent the proteins in the cheese from separating or coagulating when it is heated.

ACIDS CAN PREVENT CHEESES FROM BEING STRINGY

To avoid stringiness, food guru Shirley Corriher advocates sprinkling cheese with a little wine or lemon juice before melting it. Just as wine prevents stringiness in fondue, the addition of lemon juice can keep mozzarella from becoming a stringy mass when you toss it with hot pasta.

OVERHEATING CAN CAUSE CHEESE TO BECOME TOUGH

When using cheese as a topping, if you add it toward the end of baking or broiling, about five to ten minutes before the dish will be finished, you can avoid toughness. Adding it then means you can heat it just long enough to melt it, but not so long that it becomes leathery. When broiling cheese, keep it 3 to 4 inches from the heat source and broil it quickly under high heat.

ADDITIONAL CONSIDERATIONS FOR COOKING WITH CHEESE

- Cheeses that are high in fat make good melting cheeses, as do soft, moist cheeses. Both are less apt to become stringy when melted properly. Low-fat cheeses are not good melting cheeses because they are higher in proteins, which cause stringiness and leatheriness.

- Harder cheeses can withstand higher temperatures than softer ones because more of their protein was broken down into small fragments during the cheesemaking process.

- The better the quality of the cheese in a dish, the better the dish will be.

- Heat can change the flavor of a cheese. For example, the flavor of blue cheese is intensified when it is heated. The flavor of cheeses such as goat cheese, though, becomes less pronounced.

- Measure cheese accurately for cooking. Weight is the best way to measure cheese for recipes. For instance, 4 ounces hard cheese such as Gruyère equals 1 cup shredded cheese, whereas 4 ounces cream cheese equals ½ cup and 4 ounces crumbled feta equals ¾ cup.

- Some cheeses begin to separate at a temperature as low as 150°F.

- In fondue, the addition of the alcohol, either white wine or kirsch, lowers the boiling point and prevents the protein in the cheese from curdling.

Serving Cheese

How to Cut Cheese

SMALL CHEESES SHOULD BE SERVED whole. Pieces of larger cheeses can be served in the cut shapes in which they were purchased, usually wedges or large chunks. If you have a wheel of cheese, it's nice to cut a wedge out of the cheese and place the wedge beside the cheese. People can feel intimidated when they encounter a whole cheese and may not want to be the first to cut into it. One of the other cheeses can be sliced and fanned out to create an interesting presentation. But don't cube cheese; it will dry out, and cubes are not aesthetically pleasing.

The shape of the cheese often dictates how it should be cut. If you have a large wheel of cheese, first cut it in half, then cut the half into quarters, and finally into smaller wedges. The rind should always be distributed evenly among the pieces. It is easiest to cut cheese when it is cold.

If you are planning to serve cheeses precut on individual serving plates, adhere to these same rules. The cheeses should be cut into a variety of different shapes. One attractive way to cut a wedge of cheese for serving is to cut across it horizontally so that you have little triangles. Soft cheeses can easily be shaped into little balls and rolled in herbs or formed into other shapes.

How to Display Cheeses on a Tray

Because most cheeses are white, I like to display them on a plate or tray with a dark background. If you are using a light-colored plate or silver tray, large dark green leaves, such as grape leaves, show off cheeses well. Other large herb leaves or unsprayed lemon leaves also work well. Lacking fresh leaves, you can often find attractive paper leaves at cheese shops. You can use any type of wooden cutting board, a slab of granite or marble, ceramic tiles, plates or trays made of wicker, straw, or reeds. Even a cake pedestal can work well and give some height to your cheese arrangement.

Remember that presentation is of prime importance. Garnish the tray attractively but simply using fresh herbs, fruits, and/or edible flowers.

Arranging Cheeses for Serving

A variety of sizes and shapes of cheese makes for the best presentation. For aesthetics, one of the cheeses can be sliced and fanned. Use a tray or plate that is large enough to keep the cheeses from touching each other; they should have room to breathe. Don't place a very strong cheese next to a mild cheese, since the milder cheese might pick up the flavor of the strongly flavored cheese. Each cheese should have its own knife, and there should be enough space to cut easily into the various cheeses.

Serving Temperature for Cheese

Cheese should be served at room temperature (around 70°F.) for the best flavor, texture, and aroma. Always remove the cheeses from the refrigerator at least thirty minutes, and up to an hour, before serving them. The time depends on the size of the cheese pieces: Larger cheeses take a longer time to come to room temperature.

If you have a large piece of cheese and you don't plan to serve it all, it's best to cut off only what you plan to serve and return the rest of the cheese to the refrigerator quickly. Moving a cheese back and forth from the refrigerator causes it to spoil more quickly. And the longer a cheese stays at room temperature, the more moisture it loses.

Unwrap the cheeses and arrange them on the tray or serving piece ahead of time. If one of the cheeses is extremely runny or pungent, though, it should be kept wrapped and separate from the others until serving time. After arranging the cheeses on the tray, it's a good idea to loosely cover them with plastic wrap or a barely damp clean dish towel to keep them from drying out until serving time.

Accompaniments for Cheese

The accompaniments you choose should accent and complement the cheeses you are serving. They should allow the flavors and textures of the cheeses to shine with their own distinctive merits. Accompaniments can be placed on the tray with the cheeses, served separately, or placed nearby in small bowls or dishes.

The accompaniments depend upon the particular cheeses and when they will be served. Will they be served as an appetizer or as a prelude to dessert? Or will they be served as part of a meal? Which meal—breakfast, lunch, or dinner? Match sweet with salty, piquant, and/or sharp cheeses: Gorgonzola and dates, or Cheddar and chutney. Be careful not to overpower a cheese with the accompaniments. Some good accompaniments are:

Cured meats: Prosciutto, salami, or serrano ham from Spain.

Salads: Green salads of fresh herbs and field greens, simply dressed.

Olives: Green or black olives, along with olive spreads, tapenades, and capers.

Vegetables: Roasted red bell peppers, Italian pickled vegetables, and freshly shelled and peeled fava beans.

Fruits: Fresh ripe fruits such as figs, grapes, apples, pears, plums, and seasonal melons. (Sliced apples and pears should be dipped into water with freshly squeezed lemon juice to prevent discoloration). Dried fruits like dates are also good, but steer clear of citrus fruits, except for candied citrus rinds or candied fruits in syrup.

Toasted nuts: Almonds, hazelnuts, pecans, and walnuts.

Chutneys, fruit pastes, and cakes: Various chutneys and *mostardas* (Italian sweet-sour fruit condiments) as well as quince, fig, pear, and guava pastes from Spain and Mexico are particularly good.

Honey: Wildflower and herbal honeys drizzled over cheese not only are delicious but also make a nice presentation.

Garnishes for Cheese

First impressions are the most important. Remember, first we eat with our eyes, so be sure to spend a little time and energy garnishing your cheese tray. Fresh herbs, whole nuts, dried fruits, and even flowers add so much. Simplicity is always best. Use garnishes as accents to set off the cheeses.

Breads and Crackers for Serving Cheese

Serve mild cheeses with mild-tasting breads like plain baguettes. More assertive cheeses go nicely with stronger-tasting multigrain breads or even fruit and nut breads. Sourdough bread is good with more strongly flavored cheeses, but it can overpower some more subtly flavored cheeses. Hearth-baked breads with wonderful thick, rustic crusts are fabulous with any cheese. Always choose breads that have a good texture.

Choose different breads for different cheeses, such as olive bread for soft white spreadable cheeses like fresh goat cheese. Try toasted nut and herb breads with other soft spreadable cheeses such as Brie and triple-crèmes. Multigrain breads are good with Cheddars and other hearty aged cheeses. Be careful not to choose a bread that has such a strong overpowering flavor that it would detract from the cheese.

Bread should be served sliced. It can be heated, but it doesn't have to be. You can also slice some of the bread very thin and toast it so that you have a variety of textures. Serve bread in baskets or on a separate platter to keep it from getting soggy from the cheese.

There are any number of other possibilities, including crackers, ginger cookies, lavosh, and bread sticks. Crisp flatbreads are great too, and I love those Scandinavian crackers. Generally, plain unflavored crackers are best, since they won't compete with the flavor and aroma of the cheese.

Cheese Serving Utensils

Any small knife is good for serving cheese. Butter knives work very nicely for soft cheeses, and so do small paring knives. Choose a knife with a wider blade if the cheese is soft and spreadable. A sharp knife is necessary for harder cheeses; steak knives can work well. Sometimes you can find special little cheese knives in antiques stores.

Place one knife by each cheese on your tray. That way, each cheese can always be cut with the same knife and flavors will not be transferred from cheese to cheese. Also, this allows more than one person to serve himself from the cheese tray at one time.

There are some specialized knives for serving specific cheeses: In Italy, wedge-like almond-shaped knives with round wooden handles are used for extremely hard cheeses such as Parmigiano-Reggiano, because they can be used to crack off and split the cheese into chunks and pieces. Cheese planes are popular in Scandinavia; they are pulled across the flat surface of semi-soft and hard cheeses to shave off very thin slices. Cheese wires can be used to cut cheeses. A rolling cheese cutter with a wire is good for semi-soft to firm cheeses. Another such tool in this category is the French *roquefortaise*, a wire butter knife that allows the cheese to be cut without damaging its fragile interior. In France, a special tool called a *girolle* is used for Tête de Moine; it is inserted into the center of the wheel and then scraped over the surface in a clockwise motion to make thin shavings of cheese, which are then gathered together to make cheese flowers. In England, a special scoop is used to dig out the center of Stilton. Another special cheese knife has a slightly curved blade and a pronged point, and it is handy for cutting and then spearing semifirm and firm cheeses. There are small cheese cleavers as well. You can even use tightly held and stretched dental floss in place of a wire cheese cutter when cutting soft and very creamy cheeses.

For cutting large cheese wheels, professionals often use a large two-handled knife, shaped like a flat mezzaluna. Sturdy professional wire cutters are popular for cutting wheels into wedges. Another popular choice is a chef's knife with large holes in the blade that keep cheese from sticking to the blade. Or you can dip the knife into hot water and wipe it dry between slices if you need to cut large amounts of cheese.

Making Cheese at Home

WHEN I BEGAN THE MOZZARELLA Company, I had never made cheese at home. Ignorance was bliss. Fortunately for me, I learned to make cheese in my factory with a cheese professor there to instruct me each and every step of the way. I have always made cheese in large quantities, and the quantities have only become larger over the years. I have also had the good fortune to purchase equipment and supplies from commercial companies whose reputation for quality is impeccable.

Surprisingly, it turned out to be much more difficult to make cheese at home than I had expected. It is hard to maintain the proper temperatures needed when working with smaller quantities of milk and cheese. It is also difficult to find or improvise the proper equipment and supplies: There is only one place I know of—the New England Cheesemaking Supply Company in Ashfield, Massachusetts (see Sources, page 374). It is owned by Ricki Carroll, who years ago wrote the definitive home cheesemaking book, *Cheesemaking Made Easy*. The company sells cheesemaking ingredients, equipment, and supplies in sizes and quantities that are convenient for home cheesemaking. I heartily recommend Ricki's book to anyone who would like to go beyond the cheese recipes that I offer.

Over the years, I have developed and devised all the recipes that we use for our cheeses through experimentation. Many variables go into making cheese, and I urge you to do your own experiments and try different techniques. Be sure to take notes, record times and temperatures, and so on, so that you can go back and analyze one batch against another. Also be aware that things won't always work out as you plan. Milk is a living organism, and it is different each and every day. Invariably things go wrong and you won't know why. But don't give up. Be flexible. More than likely, something good will come out of your experiment and it will be something you will be able to use some way or another. Just remember that you need to be willing to be creative.

Milk

The source of the milk is of primary importance. Usually when milk is pasteurized, it is homogenized, which means that its fat globules are broken up into tiny particles so that they will stay evenly distributed throughout the milk and will no longer rise to the top when the milk stands undisturbed for a period of time. During homogenization, the composition of the milk is changed, and this in turn will affect the cheesemaking process.

The best milk to use for cheesemaking is raw milk; however, it's available only from a farm. I like to buy raw milk and pasteurize it myself so that I have more control over the bacteria present, but locating raw milk is probably out of the question for most home cheesemakers. If you do find this type of milk, be sure to pasteurize it (see below) before making a fresh cheese or a cheese you don't plan to age for at least sixty days.

The next best milk to use is milk that has only been pasteurized, not homogenized. You may find this type in a market near you. An easy way to recognize this milk is by its old-fashioned glass bottle. And finally, there is homogenized milk, the milk found in all supermarkets. All of the recipes in this chapter except the one for Aged Tomme will work with homogenized milk, but the cheeses will be better if you are able to use pasteurized milk that has not been homogenized.

If you buy raw milk at a farm, you should be sure to pasteurize it before you make fresh cheese. When milk is pasteurized, the harmful bacteria that cause brucellosis and other such problems are destroyed. The best method of pasteurization for cheesemaking is to heat the milk to 145°F. and hold it at that temperature for 30 minutes. Pasteurizing at this low temperature kills the smallest amount of good bacteria while eliminating all the harmful bacteria.

The next consideration is the fat content of the milk. Whole milk has a fat content of about 4 percent. The various other milks have lesser amounts of butterfat, down to skimmed milk, from which virtually all the fat has been removed. All of the recipes in this chapter, except the cottage cheese, were developed using whole milk. Depending on your preferences and health considerations, choose the milk you prefer. You may need to experiment with milks of varying butterfat content. Generally speaking, the lower the amount of fat in the milk, the harder the resultant cheese.

If a recipe, such as the ones for mascarpone and triple-crème cheese, calls for cream, buy heavy cream. This cream usually has 40 percent butterfat. It is best to steer clear of cream that is labeled ultra-pasteurized, because it has been heat-treated at a very high temperature and therefore contains few or no active bacteria and is virtually sterile.

Equipment

As for utensils, use stainless steel, glass, or enamel. Do not use aluminum unless it is coated. A large stainless steel or enameled stockpot or soup pot works very well. You'll also need another larger pot to hold the water bath that will heat the stockpot (unless you use the oven method). A large canning pot works well for this.

For stirring the milk, you'll need a stainless steel or heatproof plastic spoon. For cutting the curds, you'll need a knife with a long blade that will reach down to the bottom of the pot. A stainless steel perforated ladle or spoon is good for ladling the curds out into the cheesecloth. You'll also need a plastic or stainless steel colander. If you don't have a cheese mold, you can improvise by drilling or punching holes in the sides and bottom of flexible plastic containers.

For cheesecloth, I have found that unbleached muslin works very well. I prefer muslin to gauze cheesecloth because you have to use only one thickness and it retains the milk solids better. Flour-sack dish towels also work well, as do old sheets and pillowcases. If you use cheesecloth gauze, you will have to use several thicknesses to prevent the curds from passing through the cloth.

You will also need a good thermometer, one that measures temperatures between 70° and 212°F. I find the instant-read digital thermometers the easiest to work with. Before beginning, make sure yours is accurate by testing the temperature reading in boiling water—it should read 212°F.—and in a glass of ice and water—it should read 32°F. Temperature is critical during cheesemaking: Too low, and the cultures won't grow because the development of lactic acid is retarded; too high, and the bacteria may die in the culture, so there's nothing left to develop. It is important to regulate the temperature of the milk carefully and accurately as it incubates and coagulates. One easy method is to keep the pot in the oven, regulated to the desired incubation temperature. Or keep the pot with the milk or cheese in a larger pot filled with water kept at the incubation temperature.

Sanitation

Sanitation is of great importance. All utensils should be dipped into a sanitizing chlorine-and-water solution prior to each and every contact with the milk or cheese to avoid bacterial cross-contamination, so you'll need to have some household bleach on hand.

Cultures

Basically speaking, cultures are selected bacteria used to inoculate the milk. They replace the bacteria that are killed during pasteurization. There are two basic types of cultures: mesophilic and thermophilic. Mesophilic cultures are those that multiply and function at temperatures between 70° and 100°F. Thermophilic cultures are those that work at temperatures over 100°F.

The New England Cheesemaking Supply Company sells packets of freeze-dried cultures that will inoculate 2 gallons of milk each (see Sources, page 374). If you are making cheese using a smaller quantity of milk than 2 gallons, the easiest way to deal with the cultures is to bring 1 cup of milk to a boil and then cool it to 90°F. for mesophilic cultures or 100°F. for thermophilic cultures. Pour the entire packet of cultures into the milk, stir well to mix the cultures into the milk, and then cover with plastic wrap and allow to propagate until ready to use. Use the proportionate amount of culture for the amount of milk you have. Do not attempt to save the cultures for more than twenty-four hours, as wild bacteria may develop and contaminate the cultures.

You can also inoculate your milk with buttermilk in place of mesophilic cultures or acidophilus yogurt in place of thermophilic cultures. Results will vary depending on the freshness of the buttermilk or yogurt, but it's fun to experiment.

Coagulants

There are two ways to coagulate milk—by direct introduction of acid or by using cultures and rennet. With the direct-acid method, an acid such as lemon juice, vinegar, or citric acid is stirred into the milk. Cheeses made with this procedure develop curds that get soft but do not melt when heated. Ricotta and queso blanco are examples of cheese made in this method.

Rennet is a coagulant; it is the enzyme that causes the milk to coagulate. Originally, rennet came from the stomach lining of an unweaned kid. Now most rennet is microbial- or vegetable-based. It comes in tablet or liquid form. Rennet is very concentrated, so it must always be dissolved in a copious amount of fresh water before it is added to the milk. Generally, the rennet works in tandem with the lactic acid, producing cultures to coagulate milk in about 25 to 30 minutes. If coagulation takes place more rapidly, try reducing the amount of rennet the next time you make the cheese. The amount of rennet and length of time for coagulation determine the firmness of the curd, and if you add too much rennet, the curds can become rubbery. Cheeses made with cultures and rennet melt readily when heated.

It is very difficult to make good cheese at home and much simpler and a lot more convenient to buy it. But it's fun to experiment. As a beginner, you should stick to the simple fresh cheeses like ricotta, mascarpone, cream cheese, and queso blanco. Once you have mastered the fresh cheeses, move on to the aged cheeses. These cheeses are more complicated to make and present challenges because of the ambient conditions that are required for the aging process.

Mozzarella is even more difficult, because stringing the curds involves monitoring the pH of the cheese, a very difficult thing to do at home. As much as I would like to give you a foolproof recipe for mozzarella, I can't. I have tried and tried to make it at home, but I have failed each and every time. Perhaps I just know too much about proper factory mozzarella production, whereas ignorance would allow me to succeed. Instead, I recommend that you buy curds from a store that strings mozzarella daily. Alternatively, Ricki Carroll of the New England Cheesemaking Supply Company has developed a kit for making fresh mozzarella in a microwave (see Sources, page 374).

One final note of prime importance is cleanliness—you don't want to introduce foreign bacteria that could disturb your cheesemaking. Be careful, also, to adhere to the temperatures given. They are critical to the success of each recipe. Patience is another necessary ingredient, because there are so many variables, and it can take longer than expected for the cheese to mature and drain. But don't give up—even if the cheese doesn't turn out as you expect, you can always turn it into something else. I know this, for sure, from experience.

Crème Fraîche

Crème fraîche is a thickened cream. My crème fraîche is thick but pourable; some supermarket brands may be closer to the consistency of sour cream. Its thickness depends on its acid development. If you prefer it to be very thick, let it sit out of the refrigerator for a longer period of time. Crème fraîche can be used in place of sour cream or heavy cream. It is commonly used in French cooking, and French housewives always seem to have some sitting out thickening for the next day's dinner. It is also wonderful slightly sweetened with sugar and served with desserts.

MAKES 3 CUPS

2 cups heavy cream   ¼ cup yogurt with acidophilus cultures
¾ cup buttermilk

PREPARE A sanitizing solution of 1 quart water and 1 tablespoon household bleach.

RINSE OUT a glass quart jar or a stainless steel bowl with the sanitizing solution.

PLACE THE cream, buttermilk, and yogurt in the jar or bowl. Using a sanitized spoon, stir vigorously to mix. Cover the container with plastic wrap and set aside at room temperature for 4 to 8 hours, or overnight, until thickened. If it is not as thick as you would like it, leave at room temperature for several hours longer. Refrigerate once the crème fraîche has almost reached the desired consistency. It will continue to thicken as it chills. Use within 1 week.

Queso Blanco

Queso blanco can be used in place of pot cheese or farmer cheese. It is good in pastries, as well as in Mexican dishes of all types. But because an acid is used to curdle the milk, rather than cultures and rennet, queso blanco does not melt when heated; it just gets soft.

MAKES 2 (12-OUNCE) CHEESE ROUNDS

1 gallon homogenized whole milk	¼ to ½ cup white distilled vinegar
1 cup yogurt with acidophilus cultures	½ to 1 teaspoon salt, or to taste

PREPARE A sanitizing solution of 1 quart water and 1 tablespoon household bleach.

RINSE A large stainless steel or enameled stockpot or soup pot with the sanitizing solution and pour the milk into the pot. Using a sanitized spoon or whisk, stir in the yogurt. Cover the pot and set aside at room temperature for 4 hours.

REMOVE THE lid, place the pan over medium heat, and heat the mixture to 185°F., stirring as necessary so the milk does not scorch on the bottom of the pot. Remove from the heat. Slowly drizzle ¼ cup of the vinegar into the milk, stirring constantly with a sanitized spoon. Continue to add up to ¼ cup more vinegar, adding only enough to coagulate the curds. You will recognize the distinct change when the curds form: They will be white and will separate from the whey, which will be yellowish in color. You may not need to add all the vinegar. Cover the pot and set aside for 5 to 10 minutes.

RINSE A colander and a large piece of muslin or several layers of cheesecloth in the sanitizing solution. Wring out the cloth to release the excess water. Line the colander with the cloth and set the colander in the sink or over a large bowl. Pour the curds into the colander, letting the whey drip through. Drain for 10 minutes or until the curds are cool enough to handle.

PREPARE TWO ring-shaped molds for the cheese by cutting the bottoms off two sour cream containers or two flat and squatty ½-pint plastic containers. Dip the molds into the sanitizing solution and set on a flat plate or sheet pan lined with plastic wrap. Wash your hands and dip them into the sanitizing solution. Transfer the cheese to a large sanitized bowl and knead the salt into the cheese. Taste and add more salt if necessary.

DIVIDE THE curds in half. Place half in each mold, pressing and packing to compact them, and flatten the tops. Cover with plastic wrap and refrigerate for at least several hours, or until firm. Use within 1 week.

Ricotta

Fresh ricotta is very mild and has a delicate, milky flavor. It can be used in savory dishes as well as desserts. It is fabulous on pasta dressed simply with extra virgin olive oil and black pepper. It's even good for breakfast, with fruit or spread on bread.

Ricotta salata is a salty, dried version of ricotta that has been aged to develop a sharper flavor. The longer it is aged, the sharper the flavor. Ricotta salata can be grated and served over pasta and salads.

Traditionally, ricotta is made from whey, but since whey is available only as a by-product of making cheese, it is highly unlikely that you will want to make ricotta from whey. My ricotta recipe uses milk as the primary ingredient.

MAKES ABOUT 1 POUND 10 OUNCES, OR 3¼ CUPS

1 gallon homogenized whole milk	½ cup freshly squeezed lemon juice
1 cup heavy cream	Salt to taste (optional)

PREPARE A sanitizing solution of 1 quart of water and 1 tablespoon of household bleach.

RINSE A large stainless steel or enameled stockpot or soup pot with the sanitizing solution and pour the milk and cream into the pot. Place over medium-high heat and bring to a boil, stirring as necessary with a sanitized spoon so the milk doesn't scorch on the bottom of the pot. Reduce the heat to low and stir in the lemon juice. Continue stirring slowly until the milk curdles and white curds float to the top. Remove from the heat and cover. Wait for 5 minutes while the curds solidify slightly and become firmer.

RINSE A colander and a large piece of muslin or several layers of cheesecloth in the sanitizing solution. Wring out the cloth to release the excess water. Line the colander with the cloth and set the colander in the sink or over a large bowl.

USING A sanitized perforated spoon, gently ladle the curds into the colander. Let the whey drain for 30 minutes, or until the ricotta is still moist but fairly dry. After about 15 minutes, lift the edges of the cloth toward the center of the colander to loosen the cheese from the cloth and facilitate draining. If the ricotta is still too liquid and runny in texture after 30 minutes, gather the edges of the cloth together using one hand, wrap a piece of kitchen string around the gathered cloth to form a bag, and tie it closed. Hang the bag containing the cheese from the faucet or the handle of a kitchen cabinet door and allow the excess whey to drip from the bag into the sink or a bowl. If adding salt, transfer the ricotta to a sanitized bowl and stir in the salt. Place the ricotta in an airtight container and store it in the refrigerator. Use within 5 days.

Ricotta Salata

Follow the recipe above to the point of covering the pot and waiting 5 minutes for the curds to solidify. Then return the stockpot to low heat and gently heat the curds for 5 minutes, without stirring. Remove from the heat, cover, and wait for 5 minutes. Ladle the curds into a sanitized colander lined with sanitized muslin or several layers of cheesecloth, sprinkle with 1 tablespoon salt, and stir to mix in. Drain in the sink or over a large bowl for 30 minutes.

Gather up the edges of the cloth, press the curds together, and tie the cloth with a string to form a bag. Hang the bag from the faucet or from the handle of a cabinet door and let drain, into the sink or a bowl, for several hours. Take the cheese down and twist the cloth to compact the cheese even more.

Place the cheese, still wrapped in the cloth, in the colander, set it in the sink or over a bowl, place a weight, such as a heavy saucepan partially filled with water, on top of the cheese, and press it for 1 hour.

Remove the cloth and turn the cheese over, to keep it from sticking to the cloth later, rewrap it in the cloth, and return to the colander. Replace the weight on top of the cheese and leave at cool room temperature, 70°F. or less, to drain for 12 hours. (If the weather is hot, drain the cheese in the refrigerator for 24 hours.)

To age the cheese, unwrap it and sprinkle lightly with salt, rubbing it into the cheese. Wrap in plastic wrap, and refrigerate. Each day for 1 week, sprinkle the cheese lightly with salt and rub it into the exterior. Also check the cheese daily for mold. If mold appears, scrape it off, sprinkle the affected area with salt, and rub it in. Replace the plastic wrap daily. If the cheese begins to get mushy or soft on the exterior, remove the plastic wrap, sprinkle the cheese with salt, rubbing it in, place on a paper towel on a plate, and refrigerate uncovered for a few days, until it dries slightly. Age the cheese for a total of 2 to 4 weeks. The longer it ages, the more flavorful it will become.

To serve, the cheese can be crumbled or grated.

MAKES 1 CHEESE ROUND WEIGHING ABOUT 1½ POUNDS.

Sue's Cottage Cheese

Sue Conley and Peggy Smith own a small cheese factory in the town of Tomales, California, north of San Francisco, called the Cowgirl Creamery. Sue is famous for her cottage cheese, which she sells on Saturdays at the Ferry Market in San Francisco.

MAKES ABOUT 1 POUND 12 OUNCES, OR 4 CUPS

1 gallon nonfat milk

1 cup buttermilk

1 tray ice cubes

½ to 1 cup (4 to 8 ounces) crème fraîche, homemade (page 68) or store-bought

Salt to taste

PREPARE A sanitizing solution of 1 quart water and 1 tablespoon household bleach.

RINSE A stainless steel or enameled stockpot or soup pot with the sanitizing solution and pour the milk into the pot. Place the pot in a large bowl or larger stockpot and surround the milk pot with warm water (90°F.). With a sanitized spoon, stir in the buttermilk. Leave the milk in the water bath to incubate for 24 hours, or until a firm, custard-like curd forms. The temperature of the milk will slowly decrease from 90° to 70°F. (room temperature).

RINSE A long knife in the sanitizing solution and cut the curd into smaller curds: First cut the curd, top to bottom, into slices ½ inch apart, then cut again at right angles into ½-inch slices. Then, using the knife or a sanitized ladle, cut the curds horizontally at an angle from the bottom of the pot upward into ½-inch cubes. Leave undisturbed for 15 minutes.

Place the pot, still in the water bath, over medium heat and cook slowly until the curds and whey reach 120°F. The temperature should not rise more than 1 degree a minute, so this process will take up to 1 hour. (If you cook the curds too quickly, the outer skin of the curd will be too firm and the inside will be too mushy.) Stir very gently just a few times until the temperature reaches 90°F., then stir constantly until it reaches 120°F.

RINSE A colander and a large piece of muslin or several layers of cheesecloth in the sanitizing solution. Wring out the cloth to release the excess water. Line the colander with the cloth and set the colander in the sink or over a large bowl. Using a sanitized perforated spoon, ladle the curds into the colander and let drain for 15 minutes.

Fill a large bowl with the ice cubes and some cold water. Remove the curds, still wrapped in the muslin, from the colander and gather up the edges of the muslin like a bag. Holding the cloth together so the curds stay inside, dip the bag into the ice water and swirl it around for about 5 minutes to wash off the curds. Return the curds, still in the muslin, to the colander and drain for 1 hour.

Place the curds in a sanitized bowl, add crème fraîche as desired, and stir. Season to taste with salt. Cover tightly and refrigerate. Use within 1 week.

Mascarpone

Mascarpone is usually made with tartaric acid, but because tartaric acid is hard to find, I developed this recipe using yogurt. If you're in a hurry, you can skip the step of heating the cream to 195°F., but I like the flavor the cooked cream gives the cheese.

Mascarpone is good for desserts as well as for savory dishes. It adds a special creaminess and richness. You can also use it in place of clotted cream for scones and in place of cream cheese on bagels.

MAKES ALMOST 2 CUPS

2 cups heavy cream	¾ cup buttermilk
One 10-pound bag ice	¼ cup yogurt with acidophilus cultures

PREPARE A sanitizing solution of 1 quart water and 1 tablespoon household bleach.

RINSE A large stainless steel or enameled saucepan with the sanitizing solution and pour the cream into the saucepan. Place the pan over medium heat and stir with a sanitized spoon to keep the cream from scorching until it reaches 195°F. Fill a large bowl with the ice and a little water. Place the pan in the ice bath to cool, and stir until the cream reaches 90°F. Remove the pan from the ice bath.

POUR THE cream into a sanitized stainless steel or glass bowl, add the buttermilk and yogurt, and stir to combine. Cover and set aside at room temperature to incubate for 8 hours, or until the mixture thickens and becomes stiff. Refrigerate for several hours; it will thicken even more as it chills.

RINSE A colander and a large piece of muslin or several layers of cheesecloth in the sanitizing solution. Wring out the cloth to release the excess water. Line the colander with the cloth and set it in a shallow pan or over a large bowl. Slowly pour the cream into the colander. Let the mascarpone drain at room temperature for 4 hours, or until it is very thick and stands in soft peaks when stirred with a spoon. Alternatively, place it in the refrigerator to drain overnight.

REMOVE THE mascarpone from the cloth, place in a sanitized bowl, stir, and cover with plastic wrap. Refrigerate until ready to use; use within 1 week.

THE MASCARPONE can be used as is or heated in a recipe. It can also be whipped; make sure, however, that it is very cold before whipping it, or it may separate because it is so high in butterfat.

Fresh Cream Cheese

Cream cheese is a simple cheese to make at home. The entire cheesemaking process will take at least three days, but not much of that involves actual work, and the finished product is well worth the effort. This fresh cream cheese won't look like store-bought cheese. It will be soft and appear a little dry and crumbly, but it smoothes out easily once it warms to room temperature and is stirred. It can be whipped using the food processor or a hand mixer, but be careful not to over-process it because it can break down very quickly and become runny. Use it in cheesecakes, fruit tarts, or vegetable dips. Of course, it's great on bagels too.

MAKES ALMOST 2 POUNDS, OR 4 CUPS

1 gallon homogenized whole milk

One 10-pound bag ice

1 packet mesophilic cultures (see Note)

4 drops vegetable rennet (see Note)

1 to 2 teaspoons salt, or to taste

PREPARE A sanitizing solution of 1 quart water and 1 tablespoon household bleach.

RINSE A large stainless steel or enameled stockpot or soup pot with the sanitizing solution and pour the milk into the pot. Heat over medium heat, using a sanitized spoon to stir as necessary to keep the milk from scorching, until it reaches 165°F. While the milk is heating, fill the sink or a large bowl with the ice and a little water.

ONCE THE milk has reached 165°F., remove the pot from the heat and place it in the ice bath. Stir occasionally until it cools to 90°F.; this should take about 20 minutes. Transfer the milk to a sanitized bowl. Add the mesophilic cultures to the milk (the instructions on the package say that one packet inoculates 2 gallons milk, but you should use the whole packet for this recipe) and stir well for 1 minute. Cover with plastic wrap and then with a dish towel. Set aside, undisturbed, in a warm place (70° to 80°F.) for 45 minutes; an unheated oven is a good place.

DILUTE THE rennet in ½ cup cold water, stirring well. Add this to the inoculated milk and stir in a figure-eight pattern for 1 minute. (The rennet is very concentrated, so the dilution and stirring are critical.) Cover the container with clean plastic wrap and then with a dish towel and set aside, undisturbed, in a warm place (70° to 80°F.) until whey (clear yellow liquid) appears on top and the curd is firm enough for you to press gently on it without breaking it. This should take between 18 and 28 hours: When the milk is properly coagulated, the curd will resemble white gelatin or yogurt and be firm enough to hold its shape on a spoon. (If this doesn't happen within the given time range, the room temperature may be too cool or the cultures may be slow in their acid development; just wait a few more hours and test the curd for coagulation again.) To test the curd, wash your hands and dip them into the sanitizing solution. Dip your forefinger into the coagulated milk and slowly raise it to the surface, with your finger extended horizontally. The curd should rise up slightly and then there will be a clean breaking line in the curd if the milk is properly coagulated.

RINSE A colander and a large piece of muslin or several layers of cheesecloth in the sanitizing solution. Wring out the cloth to release the excess water. Line the colander with the cloth and set the colander in the sink or over a large bowl. (If you want to save the high-protein whey for cooking or baking, set the colander over the bowl.)

ONCE THE curd has coagulated, use a sanitized ladle or a mesh skimmer to carefully scoop the curd into the colander. When transferring the curds, be careful to break it up as little as possible. If the curd is shattered, it will expel more whey and that will make the cheese drier and less flavorful. Fold the excess fabric over the curd and set the colander in a large bowl. Cover the bowl with plastic wrap and place it in the refrigerator for 24 hours to drain and chill.

TRANSFER THE cheese to a sanitized bowl, stir it with a spoon, and add salt to taste. Cover tightly and refrigerate; use within 1 week.

Note: The cultures and rennet are available from the New England Cheesemaking Supply Company (see Sources, page 374.)

Aged Tomme

This recipe involves lots of steps and takes about six hours to complete. (A lot of the time is spent waiting, so make sure to have a good book to read or a project to do in between steps.) But it is fun to come up with a cheese that you can age.

To make this cheese, you'll need to buy milk that has been pasteurized but not homogenized. You can often find it in glass bottles at natural foods stores and in specialty markets. You can use either cow's milk or goat milk, but the resultant cheese will be dramatically different. The cheese made from cow's milk will be much milder and have a less pronounced flavor. Try making one cheese from each milk, and decide which you prefer.

You could also use raw milk, which you would have to buy directly from a farmer. If you want to make the cheese from raw milk without pasteurizing it, to be safe you will need to age the cheese for at least 60 days before eating it. (If following this procedure, omit the first step of the recipe of heating the milk to 165°F. for 30 minutes, and begin with heating your milk to 100°F.)

MAKES 1 CHEESE ROUND, ABOUT 14 OUNCES

1 gallon plus 2 cups pasteurized (not homogenized) whole cow's milk or goat milk

1 packet mesophilic cultures (see Note)

1 packet thermophilic cultures (see Note)

One 10-pound bag of ice

¼ tablet rennet (see Note)

Salt

PREPARE A sanitizing solution of 1 quart water and 1 tablespoon household bleach.

RINSE A large stainless steel or enameled stockpot or soup pot with the sanitizing solution and add 1 gallon of the milk. Heat the milk over medium heat to 165°F., then hold at that temperature for 30 minutes. This can be done by placing the pot in a larger pan containing 165° to 170°F. water, set over low heat, or in an oven heated to 165°F. Use a thermometer to maintain a constant temperature, and stir the milk occasionally.

IN THE meantime, fill a medium saucepan half-full with ice and cold water. Bring the remaining 2 cups milk to a boil in a small sanitized saucepan. Immediately remove from the heat and place in the ice bath; using a sanitized spoon, stir until the milk cools to 100°F. Pour 1 cup milk into each of two sanitized glasses. Add the mesophilic cultures to one glass and the thermophilic cultures to the other glass of milk and stir each well to mix. Cover with plastic wrap, mark the glasses, and set aside.

FILL THE sink with cold water and the remaining ice. Once the stockpot of milk has remained at 165°F. for 30 minutes, place it in the ice water bath and, using a sanitized spoon, stir to cool to 100°F. (Begin here if using raw milk. Heat milk to 100°F. and continue.) Remove from the ice bath. Add ½ cup of the mesophilic cultured milk and all of the thermophilic cultured milk to the milk and stir well with a sanitized spoon. (Discard the remaining cultured milk or cover tightly and refrigerate for use within 12 hours.) Place stockpot either in a large bowl or pot of 100°F. water or in a 100°F. oven. Let the milk incubate for 1½ hours while you carefully regulate the oven or water bath by turning the heat on and off to maintain a constant temperature; checking constantly with a thermometer.

WHEN THE milk has incubated for about 1 hour and 15 minutes, dissolve the rennet tablet in 1 tablespoon of water, stirring and breaking up the tablet. Then stir 1½ teaspoons of the dissolved rennet into ¼ cup cold water. Set aside.

WHEN THE milk has incubated for 1½ hours, remove it from the water bath or oven, pour the diluted rennet into the milk, and, using a sanitized spoon, stir vigorously in a figure-eight pattern for 1 minute. Stop the movement of the milk by holding the spoon still in the milk, and return the milk to the 100°F. water bath or the 100°F. oven to coagulate for 25 to 30 minutes. Keep the oven or water bath regulated so the temperature of the milk remains at 100°F.

SANITIZE A long knife and cut the curd mass into smaller curds: First cut through it, top to bottom, into slices about ½ inch apart, then cut it again at right angles, top to bottom, into slices about ½ inch apart. Using the sanitized knife or a ladle, cut the curds horizontally at an angle from the bottom of the pot upward into ½-inch cubes. Let stand for 5 minutes.

USING A sanitized perforated spoon, carefully fold over the curds from the bottom and sides of the pot, gently cutting any that are larger than the others with the edge of the spoon. Return the pot to the 100°F. water bath or 100°F. oven to incubate; keep the temperature of the curds at 100°F. After 15 minutes, stir the curds, using the spoon, from the bottom to the top again; then repeat after 15 minutes more. Each time, cut up any large curds with the spoon as you stir. Stir the curds once more, cutting them into slightly smaller, uniformly sized pieces with the knife. Return the pot to the water bath or the oven, slowly increasing the temperature to about 110°F. by turning on the heat under the pot or in the oven.

YOU CAN improvise a cheese mold by using an ice pick to punch ⅛-inch-wide holes in the sides and the bottom of a thick, flexible plastic bowl or container, spacing them about ½ inch apart. Make sure to punch the holes from the inside, so that the muslin or cheesecloth will not snag or catch on the edges of the holes. Alternatively, you can use a colander. Rinse the mold or colander and a large piece of muslin or several layers of cheesecloth in the sanitizing solution. Wring out the cloth to release the excess water. Line the mold with the cloth. Set over a pan or in the sink.

REMOVE THE pot from the water bath or oven and drain off about 8 cups of whey by using a sanitized cup and scooping the whey into the colander and allowing it to drain away, capturing any curds in the cloth; return these curds to the pot. Add 8 cups warm water (about 115°F.) to the curds. Increase the water bath or oven temperature to 140° to 150°F. Return the pot to the water bath or oven and heat the curds, stirring every 5 minutes to keep them from matting together, until the temperature of the curds and whey is 115°F.; the temperature of the curds should not rise more than 2 degrees every 5 minutes. Once or twice during the stirring and heating process, cut the curds smaller, using the knife, so that they are finally about the size of a corn kernel.

REMOVE THE pot from the heat, pour the curds into the lined mold or colander, and let the whey drain away. Twist the cloth tightly around the curds and squeeze and press out as much whey as you can, then return the curds, still wrapped in the cloth, to the mold or colander. Place a heavy saucepan on top of the curds to weight them down and press for 30 minutes.

REMOVE THE cloth and turn the curds over, to keep them from sticking to the cloth later, then rewrap them in the cloth. Twist the cloth closed and turn the cloth bag upside down in the mold or colander. Fill the saucepan full of water and place on top of the curds to weight them down and press them for 8 to 10 hours at cool room temperature (about 70°F.).

REMOVE THE cloth, sprinkle ¼ teaspoon of salt over the cheese, and rub it into the exterior of the cheese. Place the unwrapped cheese in a colander to allow for air circulation and place in the refrigerator to age. Turn it and rub it with salt daily for 2 weeks. Each day, check to make sure other food is not stacked around the cheese and that there is room for air to circulate around it. Once the exterior of the cheese is dry, wrap it in plastic wrap and continue to age it in the refrigerator for 1 to 2 months total. If mold develops, scrape it off, rub the cheese with salt, and rewrap it in clean plastic wrap.

Note: The cultures and rennet are available from The New England Cheesemaking Supply Company (see Sources, page 374).

VARIATIONS

Black Pepper Tomme

Soak 1 to 2 tablespoons whole black peppercorns in ½ cup hot water for 30 minutes. Drain the peppercorns and stir them into the curds prior to draining and placing in the mold.

Herbed Tomme

After 2 weeks of rubbing the cheese with salt daily, completely cover the cheese on all sides with ¼ cup dried herbes de Provence. Continue to age.

Basic Recipes

I have been using this recipe to make my own seasoning salt forever, and I season nearly everything I cook with it. I make up a big batch, put some in one of those tin shaker cans right next to my stove, and store the rest in a Mason jar in the pantry. I sometimes make it to give away at Christmastime in little saltshakers. This recipe originally came from one of my mother's friends, and way back in the early days, I think it might have contained MSG, although I've never included it in my recipe. Make sure to use fresh spices, as they have so much more potency than tired old ones.

MAKES ABOUT 4 CUPS

2¾ cups salt (about 26 ounces)

6 tablespoons ground black pepper (about 1½ ounces)

½ cup cayenne pepper (about 2 ounces)

3 tablespoons garlic powder (about 1 ounce)

¼ cup chili powder (about 1 ounce)

COMBINE ALL the ingredients in a bowl and stir well. Be careful not to sneeze!

STORE IN a cool, dark place. The salt will keep for 1 year.

Basil Pesto

I couldn't live without basil. It adds a wonderful piquant flavor to any dish it graces. In Italian, *pesto* means "pounded" or "mashed" and that's because pesto is traditionally made with a mortar and pestle. The most famous pesto comes from Liguria, a region of northern Italy on the Mediterranean coast. It's usually made with basil, pine nuts, garlic, olive oil, salt, and Pecorino. In recent years, American chefs have created many wonderful new pestos that run the gamut from sun-dried tomato to cilantro.

I always make pesto during the summer, especially when I have an overabundance of fresh basil. I prefer to use walnuts because I like their flavor and because they aren't as expensive as pine nuts.

Because it is made without cheese, my pesto can be frozen and kept for months. A clever way to freeze the pesto and have it available later in small amounts is to pour it into an ice-cube tray. Once the cubes are frozen, place them in a tightly closed container in the freezer. They can be used later for flavoring sauces, soups, and pasta dishes.

MAKES ABOUT 1 ½ CUPS

2 large cloves garlic, peeled

½ cup walnuts

½ teaspoon salt

2 cups tightly packed fresh basil leaves

⅓ cup extra virgin olive oil, plus extra if storing

PREPARE THE pesto in the work bowl of a food processor fitted with a steel blade. With the motor running, drop the garlic through the feed tube to mince it. Stop the machine, add the walnuts and salt, and pulse to coarsely chop the nuts. Add the basil and process until finely chopped. With the machine running, pour the olive oil through the feed tube and process to a puree.

USE AT once, or store in an airtight container in the refrigerator. Cover the top of the pesto with a layer of olive oil to help keep the color bright green. If necessary, drizzle additional oil over the top of the remaining pesto as you use it. The pesto will keep for several months.

Chicken Broth

There are as many ways to make a good chicken broth as there are types of soup, and yet so many people continue to open cans of stock. This is my personal method, and I assure you it could not be easier or more delicious. This recipe makes about six cups, and I like to make it in advance and store it in my freezer. I always feel as if broth in the freezer is like money in the bank.

MAKES ABOUT 6 CUPS

1 broiler-fryer chicken (2½ to 3½ pounds)

2 carrots, cut into chunks

1 onion, studded with 4 whole cloves

2 ribs celery, cut into chunks

1 tomato, cored and quartered

2 teaspoons salt

¼ teaspoon whole black peppercorns

12 cups water

1 teaspoon dried herbes de Provence

PLACE THE chicken in a large soup pot or stockpot. Add the carrots, onion, celery, tomato, salt, and peppercorns. Add the water, place the pot over high heat, and bring to a boil. Adjust the heat so the liquid boils slowly. Remove the foam as it rises to the top with a skimmer or a large flat spoon, and discard. (The foam would make the stock cloudy.) After about 15 minutes of skimming, add the herbes de Provence, lower the heat to a slow simmer, and cook for 30 minutes. Turn the chicken over and cook for 30 minutes longer, or until the meat is beginning to fall off the bones.

REMOVE THE pot from the heat. Take out the chicken and vegetables, discard the vegetables, and reserve the chicken for another use. Set the broth aside to cool for 30 minutes to 1 hour.

WHEN COOLED, strain the broth into a large container. Cover and refrigerate for several hours, until the fat rises to the surface and congeals.

REMOVE AND discard the congealed fat. There should be about 6 cups of broth. If there is more, reduce the broth over high heat until 6 cups remain; if there is less, just add water.

THE BROTH will keep for 5 days refrigerated and several months if frozen.

Crêpes

The thin little pancakes called crêpes are very versatile. They can be used in both savory and sweet dishes and make the easiest dishes look elegant. They are quick and simple to make. Best of all, extras can be frozen for later use.

MAKES ABOUT 16 (6-INCH) CREPES

2 large eggs

1 cup milk

1 cup unbleached all-purpose flour

Pinch of ground nutmeg

½ teaspoon salt

2 tablespoons clarified unsalted butter, melted (see Box below)

Clarified butter or vegetable oil, for the pan

COMBINE THE eggs, milk, flour, nutmeg, salt, and melted butter in the work bowl of a food processor fitted with the steel blade or in a blender. Pulse to mix well, scraping the sides as necessary. Cover and refrigerate the batter for at least 1 hour.

HEAT A crêpe pan or small nonstick skillet, about 6 inches in diameter, over medium-high heat. Brush the pan with butter or oil. Ladle 2 tablespoons of the batter into the pan while tilting and swirling the pan to cover the bottom with a thin film of batter. Cook for about 15 seconds, or until the top begins to appear dry. Using a small spatula or your fingers, turn the crêpe over and cook the other side for 5 seconds, or until lightly browned and cooked through. (The two sides will be different colors; generally the browner first side is the one used as the outside in any rolled crêpe recipe.) Slide the crêpe out of the pan onto a plate. Continue cooking in this fashion, stacking the crêpes, until the batter is gone.

THE CRÊPES can be used immediately or stored in the refrigerator or freezer for later use. To store, place small squares of waxed paper between the crêpes and wrap the stack tightly in plastic wrap. The crêpes will keep for 5 days refrigerated and several months if frozen.

Clarifying Butter

To clarify butter, place 8 tablespoons (1 stick) butter in a small saucepan and melt over low heat. Remove from the heat and let stand for 5 minutes, or until the milk solids sink to the bottom, leaving the clear yellow liquid, clarified butter, on top. Skim (or carefully pour) off the clarified butter and discard the milk solids. Alternatively, you can chill the melted butter, then remove the hardened clarified butter. Clarified butter keeps for weeks in the refrigerator.

Homemade Pasta Dough

When I lived in Italy, you could pass by almost any doorway and look inside to see pasta being made. In Italian, pasta called *fatta in casa* means made at home. Despite many attempts, I have never mastered the Italian technique of spreading flour on a board, making a well, and then stirring in the eggs and water with a fork. Italians say it's simple, but not for me. Instead, I devised this recipe for the food processor. It's easy as can be.

Once made, the pasta dough can be rolled out by hand or run through a hand-cranked or electric pasta machine into sheets and then cut into ribbons or other shapes.

MAKES ABOUT ½ POUND

1 cup unbleached all-purpose flour

½ teaspoon salt

1 tablespoon water

1 large egg

1 tablespoon extra virgin olive oil

PLACE THE flour and salt in the work bowl of a food processor fitted with a steep blade. Add the water, egg, and olive oil and process until a ball forms on the blade that cleans the sides of the bowl. Remove the dough and pat it into a disk. Wrap the dough with plastic wrap and set aside for 30 minutes, or until ready to roll out.

DUST THE ball of dough with flour and knead it briefly on a floured board. Roll it out by hand, using a rolling pin, or roll through a pasta machine to the desired thickness, then cut into ribbons or another shape. The pasta should be used the day it is made.

Paula's Tomato Sauce

This is my favorite tomato sauce recipe. It's great for spaghetti, for lasagne, for pizza, and for meat dishes, and it's a snap to make. If you're in a hurry, drain away the excess tomato juice and just puree the tomatoes. The sauce will cook much faster.

I prefer seasoning the sauce with fresh basil; dried oregano or other herbs work just as well.

MAKES 2½ CUPS

2 tablespoons extra virgin olive oil

3 cloves garlic, minced (2 teaspoons)

2 (14.5-ounce) cans peeled whole tomatoes in juice

6 leaves fresh basil, minced

Salt and freshly ground black pepper to taste

HEAT THE olive oil in a medium saucepan over medium heat. Add the garlic and cook until it is fragrant and golden brown. Remove the tomatoes from the cans and coarsely chop by hand or using a food processor. If a smooth sauce is desired, puree the tomatoes in the work bowl of a food processor fitted with a steel blade. Add the tomatoes to the pan, along with the juice from the cans, and cook over medium heat, stirring occasionally, until the sauce becomes thick, for 15 to 30 minutes, depending on how finely the tomatoes were chopped and the thickness of their juice. Remove the sauce from the heat, stir in the basil, and season with salt and pepper. The sauce keeps, covered and refrigerated, for up to 1 week. Frozen, it will keep for several months.

Appetizers

Mushrooms Stuffed with Ricotta and Prosciutto

This recipe was inspired by Ann Clark, a cookbook author and former cooking school owner. For years, she taught cooking classes at her Austin school, La Bonne Cuisine. She also owned a widely respected catering business, and she often served a dish like this one.

MAKES ABOUT 2½ CUPS STUFFING
SERVES 8 TO 12

16 medium or 12 large shiitake or cremini mushrooms

RICOTTA STUFFING
8 ounces ricotta, homemade (page 70) or store-bought, well drained (1 cup)

3 tablespoons heavy cream

4 thin slices prosciutto, chopped (2½ ounces)

3 tablespoons finely chopped fresh flat-leaf parsley

1 tablespoon finely chopped fresh basil

½ teaspoon finely chopped fresh thyme

2 tablespoons finely chopped fennel bulb

1 ounce Parmigiano-Reggiano, grated (¼ cup)

Salt to taste

½ teaspoon freshly ground black pepper

Sprigs of fresh parsley, basil, and/or thyme, for garnish

PREHEAT THE oven to 375°F.

RUB THE mushrooms with a damp cloth to remove any dirt. Remove the stems and finely chop them. Set aside the mushroom caps for stuffing.

FOR THE Ricotta Stuffing, beat the ricotta with the cream in a medium bowl. Add the prosciutto, parsley, basil, thyme, fennel, Parmigiano, and the reserved mushroom stems and stir to combine. Season with salt and the pepper.

LIGHTLY OIL a baking pan just large enough to hold the stuffed mushrooms in a single layer. Mound a portion of the stuffing in each mushroom cap, smoothing the top, and place the stuffed mushrooms in the baking pan.

BAKE FOR 7 to 10 minutes, or until the filling is heated through and the mushrooms are just beginning to soften. Remove from the oven.

PLACE THE mushrooms on a serving platter, garnish with sprigs of fresh herbs, and serve warm.

Baked Camembert
with Green Tomatillo Salsa

This recipe was inspired by Patricia Quintana, a Mexican chef and cookbook author who studied cooking in France. Today she often uses her classic French training when preparing magical Mexican food. This recipe is the perfect marriage of a French cheese and a Mexican sauce. The sauce is easy to make and very versatile.

Tomatillos resemble little green tomatoes covered with papery husks. They are quite acidic, and that's why I add a small amount of sugar to the salsa.

Serve the dish with tortillas for a light lunch or as an hors d'oeuvre. The sauce is also good on grilled chicken, poached salmon, and even enchiladas.

MAKES ABOUT 1 ½ CUPS SALSA
SERVES 6

GREEN SALSA

½ small white onion, unpeeled

2 cloves garlic, unpeeled

3 serrano chiles

1 jalapeño chile

8 tomatillos, husks removed and washed

1½ cups coarsely chopped fresh cilantro (1 large bunch) *or* 1¼ cups fresh chopped cilantro plus ¼ cup chopped fresh epazote *or* 1 cup chopped fresh cilantro plus ½ cup chopped fresh hoja santa

2½ tablespoons extra virgin olive oil

2 tablespoons freshly squeezed lime juice, or to taste

¼ teaspoon salt, or to taste

Pinch of sugar, or to taste

1 whole Camembert (8 ounces)

Fresh cilantro leaves, for garnish

Roasted red pepper strips, for garnish

12 (8-inch) flour tortillas, warmed and cut into quarters

FOR THE Green Salsa, preheat the broiler.

CUT THE onion into 2 pieces. Place the onion, garlic, chiles, and tomatillos on a baking sheet and position the pan 3 inches from the broiler. Roast the vegetables, turning as necessary, until the skins of the chiles are blistered and the onions, garlic, and tomatillos are deeply browned or blackened. Remove the vegetables from the heat, place in a bowl, cover with plastic wrap, and allow to steam until cool.

WHEN COOL, remove and discard any blackened skins. Put all of the vegetables in the work bowl of a food processor fitted with a steel blade or a blender and pulse until the mixture is uniformly chopped. Add the cilantro, oil, lime juice, salt, and sugar. Blend to the desired consistency, as coarse or smooth as you like. Taste the salsa and add additional salt, sugar, or lime juice if necessary. Set aside at room temperature to allow the flavors to blend while you prepare the cheese.

PREHEAT THE oven to 350°F.

PLACE THE Camembert on a baking sheet and bake for 15 minutes.

POUR THE salsa into a large shallow serving dish. Using a large spatula, carefully place the heated cheese on the salsa. Garnish the cheese with cilantro leaves and bell pepper strips. Serve with the warmed tortillas.

VARIATION

Camembert Wedges with Green Salsa

To serve the Camembert on individual plates, as an entrée or an appetizer, bake the cheese for only 5 minutes. Cut it into 6 wedges. Pour ¼ cup of sauce onto each individual serving plate and top with a wedge of heated Camembert. Garnish with cilantro leaves and bell pepper strips. Accompany each serving with 2 heated tortillas rolled up like cigars.

For full persuasion Camembert, like a good orator, should stop short just this side of fluency.

–Clifton Fadiman

Beggar's Purses Filled with Herbed Ricotta in Red Bell Pepper Sauce

Beggar's purses are so named because they resemble small pieces of cloth tied up with string to hold a few coins. You just gather up the crêpes into little sacks and then tie them with chive strings. I love to serve them as an appetizer, particularly at dinner parties, because they are so full of fresh herbal flavors.

The flavor of fresh herbs is very important to me, and I have always had an herb garden, even if I've had to grow the herbs in flowerpots in a window box, as I did when I lived in an apartment in Italy. Nowadays I dash out of the kitchen into the garden while I'm cooking to snip herbs for my dishes. I'm convinced they are most fragrant and flavorful this way.

**MAKES ABOUT 1½ CUPS SAUCE
MAKES ABOUT 1 CUP FILLING
SERVES 4 OR 8**

RED BELL PEPPER SAUCE

1 tablespoon extra virgin olive oil

2 red bell peppers, cored, seeded, and coarsely chopped

2 tablespoons minced onion

1 clove garlic, minced

½ cup chicken broth, homemade (page 81) or store-bought

¼ teaspoon minced fresh thyme

Salt and freshly ground black pepper to taste

RICOTTA FILLING

8 ounces ricotta, homemade (page 70) or store-bought, well drained (1 cup)

2 tablespoons minced fresh chives

½ teaspoon minced fresh thyme

½ teaspoon minced fresh oregano

1 large egg, lightly beaten

8 Crêpes (page 82)

8 fresh chives, about 4 to 5 inches long

FOR THE Red Bell Pepper Sauce heat the oil in a large skillet. Add the bell peppers, onion, and garlic and sauté for 5 minutes over medium heat. Add the chicken broth, cover, and steam for 5 to 7 minutes, or until the vegetables are tender. Remove from the heat and add the thyme.

TRANSFER THE mixture to the work bowl of a food processor fitted with a steel blade or a blender and puree until smooth, or pass it through a food mill fitted with a medium disk. Pour the sauce into a small saucepan, season with salt and pepper, cover, and set aside.

PREHEAT THE oven to 350°F.

FOR THE Ricotta Filling, combine the ricotta, herbs, and egg in a food processor fitted with a steel blade or a medium bowl. Blend until the mixture is smooth and light. Place 1½ to 2 tablespoons of the mixture in the center of each crêpe. Gather up the edges of each crêpe to enclose the filling and use a chive to tie each bundle near the top to form a beggar's purse.

LIGHTLY BUTTER a deep baking dish just large enough to hold the purses. Place the purses in the dish and cover with foil. Place in the oven and heat for 20 minutes.

TO SERVE, reheat the sauce over low heat, spoon a shallow pool of sauce onto each small heated serving plate, and set 1 or 2 purses on top of the sauce.

A poet's hope: to be,
like some valley cheese,
local, but prized elsewhere.
–W. H. Auden

Baked Brie with Mushrooms, Walnuts, and Dried Cranberries

My friend Kris Ackerman is famous for her baked Brie, which she first developed for her cooking school. Her students and friends loved the recipe so much that now she has a business selling the cheeses, ready to bake. The Brie is baked at the last moment and emerges from the oven encased in a feathery golden-brown phyllo crust that comes up around the cheese like a wispy collar. Mushrooms, walnuts, and cranberries add a sweet and savory accent to the warm cheese.

It's a perfect appetizer for a cocktail party. This recipe calls for a mini Brie. If you are having a large party, use a large Brie and double the other ingredients.

SERVES 6 TO 10

1 whole mini Brie (1 pound)

1 tablespoon cognac or brandy

2 teaspoons unsalted butter

4 ounces mushrooms, trimmed and sliced (1 cup)

¼ cup walnuts, toasted and coarsely chopped

1 tablespoon dried cranberries or dried cherries

10 sheets frozen phyllo dough, thawed and cut into 12-inch squares

4 tablespoons (½ stick) unsalted butter, melted

1 bunch grapes, for garnish (optional)

1 baguette, sliced, for serving

PLACE THE cheese on a plate, pierce the top of the cheese with the tip of a knife in several places, and drizzle the cognac over the cheese. Let stand at room temperature while you prepare the other ingredients.

MELT THE butter in a large skillet and sauté the mushrooms over high heat until golden brown. Remove from the heat and set aside to cool.

ARRANGE THE cooled mushrooms on top of the Brie, followed by the walnuts and cranberries. Set aside.

LAY THE phyllo dough sheets on a dry work surface and cover with a damp towel. Brush a baking sheet with some of the melted butter. Lightly brush a sheet of phyllo dough with melted butter. Lay the dough on the cookie sheet. Repeat the process with 4 more sheets, laying each one at an angle to the previous one. Brush 4 more sheets of dough and lay them at angles to each other on top of the cheese. Pick up the cheese, tuck the overhanging pieces of dough under it, and carefully center the cheese on the sheets of dough on the baking sheet. Gather up the edges of the bottom layers of dough and bring them up toward the top of the cheese. Brush the remaining sheet of dough with melted butter and tear it into 2-inch strips. Wrap the strips around the cheese to create a smooth collar. Brush the collar with additional butter. Cover the Brie loosely with plastic wrap, and refrigerate until ready to bake.

ABOUT 30 minutes before serving, preheat the oven to 400°F.

PLACE THE Brie in the oven and bake for 20 minutes, or until lightly browned. Remove from the oven and let cool for 10 minutes.

TO SERVE, transfer the Brie to a serving platter. Garnish with grapes if desired and serve with the bread.

A perfect Brie cannot be produced by standardized methods; it is the end product of a series of miracles. Essays are writ by fools like me, but only God can make a Brie.

–Clifton Fadiman

Parmigiano Cheese Puffs

Becky Wasserman, a *négociante* who arranges to sell and export French wines to America, has lived in Burgundy for years, in a quaint stone farmhouse outside Beaune. Limestone cliffs tower above, grapes grow everywhere, a little river meanders down the valley, and ancient trees bend over the narrow road. She is a wonderful cook, and lunches *chez Becky* are a special treat. The wines she represents are among the most special in all of Burgundy, and she often presents them with nibbles such as these cheese puffs.

In Burgundy, cheese puffs similar to these are traditionally made with Gruyère cheese and called *gougères*. Often they are arranged in a ring so that they bake together, like monkey bread. I prefer to make them as little individual cheese puffs, and I've discovered they are even more delicious made with Parmigiano-Reggiano. They go well with all wines, especially reds like Burgundy.

MAKES ABOUT 22 PUFFS

½ cup water or milk

4 tablespoons (½ stick) unsalted butter

½ cup unbleached all-purpose flour

½ teaspoon dry mustard

¼ teaspoon salt

⅛ teaspoon white pepper

4 large eggs

5 ounces Parmigiano-Reggiano, grated (1¼ cups)

PREHEAT THE oven to 400°F. Line a baking sheet with parchment paper or grease it with butter.

COMBINE THE water and butter in a medium saucepan over medium-high heat and bring to a boil. Sift the flour, dry mustard, salt, and white pepper together. When the water boils, remove the pan from heat and add all of the flour mixture at once. Stir the mixture with a wooden spoon until the flour is completely absorbed and the mixture is smooth. Return the pan to low heat and continue to cook, stirring constantly, for 1 to 2 minutes, or until the dough pulls away from the sides of the pan. Remove the pan from the heat and add 3 of the eggs, one at a time, beating well with a handheld mixer or a whisk after each egg is added. When the eggs are well incorporated, stir in 1 cup of the Parmigiano.

BEAT THE remaining egg with a fork to use as an egg wash and set aside. Using a small ice cream scoop or a tablespoon, drop tablespoonfuls of the dough onto the prepared baking sheet 1½ to 2 inches apart. Gently brush the top of each dough ball with the egg wash and sprinkle with the remaining ¼ cup cheese.

BAKE FOR 15 to 20 minutes, or until golden brown and puffed. The outside will be crispy and the inside soft and hollow. Transfer the puffs to a rack to cool slightly. Serve warm.

I don't want the cheese, I just want to get out of the trap.

–Latin proverb

Spicy Cheddar Cheese Straws

When I was a child, friends of my parents always gave our family tins of cheese straws as Christmas gifts. I would sneak downstairs into the living room and pry open the tins that were carefully placed under the Christmas tree. I can still remember the intense and cheesy aroma that escaped from the tin when it was opened. And I can still taste the spicy flavor of the cheese straws.

These cheese straws are great with wine and cocktails. They make a fine accompaniment to soups and salads. One word of caution: You won't be able to eat just one.

MAKES ABOUT 36 STRAWS

8 ounces sharp Cheddar, shredded (2 cups)

4 tablespoons (½ stick) unsalted butter, softened

1½ teaspoons grated onion

½ teaspoon Worcestershire sauce

3 dashes Tabasco sauce

¼ teaspoon dry mustard

¼ teaspoon cayenne pepper

½ teaspoon salt

1 cup unbleached all-purpose flour

1 ounce Parmigiano-Reggiano, grated (¼ cup)

PLACE THE Cheddar, butter, onion, Worcestershire, Tabasco, dry mustard, cayenne, and salt in the work bowl of a food processor fitted with a steel blade. Process until combined and smooth. Add the flour and pulse just until the flour begins to disappear and the dough is in pea-sized balls; be careful not to overmix the dough.

TURN THE dough out onto a lightly floured surface. Knead it quickly and gently until the dough comes together. Divide the dough into thirds. Wrap each with plastic wrap and refrigerate for at least 1 hour.

PREHEAT THE oven to 350°F. Line a baking sheet with parchment paper.

PAT OR roll each piece of dough into a rectangle about 6 x 4 x ½ inches. With a sharp knife, cut the dough crosswise into ½-inch strips. Pick up each strip of dough, gently twist it like a corkscrew, and set on the parchment-lined baking sheet, placing the strips 1½ inches apart. Sprinkle the strips with the Parmigiano.

BAKE FOR 12 to 15 minutes, or until lightly browned. Let stand for 5 minutes, then transfer the cheese straws with a spatula to a wire rack to cool.

SERVE, OR store in a tightly covered container for up to 5 days.

Cheddar Cookies

Roll out each piece of dough on a lightly floured surface to a ¼-inch thickness. Using a cookie cutter, cut the dough into 2½-inch circles and place on the baking sheet. Place a toasted pecan half on each cookie. Bake for 10 to 12 minutes.

MAKES 36 TO 40 (2½-INCH) COOKIES

Cheddar Olive Balls

Drain about 30 pimiento-stuffed Spanish olives and dry with paper towels. Pinch off heaping teaspoonfuls of the dough and wrap around each olive. Place seam side down on the pan and bake for 12 to 15 minutes, or until lightly browned.

MAKES ABOUT 30 BALLS

Savory Herbed Cheesecake

Savory cheesecakes can be served at cocktail buffets, as an appetizer, or even as the entrée for a light lunch or supper. The Parmigiano-and-rosemary crust of this elegant cheesecake is crisp, crunchy, and flavorful, and the creamy cheesecake is accented with crunchy red bell peppers and carrots.

I'm an artist at heart and I love decorating the top of this cheesecake. Carrots and red bell peppers can be cut into shapes to form dragonflies and flower petals, and parsley can be used for stems and leaves. Geometric patterns and designs can also be quite whimsical and attractive. You can even use vegetables and herbs to write out messages atop the cake. Let your imagination take you where it leads you.

SERVES 12

CRUST

4 ounces Parmigiano-Reggiano, grated (1 cup)

1 cup dried bread crumbs

½ teaspoon minced fresh rosemary

5⅓ tablespoons (⅓ cup) unsalted butter, melted

FILLING

10 cloves garlic, unpeeled

⅓ cup extra virgin olive oil

1½ pounds (3 cups) cream cheese, homemade (page 74) or store-bought, softened

1 cup (8 ounces) Crème Fraîche, homemade (page 68) or store-bought, or sour cream

3 large eggs

3 tablespoons unbleached all-purpose flour

1 teaspoon salt, plus extra to taste

2 tablespoons minced fresh flat-leaf parsley

1 tablespoon minced fresh chervil

1 tablespoon minced fresh basil

1 tablespoon minced fresh oregano

1 tablespoon minced fresh sage

⅓ cup finely diced red bell pepper

⅓ cup finely diced carrot

Freshly ground black pepper to taste

2 large egg whites, at room temperature

Additional herbs and/or vegetables, for decoration (optional)

FOR THE crust, mix all the ingredients together in a small bowl. Press the mixture into the bottom and up the sides of a 9-inch springform pan. Refrigerate while you make the filling.

FOR THE filling, preheat the oven to 350°F.

PLACE THE unpeeled cloves of garlic in a small ramekin or ovenproof dish and drizzle with the olive oil.

BAKE, UNCOVERED, for 10 to 15 minutes, or until soft when tested with the tip of a knife. Remove and set aside to cool slightly. Reduce the oven temperature to 325°F.

SQUEEZE THE roasted garlic out of the skins and mash or chop the garlic to a puree.

COMBINE the garlic puree, cream cheese, crème fraîche, whole eggs, flour, and salt in the work bowl of a food processor fitted with a steel blade. Process for 2 minutes. Add the parsley, chervil, basil, oregano, and sage and process for 1 minute. Pour the cream cheese mixture into a large bowl. Stir in the red pepper and carrot. Season with salt and pepper to taste.

IN A clean bowl, beat the egg whites until soft peaks form. Blend a spoonful of egg whites into the cream cheese mixture, then gently fold in the remaining egg whites.

POUR THE cheesecake batter into the chilled crust. Line a baking pan with foil and set the springform pan on top of the foil (to catch any drips). Using the additional herbs and vegetables, float a design on top of the batter. Alternatively, you can decorate the cheesecake after it is baked.

PLACE THE cheesecake in the oven and bake for about 45 minutes. When done, the cake will have risen and the center will be almost set. Turn the oven off and allow the cheesecake to remain in the oven for 1 hour longer, without opening the door. Don't worry if the cake is cracked. Remove the cheesecake and set it on a rack to cool for 1½ hours.

REMOVE THE outer ring of the springform pan. Loosen the cheesecake from the bottom of the pan, using a knife, and slide it onto a serving plate.

SERVE AT room temperature, or cover with plastic wrap and refrigerate overnight. Remove the cheesecake from the refrigerator at least 2 hours before serving and allow it to come to room temperature. If desired, decorate the top of the cheesecake using herbs and/or vegetables, as described in the introduction to the recipe on the opposite page.

THE CHEESECAKE is lovely served whole for a cocktail buffet party, but it can also be cut into wedges and served on individual plates.

VARIATION

Savory Stilton Cheesecake

Reduce the cream cheese to 12 ounces (1½ cups) and add 12 ounces Stilton, crumbled (about 2 cups).

Chile con Queso

Here are two versions of an old standby. The old-fashioned version is similar to one I made as a teenager in Fort Worth. It was very popular for after-school parties in the 1950s. The Velveeta makes it creamy and smooth, while the fire comes from the Rotel, canned tomatoes with chiles. The second is an updated gourmet version, with high-class ingredients. Either way, Chile con Queso must be served warm (otherwise it solidifies).

Fritos corn chips are my favorite accompaniment to this dip, but baked or fried tortilla chips are also good.

MAKES 2½ CUPS
SERVES 6 TO 8

Old-Fashioned Texas Version

1 tablespoon vegetable oil

1 small onion, minced (½ cup)

2 cloves garlic, minced

2 jalapeño chiles, stems and seeds removed and minced

1 (10-ounce) can Rotel diced tomatoes with green chiles

1 pound Velveeta or processed American cheese, cut into ½-inch cubes

Fritos corn chips, tortilla chips, or cut-up vegetables, for serving

HEAT THE oil in a medium saucepan and sauté the onion, garlic, and jalapeños until soft. Add the tomatoes with their liquid and cook over medium heat for about 5 minutes, to reduce the liquid. When the tomatoes begin to look dry, reduce the heat to medium-low and start adding the cheese, 1 handful at a time, stirring over medium-low heat until the cheese melts; wait for each handful to melt before adding more cheese.

SERVE IN a chafing dish or fondue pot to keep the queso warm. Serve with corn chips, tortilla chips, or cut-up vegetables.

Gourmet Version

1 small onion, unpeeled, quartered	4 teaspoons cornstarch
3 cloves garlic, unpeeled	Salt
3 Anaheim chiles	½ cup heavy cream
3 jalapeño chiles	1 teaspoon ground cumin
3 plum tomatoes	1 teaspoon pure ground chile powder
8 ounces Caciotta or Monterey Jack, shredded (2 cups)	1 dried árbol chile, for garnish
8 ounces Cheddar or Longhorn, shredded (2 cups)	Corn chips, tortilla chips, or cut-up vegetables, for serving

PREHEAT THE broiler.

PLACE THE onion, garlic, chiles, and tomatoes on a baking sheet. Broil them 3 inches from the heat, turning with tongs as necessary until their skins are blackened on all sides. Remove from the broiler, place in a bowl, cover with plastic wrap, and allow to steam until cool.

ONCE THEY are cool enough to handle, remove the skins from the onion and garlic. Remove the blackened skins and seeds from the chiles and discard. Peel the tomatoes, cut in half; squeeze out the seeds and juice and discard. Place the onions, garlic, chiles, and tomatoes in the work bowl of a food processor fitted with a steel blade and pulse to chop coarsely. (There will be about 1½ cups of chopped vegetables.) Set aside.

MIX THE shredded cheeses with the cornstarch and toss with ½ teaspoon salt.

COMBINE THE cream, cumin, and chile powder in a 2-quart saucepan and heat over low heat. When the cream is warm, gradually stir in the shredded cheese, handful by handful; wait for each handful of cheese to melt before adding the next. When all of the cheese is melted, gradually stir in the chopped vegetables. Add salt, to taste.

SERVE THE queso in a chafing dish or fondue pot to keep it warm. Float the chile árbol on top as a garnish. Serve with corn chips, tortilla chips, or cut-up vegetables.

Cowboy Cheese Dip

Mary Joe Reynolds and I have been friends since we grew up one house apart on Spanish Trail in Fort Worth. Now she runs the Long X, her family's century-old ranch out in the Davis Mountains in West Texas. It's a huge ranch with an old, rambling white adobe headquarters building where cowboys, neighbors, and friends often congregate in rocking chairs to spin tales in front of a blazing fire in the huge stone fireplace.

Mary Joe is a master at whipping up simple yet delicious dishes at the drop of a cowboy hat. This is one she often makes with our cheese.

**MAKES ABOUT 3½ CUPS,
SERVES 8 TO 10**

1 tablespoon extra virgin olive oil

1 medium onion, chopped (¾ cup)

2 cloves garlic, minced

8 ounces lean ground beef

½ cup milk, or more if needed

12 ounces Velveeta or processed American cheese, cut into ½-inch cubes

8 ounces Ancho Chile Caciotta (see Note) or pepper Jack, cut into ½-inch cubes

1 teaspoon pure chile powder, or to taste

Salt and freshly ground black pepper to taste

Corn chips or tortilla chips, for serving

HEAT THE oil in a heavy saucepan over medium heat and sauté the onion and garlic until they begin to soften. Add the beef, raise the heat, and sauté until cooked through, about 4 minutes. Drain off any excess fat if necessary.

ADD THE milk to the pan, reduce the heat to medium-low, and begin adding the cheese one handful at a time, blending until melted after each addition. When all of the cheese is melted, season the dip with chile powder and salt and pepper. The dip should be thick enough to coat a corn chip; adjust the consistency with more milk if necessary.

SERVE THE dip in a chafing dish or fondue pot so that it stays warm and liquid. Serve with corn chips or tortilla chips.

Note: Ancho Chile Caciotta is available from the Mozzarella Company (see Sources, page 373).

Ancho Chile and Sun-Dried Tomato Salsa with Goat Cheese

The inspiration for this dish comes from Patricia Quintana, a chef and cookbook author from Mexico City. I first tasted this salsa in Austin at the Texas Hill Country Wine Festival. After her cooking class there, Patricia had lots of salsa left, so she came to my booth, where I was passing out cheese, and suggested I serve her leftovers with my goat cheese. They were delicious together. We found someone who had chips and brought those to the booth. It was a great match, and everyone loved it.

The sun-dried tomatoes sweeten and soften the salsa. You'll find that mild fresh goat cheese is the perfect match for this spicy, vinegary salsa. This is a great hors d'oeuvre to serve before a Mexican meal, or anytime, for that matter.

MAKES ABOUT 1 CUP, SERVES 6

4 large dried ancho chiles	3 tablespoons red wine vinegar
10 dry-packed sun-dried tomato halves	½ teaspoon dried oregano
½ small onion, thinly sliced	⅛ teaspoon salt
2 cloves garlic, minced	5 ounces (⅔ cup) fresh goat cheese
¼ cup extra virgin olive oil	Tortilla chips, for serving

SLIT THE ancho chiles lengthwise. Remove the seeds and discard. Place the chiles and tomatoes in a dry skillet. Toast them over medium heat, flattening the chiles and tomatoes with the back of a spatula and turning them several times, until aromatic and slightly darkened. Watch carefully, as they can burn quickly. Transfer the chiles and tomatoes to two separate bowls and cover each with hot water. Let them sit until plumped and pliable, about 15 minutes for the tomatoes and 30 minutes for the chiles; to keep them immersed in the water, push them down with the back of a spoon every 5 minutes or so.

REMOVE THE tomatoes from the water, pat dry, and cut into ¼-inch julienne strips. Place in a bowl.

REMOVE THE chiles from the water, pat dry, and remove any remaining seeds, the ribs, and stems. Cut into ¼-inch julienne strips. Add to the tomatoes, then add the onion, garlic, oil, vinegar, oregano, and salt. Let the salsa stand at room temperature for at least 1 hour so that the flavors blend.

TO SERVE, put the salsa in a shallow dish. Slice the goat cheese into 1-inch-thick rounds and place on top of the salsa, or coarsely crumble it over the salsa. Serve at room temperature accompanied by tortilla chips.

Bruschetta Topped with Goat Cheese and Tomatoes

I remember when I lived in Italy driving past olive groves where huge white cloths lay on the ground. The olive pickers climbed the trees and shook the branches so that the ripe olives would fall to the ground, on top of the cloths. Each evening, the day's olives would be taken to the local mill, where they were placed in a stone basin. A huge stone wheel would then roll over the olives and crush them, pressing out their oil. That first oil, green in color and fruity and peppery in taste, would trickle down into huge earthen cisterns. This first cold pressing yields the oil called extra virgin.

Since the olives were picked in the cool days of late fall and early winter, the olive pickers would often build fires to keep themselves warm. They would gather round the fires and toast giant slices of bread, rub them with raw garlic cloves, and drizzle the bread with the newly pressed extra virgin olive oil. In Italy, this original bruschetta became a popular snack and was always consumed with local red wine.

Nowadays bruschetta has evolved into toasted pieces of bread topped with any number of ingredients. Jim Severson serves one of my favorite modern versions at Sevy's Grill in Dallas, and it is the inspiration for my recipe.

SERVES 6 TO 12

2 medium ripe tomatoes, peeled and finely chopped (about 2 cups)

1 clove garlic, minced, plus 2 cloves garlic, unpeeled, cut in half

2 tablespoons extra virgin olive oil

2 leaves fresh basil, chopped, plus 12 whole leaves for garnish

½ teaspoon salt

Freshly ground black pepper to taste

12 diagonal slices baguette (⅓ to ½ inch thick)

6 ounces (¾ cup) fresh goat cheese

PLACE THE tomatoes, minced garlic, olive oil, basil, salt, and pepper in a small bowl. Gently mix together and set aside to marinate for at least 15 minutes.

TOAST THE bread on both sides until light brown. While the toast is still warm, rub the top of each piece with the cut side of a garlic clove.

SPREAD EACH slice of toast with 1 tablespoon of the goat cheese. Drain the chopped tomato mixture, and top the goat cheese with it.

GARNISH EACH bruschetta with a basil leaf and serve on a large platter.

Cheddar Cheese Ball with Chutney

This is my updated version of an old-fashioned cheese ball. It is a perfect party food for any season of the year, although it is often associated with Christmas cocktail buffets. The combination of curry powder and chutney is good because it's both spicy and sweet. Rolling the cheese ball in chopped scallions rather than the traditional nuts gives it a fresh appearance. And it doesn't have to be a cheese *ball*—it could be a pyramid, a cylinder, or any other shape you desire.

SERVES 8

6 ounces (¾ cup) cream cheese, home-made (page 74) or store-bought, softened

4 ounces sharp Cheddar, shredded (1 cup)

3 tablespoons dry sherry

¾ teaspoon curry powder

¼ teaspoon dry mustard

¼ teaspoon salt

5 scallions, trimmed and finely chopped

10 fresh chives, minced

½ cup mango chutney

Scallion curls, for garnish (see Note)

PLACE THE cream cheese, Cheddar, sherry, curry, mustard, and salt in the work bowl of a food processor fitted with a steel blade. Blend until well combined and smooth. Remove the cheese mixture from the bowl and wrap in waxed paper or plastic wrap, shaping it into a ball or another desired shape. Refrigerate for at least 30 minutes.

MIX THE scallions and chives on a sheet of waxed paper or plastic wrap. Roll the chilled cheese in the scallions and chives, gently pressing them into the surface. Refrigerate for 1 hour before serving.

AT SERVING time, spread the chutney on a serving platter. Place the cheese ball on top of the chutney. Garnish with scallion curls. Serve with crackers.

Note: To make scallion curls, trim the roots off each scallion and remove and discard all but 1½ inches of the green part. Using a sharp knife, "feather" the green part, thinly slicing it lengthwise. Drop the scallions into a bowl of ice water and soak for 15 to 20 minutes, or until the green ends are curled.

Endive Canoes Stuffed with Blue Cheese

This dish is fabulous when made with the wonderful American blue cheese from Iowa called Maytag Blue. Yes, it's from those same folks who make the washing machines!

Legend is that the Maytag family had a wonderful herd of prized dairy cows in Iowa that produced copious quantities of rich milk after grazing on their amber-waving Midwestern grain. In order to make the prized herd pay for itself, one Mr. Maytag decided to make cheese. It's an American original, found on restaurant menus across the country as well as in gourmet stores.

**MAKES ABOUT 18 LARGE HORS D'OEUVRES
SERVES 6**

2 to 3 heads Belgian endive

8 ounces Maytag Blue or Danish Blue cheese, crumbled (1½ cups)

½ cup (4 ounces) crème fraîche, home-made (page 68) or store-bought, or sour cream

5 toasted walnut halves, finely chopped

¼ red bell pepper, finely chopped

1 rib celery, finely chopped

1 strip bacon, cooked until crisp, and finely chopped (optional)

REMOVE ANY bruised outer leaves from the endive and discard. Carefully peel the remaining large endive leaves off the heads, rinse them in cold water, and set them aside on a damp towel to dry. There should be 18 large leaves. (Save the remaining endive for another use.)

MIX THE blue cheese and crème fraîche together in the work bowl of a food processor fitted with a steel blade, pulsing until smooth. Or mash the blue cheese and crème fraîche together with a fork until smooth.

SPREAD 2 to 3 teaspoons of the cheese mixture down the center of each of the endive leaves, using a knife; or pipe it, using a pastry bag fitted with a large tip.

ARRANGE THE leaves on a serving platter. Sprinkle the walnuts, bell pepper, celery, and bacon, if using, on top of the filled canoes. Serve at once, or refrigerate for a short time until ready to serve.

Stuffed Cherry Tomatoes

Cut off the tops of 1 pint of cherry tomatoes. Scoop out the centers with a small spoon or your finger and discard. Spoon or pipe the blue cheese mixture into the hollowed-out tomatoes. Sprinkle the chopped walnuts, vegetables, and bacon on top.

It is better to scrape the cheese than to peel it.

–Danish proverb

Jalapeño Chiles Stuffed with Pimiento Cheese

This is a famous old Texas dish. It's not nearly as hot as it sounds, because the old adage is true—dairy products calm the fire of hot foods. When I was growing up, jalapeños were widely available in Texas but scarce in other parts of the country. Now they are found everywhere in the United States and even in Europe and Australia.

Jalapeños are considered to be a hot chile, but actually they are pretty tame when compared to hotter chiles such as the habanero. A jalapeño's heat depends on which strain or subspecies of jalapeño it is, so you never know how hot it will be until you taste it. And a large part of the fire is in the seeds and membranes, so once these are removed, you have lost much of the heat.

You can use either fresh or canned chiles for this recipe. The fresh jalapeños will be the hottest, followed by the pickled jalapeños; sweet banana peppers will be mild. A combination of all three will provide something for all as well as a colorful presentation. Wear gloves while preparing the chiles or wash your hands well in soapy water after handling them. Be careful not to touch your eyes or any tender part of your body after handling chiles, because the capsicum oil will remain on your skin and can easily irritate.

This recipe makes more pimiento cheese than you will need to stuff the jalapenos. You'll be glad, because you can make wonderful cheese sandwiches—grilled or regular—with the leftovers.

MAKES ABOUT 1½ CUPS PIMIENTO CHEESE
SERVES 6

PIMIENTO CHEESE
8 ounces Cheddar, Longhorn, or Colby, coarsely shredded (2 cups)

2 tablespoons grated onion

1 (2-ounce) jar chopped pimientos, with their juice

2 tablespoons Dijon mustard

½ cup mayonnaise

10 fresh jalapeño chiles, jarred whole pickled jalapeños, or small sweet banana chile peppers

Pimiento or roasted red bell pepper strips, for garnish

FOR THE Pimiento Cheese, place the cheese in a medium bowl and add the onion, pimientos with their juice, mustard, and mayonnaise. Blend well with a spoon. Set aside while you prepare the chile peppers.

CUT EACH chile lengthwise in half and remove and discard the seeds, veins, and stems.

MOUND 1 to 2 teaspoons of the pimiento cheese into each pepper half. (The leftover cheese can be kept for up to 1 week in a tightly closed container in the refrigerator.)

TO SERVE, arrange the chiles on a platter. Garnish with pimiento strips.

Hey Man, I'm drinking wine, eating cheese, and catching some rays.
–Donald Sutherland as Oddball
in *Kelly's Heros*

Sun-Dried Tomato and Basil Pesto Mascarpone Torta

I created this torta years ago to sell at our retail shop at the Mozzarella Company. It was loosely modeled on the mascarpone tortas made in one of my favorite shops in Milano. Their tortas are extraordinary, made with basil and pine nuts, Gorgonzola, candied figs, and other ingredients.

This is a very pretty dish because the mascarpone is mixed with the tomatoes and basil to create pink and green layers. It can be decorated with sun-dried tomato strips, pine nuts, and fresh herbs. Try molding it in an unusual mold—low or tall, fluted or straight sided, small or large.

This torta is great for parties because it is soft and spreadable. And, best of all, it goes with both red and white wine.

SERVES 8 TO 12

1 pound (2 cups) mascarpone, home-made (page 73) or store-bought

2 tablespoons finely chopped oil-packed sun-dried tomatoes, or more to taste plus 1 to 2 oil-packed sun-dried tomato halves, sliced into strips

2 tablespoons Basil Pesto (page 80), or more to taste

4 ounces Texas Basil Caciotta (see Note) or other mild cheese, such as low-moisture mozzarella or Monterey Jack

¼ cup toasted pine nuts, for garnish

Fresh herb sprigs, for garnish (optional)

Crackers, plain water biscuits, or toasted slices of baguette, for serving

DIVIDE THE mascarpone in half and place in two bowls. Stir the finely chopped sun-dried tomatoes into one bowl of mascarpone and the pesto into the other. Taste the mixtures and adjust the flavors if desired.

THINLY SLICE the caciotta, using a cheese plane or a wire cheese cutter, as the cheese is soft.

LINE A small bowl, about 2 cups in capacity, or similar mold with plastic wrap, letting the excess extend over the sides. Arrange the strips of sun-dried tomato in a pattern on the bottom. Gently spoon enough of the tomato or pesto mascarpone into the mold to make a layer about 1 inch thick. Place a few slices of cheese over the mascarpone and gently press down to evenly distribute the mascarpone underneath. Repeat the procedure, alternating the two colors of the mascarpone, with slices of cheese in between, until all the mascarpone is used. Top the last layer with the remaining Caciotta and gently press down to compress the layers of cheese. Bring the sides of the plastic wrap up and cover the top. Press down again. Refrigerate for several hours, or overnight.

ABOUT 30 minutes before serving, spread open the plastic wrap covering the top of the cheese, invert the torta on a serving platter, and remove the mold. Carefully peel away the plastic wrap. Garnish with the pine nuts and herb sprigs, if desired.

SERVE THE torta at room temperature with crackers, biscuits, or toasted French bread.

Note: Texas Basil Caciotta is available from the Mozzarella Company (see Sources, page 373).

Age is not important unless you're a cheese.

–Helen Hayes

Artichoke, Spinach, and Goat Cheese Spring Rolls

These spring rolls were inspired by a dish that Lissa Doumani and Hiro Sone served to me at Terra, their delightful restaurant in St. Helena in the Napa Valley. Hiro is a Japanese chef and a master at combining Asian ingredients with California products.

The spring rolls, wrapped in rice flour paper, are meant to be served cold. The same filling can be used for an egg roll variation; they are fried and served warm. Both are delicious and quite unusual.

MAKES 8 SPRING ROLLS, MAKES ABOUT ½ CUPS SAUCE, SERVES 4 TO 8

DIPPING SAUCE

½ cup seasoned rice vinegar

¼ teaspoon fish sauce

¼ teaspoon finely grated peeled fresh ginger

1 tablespoon coarsely grated carrot

1 tablespoon minced fresh cilantro

¼ teaspoon minced garlic (optional)

Sugar to taste

SPRING ROLLS

1 can (8.5 ounces) artichoke hearts or 4 large artichokes

Salt

2 tablespoons freshly squeezed lemon juice

4 ounces (½ cup) fresh goat cheese, crumbled

¼ teaspoon grated peeled fresh ginger

Dash or up to 5 drops hot chile sauce

2 cups julienned spinach leaves

2 cups julienned lettuce leaves

15 large leaves fresh basil, cut into very thin strips

15 large leaves fresh mint, cut into very thin strips

10 stems fresh cilantro, leaves only, cut into very thin strips

1 carrot, peeled and cut into long strips with a vegetable peeler

¼ cup matchstick julienne of red bell pepper (1 inch long)

8 square or round rice paper wrappers

FOR THE Dipping Sauce, mix all the ingredients together. Transfer to a small serving bowl and set aside at room temperature while you prepare the spring rolls.

FOR THE Spring Rolls, drain the canned artichokes, if using, and rinse under cold water. Squeeze out the excess liquid and roughly chop them by hand or in the work bowl of a food processor fitted with a steel blade. (You should have about 1 cup.) Sprinkle with the lemon juice.

OR, IF using fresh artichokes, cut away the leaves, stems, and chokes with a sharp knife. Rinse the artichoke hearts and rub with the lemon juice. Heat 1 inch water in a heavy saucepan fitted with a steaming basket, add the artichoke hearts, cover, and steam over medium heat for 20 minutes, or until tender. Remove from the pan and set aside on a plate to cool. Chop the artichoke hearts by hand or in the work bowl of a food processor fitted with a steel blade into ¼-inch pieces and season with salt.

PLACE THE chopped artichokes in a medium bowl and add the goat cheese, ginger, ⅛ teaspoon salt, and the chile sauce. Mix well. On a large sheet of waxed paper, divide the mixture into 8 portions. Toss the spinach, lettuce, basil, mint, and cilantro together and divide into 8 piles. Mix the carrots and bell pepper together and divide into 8 portions.

TO ASSEMBLE the spring rolls, one at a time, soak the rice paper wrappers in cool water for about 3 minutes. Remove them as they soften and lay on a damp towel to drain; cover with another towel to blot dry. Place a softened wrapper on a work surface, with a point facing you. Moisten the edges of the wrapper with water. Place a portion of the lettuce mixture across the top of the wrapper, about ¾ inch down from the point. Top with a portion of the artichoke and cheese mixture, then of the carrot and pepper mixture. Fold the top of the wrapper down over the cheese and vegetables and roll snugly for a complete turn. Fold the sides inward over the rolled section and continue rolling (moistening the paper again if necessary) until you have a tightly sealed roll. Repeat with the remaining rolls. Refrigerate the spring rolls until chilled. (The rolls can be prepared several hours in advance.)

TO SERVE, cut each roll in half on the diagonal. Serve with the dipping sauce.

VARIATION

Artichoke, Spinach, and Goat Cheese Egg Rolls

Prepare the filling as for the spring rolls. Substitute egg roll wrappers for the rice paper wrappers. The egg roll wrappers are ready to use; simply brush away any excess flour on the wrappers with a pastry brush. Fill the egg roll wrappers, rolling in the same manner and moistening the edges with water to seal them. Heat about ½ inch vegetable oil in a large pan over medium heat until hot but not smoking (about 350°F.). In batches, gently slide the egg rolls into the pan, without crowding, and quickly fry, turning with tongs, until golden on all sides. Remove and drain on paper towels. Cut each roll in half on the diagonal. Serve hot with the dipping sauce.

MAKES 8 EGG ROLLS
SERVES 4 TO 8

Grilled Zucchini Cigars Stuffed with Feta and Mascarpone

I've named these stuffed little vegetable rolls cigars because they are about the size of Toscanos, the small, stubby cigars that many Italian men smoke.

When I lived in Italy, the best thing of all was to be invited out to the countryside for Sunday lunch in the home of one of the *contadini* who worked in the vineyards. Their meals always lasted for hours and included many courses: antipasti, then homemade pasta, followed by roasted meats, and finally salad and fruit. Simple and hearty wines produced on the property always accompanied the meal.

Arrange these cigars on an antipasto platter with an assortment of cured meats such as prosciutto, salami, and capocollo. Garnish the platter with lots of olives and anything else that suits your fancy.

MAKES 16 ROLLS
SERVES 4 TO 8

1 large or 2 small zucchini

1 tablespoon salt

About ¼ cup extra virgin olive oil

2 ounces feta, crumbled (⅓ cup)

2 tablespoons (1 ounce) mascarpone, homemade (page 73) or store-bought, very cold

1 teaspoon finely chopped capers

¼ teaspoon dried oregano

Salt and freshly ground black pepper to taste

Toothpicks (optional)

Cured meats (optional)

Olives (optional)

Sprigs of fresh mint or watercress, for garnish (optional)

Edible flowers, for garnish (optional)

SLICE THE zucchini diagonally about ⅛ inch thick into the longest possible slices. (You should have 16 slices.) Sprinkle the slices with the salt and place in a colander to drain for 30 minutes.

PREHEAT A charcoal or gas grill to high heat, or preheat the broiler.

RINSE THE zucchini slices with cold water and pat dry. Lay them out on a baking sheet and brush with olive oil. Grill or broil the zucchini slices until marked or browned on each side. Do not overcook, or the zucchini will become too soft to stuff. Transfer the slices to a work surface or rack to cool.

PLACE THE feta in the work bowl of a food processor fitted with a steel blade and process until smooth. Add the mascarpone and process briefly. Add the capers and oregano. Process briefly to mix; don't overprocess, or the mascarpone may separate. Season to taste with salt and pepper.

SPREAD THE cheese mixture on the zucchini slices and roll up to form cigar shapes. Secure with toothpicks if necessary. Refrigerate for at least 30 minutes, so the filling becomes firm.

AT SERVING time, remove any toothpicks and arrange the rolls on a serving platter, with cured meats and olives, if desired. Garnish with the sprigs of mint or watercress and/or edible flowers, if desired.

VARIATION

Eggplant Rolls Filled with Ricotta and Mascarpone

Cut 1 small eggplant lengthwise into slices about ¼ inch thick. Salt and drain the slices, then grill or broil the eggplant as directed above. Substitute 4 ounces (½ cup) well-drained ricotta for the feta. Make eggplant cigars as above and refrigerate. To serve, remove any toothpicks and cut the rolls into 1-inch-long pieces. Stand the pieces on end on a serving platter. Garnish with sprigs of fresh herbs and red bell pepper strips.

Potato Pancakes with Smoked Salmon and Dilled Mascarpone

Potatoes, smoked salmon, and dill are a classic Russian combination. In this recipe, the warm potato pancakes melt the dilled mascarpone and gently warm the smoked salmon, making it even more flavorful.

This dish reminds me of a fabulous trip we took to St. Petersburg, where we visited the most magnificent palaces, resplendent with opulent and glorious furnishings. Peter the Great and his daughter-in-law Catherine modeled the city upon Venice. All the buildings that line the canals are baroque in style and painted in various pastel colors. It is far from bleak; in fact it seems almost more Venetian than Venice.

From her pictures, it appears that Catherine the Great enjoyed feasting. I can only imagine that one of her European-trained chefs might have created something similar to this for her.

Make the potato pancake mixture as close to cooking time as possible so the potatoes do not discolor or become watery.

MAKES ABOUT 1 CUP DILLED MASCARPONE
MAKES 12 (3- TO 4-INCH) PANCAKES
SERVES 6

DILLED MASCARPONE

4 ounces (½ cup) mascarpone, homemade (page 73) or store-bought, cold

½ cup (4 ounces) crème fraîche, homemade (page 68) or store-bought, or sour cream

½ teaspoon grated lemon zest

2 teaspoons freshly squeezed lemon juice

¼ cup snipped fresh dill

8 dashes Tabasco sauce

Salt and freshly ground black pepper to taste

POTATO PANCAKES

2½ pounds Yukon Gold potatoes, peeled

1 small onion

3 tablespoons minced shallots

2 large eggs, lightly beaten

½ cup (4 ounces) crème fraîche, homemade (page 68) or store-bought, or sour cream

1 ounce Parmigiano-Reggiano, grated (¼ cup)

2 tablespoons unbleached all-purpose flour

¾ teaspoon salt

1 teaspoon freshly ground black pepper

8 tablespoons (1 stick) unsalted butter

12 slices smoked salmon (12 ounces total)

12 sprigs fresh dill, for garnish

½ red bell pepper, diced, for garnish

2 tablespoons finely minced fresh chives, for garnish

FOR THE Dilled Mascarpone, blend the mascarpone and crème fraîche together in a bowl until smooth and well mixed. Stir in the lemon zest, lemon juice, dill, Tabasco, and salt and pepper. Refrigerate until serving time.

FOR THE Potato Pancakes, preheat the oven to 400°F. Set a baking pan large enough to hold 12 potato pancakes near the stove.

PEEL AND grate the potatoes, and then the onions, using the grating blade of a food processor or by hand. Place the potatoes and onion in a large bowl and add the shallots, eggs, crème fraîche, cheese, flour, salt, and pepper. Stir all of the ingredients together.

MELT 2 tablespoons of the butter in a large nonstick skillet over medium heat. Scoop up a heaping ¼ cup of the potato mixture and place in the skillet. Using a spatula, shape the pancake into a round, smoothing the top and sides. Add 1 or 2 more pancakes to the pan, without crowding, and cook for 3 minutes on one side. Turn the pancakes and cook for an additional 4 minutes, or until lightly browned on both sides. Remove the pancakes as they are cooked and put them on the reserved baking pan in a single layer. Wipe out the skillet if necessary and melt more butter to cook the additional pancakes. Continue until all are cooked.

JUST BEFORE serving, place the baking pan with the pancakes in the oven for 3 minutes, or until they are hot and cooked through.

TO SERVE, spread about 1 tablespoon of the dilled mascarpone on each warm pancake. Arrange the smoked salmon slices artfully on top and garnish with the dill sprigs. Place 2 pancakes on each heated serving plate and garnish the plates with the diced bell pepper and chives.

Fontina Rice Supplì

Where I lived in Perugia, there were lots of inconspicuous doorways that led into tiny food shops called *tavole calde* (hot tables), so called because they sold food that was kept warm on steam tables. One I liked very much was located on a narrow pedestrian street lined with medieval buildings in the center of town. My favorite purchase was their *supplì*, fritter-like rice balls filled with mozzarella. They called them *telefoni* because when served piping hot, the molten mozzarella in the center formed strings that resembled telephone wires when the *supplì* were broken in half.

These are great served as an appetizer from a platter garnished with olives and giant caperberries.

MAKES 16 SUPPLÌ
SERVES 4 TO 6

¾ cup Arborio rice (or 1½ cups leftover risotto)

½ teaspoon salt

2 large eggs

2 ounces Fontina, shredded (½ cup)

¼ cup minced fresh flat-leaf parsley

1 teaspoon minced fresh oregano

½ teaspoon minced garlic

2 ounces fresh mozzarella, cut into 16 cubes

½ cup unbleached all-purpose flour

1 cup fresh bread crumbs

1½ cups vegetable oil

16 (3-inch) stiff sprigs fresh rosemary, for garnish (optional)

1½ cups Paula's Tomato Sauce (page 84), or store-bought, warmed

Olives and/or giant caper berries, for garnish

TO MAKE the rice, bring 2 cups water to a boil in a medium saucepan. Stir in the rice and salt, reduce the heat to low, and simmer, uncovered, for 14 to 16 minutes, until the rice is al dente. Stir the rice occasionally so it does not stick to the bottom of the pan. When the rice is cooked, remove the pan from the heat. The water should have been absorbed; if not, drain the rice in a colander. If using leftover risotto, begin recipe at this point.

Beat 1 of the eggs into the rice. Set the rice aside to cool for about 10 minutes (or continue with the cold leftover risotto). Stir the Fontina, parsley, oregano, and garlic into the rice. Pinch off a large olive-sized portion of rice and mold it around a cube of mozzarella, taking care to completely enclose the cheese. Put on a plate and continue to shape the *supplì*. Set aside and refrigerate until ready to fry.

ABOUT 20 minutes before serving, beat the remaining egg in a shallow bowl. Place the flour and bread crumbs on separate plates or on waxed paper.

HEAT THE oil in a large skillet over medium heat until hot but not smoking (about 350°F.). Carefully roll each supplì in the flour, then in the egg, and finally in the bread crumbs. In batches, fry the supplì in the hot oil until golden on all sides, turning as necessary with tongs or a spatula; be careful not to crowd the pan. Watch carefully, as they cook quickly. Remove as browned and drain on paper towels.

INSERT A rosemary skewer into each supplì if desired; these serve as handles for dipping the supplì into the tomato sauce. Pour the tomato sauce into a bowl, place it on a heated platter, and surround with the supplì. Serve hot.

Some cultures are defined by their relationship to cheese.

–Mary Stuart Masterson as Joon,
in *Benny & Joon*

Grilled Mozzarella Bundles
with Sun-Dried Tomato–Basil Pesto

When I drive up to the Napa Valley from San Francisco, the landscape reminds me of Umbria, with its wide valley covered with vineyards and its sun-scorched, golden hills forming the backdrop. One of my favorite restaurants is Tra Vigne, whose name means "in the midst of the grapevines."

Michael Chiarello is the genius behind Tra Vigne. Michael loves fresh mozzarella as much as I do, and he is a master at coming up with innovative mozzarella recipes like this one. Not only is the prosciutto an integral part of the flavor of this dish, it also keeps the mozzarella from oozing out when the bundles are grilled.

MAKES ABOUT 1 CUP SAUCE
MAKES 8 BUNDLES
SERVES 4 TO 8

SUN-DRIED TOMATO-BASIL SAUCE

12 dry-packed sun-dried tomato halves

¼ cup Basil Pesto (page 80)

⅓ cup extra virgin olive oil

2 tablespoons balsamic vinegar

Salt and freshly ground black pepper to taste

MOZZARELLA BUNDLES

8 large radicchio leaves

8 ounces fresh mozzarella cheese, cut into 8 slices

8 very thin slices prosciutto (4 to 6 ounces)

Olive oil, for brushing

8 (8-inch) pieces cotton kitchen string

¼ cup toasted pine nuts, for garnish

FOR THE Sun-Dried Tomato–Basil Sauce, place the tomatoes in a bowl, cover with hot water, and let plump for 20 minutes.

DRAIN AND finely chop the tomatoes. You should have about ¼ cup. Place them in a bowl and add the pesto, oil, vinegar, and salt and pepper. Blend with a whisk or, for a smoother sauce, place all of the ingredients in the work bowl of a food processor fitted with a steel blade and blend well. Set aside while you prepare the bundles.

FOR THE Mozzarella Bundles, prepare a hot fire using hardwood charcoal, charcoal briquettes, or wood, or heat a gas grill to high. (Alternatively, the bundles can be sautéed in a small amount of olive oil.)

PLACE A large pan of water over high heat and bring to a boil. Blanch the radicchio leaves by dipping them into the boiling water for about 5 seconds. Remove them with tongs and plunge them into a bowl of ice water to stop the cooking. When cool, remove the leaves and place on paper towels to drain. They should be limp and pliable.

WRAP EACH slice of mozzarella in a slice of prosciutto. Wrap the bundles with the radicchio, taking care to enclose them completely. Secure each bundle with string, as if you were wrapping a package. Brush each with olive oil.

GRILL THE bundles (or cook in a little olive oil in a sauté pan over medium-high heat) for about 3 minutes on each side, or until nicely browned, turning the bundles with tongs or a spatula, so as not to pierce them. Transfer them to a heated platter.

TO SERVE, drizzle the sauce over the bundles and sprinkle with the pine nuts. Serve warm.

I love cheese! It's a marvelous product, inscribed in that great trinity of the table, which it forms with bread and wine.

—Joël Robuchon

Portobello–Goat Cheese Napoleons

There's a new, very chic hunting lodge southwest of Dallas, near Glen Rose, called Rough Creek Lodge. Architecturally, it is stunning, with several modern two-story buildings built along a limestone ridge overlooking a small lake. It's located in the middle of the desolate Texas prairie.

Even if you don't hunt, the tranquillity of the location and its magical setting in the midst of the rolling hills of Central Texas are enough to warrant a visit. The accommodations and service are stellar, as is the kitchen run by Gerard Thompson, who is widely recognized for his creativity. One evening he served us a napoleon that was my inspiration for this recipe.

You will need eight two-inch-deep by two-inch-diameter round molds such as cookie cutters, cut PVC pipe, or small empty cans. Small plastic drinking cups could also serve as molds. It is ideal to have eight molds, but the same one can be used over for each napoleon; just empty the mold after constructing each napoleon by gently pushing it out.

MAKES 8 TEASPOONS DRESSING
MAKES 8 (2-INCH) NAPOLEONS
SERVES 8

TARRAGON DRESSING

2 tablespoons extra virgin olive oil

½ tablespoon freshly squeezed lemon juice

½ teaspoon minced fresh tarragon

Salt and freshly ground black pepper to taste

NAPOLEONS

8 ounces (1 cup) fresh goat cheese

¼ teaspoon minced garlic

¼ teaspoon minced fresh tarragon, plus a few sprigs for garnish

Salt and freshly ground black pepper to taste

12 ounces portobello mushroom caps

2 tablespoons extra virgin olive oil

2 red bell peppers or pimientos

FOR THE Tarragon Dressing, blend the oil, lemon juice, tarragon, and salt and pepper in a blender or the work bowl of a food processor fitted with a steel blade. Set aside.

FOR THE Goat Cheese Napoleons, prepare a hot fire using hardwood charcoal, charcoal briquettes, or wood, or preheat a gas grill to high; or preheat the broiler.

MIX THE goat cheese with the garlic and tarragon in a small bowl. Season with salt and pepper to taste. Set aside.

BRUSH THE mushrooms with the olive oil. Grill or broil the mushrooms on both sides until they begin to brown and their juices just begin to exude. Remove from the heat and set aside in a single layer to cool. Place the peppers on the grill or under the broiler and cook, turning as necessary, until the skins are blackened. Place in a bowl, cover with plastic wrap, and let steam until cool.

WHEN THE mushrooms have cooled, cut them on the bias into thin slices, to expose the maximum amount of interior surface. Sprinkle with salt and pepper; set aside. Remove the charred skins, stems, seeds, and membranes from the roasted peppers. Set aside.

LIGHTLY OIL a 2-inch-round mold or spray it with cooking spray. To build the napoleons, trim the mushrooms and peppers as necessary to fit the diameter of the mold. Place a layer of the mushrooms in the mold. Top the mushrooms with a thin layer of the goat cheese mixture, about 2 teaspoons. Gently spread the goat cheese into an even layer. Top with a layer of roasted peppers and then another layer of the goat cheese mixture. Continue in this fashion until you have about 4 layers of vegetables and 3 layers of goat cheese, ending with a layer of peppers on top. Repeat to make 7 more napoleons. Refrigerate for at least 30 minutes before serving.

TO SERVE, push the napoleons out of the molds, if necessary. Insert a sprig of tarragon in the top of each napoleon like a plume, place the napoleons on serving plates, and drizzle about 1 teaspoon of the dressing over the top of each one.

Crispy Pita Points Topped with Spinach and Feta

One of my greatest pleasures in Greece was wandering around the vast marketplace of Athens, up and down the narrow, crowded streets. There are tiny stores side by side in every nook and cranny, selling everything from cheese to sponges. Unlike our supermarkets, there is a separate vendor for each type of product, so that you'll need to stop at four or five different stores to put together one meal, but you'll be assured of the very finest quality and freshness. In my wanderings, I found one store filled with nothing but barrels and barrels of olives, next door to a cheese seller, which in turn was next to a bread shop. I like to imagine them trading their goods with each other at the end of a long day to put together the perfect snack.

While this may not be a traditional recipe, it a very Greek dish because it contains all the quintessential Greek ingredients: spinach, feta, pine nuts, oregano, and Calamata olives.

MAKES 36 PITA POINTS
SERVES 12

6 rounds pita bread, cut into 6 wedges each

¼ cup extra virgin olive oil

Salt, preferably freshly ground sea salt, and freshly ground black pepper to taste

1 tablespoon dried oregano

¼ cup pine nuts

1 bunch spinach (about 12 ounces)

2 cloves garlic, minced

25 Calamata olives, pitted and chopped, plus whole olives for garnish

8 ounces feta cheese, crumbled (1½ cups)

PREHEAT THE oven to 350°F.

USING 2 tablespoons of the oil, brush each pita wedge with oil and sprinkle with salt and pepper. Place the wedges of pita bread on a baking sheet, place in the oven, and toast, turning as necessary, until nicely browned and dry on both sides, about 20 minutes. Remove from the oven and transfer to a rack to cool. (Leave the oven on.) Immediately crush the oregano between your fingers and sprinkle over the pita toasts.

PLACE THE pine nuts on the same baking sheet and toast them in the oven to a golden brown, about 3 to 5 minutes.

CUT THE stems from the spinach leaves by cutting across the bunch before untying it. Wash the spinach leaves and shake off the excess water. Place the leaves in a large saucepan, sprinkle with salt, cover the saucepan, and cook over medium heat until wilted, about 5 minutes. Transfer the spinach to a colander to drain.

WHEN THE spinach is cool enough to handle, squeeze the excess moisture out of it with your hands or the back of a spoon. You should have about ⅔ cup packed spinach. Place on a cutting board and finely chop.

HEAT THE remaining 2 tablespoons oil in a skillet over medium heat. Add the minced garlic and sauté briefly. Add the chopped spinach and cook until dry, about 2 minutes. Add the chopped olives, the pine nuts, and salt and pepper to taste. Mix well and remove from the heat. Add the feta cheese and stir to blend.

PLACE A teaspoon of the spinach mixture on each pita point and spread it out to cover the pita. Arrange on a serving platter, garnish with olives, and serve warm or at room temperature.

Well, many's the long night I've dreamed of cheese—toasted mostly—and woke up again, and here I were.

–Robert Louis Stevenson

Salads

Greek Salad with Feta and Mint

Once on a trip to Greece I missed my connecting flight to Metsovo, a village in the northern part of the country, and had to hire a taxi at the Athens airport to drive me seven hours across the Greek countryside. My friends who had arrived in Metsovo by air all felt sorry for me, but actually I had a great adventure and relished the views of Greece from the windows of the taxi rather than from the air. As we drove north and approached the mountains, the taxi driver decided it was time to stop for a light meal. We pulled into a little family-run restaurant he knew that was attached to a gas station. I ordered a salad and was so overwhelmed by its freshness and simplicity that I have recreated it for you here. I particularly liked the way the feta was served in a big slab, teetering on top of the salad.

SERVES 4 GENEROUSLY

2 sweet onions, such as Texas 1015, Vidalia, or Walla Walla

3 small cucumbers, peeled and sliced ⅓ inch thick

3 ripe tomatoes, peeled and cut into 8 wedges each

¼ cup extra virgin olive oil

2 tablespoons red wine vinegar

Salt and freshly ground black pepper to taste

8 ounces feta, cut into 4 slabs

½ teaspoon dried oregano or 1 teaspoon minced fresh oregano

4 sprigs fresh mint

THINLY SLICE the onions, rinse under cold water, and drain on paper towels. Combine the onions, cucumbers, and tomatoes in a large salad bowl and toss with the oil, vinegar, and salt and pepper.

TO SERVE, divide the salad among four large serving plates or shallow bowls. Place a slab of feta on top of each. Sprinkle with the oregano and garnish with the fresh mint.

Baked Goat Cheese Salad

Few things are more delicious than warm goat cheese. When goat cheese is heated, its flavor is quite mild and less pronounced and its texture is exceedingly soft, almost runny. When goat cheese first began to gain popularity in the United States in the mid- to late 1980s, this dish could be found on menus in many restaurants serving American regional cuisine.

This salad is the perfect first course to serve at a dinner party, because almost everything can be prepared in advance and all you'll need to do at the last moment is toss the salad, heat the goat cheese, and place a warm disk of cheese on top of each salad. Make sure to serve the salad with crusty French bread, because the warm cheese just begs to be spread on bread. I would also suggest you serve a Sauvignon Blanc or Sancerre, perfect wines for pairing with goat cheese.

MAKES ½ CUP VINAIGRETTE
SERVES 4

BAKED GOAT CHEESE

8 to 10 ounces fresh goat cheese
(2 rounds of chèvre or 1 log Montrachet)

3 sprigs fresh thyme

1 sprig fresh rosemary

1 sprig fresh oregano

½ cup extra virgin olive oil

1 cup fresh bread crumbs

SALAD

1 bunch watercress

1 small head radicchio

½ head Bibb or Boston lettuce, washed and dried

HERBED BALSAMIC VINAIGRETTE

2 tablespoons balsamic vinegar

½ teaspoon Dijon mustard

Salt and freshly ground black pepper to taste

FOR THE Baked Goat Cheese, cut each round of goat cheese horizontally in half so you have 4 disks of cheese about ½ inch thick. If using Montrachet, slice the log into 4 rounds. Strip the leaves off the herbs. Pour the oil into a shallow bowl just large enough to hold the cheese in one layer. Sprinkle the herbs over the oil. Lay the goat cheese in the oil. Let the cheese marinate at room temperature for 30 minutes, turning once after 15 minutes.

FOR THE Salad, cut the stem ends off the watercress and radicchio before you untie the bunches. Wash them, drain, and dry, using a spinner or dish towels. Wrap in paper towels or dish towels and refrigerate.

JUST BEFORE serving, preheat the oven to 400°F.

REMOVE THE goat cheese from the oil, letting the oil drain off (reserve the oil), and roll the cheese in the bread crumbs. Sprinkle any remaining crumbs on top. Place on a small baking pan. Place in the oven and bake for 2 to 3 minutes, or until lightly browned and just heated. Be careful not to overheat the cheese, or it will melt completely. Remove and set aside.

MEANWHILE, FOR the Herbed Balsamic Vinaigrette, whisk the vinegar, mustard, and salt and pepper together in a small bowl. Drizzle in the reserved oil and herbs, whisking constantly until emulsified and thickened. Set aside.

TEAR THE lettuces into bite-sized pieces and place in a large salad bowl. Pour the vinaigrette over the leaves and toss until well coated. Divide the salad among four plates.

USING A spatula, gently remove each warm goat cheese disk from the pan and place it atop a salad. Serve immediately.

My favorites are authentic, the real thing, palpably linked to the milks from which they are made and to their geographic origins. To taste them is to appreciate the link that must take place for a cheese to achieve greatness—a concomitance of soil and herbage, beast and human, climate and the passage of time.

–Steve Jenkins

Green Salad with Apples and Goat Cheese

I love the combination of green apples and toasted nuts because the apples are so juicy and tart, while the nuts are crunchy and rich. The addition of a creamy, tangy goat cheese seems to even out and intensify the flavors.

When I went to Mary Baldwin College in Virginia, we had a special day called Apple Day. One morning each fall we would awaken to the news that all our classes had been canceled for the day and we were to proceed posthaste to the orchards outside of town to pick apples. We would spend the day picking all the apples we could carry, which we were free to take back to the dorm. I ate apples galore for a month thereafter.

If only I had known of goat cheese then, I would have enjoyed the apples even more.

MAKES ABOUT ⅓ CUP VINAIGRETTE
SERVES 4 TO 6

BALSAMIC VINAIGRETTE
1 tablespoon balsamic vinegar
1 teaspoon freshly squeezed lemon juice
½ teaspoon salt
Freshly ground black pepper to taste
⅓ cup extra virgin olive oil

SALAD
½ cup pecan halves
1 tart green apple, cored but not peeled
1 teaspoon freshly squeezed lemon juice
½ head romaine lettuce, washed and dried
½ head red leaf lettuce, washed and dried
4 ounces fresh goat cheese, crumbled (½ cup)

FOR THE Balsamic Vinaigrette, place the the vinegar, lemon juice, salt, and pepper in a small bowl and whisk to combine. Slowly drizzle in the oil in a thin stream, whisking constantly until thickened and emulsified. Set aside.

FOR THE Salad, preheat the oven to 350°F.

PLACE THE pecans on a small baking sheet and bake them for 5 minutes, or until golden brown and aromatic. Be careful not to burn them. Remove and let cool, then coarsely chop.

CUT THE apple into very thin slices, place in a large salad bowl, and toss with the lemon juice.

JUST BEFORE serving time, tear the lettuce leaves into bite-sized pieces and add to the apple. Add the pecans and vinaigrette and toss to combine well. Sprinkle with the goat cheese and toss again.

TO SERVE, arrange the salad on chilled salad plates.

I have fed too many teenagers to have illusions. Given a choice between cheese, for example, they will skirt the Pont l'Evêque, the Reblochon, the Appenzeller and the Triple Crème, and head with unerring aim for the prepackaged process slices or the supermarket Swiss (which has the texture, but nowhere near the flavor, of rubber gloves).

–Robert Farrar Capon

Caesar Salad with Pecorino

Caesar salad is said to have originated in a restaurant in Tijuana, Mexico, in the 1920s. Often it is prepared tableside with great flourish.

Classically, Caesar salad is made with Parmigiano cheese. However, I have created my version using all sheep milk cheeses. Pecorino is a hard sharp cheese suitable for grating. It is traditionally made in the countryside near Rome. Pepato, a semi-soft sheep milk cheese that is studded with black peppercorns, is much milder despite the kick from the pepper. It is too soft to grate, so it must be shredded or shaved. It usually is imported from Italy; however, Eric Liebetrau of Park Cheese in Wisconsin makes a wonderful pepato (see Sources, page 373).

MAKES ½ CUP DRESSING
MAKES 4 CUPS CROUTONS
SERVES 4

BLACK PEPPER-PECORINO CROUTONS

½ baguette

¼ cup extra virgin olive oil

1 clove garlic, minced

Seasoning Salt (page 79) or store-bought, to taste

Freshly ground black pepper to taste

½ to 1 ounce Pecorino Romano, grated (2 to 4 tablespoons)

CAESAR SALAD DRESSING

2 cloves garlic, minced

3 to 6 anchovy fillets, with their oil

2 tablespoons freshly squeezed lemon juice

1 very fresh large egg yolk

6 tablespoons extra virgin olive oil

1 teaspoon salt

1 teaspoon coarsely ground black pepper

1 head romaine lettuce, washed and dried

4 ounces pepato or Pecorino Romano, shaved into long wide strips with a vegetable peeler or mandoline

FOR THE Black Pepper–Pecorino Croutons, cut the bread into ½-inch-thick slices and then cut the slices into quarters. Cut into smaller pieces if necessary. (There should be about 4 cups bread cubes.)

HEAT THE oil in a large nonstick skillet over medium-high heat. Add the garlic and cook for about 30 seconds, then add the bread. Stir and toss the bread for 3 to 4 minutes, until coated on all sides with oil and beginning to brown. Sprinkle with the seasoning salt and pepper and continue stirring and tossing the bread cubes for 3 to 5 minutes more, or until brown and crunchy. Remove the skillet from the heat, immediately sprinkle the Pecorino

Romano on top, and toss to coat the croutons with the cheese. Set aside to cool. (The croutons can be stored in an airtight container for up to 3 days.)

FOR THE Caesar Salad Dressing, place the garlic and anchovies in a small bowl and mash to a paste, using the back of a spoon, or pound to a paste using a mortar and pestle. Transfer to a large salad bowl. Add the lemon juice and whisk to mix, then add the egg yolk and whisk to combine. Place the bowl on a folded damp towel to help stabilize it. Slowly drizzle the oil into the bowl, whisking constantly until emulsified and thick. Season with salt and pepper. (The dressing can also be made in a food processor fitted with a steel blade: Combine the garlic, anchovies, and lemon juice in the work bowl. Add the egg yolk, salt, and pepper and blend. While the processor is running, slowly drizzle the oil through the feed tube in a steady stream and process until emulsified and thickened.)

COVER AND refrigerate the dressing if not serving immediately. Use the dressing as soon as possible, because of the raw egg yolk; discard any unused dressing after a couple of days.

JUST BEFORE serving time, tear the lettuce into 1- to 2-inch pieces and place in the salad bowl with the dressing. (Or place in a salad bowl and add the dressing.) Toss the lettuce with the dressing until well coated. Add the croutons and the shaved cheese and toss again.

DIVIDE THE salad among four chilled salad plates and serve immediately.

Note: It's generally safe to use raw eggs in your recipes, as long as they are very fresh grade A or AA, and have been properly refrigerated. There is, however, a slight risk of *Salmonella enteritidis* and other illnesses related to the consumption of raw eggs. I have made this recipe many, many times without any problem, but if you want to be absolutely safe, you can either cook the egg yolks over a hot water bath or in a double boiler to a temperature of 145°F. or substitute pasteurized eggs (found in the grocer's refrigerated dairy case) for the raw eggs in this recipe. As a precaution, pregnant women, babies, young children, the elderly, and all those whose health is compromised should always avoid raw eggs.

VARIATION

Grilled Caesar Salad

Preheat a gas or charcoal grill to high and adjust the rack so that it is 3 inches from the heat source. When the fire is hot and coals are covered with gray ash, cut 1 head Romaine lettuce, washed and dried, lengthwise into quarters. Spray or brush the grill with vegetable oil. Place the lettuce quarters directly on the grill, cut side down. Turn the lettuce quarters as the edges of the leaves begin to turn dark brown until all sides are charred but not burned. Place the lettuce wedges on serving plates, drizzle liberally with the dressing, and sprinkle with the pepato shavings, croutons, and freshly ground black pepper. Serve immediately.

Iceberg Wedges with Creamy Gorgonzola Dressing

No one food brings us back to the 1950s as quickly as iceberg lettuce. Suddenly, it's the vogue again, and is being served in upscale steak houses across the country, cut into wedges, just as it was in the 1950s. Some things never change!

While the original blue cheese dressing typically came from a bottle, I have updated the salad by creating a dressing made with Gorgonzola, the soft rich blue cheese from northern Italy.

This recipe makes 2 cups of dressing, so you'll have leftovers. Store the unused dressing in the refrigerator in a tightly sealed glass jar for up to 2 weeks. It is also delicious served with cut-up raw vegetables as an hors d'ouevre or over warm steamed vegetables. Not to mention buffalo chicken wings.

MAKES ABOUT 2 CUPS DRESSING
SERVES 4

CREAMY GORGONZOLA DRESSING

8 ounces Gorgonzola, crumbled (1½ cups)

⅓ cup mayonnaise

⅓ cup (3 ounces) sour cream or Crème Fraîche, homemade (page 68) or store-bought

⅓ cup milk

¼ teaspoon minced garlic

½ teaspoon Worcestershire sauce

1 teaspoon white wine vinegar

1 teaspoon freshly squeezed lemon juice

½ teaspoon salt, or to taste

1 teaspoon freshly ground black pepper, or to taste

3 large leaves fresh basil, chopped

1 head iceberg lettuce

2 ounces Gorgonzola, crumbled (⅓ cup)

4 sprigs fresh basil for garnish

FOR THE Creamy Gorgonzola Dressing, combine half the Gorgonzola, the mayonnaise, and sour cream in the work bowl of a food processor fitted with a steel blade and puree until smooth. Add the milk, garlic, Worcestershire, vinegar, lemon juice, salt, and pepper. Blend well. Add the remaining Gorgonzola and pulse quickly just until it is coarsely chopped into good-sized chunks. Transfer to a medium bowl and adjust the seasonings. Fold in the basil, cover, and refrigerate. (This is a thick dressing that gets thicker upon chilling. If it is too thick, it can be thinned by whisking in additional milk before serving.)

WASH AND dry the lettuce. Cut into quarters and remove the core.

TO SERVE, place each wedge of lettuce on a chilled salad plate. Top with 3 to 4 tablespoons of the dressing, sprinkle the Gorgonzola on top, and garnish with the basil sprigs.

On Limburger:
The rankest compound of villainous smell
That ever offended nostril.

–Shakespeare

Frico Salad with Fennel and Orange

These lacy cheese wafers called fricos come from Friuli, a region of Italy that lies north of Venice and touches Yugoslavia on the east. In Italy, the cheese used most often for making fricos is a firm cow's milk cheese called Montasio. If this is not available, I like to use smoked Scamorza or provolone, but other cheeses, such as Monterey Jack or Cheddar, can be used quite easily.

Fricos can be made in a nonstick skillet or on a nonstick baking sheet in a 400°F. oven. I prefer the skillet version, because it is easier to watch the progress of the melting cheese and I feel more in control.

**MAKES ABOUT ½ CUP VINAIGRETTE
SERVES 4**

ORANGE VINAIGRETTE

¼ cup freshly squeezed orange juice

1 tablespoon red wine vinegar

Salt and freshly ground black pepper to taste

¼ cup extra virgin olive oil

SALAD

1 fennel bulb

½ red onion, thinly sliced

1 orange, peeled and segmented

4 ounces field greens, washed and dried

Salt and freshly ground pepper to taste

FRICOS

4 ounces smoked mozzarella, scamorza, Cheddar, provolone, or Montasio, shredded (1 cup)

FOR THE Orange Vinaigrette, place the orange juice, vinegar, and salt and pepper in a small bowl and whisk together. Drizzle in the oil, whisking constantly until the dressing is thick and emulsified.

FOR THE Salad, remove and discard the stalks from the fennel and very thinly slice the bulb. Place in a large salad bowl and add the onion. Drizzle with the vinaigrette, toss to coat, and set aside to marinate for at least 15 minutes, or up to 1 hour.

PEEL THE orange, removing the bitter white pith. Using a sharp knife, slice between the membranes to release the orange segments; set aside.

JUST BEFORE serving time, add the greens and oranges to the fennel, sprinkle with salt and pepper, and toss until the greens are well coated. Adjust the seasonings, if necessary.

FOR THE fricos, heat a large nonstick skillet over medium heat. Place one-eighth of the shredded cheese in a mound in the skillet. Cook until the bottom is browned, several minutes. Use a spatula to remove cheese from the skillet and place on paper towels to drain. Repeat to make 8 fricos in all.

TO SERVE, divide the salad among four salad plates and top each with 2 fricos. Serve immediately.

If there was a food place, I was like cottage cheese, or maybe the lettuce. I had really so little to do on that show.

**–Didi Conn, on her role
in the TV show *Benson***

Chopped Chef's Salad with Cheddar

Chopped salads have gained popularity in recent years, and they are currently the rage on restaurant menus from New York to California.

The ingredients in this salad are similar to those in a chef's salad or Cobb salad. They are all chopped and then tossed together.

**MAKES ABOUT ¾ CUP VINAIGRETTE
SERVES 4 TO 6 AS A MAIN COURSE**

CAPER VINAIGRETTE

⅓ cup drained capers

½ cup extra virgin olive oil, plus extra as needed

¼ cup red wine vinegar

¼ teaspoon minced garlic

½ teaspoon salt

½ teaspoon freshly ground black pepper

SALAD

1 bunch arugula, washed and dried

1 small head radicchio, washed and dried

1 small head Romaine lettuce, washed and dried

4 ounces sharp Cheddar, cut into ¼-inch pieces

4 ounces sliced smoked turkey, cut into ¼-inch pieces

2 hard-boiled eggs, peeled and cut into ¼-inch pieces

¼ cup black olives, pitted and cut into ¼-inch pieces

1 small red bell pepper, cored, seeded, and cut into ¼-inch pieces

1 small carrot, cut into ¼-inch pieces

FOR THE Caper Vinaigrette, pat the capers dry with paper towels. Place ¼ cup oil in a small skillet and heat over medium heat until hot but not smoking. Slowly slide the capers into the oil and fry for 2 to 3 minutes, or until the capers burst open and all their water has evaporated, so the sizzling ceases. Remove with a slotted spoon and drain on paper towels; set aside. Let the oil in the skillet cool.

WHISK THE vinegar, garlic, salt, and pepper together in a small bowl. Pour the reserved oil into a measuring cup and add additional oil to make ½ cup. Slowly drizzle into the vinegar mixture and continue whisking until emulsified and smooth. Set aside.

FOR THE Salad, cut the stem ends off the arugula before you untie the bunch. Wash and dry, using a spinner or dish towels. Wrap the lettuces in paper towels or dish towels and refrigerate.

JUST BEFORE serving, cut the arugula, radicchio, and lettuce into pieces about ½ inch in size. (You should have about 3 cups of each.) Combine the greens, Cheddar, turkey, eggs, olives, bell pepper, and carrot in a large salad bowl. Add the vinaigrette and toss well.

TO SERVE, divide the salad among four to six large chilled serving plates. Sprinkle the capers over the top.

I am grateful to have learned young that cheese has an important place in a menu. It isn't something to serve with apple pie, and it isn't something to cut into nasty little cubes and serve with crackers. Early in life I learned to see the beauty of great slabs or rounds of cheese on the table, and I still respond to the sight of a well-stocked cheese tray properly presented.

–James Beard

Field Greens with Pears and Blue Cheese

Shelley Barsotti, a great cook and one of the owners of a catering company in Dallas called Food Company, gave me this recipe. It is a perfect salad to enjoy with wine because it is not very acidic, and the port, blue cheese, pears, and walnuts create a culinary symphony. They were also a favorite of M. F. K. Fisher, the illustrious food writer, who waxed eloquent on their combined flavors in many essays.

I suggest serving this salad following the main course, as is the custom in Europe. It makes a lovely ending to a meal, especially if you have a little red wine left in your glass.

MAKES 1 ¼ CUPS DRESSING
SERVES 4

PORT-SHALLOT DRESSING

2 cups ruby port

½ cup thickly sliced shallots

1 tablespoon red wine vinegar

½ cup extra virgin olive oil

Salt and freshly ground black pepper to taste

SALAD

2 pears

4 to 6 ounces mixed field greens (4 to 6 cups), washed and dried

1 cup toasted walnuts, coarsely chopped

8 ounces Maytag blue cheese, crumbled (1½ cups)

Salt and freshly ground black pepper to taste

FOR THE Port-Shallot Dressing, place the port in a small heavy saucepan over medium heat. Add the shallots and bring to a boil. Reduce the heat to low and cook for 15 minutes, or until the port is reduced to ⅔ cup without the shallots. Set aside to let cool.

POUR THE port and shallots into the container of a blender and puree. Add the vinegar and blend well. While the motor is running, drizzle the oil through the hole in the blender top and continue to blend until emulsified and smooth. Season with salt and pepper to taste. Set aside; refrigerate if not using immediately.

FOR THE Salad, just before serving time peel, core, and slice the pears. Combine the greens, pears, walnuts, and blue cheese in a large salad bowl. Drizzle half the dressing over the top and toss. Drizzle in the remaining dressing, tossing until the greens are well coated— you may not need to add all the dressing. (Leftover dressing can be kept refrigerated for up to 1 week for another use.) Season with salt and pepper and toss again.

TO SERVE, place on chilled salad plates.

Roasted Beet Salad with Feta

Of all the root vegetables, beets are my favorites. I love their deceptively sweet taste. Nowadays they are available in new and different varieties, such as golden beets and even tiny baby white beets. Roasted, they become even sweeter, so I like to cut the sweetness slightly with balsamic vinegar and then contrast the sweetness with the saltiness of the feta. I also like the Russian combination of beets and dill.

MAKES ½ CUP DRESSING
SERVES 6

2 pounds beets

¼ cup extra virgin olive oil

Salt and freshly ground black pepper to taste

LEMON DRESSING

2 tablespoons freshly squeezed lemon juice

¼ cup extra virgin olive oil

3 tablespoons chopped fresh dill

½ teaspoon grated lemon zest

4 ounces feta, crumbled (¾ cup)

1 tablespoon cracked black pepper

Salt to taste

PREHEAT THE oven to 350°F.

WASH THE beets and trim the stems to ½ inch. Coat the beets with ¼ cup of the oil and sprinkle with salt and pepper. Lay the beets in a shallow roasting pan just large enough to hold them in a single layer, tightly cover with aluminum foil, and roast for 30 to 45 minutes, or until tender. Remove from the oven, uncover and continue to roast for 15 minutes, and place on a rack to cool.

PEEL THE beets, using a sharp knife, and cut into wedges. Place in a bowl.

FOR THE Lemon Dressing, whisk the lemon juice, oil, dill, and lemon zest together in a bowl.

TO SERVE, pour the dressing over the beets. Toss to combine. Sprinkle the feta and pepper over the beets. Toss to combine and add salt to taste. Serve at room temperature.

Paula's Mozzarella and Tomato Salad

This is my favorite salad of all. It was the one thing that I missed most when I left Italy for Texas, and I finally had to start the Mozzarella Company just so I could get fresh mozzarella for this salad!

It is known in Italy as *insalata caprese,* because legend has it that the salad was first made on the Isle of Capri, in the Bay of Naples. There is a lot of discussion as to whether the salad is best with *mozzarella di bufala* (made from the milk of water buffalo) or with *fior di latte,* fresh mozzarella made from cow's milk. You be the judge. Most important is that the mozzarella be fresh.

When we began the Mozzarella Company in 1982, our first really prestigious account was the Mansion on Turtle Creek, and they have served our cheese in this salad ever since. Chef Dean Fearing's version is similar to the King of Naples Salad (see variation below), but his dressing is a vinaigrette laced with fresh basil.

SERVES 4

2 large ripe tomatoes, peeled and sliced ¼ inch thick

8 ounces fresh mozzarella, sliced ¼ inch thick

¼ teaspoon salt

¼ teaspoon freshly ground black pepper

2 tablespoons extra virgin olive oil

8 leaves fresh basil

ARRANGE THE tomato and mozzarella slices on a platter or individual salad plates, overlapping the slices and fanning them out like a deck of cards. Sprinkle with the salt and pepper. Drizzle with the oil. Garnish with the basil: Cut it into very thin slices or tear into bits and sprinkle on top or leave the leaves whole and tuck them here and there between the mozzarella and tomato slices. Serve immediately.

VARIATIONS

King of Naples Salad

This is called the King of Naples salad because the red, white, and green of this dish reflect the colors of the flag of Italy. Peel, pit, and slice 1 avocado into ¼-inch-thick slices. Brush with freshly squeezed lemon juice to prevent darkening. Arrange an overlapping row of the tomato slices on one side of a platter, an overlapping row of the avocado slices on the other side, and an overlapping row of the mozzarella slices down the middle. Sprinkle with the salt and pepper, drizzle with the oil, and garnish with several sprigs of basil, emanating from the fresh mozzarella like a plume.

Stacked Mozzarella Tomato Salad

Rather than spreading out the tomato and mozzarella slices, stack them, alternating them, to form 4 towers. Make a basil vinaigrette by whisking together 2 tablespoons extra virgin olive oil, ½ teaspoon red wine vinegar, and 1 tablespoon Basil Pesto (page 80). Place on salad plates, drizzle the vinaigrette over the towers, and garnish with fresh basil as above.

Wine and cheese are ageless companions, like aspirin and aches, or June and moon, or good people and noble ventures.

–M. F. K. Fisher

Wild Rice and Smoked Chicken Salad with Blue Cheese

Wild rice really isn't rice at all. It is actually a long-grained marsh grass that is native to the northern Great Lakes area. Its nutty and crunchy texture makes it a great addition to this salad, which is much more flavorful than your usual chicken—or turkey—salad. I use this as a great way to recycle leftovers, and sometimes even look forward to the day after Thanksgiving!

MAKES ABOUT ¾ CUP DRESSING
SERVES 6 TO 8

WILD RICE SALAD

2 cups wild rice rinsed and drained (or 1 cup wild rice and 1 cup long-grain white rice)

8 ounces smoked or cooked chicken, turkey, or ham, cut into ¼-inch pieces (1 cup)

½ cup golden raisins

½ cup chopped toasted pecans

1 carrot, shredded

1 rib celery, cut into ¼-inch pieces

1 head red-tipped or regular Romaine lettuce, washed and dried

4 ounces Maytag Blue cheese, crumbled (¾ cup)

ORANGE DRESSING

2 tablespoons rice wine vinegar

¼ cup freshly squeezed orange juice

½ cup extra virgin olive oil

Salt and freshly ground pepper to taste

FOR THE Wild Rice Salad, place the wild rice in a large saucepan and cover with water by 2 inches. Place over medium-high heat and bring to a boil. Reduce the heat, cover, and simmer for 30 to 45 minutes, or until the rice grains are beginning to open and are tender. The cooking time will vary depending on the age—and dryness—of the rice. (If using white rice, cook separately according to the package directions.) Drain the rice in a colander and rinse with cold water. Shake to remove the excess water.

MEANWHILE, FOR the Orange Dressing, combine the vinegar and orange juice in a small bowl. Slowly drizzle in the oil, whisking constantly until emulsified and thick. Season with salt and pepper. Set aside.

PLACE THE rice in a large bowl and add the chicken, raisins, pecans, carrot, and celery. Toss to combine. Pour the dressing over the salad and toss to coat.

TO SERVE, line a platter or salad bowl with the Romaine lettuce leaves. Arrange the salad on top of the lettuce and sprinkle with the blue cheese. Serve at room temperature.

Fruit Salad with Honey-Ricotta Dressing

Fruit salads are wonderful in the summertime. This honey-ricotta dressing is a light accompaniment. Its citrus undertones complement the sweet fruits.

MAKES ABOUT 1 CUP DRESSING
SERVES 6

HONEY-RICOTTA DRESSING

4 ounces ricotta, homemade (page 70) or store-bought, well drained (½ cup)

1 tablespoon honey

⅓ cup freshly squeezed orange juice

½ teaspoon grated orange zest

1½ teaspoons chopped fresh mint

1 tablespoon Grand Marnier (optional)

FRUIT SALAD

½ pineapple

1 pint strawberries

2 kiwis

1 small bunch red grapes

1 medium apple or pear

Juice of ½ lemon

Confectioners' sugar, for garnish

Several sprigs fresh mint, for garnish

Edible flowers, for garnish (optional)

FOR THE Honey-Ricotta Dressing, place the ricotta, honey, and orange juice in the container of a blender or food processor fitted with a steel blade. Puree until light and smooth, 2 to 3 minutes. Add the orange zest and mint and puree briefly. Transfer to a bowl and stir in the Grand Marnier if desired. Cover and refrigerate.

FOR THE Fruit Salad, peel and slice or chop the fruits as desired (see below). Brush the apple or pear with the lemon juice to keep it from discoloring.

THIS SALAD may be served in several ways: One way is to toss bite-sized pieces of all the fruits with the dressing and serve in martini or other stemmed glasses. Another way is to layer the chopped fruits in a clear glass bowl or parfait glasses, alternating layers of fruits with the dressing, and top the final layer with a sprinkling of confectioners' sugar and a drizzle of the remaining dressing. A third way is to arrange the fruits on a platter, either sliced or whole, and serve the dressing on the side. In any case, a final dusting of confectioners' sugar enhances the sweetness of the fruit. Garnish with fresh mint and edible flowers, if desired.

Waldorf Salad with Brie

Waldorf salad is said to have originated at the venerable hotel by that name in New York City in the 1890s. I have always loved to stay at the Waldorf because it seems so grown-up and sophisticated. I like the salad because of the crunchiness of the apples and celery, the bright acidity and sweetness of the grapes, and the toasty richness of the walnuts. The Brie complements and enhances the salad with its rich and creamy texture—it is a great addition to this classic salad.

MAKES ¾ CUP DRESSING
SERVES 5

BRIE DRESSING

2 ounces Brie, rind removed, cut into ½-inch cubes

½ cup mayonnaise

2 tablespoons champagne vinegar or apple cider vinegar

1 teaspoon freshly squeezed lemon juice

1 teaspoon Dijon mustard

½ teaspoon minced shallot

1 teaspoon chopped fresh flat-leaf parsley

Salt and freshly ground black pepper to taste

Milk or water (optional)

WALDORF SALAD

3 medium crisp, tart apples, cored but not peeled, chopped into ½-inch cubes (about 3 cups)

3 ribs celery, strings removed with a peeler and sliced (about 1½ cups)

1½ cups coarsely chopped toasted walnuts

1 cup red grapes, cut in half

4 ounces Brie, rind removed, if desired, cut into ½-inch cubes (⅔ cup)

2 bunches watercress

FOR THE Brie Dressing, combine the Brie, mayonnaise, vinegar, lemon juice, mustard, shallot, parsley, and salt and pepper in the work bowl of a food processor fitted with a steel blade or in a blender. Process until smooth. Adjust the seasonings if necessary. The dressing may be thinned with milk or water if desired. Cover and refrigerate.

FOR THE Waldorf Salad, place the apples, celery, walnuts, grapes, and Brie in a large salad bowl. Toss together. Add the dressing and toss again to coat. Cover and refrigerate until chilled.

CUT 1 inch off the stems of the watercress before you untie the bunch. Wash and dry the watercress. Tear into bite-sized pieces. Wrap in a dish towel and refrigerate.

TO SERVE, divide the watercress evenly among five chilled salad plates. Top with the salad. Serve chilled.

Soups

I first enjoyed this soup when I lived in Perugia. It was a specialty of Cesarino, a tiny trattoria just below my apartment. In the years before I had a telephone, I used to drop a basket on a rope downstairs to the front door of the restaurant and swing it back and forth until someone noticed it. There would be a note inside with my order. When it was ready, Gigo, the waiter, would ring my doorbell and I'd know that dinner was in my basket and I'd hoist it up to my apartment.

The soup is ultra-simple to make. With the egg and cheese froth suspended in it, a simple chicken broth is transformed into a satisfying and complete meal.

MAKES ABOUT 7 CUPS
SERVES 4 TO 6

6 cups chicken broth, homemade (page 81) or store-bought

4 large eggs

1 ounce Parmigiano-Reggiano, grated (¼ cup)

Pinch of ground nutmeg

2 tablespoons minced fresh flat-leaf parsley

BRING THE broth to a lively boil in a large saucepan.

MEANWHILE, WHISK the eggs in a small bowl. Add the cheese, nutmeg, and parsley and whisk until completely incorporated.

SLOWLY POUR the egg mixture into the broth, whisking constantly. Continue to whisk for 3 to 4 minutes. When cooked, the eggs will be in tiny pieces suspended on the top of the broth.

SERVE IMMEDIATELY, in large heated soup bowls.

Ancho Chicken Broth with Goat Cheese–Stuffed Squash Blossoms

The broth in this soup is colored pink by the ancho chiles. Its charm lies in the manner in which it is served: You place matchstick vegetables in the bottom of each soup dish, then ladle the hot soup on top of the raw vegetables.

Squash blossoms are the flowers produced by both winter and summer squash. They are fragile and soft, easily opened and stuffed with goat cheese. Squash blossoms are available year-round in specialty produce markets as well as in Italian and Latin American food stores. If squash blossoms are not normally available in your market, the produce manager may be able to order them. If you have access to a garden, harvest your own that morning. (If squash blossoms are out of the question, the goat cheese can be formed into little 1-inch balls and rolled in minced parsley to coat them.)

Cut the vegetables into matchsticks about ⅛ inch in size using a sharp knife, food processor, or mandoline.

MAKES 4 CUPS
SERVES 4

2 dried ancho chiles

4 cups chicken broth, homemade (page 81) or store-bought

2 tablespoons extra virgin olive oil

¼ teaspoon minced garlic

½ cup matchstick julienne of shiitake mushroom caps

¼ cup matchstick julienne of yellow squash

¼ cup matchstick julienne of zucchini

¼ cup matchstick julienne of carrots

8 squash blossoms

2 ounces (¼ cup) fresh goat cheese

3 sprigs fresh cilantro, leaves only, for garnish

RINSE AND dry the chiles. Slit them lengthwise and remove and discard the seeds and stems. Place the chiles in a dry skillet and quickly and lightly toast them over medium heat, flattening them with the back of a spatula and turning them several times, until aromatic and barely toasted. Watch carefully, as they can burn quickly. Coarsely chop the chiles.

POUR THE broth into a medium saucepan and place over medium heat. Add the chiles and simmer until the broth is rose-colored, about 20 minutes. The longer the anchos steep in the broth, the darker and spicier the broth will be. Strain the broth using a fine-mesh sieve or a strainer lined with several layers of cheesecloth and return to the saucepan. Set aside.

HEAT THE oil in a small skillet over medium heat. Add the garlic and mushrooms and sauté until tender. Remove from the heat and set aside to cool. When cooled, toss with the squash, zucchini, and carrots.

GENTLY OPEN the squash blossoms and remove the yellow stamens. Fill each blossom with 1 to 2 teaspoons of the goat cheese.

TO SERVE, reheat the broth. Divide the julienned vegetables among four large shallow soup bowls. Ladle the broth over the vegetables and float the squash blossoms on top. Alternatively, set the balls of parsley-rolled goat cheese on top (see page 146). Garnish with the cilantro leaves. Serve immediately.

Cheese is probably the best of all foods, as wine is the best of all beverages.

–Patience Gray

Tomato Soup with Dilled Havarti

Tomatoes and dill are perfect mates. In the summertime, you can make this soup using fresh tomatoes, and it is even more delicious. When I moved into an apartment for the first time after college, I planted tomatoes and dill. They grew along the fence in our tiny backyard. Ever since then, I've been completely convinced that home-grown tomatoes are always best. And nowadays, so many interesting heirloom varieties are available. My husband, Jim, grows great old-fashioned tomatoes in our backyard. I think they're even better than those found at many farmers' markets.

MAKES ABOUT 5 CUPS
SERVES 4

½ cup extra virgin olive oil

2 cloves garlic, minced

¼ cup minced scallions (both green and white parts)

6 plum tomatoes, peeled, seeded, and chopped

1 (14.5-ounce) can Italian plum tomatoes, chopped, with their juice

¼ cup dry white wine

3 cups chicken broth, homemade (page 81), or store-bought

Salt and freshly ground black pepper to taste

4 ounces Havarti with dill, shredded (1 cup)

4 sprigs fresh dill

HEAT THE olive oil in a large heavy soup pot over medium heat. Add the garlic and sauté for 2 minutes, or until fragrant and nutty brown. Add the scallions and sauté for about 1 minute. Add all the tomatoes, including their juice, and cook, stirring, until the tomatoes are tender, about 15 to 20 minutes.

ADD THE wine and cook for 5 minutes. Add the chicken broth and cook, stirring occasionally, for 10 minutes. The soup can be served as it is, chunky, or pureed in a blender or passed through a food mill for a smoother texture.

TO SERVE, pour into heated large shallow soup bowls. Sprinkle the cheese over the soup, garnish each bowl with a dill sprig, and serve hot.

Fennel-Asiago Bisque

One winter during the years that I lived in Italy, I was invited to join friends in the Dolomites for a week of skiing. We stayed in a tiny mountain village near Asiago. One snowy day, we decided to forgo skiing and instead drove to Asiago. When we arrived, we headed straight to a small cheese factory. I can still picture the low cement-block building with steam billowing out the windows where the cheese was being made.

This soup is wonderfully thick and quite rich and creamy. The bacon makes it even heartier. It's perfect for a cold winter's meal.

MAKES 4 CUPS
SERVES 4

2 leeks

2 fennel bulbs

2 tablespoons unsalted butter

¼ cup dry white wine

2 cups chicken broth, homemade (page 81), or store-bought

¾ cup heavy cream

2 thick strips bacon, cooked until crisp

1 ounce Asiago, grated (¼ cup)

CUT THE green tops and roots off the leeks and discard. Wash the leeks well, as they tend to have sand between the layers. Chop the leeks into ½-inch pieces. (You should have about 1½ cups.)

REMOVE THE feathery tops and the stalks from the fennel bulbs, reserving 4 sprigs for garnish. Chop the fennel into ½-inch pieces. (You should have about 6 cups.)

MELT THE butter in a large heavy soup pot over medium heat. Add the leeks and fennel and sauté for 5 minutes, or until they just begin to color. Add the white wine and cook until the wine is reduced by half, about 5 minutes. Add the chicken broth and simmer until the vegetables are tender and the broth is reduced by half, about 20 minutes. Remove the soup from the heat and let cool slightly.

POUR THE soup into the container of a blender and puree—depending on the size of the blender container, you may have to do this in batches. Pour the soup into a clean pan and place over low heat. Add the cream and simmer gently for 10 minutes, stirring to prevent sticking. In the meantime, cook the bacon in a small skillet over medium heat until crisp. Drain on paper towels and coarsely chop. Remove the soup from the heat and stir in the cheese.

TO SERVE, divide the soup among four heated shallow soup bowls. Garnish with the bacon and the reserved fennel tops. Serve hot.

Onion Soup with Baked Stilton Crust

For me, onion soup will forever elicit memories of Paris and the old cafés and bistros in the area around Les Halles. For many years, Les Halles was a wholesale market district in the heart of Paris. (It was eventually torn down and the Pompidou Center built on that site.) You could go there at any hour of the night and see men carrying whole sides of beef down the street or farmers arriving laden with their crops—it was where Paris never slept. We used to go there very late at night, sit in a bustling café, and order the onion soup that was always served steaming with hot molten cheese on top and dribbling down the sides. Decadent and rich, this soup can cure a multitude of ills.

I make my onion soup primarily with Stilton, an English blue-veined cheese, which is both richer and hardier than Gruyère.

MAKES ABOUT 6 CUPS
SERVES 4

2 tablespoons unsalted butter

3 large yellow onions, halved lengthwise and thinly sliced crosswise

¼ cup dry Marsala wine or sherry

5 cups chicken broth, homemade (page 81), or store-bought

1 bay leaf

8 whole black peppercorns

1 whole clove

Salt and freshly ground black pepper to taste

1 baguette, cut into ¼-inch-thick slices

8 ounces Stilton, crumbled (1½ cups)

1 ounce Gruyère, shredded (¼ cup)

A small square of cheesecloth and a piece of kitchen string

MELT THE butter in a large heavy saucepan over low heat. Add the onions and sauté slowly until they turn brown and caramelize. This may take up to 40 minutes.

ADD THE marsala and stir to loosen all the browned bits of onion. Add the chicken broth and bring to a boil. In the meantime, make a sachet by wrapping the bay leaf, peppercorns, and clove in the cheesecloth and tie with kitchen string.

ADD THE sachet to the soup, reduce the heat to low, and simmer for 20 minutes. Remove and discard the sachet.

IN THE meantime, toast the bread. Combine the Stilton and Gruyerè in a small bowl and mash together with a fork. Spread generously on the toasts. Reserve any remaining cheese.

PREHEAT THE broiler to high. Adjust the rack so that the top of the soup bowls will be about 3 inches from the heat source.

DIVIDE THE soup among four ovenproof soup bowls or crocks. Place the bread on top of the soup, completely covering it. Sprinkle any remaining cheese over the top. Place the bowls on a baking sheet, place under the broiler, and broil for 3 minutes, or until the cheese is bubbly and beginning to brown. Remove and serve at once.

How can anyone govern a nation [France] that has 246 different kinds of cheese?

–Charles de Gaulle

Cheddar Cheese–Beer Soup with Black Pepper Croutons

This reminds me of the kind of hearty food that is served in Wisconsin up along Lake Michigan on cold winter nights. When I was at Kemper Hall, a boarding school in Kenosha, one winter was so cold that the lake was frozen solid one mile out from the shore. So I know that warm foods like this are a necessity.

This is a great soup to take along on a camping or hunting trip, in a Thermos bottle, then served in mugs or just passed around the campfire for a swig.

MAKES ABOUT 1½ CUPS CROUTONS
MAKES ABOUT 6 CUPS SOUP
SERVES 4 TO 6

BLACK PEPPER CROUTONS
2 tablespoons olive oil
4 slices stale white bread, cut into ½-inch cubes
2 cloves garlic, minced
1 teaspoon coarsely ground black pepper

CHEDDAR CHEESE-BEER SOUP
3 tablespoons olive oil
1 medium onion, chopped (1¼ cups)
1 clove garlic, minced
1 pound red-skinned potatoes, peeled and coarsely chopped (2 cups)

1 cup beer
4 cups chicken broth, homemade (page 81) or store-bought
¼ teaspoon dry mustard
½ teaspoon Worcestershire sauce
Several dashes Tabasco sauce
6 ounces sharp Cheddar, shredded (1½ cups)
Salt and freshly ground black pepper to taste
2 tablespoons chopped fresh chives, for garnish

FOR THE Black Pepper Croutons, heat the oil in a large skillet over medium heat. Add the bread and sauté, tossing and stirring until lightly browned on all sides, 2 to 3 minutes. Sprinkle the garlic and pepper over the bread and continue to sauté, tossing and stirring, for 2 to 3 minutes, or until the bread cubes are golden brown. Remove from the heat and place on a rack to cool. (The croutons can be stored in an airtight container for up to 2 weeks.)

FOR THE Cheddar Cheese–Beer Soup, heat the olive oil in a large heavy saucepan or stockpot over medium heat. Add the onion and garlic and sauté for 5 minutes, or until translucent but not browned. Add the potatoes and sauté for 10 minutes, or until they lose their raw look. Add the beer and cook for 15 minutes. Add the chicken broth, bring to a simmer, and simmer, stirring occasionally, for 15 minutes, or until the potatoes are tender. Remove from the heat and set aside to cool slightly.

PUREE THE SOUP in a blender in two batches, if necessary, return the soup to a clean saucepan and place over low heat. Combine the dry mustard, Worcestershire, and Tabasco in a small bowl and mix until smooth. Stir into the soup and increase the heat to medium. Add the cheese one handful at a time, stirring after each addition until the cheese is melted. Season with salt and pepper.

TO SERVE, pour into large heated soup bowls. Garnish with the chopped chives and the black pepper croutons.

Beware of young women who love neither wine nor truffles nor cheese nor music.

–Colette

Tuscan White Bean and Escarole Soup with Parmigiano

The most famous beans in Tuscany are *cannellini,* large, white kidney-shaped beans. The traditional method of cooking the beans is in a Chianti wine flask. It is filled with beans, extra virgin olive oil, sage, pepper, and very little water (salt is not added until the cooking is finished, as it is said to toughen the skins of the beans). To cook the beans, the flask is placed directly on smoldering embers and left to simmer.

There are wonderful rustic little trattorias located in the hills throughout Tuscany that serve soups such as this. Fall and winter are my favorite time of year to go to these wonderful spots, because there are fewer people around, the leaves crackle underfoot when you walk across them, and there's always a welcoming and blazing fire to greet us.

This is a very thick, dense, flavorful soup. It's perfect for a cold, wintry meal.

MAKES ABOUT 8 CUPS
SERVES 6 TO 8

1 tablespoon extra virgin olive oil

2 ounces pancetta or prosciutto, sliced (½ cup)

1 cup finely chopped onions

⅓ cup finely chopped carrot

⅔ cup finely chopped celery

2 cloves garlic, minced

¼ teaspoon dried thyme

¼ teaspoon dried sage

¼ teaspoon dried rosemary

1 bay leaf

A small square of cheesecloth and a piece of kitchen string

3 cups chicken broth, homemade (page 81) or store-bought

3 cups water

1 cup dried white cannellini beans (Italian white kidney beans), picked over and rinsed

2 cups shredded escarole

Salt and freshly ground black pepper, to taste

¼ cup extra virgin olive oil, for garnish

1 ounce Parmigiano-Reggiano, grated (¼ cup), for garnish

HEAT THE olive oil in a large heavy saucepan or stockpot over medium heat. Add the pancetta and sauté for several minutes, or until the fat begins to render. Add the onions, carrot, celery, and garlic and sauté until soft. Meanwhile, place the thyme, sage, rosemary, and bay leaf on the cheesecloth square and tie with kitchen string to form a sachet.

ADD THE chicken broth, water, beans, and herb sachet to the soup. Bring the soup to a boil, reduce the heat, and cook slowly, with a lid slightly ajar, for 2 to 3 hours, or until the beans are tender. Stir the soup occasionally to keep it from sticking, and add additional water if the soup becomes too dry. (Beans vary in their dryness, so it is necessary to check them at regular intervals.)

ABOUT 10 minutes before the soup is done, stir in the escarole and simmer until it is tender, about 10 minutes. Add additional water, if the soup seems too thick. Season with salt and pepper.

TO SERVE, ladle the hot soup into large shallow bowls. Drizzle each with 2 teaspoons of the olive oil and sprinkle the Parmigiano over the top.

> This round world is a cheese to be eaten through and Jules had nibbled quite into his cheese world already at twenty-two.
>
> **–George W. Cable**

Black Bean Soup with Goat Cheese Dollops

Black beans always remind me of Guatemala. When we visited there, we had black beans at each and every meal. Guatemala is alive with brightly colored textiles and native primitive arts and crafts. Antigua, which once was the capital of the Spanish New World, is located on an earthquake fault, so the town is like a museum of romantic ruins. I particularly liked the markets where Indians spread out their colorful pieces of cloth piled high with little mountains of their homegrown black beans.

This is a hearty, peasant-style soup flavored with ancho chiles and bacon, and garnished with fried tortilla chips and goat cheese.

MAKES ABOUT 8 CUPS
SERVES 6 TO 8

BLACK BEAN SOUP

5 dried ancho chiles

1 tablespoon olive oil

3 thick slices bacon, chopped (¾ cup)

½ small onion, finely chopped (¼ cup)

3 cups cooked black beans, drained, rinsed if canned, and pureed

3 cups chicken broth, homemade (page 81) or store-bought

Salt and freshly ground black pepper to taste

GARNISH

¼ cup vegetable oil

4 corn tortillas, cut into ¼-inch strips

4 ounces (½ cup) fresh goat cheese

¼ cup (2 ounces) Crème Fraîche, homemade (page 68) or store-bought, or sour cream

FOR THE Black Bean Soup, rinse and dry the chiles. Slit lengthwise and remove and discard the seeds and stems. Place the chiles in a dry 12-inch skillet and toast them over medium heat, flattening them with the back of a spatula and turning them several times, until aromatic and slightly darkened. Watch carefully, as they can burn quickly. Remove the chiles from the pan, place in a small bowl, and pour in just enough hot water to barely cover them. Tightly cover the bowl with plastic wrap and set aside to rehydrate for 30 minutes.

WITH A slotted spoon, transfer the chiles to the container of a blender. Add ¼ cup of the soaking liquid and puree. (You should have about 1 cup puree.) Set aside.

HEAT THE olive oil in a large heavy saucepan over medium heat. Add the bacon and sauté until it renders its fat, about 5 minutes. Add the onion and sauté until soft and translucent, about 3 to 5 minutes. Add the chile puree and cook, stirring constantly, for 5 minutes. Add the beans and cook for 5 minutes, or until the mixture has thickened. Gradually stir in the chicken broth, bring the soup to a boil, and reduce the heat to low. Simmer, stirring occasionally to prevent sticking, for 20 to 30 minutes to blend the flavors. Season with salt and pepper.

MEANWHILE, PREPARE the Garnish: Heat the vegetable oil in a small skillet over medium-high heat until hot but not smoking (about 350°F.). Fry the tortilla strips, in small batches, until crisp and slightly browned, about 2 minutes. Do not crowd the pan. Transfer the strips to paper towels to drain.

MIX THE goat cheese and crème fraîche together in a small bowl until smooth.

TO SERVE, pour the soup into large heated soup bowls. Garnish each with a large spoonful of the cheese and a sprinkling of tortilla strips.

Cheese is the soul of the soil.

–Pierre Androuët

Pasta and Grains

Fettuccine ai Quattro Formaggi

Like me, Italians are crazy about cheese. They prepare pizzas and *pasta ai quattro formaggi*, which means with four cheeses. No doubt, there's probably a recipe for *insalata ai quattro formaggi* too!

There is no set standard for this dish—almost any four cheeses will do. I have chosen mascarpone as one, because it is creamy and melts so beautifully, and I chose the other three cheeses for their taste and great melting qualities. You could substitute your favorite cheeses or any combination of cheeses you find in the recesses of your refrigerator. **SERVES 4**

9 ounces fresh fettuccine

Salt

1 tablespoon unsalted butter

1 tablespoon minced shallot

8 ounces (1 cup) mascarpone, home-made (page 73) or store-bought

½ cup half-and-half

1 ounce Asiago, grated (¼ cup)

1 ounce Manchego, shredded (¼ cup)

1 ounce Gruyère, shredded (¼ cup)

Freshly ground black pepper to taste

¼ cup minced fresh flat-leaf parsley

BRING A large pot of water to a boil and add 1 teaspoon salt. Drop in the pasta and cook until al dente, about 5 minutes.

WHILE THE pasta is cooking, melt the butter in a large skillet over medium heat. Add the shallot and sauté for 2 to 3 minutes, or until golden brown. Remove the pan from the heat and stir in the mascarpone and half-and-half. Set aside.

RESERVE ABOUT ½ cup of the pasta cooking water and drain the pasta.

RETURN THE mascarpone mixture to the stove over low heat. Add the pasta to the skillet and stir gently to mix the pasta with the melted mascarpone and shallots. Sprinkle the grated Asiago, Manchego, and Gruyère over the pasta and toss to distribute the cheeses, using tongs or two large forks. Season with salt. Add some of the reserved pasta water if necessary, to moisten the pasta. Mix well to distribute the cheeses evenly and remove from the heat.

TO SERVE, place on heated plates, sprinkle copious amounts of pepper over the pasta, and finish each serving with a sprinkling of minced parsley. Serve immediately.

Red Bell Pepper Ravioli with Goat Cheese Sauce

This recipe reminds me of my friends Chena and Phil Civello, who own and operate a tiny ravioli factory in Dallas called Raviolisimo. Their ravioli are all handmade, and they sell them by the dozen. When you enter their shop, you stand at the counter while they count out their ravioli one by one.

The smooth, creamy goat cheese sauce is perfect for these fresh ravioli.

MAKES ABOUT 28 RAVIOLI
MAKES ABOUT 2 ½ CUPS SAUCE
SERVES 4 TO 6

FILLING

1 tablespoon extra virgin olive oil

¼ teaspoon minced garlic

3 red bell peppers, cored, seeded, and finely chopped (about 2 cups)

2 ounces (¼ cup) mascarpone, home-made (page 73) or store-bought

2 tablespoons ground pine nuts

1 large egg yolk

1 teaspoon minced fresh basil

GOAT CHEESE SAUCE

2 cups (1 pound) crème fraîche, homemade (page 68) or store-bought, or sour cream

4 ounces (½ cup) fresh goat cheese, crumbled

8 large fresh basil leaves, cut into very thin strips

Salt and freshly ground black pepper to taste

¾ pound Homemade Pasta Dough (page 83), store-bought fresh pasta sheets, or egg-roll wrappers

1 teaspoon salt

8 to 12 leaves fresh basil, for garnish

FOR THE Filling, heat the olive oil in a large skillet over medium heat. Add the garlic and bell peppers and sauté for 5 minutes, or until the peppers are soft and all the moisture has evaporated. Remove from the heat.

REMOVE AND reserve about one-fourth of the peppers for garnish. Combine the mascarpone, pine nuts, egg yolk, minced basil, and the remaining bell peppers in a small bowl and mix well.

FOR THE ravioli, roll out the pasta dough into long thin sheets using a pasta machine and cut into 12-inch-long strips. Or roll it out to thin sheets on a lightly floured surface, using a rolling pin, and cut into strips about 4 inches wide and 12 inches long. Alternatively, if using fresh pasta sheets, cut them into 4 x 12-inch strips.

PLACE A sheet of pasta over a ravioli form, if you have one. Spoon 1 tablespoon of the filling into each space. Moisten the pasta around the filling with water. Place another sheet of pasta on top and roll over the ravioli form with a rolling pin to press together the sheets of dough and cut the ravioli. Transfer the ravioli to a clean dry cloth dusted with flour and set aside. Repeat to make more ravioli.

IF YOU do not have a mold, then lay a pasta sheet on a lightly floured work surface and spoon equally spaced mounds of filling on top of it, about 2 inches apart; the finished ravioli should be about 2 inches square. Moisten the pasta around the mounds of filling with water and place another sheet of pasta on top. Gently press the dough together around the filling. Cut the ravioli with a sharp knife, a pastry wheel, or a fluted ravioli cutter. Place the ravioli on a clean dry cloth dusted with flour and set aside. Repeat with the remaining dough and filling.

IF USING egg-roll wrappers, proceed in a similar fashion.

FOR THE Goat Cheese Sauce, place the crème fraîche in a large skillet and heat over medium-low heat until warm; do not let it boil. Remove from the heat and stir in the goat cheese and basil. Season with salt and pepper. Set aside.

BRING A large pot of water to a boil over high heat. Add the salt. Gently place the ravioli into the water, reduce the heat to medium-low, and cook for 3 to 4 minutes, or until they float to the top and the pasta is cooked al dente. With a strainer, transfer the ravioli to a colander to drain.

RETURN THE goat cheese sauce to the stove and heat over low heat. Add the ravioli to the sauce and stir gently to coat with sauce.

TO SERVE, divide the ravioli among heated serving plates. Sprinkle with the reserved bell peppers. Garnish with the fresh basil leaves.

Pasta Primavera with Mascarpone

I'll always remember my first experience with mascarpone. I was in a small grocery store in Perugia and saw a bowl full of a white fluffy substance in the deli case. Shoppers would ask for some, and the deli man would spoon out an amount onto a piece of waxed paper, which he would then fold into a package for the customers to carry away. I couldn't imagine just what it might be— was it whipped cream, was it yogurt, or was it cream cheese? I asked a friend what it was and was told it was *mascarpone*—whatever that meant. Mascarpone, it turned out, is wonderful with pasta because it is so rich and melts so beautifully that it becomes an instant cream sauce.

Primavera means springtime in Italian, and I have chosen the quintessential springtime vegetables for this pasta dish.

SERVES 4

Salt

4 tablespoons (½ stick) unsalted butter

4 ounces snow peas, strings removed and cut on the diagonal into 1-inch pieces (1 cup)

4 ounces asparagus, tough ends removed and cut on the diagonal into ¾-inch pieces (1 cup)

1 carrot, cut into long thin strips with a vegetable peeler (⅔ cup)

¼ red bell pepper, cut into very thin julienne strips (⅔ cup)

2 scallions, trimmed and thinly sliced crosswise on the diagonal (⅔ cup)

10 large spinach leaves, stems removed

8 ounces (1 cup) mascarpone, homemade (page 73) or store-bought

9 ounces fresh pasta, such as fettuccine or tagliatelle

3 ounces Parmigiano-Reggiano, grated (¾ cup)

Freshly ground black pepper to taste

PLACE A large pot of water over high heat, bring to a boil, and add 2 teaspoons of salt.

MEANWHILE, MELT the butter in a large skillet over medium heat. Add the snow peas and sauté for a few minutes. Add the asparagus and sauté for 4 minutes. Add the carrot shreds, bell pepper, and scallions and sauté for 2 minutes. Add the spinach and immediately remove from the heat. Add the mascarpone and stir gently to distribute it. Set aside.

DROP THE pasta into the rapidly boiling water. Cook until al dente, about 5 minutes. Reserve 1 cup of the pasta water and drain the pasta in a colander. Shake briefly, then add to the skillet with the vegetables and mascarpone and place over low heat. Toss well with tongs or two forks to distribute the vegetables evenly. Sprinkle with the Parmigiano and salt and pepper to taste and lightly toss again. Add some of the reserved pasta water if necessary to moisten the pasta.

TO SERVE, divide the pasta among four heated plates or place on a heated serving platter, arranging it so the vegetables are showing on top of the pasta.

Cheese it is a peevish elf,
It digests all things but itself.
–John Ray

Paula's Lasagne al Forno

This recipe was inspired by the lasagne that Suzanne Bartolucci, one of my partners at the Mozzarella Company, prepared for our opening party in 1982. It was a great celebration because I had accomplished my dream of making fresh mozzarella in Dallas. We invited all our friends to come, and everything we served was made with our very own fresh mozzarella.

This lasagne is made very simply with fresh mozzarella and fresh ricotta flavored with spinach and basil pesto, layered between fresh pasta sheets. The sauce is my simple tomato sauce that can be made from either fresh or canned tomatoes, flavored with basil.

For years we have been making this same lasagne recipe at the Mozzarella Company. We sell it frozen. At first we made it to use up our excess cheese; now we have to make extra cheese just for the lasagne.

SERVES 6 TO 8

1 pound Homemade Pasta Dough (page 83), store-bought fresh pasta sheets, or 1 pound dried lasagne noodles

1 tablespoon salt

1 tablespoon extra virgin olive oil

FILLING

1 (10-ounce) package frozen spinach, thawed

1 pound ricotta, homemade (page 70) or store-bought, well drained (2 cups)

2 tablespoons Basil Pesto (page 80)

Salt and freshly ground black pepper to taste

2½ cups Paula's Tomato Sauce (page 84), or store-bought

1 pound fresh mozzarella, cut into thin slices

1 ounce Parmigiano-Reggiano, grated (¼ cup)

FOR THE Pasta, if using fresh pasta, use a pasta machine to roll it out to the next-to-thinnest setting. Cut the fresh pasta (homemade or store-bought) into 4 x 6 pieces or to fit the size of the pan you are using.

BRING A large pot of water to a boil over high heat. Add the salt. Cook the pasta in the rapidly boiling salted water, about 2 minutes for fresh, or 7 minutes for dried lasagne noodles, or until very al dente. Remove the pasta with a strainer and drain in a colander.

FILL A large bowl with cold water and pour in the olive oil. Immediately transfer the pasta to the bowl to cool. Once cooled, remove the pasta from the water and lay it out flat in one layer on towels to drain. (If you must stack the cooked pasta, place sheets of plastic wrap between the layers of pasta.)

FOR THE Filling, squeeze all the excess moisture from the spinach and coarsely chop it. In a bowl, mix the spinach with the ricotta and pesto. Season with salt and pepper.

PREHEAT THE oven to 375°F. Grease an 11 x 7 x 2-inch baking dish with olive oil.

SPREAD SEVERAL spoonfuls of tomato sauce over the bottom of the pan. Place a single layer of the pasta over the sauce. Crumble some of the ricotta mixture over the pasta and top with a layer of mozzarella slices. Spoon more tomato sauce over the cheese. Continue making layers in this fashion until all of the ingredients are used. The final layer should be pasta topped with tomato sauce. Sprinkle the top with the Parmigiano.

PLACE THE pan in the oven and bake for 30 to 45 minutes, or until bubbling and golden brown on top. Remove from the oven and let stand for 10 minutes before cutting.

Blessed are the cheesemakers for they are pure of heart.

—**Monty Python**, *Life of Brian*

Ricotta and Swiss Chard Cannelloni with Tomato Cream Sauce

In Italy, cannelloni is served as a first course, never as an entrée. Italians always eat a pasta or soup course before their main course. A salad normally follows the main course, then cheese, and finally fruit. Italians love to linger over a long lunch or dinner, leisurely relaxing and visiting, so it is nice to begin with a light dish like this cannelloni.

MAKES ABOUT 2 CUPS SAUCE
MAKES 15 TO 20 CANNELLONI
SERVES 4 TO 6

TOMATO CREAM SAUCE

1 tablespoon unsalted butter

¼ cup minced shallots

1 (16-ounce) can whole peeled tomatoes, drained and coarsely chopped

1 sprig fresh rosemary

½ cup heavy cream

Salt and freshly ground black pepper to taste

CANNELLONI FILLING

6 large leaves Swiss chard (1 bunch), washed

Salt

1 pound ricotta, homemade (page 70) or store-bought, well drained (2 cups)

2 large eggs

3 ounces Parmigiano-Reggiano, grated (¾ cup)

¼ teaspoon ground nutmeg

Freshly ground black pepper to taste

1 pound Homemade Pasta Dough (page 83) or store-bought fresh pasta sheets

Fresh rosemary sprigs, for garnish

FOR THE Tomato Cream Sauce, melt the butter in a medium saucepan or skillet over medium heat. Add the shallots and sauté until translucent, about 5 minutes. Add the tomatoes and cook over low heat for 20 minutes, or until the tomatoes are soft and the sauce has thickened. Add the rosemary and cook for 10 minutes, or until the sauce is thick. Pass the sauce through a food mill fitted with the medium disk, or remove the rosemary and puree the sauce in the work bowl of a food processor fitted with a steel blade or a blender. Return the sauce to the pan, add the cream, and simmer for a few minutes to thicken. Add the salt and pepper. Remove from the heat and set aside.

FOR THE Cannelloni Filling, cut the tender leafy part of the chard from the tough stalks and discard the stalks. Place the still-damp chard leaves in a dry saucepan over medium-low heat, sprinkle with ½ teaspoon salt, cover, and steam until wilted, about 3 to 5 minutes. Drain the chard in a colander and let cool, then press away the excess liquid with the back of a spoon. Finely chop. (You should have a little less than 1 cup chopped chard.)

MIX THE ricotta, eggs, and ½ cup of the Parmigiano in a medium bowl. Stir in the chard, nutmeg, and salt and pepper to taste.

PREHEAT THE oven to 400°F. Butter a 13 x 9-inch glass baking dish.

USING A pasta machine or a rolling pin on a lightly floured surface, roll the pasta (or pasta sheets) as thin as you can, so that it is almost transparent. Cut into rectangles that measure 4 x 3 inches. Lay 1 piece of pasta on a work surface with a long side facing you. Mound 3 tablespoons of filling along the lower edge, spreading it evenly to the edges, and roll up to form a tube. Place the cannelloni, seam side down, in the baking dish. Repeat until all the pasta and filling are used, making two rows in the baking dish.

POUR THE sauce over the cannelloni and sprinkle with the remaining ¼ cup Parmigiano. Place in the oven and bake for 20 to 25 minutes, or until heated through and bubbling around the edges.

TO SERVE, place 3 to 4 cannelloni on each serving plate and garnish with a rosemary sprig. Serve immediately.

VARIATION

Ricotta and Swiss Chard Cappelli

Roll out the pasta and cut it into 3-inch squares. Place 1 tablespoon of the filling near one corner of a square. Moisten the edges with water or an egg wash. Fold the pasta over the filling to form a triangle and press the edges of pasta together to seal them. Bring the two opposite points together, overlapping them slightly, moisten, and press together to form a *cappello* (pope's hat). Place on a dry towel sprinkled with flour or semolina. Repeat until all the pasta and filling are used. Set the pasta aside to dry (refrigerate if holding for longer than 30 minutes).

Cook the pasta in gently boiling salted water for 3 to 4 minutes until the capelli float to the top and are cooked al dente. Remove with a slotted spoon, shake away excess water, and place in the skillet containing the Tomato Cream Sauce. Heat, turning gently to coat the cappelli with sauce, and serve.

To serve, divide the cappelli among heated serving plates and garnish each with a sprig of rosemary. Pass the remaining Parmigiano to sprinkle on top of the cappelli.

Lisa's Seafood Penne with Mozzarella

My friend Lisa Smith, who is a very creative cook, developed this unusual pasta dish. There's a special sweetness that comes from roasting the tomato sauce in the oven. The saffron and shellfish make it somewhat reminiscent of bouillabaisse.

SERVES 6

ROASTED TOMATO SAUCE

¼ cup extra virgin olive oil

1 medium yellow onion, chopped (1½ cups)

4 cloves garlic, minced

½ fennel bulb, green tops and stalks removed, chopped (1½ cups)

½ cup dry red wine

2 (28-ounce) cans Italian plum tomatoes, coarsely chopped, with their juice

¼ teaspoon saffron threads

Salt and freshly ground black pepper to taste

4 sprigs fresh oregano

18 clams

1 pound mussels

12 jumbo shrimp or prawns, peeled and deveined

9 sea scallops, cut in half

2 teaspoons salt

1 pound dried penne pasta

8 ounces fresh mozzarella, cut into ½-inch cubes

1 tablespoon chopped fresh oregano

Freshly ground black pepper to taste

Sprigs of fresh oregano, for garnish

FOR THE Roasted Tomato Sauce, preheat the oven to 300°F.

HEAT THE olive oil a large skillet over medium heat. Add the onion, garlic, and fennel and sauté for about 7 minutes, stirring occasionally, until soft. Add the red wine and cook for a few minutes to reduce slightly. Add the canned tomatoes, along with their juice, and the saffron and stir well. Season with salt and pepper and cook over low heat for 3 to 5 minutes. Add the oregano sprigs and stir. Pour into a large shallow roasting pan at least 13 x 9 inches.

PLACE THE sauce in the oven and roast for 30 to 45 minutes until the sauce reduces slightly but is not dry.

IN THE meantime, scrub the clams and mussels. Check to make sure their shells are closed, and discard any open or broken clams or mussels. Debeard the mussels. Remove the sauce from the oven and stir it. Add the clams and mussels. Raise the oven temperature to 350°F., return the sauce to the oven, and roast for 10 minutes. Remove the pan from the oven again and add the shrimp and scallops, distributing them evenly. Return to the oven and roast for 10 minutes. Remove from the oven.

IN THE meantime, bring a large pot of water to a boil over high heat. Add 2 teaspoons salt and drop in the pasta. Cook for about 8 to 10 minutes, until slightly less than al dente. Drain in a colander; set aside.

REMOVE THE seafood from the sauce and place it on one side of a large deep heated serving platter. Cover loosely with aluminum foil and set aside in a warm place.

POUR THE pasta into the roasting pan and toss well to coat with the sauce. Add the mozzarella, oregano, and pepper and toss again. Place in the oven and roast for 5 minutes. Remove and transfer the pasta to the other side of the serving platter.

TO SERVE, garnish the platter with sprigs of fresh oregano. Serve immediately.

My studies in speculative philosophy, metaphysics, and science are all summed up in the image of a mouse called man running in and out of every hole in the Cosmos hunting for the Absolute Cheese.

–Benjamin DeCasseres

Cheddar Cheese Grits with Roasted Garlic

Cheddar cheese grits always make me think of fall and football parties. When I was growing up in Texas, they would invariably be served on sunny, crisp days before Saturday afternoon football games.

This dish is a fabulous accompaniment to barbecued or charcoal-grilled game and other meats. It is rich, creamy, cheesy, and garlicky. Today as then, whenever I serve myself cheese grits, I try to get some of the crust or sides that have browned against the baking dish. They are the best part of all.

You can also serve these grits topped with grilled asparagus if you like.

SERVES 6 TO 8

6 large cloves garlic, unpeeled

1 tablespoon extra virgin olive oil

5 cups cold water

1½ teaspoons salt

2 cups regular grits

3 shakes Tabasco

4 tablespoons (½ stick) unsalted butter

8 ounces sharp Cheddar, shredded (2 cups)

2 large eggs, lightly beaten

Freshly ground black pepper to taste

PREHEAT THE oven to 350°F.

PLACE THE garlic cloves and olive oil in a small ramekin or ovenproof dish. Roast the garlic 15 to 20 minutes, or until golden brown. Remove and set aside to cool. Raise the oven temperature to 400°F.

POUR THE water into a large deep, heavy saucepan and add the salt. Slowly stir the grits into the cold water and place over medium heat. Cook, stirring to prevent lumps from forming and sticking to the pan, for 10 minutes, or until thick and smooth. Add more water if necessary. The grits should be thick yet somewhat soupy. Remove from the heat.

IN THE meantime, remove the garlic from the ramekin, reserving the oil. Pierce the garlic skins with a sharp knife and squeeze the garlic out of the skins. With the side of a knife, crush the garlic into a paste on a cutting board.

ADD THE garlic to the grits, then add the Tabasco and butter and stir until it is melted. Stir in the Cheddar, reserving one handful of the cheese. Stir in the eggs. Season with pepper.

GREASE A 7 x 3-inch round baking dish or a 2-quart dish of similar size with the reserved garlic oil. Pour the grits into the baking dish and smooth the top with a rubber spatula. Sprinkle the reserved Cheddar over the top.

BAKE FOR 30 to 40 minutes, or until puffed and golden brown on top. Remove from the oven and let cool slightly before serving.

S'il que mange du fromage,
S'il ne le fait, il enrage.

(Cheese eaters who do not eat cheese will go mad.)

–French proverb

Polenta with Mascarpone and Porcini Mushrooms

I adore polenta. I like to serve it loose and soupy in a puddle on a plate topped with a mascarpone. The heat from the polenta melts the mascarpone so that it resembles melted butter. Here it is coupled with the intense, foresty flavors of porcini mushrooms, and I'm sure you'll adore this dish as well.

MAKES 1 ½ CUPS SAUCE
SERVES 4

MUSHROOM SAUCE

1 ounce dried porcini mushrooms

1 cup hot water

2 tablespoons unsalted butter

1 small onion, minced

1 clove garlic, minced

¼ cup dry red wine

2 tablespoons minced fresh flat-leaf parsley

Salt and freshly ground black pepper to taste

POLENTA

2 cups milk, plus additional if needed

2 cups water

1 teaspoon salt, or to taste

1 cup coarsely ground cornmeal

8 ounces (1 cup) mascarpone, home-made (page 73) or store-bought

1 ounce Parmigiano-Reggiano, grated (¼ cup)

4 sprigs fresh flat-leaf parsley

FOR THE Mushroom Sauce, rinse the mushrooms to remove any dust and dirt. Soak the mushrooms in the hot water for 30 minutes. Using a slotted spoon, lift out the mushrooms. Strain the soaking liquid through a very fine sieve or a strainer lined with several layers of cheesecloth and set aside. Slice the mushrooms into narrow strips and set aside.

MELT THE butter in a medium skillet over medium heat. Add the onion and garlic and sauté for 5 minutes, or until lightly browned. Add the mushrooms and the reserved soaking liquid and cook for several minutes. Add the red wine and simmer for several minutes longer, or until the sauce reduces and thickens. Remove from the heat, add the parsley, and season with salt and pepper. Set aside.

FOR THE Polenta, pour the milk and water into a large deep heavy pan and place over high heat. Bring to a boil and add the salt. Slowly add the cornmeal, releasing it in a steady stream from one hand while whisking constantly with the other hand. When all the cornmeal has been added, switch to a long-handled wooden spoon, reduce the heat, cook while stirring constantly, as the polenta thickens. Add additional milk as necessary to keep the polenta moist and soupy. If any lumps develop, break them up against the sides of the pan with the back of the spoon. Continue to cook, slowly stirring and adding milk, for about 30 minutes, or until the polenta is completely cooked. It should be fairly runny and soupy. Taste and adjust the seasoning.

TO SERVE, reheat the sauce. Spoon a portion of the cooked polenta onto each heated serving plate and top with one-fourth of the mascarpone. Spoon the sauce over and around the polenta, sprinkle with the Parmigiano, and garnish with the parsley sprigs. Serve immediately.

VARIATION

Polenta with Mascarpone and Ratatouille

Top the polenta with ratatouille instead of the mushroom sauce: Sauté a combination of chopped vegetables—1 bell pepper, ½ onion, 1 clove garlic, 1 eggplant, 2 tomatoes, and 1 zucchini—in olive oil for about 30 minutes, or until softened and well blended. Season with salt, freshly ground black pepper, and dried thyme. Serve warm spooned over the polenta.

Posole with Chiles, Chorizo, and Queso Fresco

Hominy is dried whole corn kernels that have been soaked in lime and then hulled. It has a distinctive taste. In the Southwestern part of the United States, it can be found in dried or frozen form. In other parts of the country, it is available canned, which is an acceptable substitute.

Posole is a Southwestern stew often prepared with shredded pork. It is also a wonderful side dish to serve with grilled meats. I always think of Mark Miller and his Coyote Café in Santa Fe when I prepare posole. His rendition is so hot with chiles that it makes beads of perspiration appear at the very memory!

SERVES 6

2 cups dried, 5 cups frozen, or 3 (15.5-ounce) cans whole hominy

1 poblano chile

1 jalapeño chile

1 small onion, unpeeled

1 clove garlic, unpeeled

1 dried ancho chile

1 dried árbol chile, if you want it hot (optional)

8 ounces chorizo sausage (optional)

1 teaspoon dried oregano

¼ cup packed fresh cilantro leaves, chopped, plus whole leaves, for garnish

Salt and freshly ground black pepper to taste

8 ounces queso fresco, crumbled (1½ cups)

6 radishes, thinly sliced, for garnish

2 limes, cut into wedges, for garnish

IF USING dried hominy, soak it overnight in water to cover. Drain, then boil in salted water for about 2 hours, or until tender. If using frozen hominy, boil in salted water for about 1 hour, or until tender. If using canned hominy, just rinse and drain.

PREHEAT THE broiler. Adjust the rack so that it is 3 inches from the heat source.

PLACE THE poblano, jalapeño, onion, and garlic on a baking pan and roast under the broiler, turning with tongs, until the skins are blackened. Remove from the heat, place in a small bowl, cover with plastic wrap, and let steam until cool. Remove and discard the blackened skins, stems, and seeds from the chiles and coarsely chop. Peel the garlic and onion and coarsely chop.

MEANWHILE, REMOVE the stems, seeds, and membranes from the dried chile(s) and discard. Toast the ancho and árbol chile, if using, in a dry skillet over low heat, shaking and turning the chile(s) until aromatic and slightly toasted. Be careful not to burn them.

Remove, place in a small bowl, cover with hot water, and cover the bowl with plastic wrap; let steep for 15 minutes to soften. Remove the chile(s) from the water, remove and discard any remaining seeds, and coarsely chop. The chile árbol is the hottest chile; use it accordingly: Half of the pepper will make the posole pretty hot, the whole pepper will make it very hot. (Be sure to wash your hands after handling any of the hot chiles and don't touch any tender parts of your body, because the capiscum oil from the chiles will remain on your hands.)

PREHEAT THE oven to 350°F. Grease a shallow 2-quart baking dish or 8-inch square baking dish with oil.

CUT THE chorizo, if using, into rounds. Heat a large skillet over medium-high heat, add the chorizo, and cook, turning with tongs, for 7 minutes, or until browned on both sides and completely cooked. Remove and drain on paper towels. Sprinkle the dried oregano over the chorizo.

PLACE THE hominy in a large bowl. Add all the chiles, the onion, and garlic and stir to mix well. Add the chorizo, if using, and stir to combine. Add the cilantro and mix well. Season with salt and pepper.

POUR THE posole into the baking dish. Sprinkle the cheese over the top. Place in the oven and bake for 30 minutes, or until the cheese is lightly browned.

TO SERVE, garnish with the radishes, cilantro leaves, and the lime wedges on the side.

Risotto with Asparagus and Parmigiano

I love northern Italy, especially the Veneto and the hill towns of Bassano and Asolo. The risottos that come from this region are always creamy and delicious. None can beat this plain and simple version, which is elegant and flavorful. It is similar to the one they serve at the Villa Cipriani, a hotel in Asolo and one of my favorite places.

SERVES 4

1 pound asparagus

4 tablespoons (½ stick) unsalted butter

½ small onion, minced (½ cup)

1 cup arborio rice

3 cups chicken broth homemade (page 81) or store-bought, heated

3 ounces Parmigiano-Reggiano, grated (¾ cup)

Salt and freshly ground black pepper to taste

BREAK OFF the tough ends of the asparagus and discard. Peel the stalks using a vegetable peeler. Cut the stalks into 1-inch pieces, and reserve the tips separately. Set the stalks aside.

MELT 2 tablespoons of the butter in a heavy 2-quart saucepan over medium heat. Add the onion and sauté for 5 minutes, or until tender but not browned. Add the rice and stir well to coat each grain of rice with butter. Sauté the rice for 3 to 4 minutes, stirring constantly, or until it begins to turn golden. Add ½ cup of the chicken broth and cook, stirring to keep the rice from sticking. Add another ½ cup broth when the liquid is almost completely absorbed. Add the asparagus stalks when the liquid is absorbed again, after about 10 minutes of cooking and stirring. Continue stirring and adding the broth ½ cup at a time for another 3 minutes. Add the asparagus tips, stir well, and cook for 2 to 3 minutes longer, adding more broth as necessary. (The total cooking time should be about 15 minutes, and the risotto should be somewhat runny and soupy at this point.) Check a rice grain to see if it is cooked, by biting it or by cutting it in two with a knife: It should be just al dente and there should be a small, thin white line inside the grain of rice.

WHEN THE rice is cooked, stir in the remaining 2 tablespoons butter and ½ cup of the Parmigiano. Season with salt and an abundant amount of pepper. Stir again and let the risotto rest for 1 minute, to absorb the excess liquid.

TO SERVE, spoon the risotto into heated shallow bowls. Sprinkle the remaining ¼ cup Parmigiano over the risotto or pass separately. Serve immediately.

Risotto with Oven-Roasted Cherry Tomatoes and Pecorino

Cut 2 cups cherry tomatoes in half and place them cut side up on a lightly oiled baking pan. Place them in a preheated 250°F. oven and bake for 2 hours. Substitute 1 cup of the tomatoes for the asparagus, adding the tomatoes in the last 5 minutes of cooking. Substitute grated Pecorino for the Parmigiano, and stir in 1 tablespoon minced fresh basil or fresh oregano with the cheese and final butter. Garnish with the remaining Pecorino.

And on a mountain, all of grated Parmesan cheese, dwell folk that do nought else but make macaroni and ravioli, and boil them in capon's broth.

–Boccaccio

Baked Gnocchi with Sage-Parmigiano Crust

I think that if I could visit just one place in all of Italy, I would choose Rome, the Eternal City. It has layers and layers of civilization, ranging from the Roman emperors to modern cinematography and *la dolce vita*. It is full of ruins, gardens, flowers, markets, antiquities, fountains, rococo churches and palaces, fabulous shopping, grand hotels, tiny shops, traffic, narrow streets . . . I love it all.

I particularly enjoy traditional Roman foods like these semolina gnocchi. Unlike the more commonly known potato gnocchi, which resemble dumplings, these are made of semolina polenta that is cooked, cooled, cut into rounds, and then baked.

SERVES 4 TO 6

3 cups milk	¼ teaspoon ground nutmeg
1 cup water	Freshly ground black pepper to taste
3 tablespoons unsalted butter	4 ounces Parmigiano-Reggiano, grated (1 cup)
Salt	
1 cup semolina (made from durum wheat)	4 sprigs fresh sage, plus 4 sprigs for garnish
3 large egg yolks	

BRING THE milk and water to a boil in a large deep heavy saucepan over medium heat. Add 1 tablespoon of the butter and 1 teaspoon salt. Slowly add the semolina, releasing it in a steady stream from one hand while whisking constantly with the other. Once all the semolina is added, switch to a long-handled wooden spoon, reduce the heat to low, and cook, stirring constantly, for 10 to 15 minutes, until the polenta is thick. Remove from the heat and let cool, stirring constantly, for about 3 minutes. Add the egg yolks one at a time, stirring well after each addition. Add the nutmeg, salt and pepper to taste, and ½ cup of the Parmigiano. Stir the mixture vigorously to combine well.

BUTTER A baking pan with low sides, like a jelly-roll pan, and spread the polenta in it to a depth of ½ to ⅓ inch. Use a rubber spatula dipped in water, or your fingertips dipped in water, to smooth the top. Refrigerate for at least 30 minutes, or until firm.

PREHEAT THE oven to 450°F. Generously butter an oval or rectangular ceramic or terracotta baking dish about 10 to 12 inches long.

CUT THE gnocchi out of the polenta with a biscuit or round cookie cutter about 2 inches in diameter; dip the cutter into cold water to keep it from sticking to the semolina. There will be odd-shaped pieces left after cutting out the rounds: Make a layer on the bottom of the baking dish using these pieces. Place the gnocchi on top in overlapping rows, making a single layer. Remove the leaves from 4 sprigs of sage and strew them over the top. Sprinkle with the remaining ½ cup Parmigiano and dot with the remaining 2 tablespoons butter.

PLACE IN the oven and bake for 15 to 20 minutes, or until golden brown on top. Serve directly from the baking dish, garnished with the remaining sage sprigs.

Never commit yourself to a cheese
without having first examined it.

–T. S. Eliot

Chilaquiles

This Mexican casserole can be served as a starch with grilled meats or Mexican stews. It's also delicious with eggs as a brunch dish. Zarela Martinez, the owner of Zarela's in New York City, serves a fantastic rendition of this dish, as does Stephan Pyles at Star Canyon in Dallas. They are my inspiration for this recipe.

Basically chilaquiles are just fried tortillas, cheese, and green sauce layered together and baked. No wonder everyone loves them!

MAKES 2 CUPS SALSA
MAKES ABOUT 1 1/2 CUPS ONIONS
SERVES 6

SALSA VERDE

10 small tomatillos, husks removed and rinsed

1 cup chicken broth, homemade (page 81) or store-bought

1 poblano chile

1 small onion, quartered

2 cloves garlic

1 cup loosely packed fresh cilantro leaves

1 tablespoon vegetable oil

Salt and freshly ground black pepper to taste

PICKLED ONIONS

1 large white onion, thinly sliced into rings

1/2 to 3/4 cup distilled white vinegar

1 dried ancho chile, stemmed, seeded, and cut into julienne strips

FRIED TORTILLAS

12 corn tortillas

1 cup vegetable oil

8 ounces mozzarella, sliced

8 ounces queso fresco, crumbled (1 1/2 cups)

6 tablespoons (3 ounces) Mexican crema or sour cream, for garnish

FOR THE Salsa Verde, place the tomatillos in a small saucepan. Cover with the chicken broth and bring to a boil. Reduce the heat and simmer for 10 minutes, or until the tomatillos just begin to soften. Remove from the heat and set aside to cool.

ROAST THE poblano pepper over an open flame or under the broiler, turning often, to blacken the skin on all sides. Wrap in plastic wrap, or place in a plastic bag and seal, and steam for 15 minutes. Remove and discard the blackened skin, seeds, and stem.

PLACE THE tomatillos and the broth, the poblano, onion, garlic, and cilantro in the container of a blender and blend for 2 to 3 minutes until the vegetables are finely chopped.

HEAT A large skillet over medium heat and add the oil. When the oil is hot, add the contents of the blender. Cook, stirring occasionally to prevent sticking, for 10 minutes. Season with salt and pepper. Remove from the heat and set aside.

FOR THE Pickled Onions, place the onion rings in a small bowl. Add just enough vinegar to barely cover them. Add the ancho chile and stir to mix. Cover with plastic wrap and set aside at room temperature to marinate for at least 30 minutes, stirring from time to time. The chile will dye the onions a rosy pink color as well as flavor them.

MEANWHILE, MAKE the Fried Tortillas: Tear or cut the tortillas into quarters. Heat the oil in a large skillet over medium-high heat until hot but not smoking, about 350°F. Fry the tortillas, in batches (be careful not to crowd the pan) for about 2 minutes, or until golden brown and crispy. Remove with a skimmer, slotted spoon, or tongs to paper towels to drain.

PREHEAT THE oven to 350°F. Lightly oil a terra-cotta or ceramic oval or rectangular baking dish about 10 to 12 inches long.

PLACE A layer of fried tortilla pieces in the bottom of the baking dish, cover with some of each of the two cheeses, and spoon some of the salsa over the cheese. Repeat the layers until all of the ingredients are used, finishing with salsa. Cover with aluminum foil.

PLACE IN the oven and bake for 30 to 40 minutes, until bubbly all over and golden brown on top.

SERVE THE chilaquiles direct from the baking dish, topping each serving with pickled onions and a dollop of sour cream.

Goat Cheese Spaetzle

Spaetzle is a tiny Austrian or German dumpling that is formed by rubbing the dough through a large mesh or sieve directly into boiling water. Once cooked and drained, it is usually sautéed in butter until slightly browned. It is luscious with grilled or roasted meats.

This version of spaetzle has a subtle hint of goat cheese, which gives it a deeper and richer flavor.

SERVES 4 TO 6

2 large eggs, lightly beaten	⅛ teaspoon ground nutmeg
4 ounces (½ cup) fresh goat cheese	4 tablespoons (½ stick) unsalted butter
½ cup milk	½ cup minced fresh flat-leaf parsley
2 cups unbleached all-purpose flour	Freshly ground black pepper to taste
Salt	

PLACE THE eggs, goat cheese, and milk in the bowl of an electric mixer and beat on medium speed until well combined. Turn off the mixer and add the flour, ½ teaspoon salt, and the nutmeg. Turn the mixer on and beat at medium speed until well mixed. The dough will be very gooey and will climb up the beaters; however, it will fall back into the bowl when you turn off the mixer. Cover the bowl and set aside at room temperature to rest for 1 hour. (The dough can be refrigerated for up to 8 hours. Be sure to let it come to room temperature before making the spaetzle.)

LINE A baking pan with paper towels. The dough will have to be forced through small holes about ¼ inch wide to form the spaetzle: I suggest using a colander, a potato ricer fitted with the larger disk, or large perforated spoon. Fill a large stockpot with 4 quarts water. Place over high heat and bring to a rapid boil; add 1 tablespoon salt.

FORCE ABOUT one-third of the dough through the selected colander, perforated spoon, or potato ricer, using the back of a wooden spoon if necessary, into the boiling water. The little squiggles of dough should be about ½ to 1 inch long. They will sink to the bottom of the water but will rise when they are cooked through, in about 5 minutes. Remove the cooked spaetzle with a skimmer or slotted spoon to a clean colander to drain. Rinse briefly with cold water, shake to drain, and spread the spaetzle out in the baking pan. Cook the remainder of the dough.

ABOUT 10 minutes before serving, melt the butter in a large nonstick pan over medium-high heat. Add the spaetzle and cook, stirring and shaking the pan, until the spaetzle are heated and lightly browned, about 5 to 8 minutes. Remove from the heat, stir in the parsley, and season with salt and pepper. Serve immediately.

Brunch

Jarlsberg and Ricotta Bread Pudding

This is an updated version of a classic strata recipe, which is basically just cheese, eggs, bread, and milk layered in a casserole and baked. It can be served as a brunch dish or as a side dish with a meat and vegetable.

The ricotta makes this bread pudding very light, while the Jarlsberg gives the dish a rich cheesy flavor. The olives and basil accent and punctuate the strata's inherent simple and homey flavors and make it sparkle.

SERVES 4 TO 6

1 tablespoon unsalted butter, softened

4 large eggs

2 cups milk

1 teaspoon Dijon mustard

1 teaspoon salt

8 slices stale white sandwich bread, torn into 2-inch-square pieces

8 ounces Jarlsberg, shredded (2 cups)

8 ounces ricotta, homemade (page 70) or store-bought, well drained (1 cup)

¼ cup pitted black and green olives, coarsely chopped

8 large leaves fresh basil, torn into small pieces

Freshly ground black pepper to taste

GENEROUSLY BUTTER an 8- or 9-inch square glass baking dish or a 2-quart round baking dish with the butter. Place the eggs, milk, mustard, and salt in a medium bowl and whisk until blended. Place one-third of the bread in a layer in the bottom of the baking dish. Pour one-third of the egg mixture over the bread to soak it. Sprinkle one-third of the Jarlsberg cheese over the bread, crumble half of the ricotta over the Jarlsberg, and sprinkle half the olives and half the basil over the ricotta. Sprinkle with pepper. Repeat for a second layer, then finish with a layer of the remaining bread, topped with the remaining eggs and Jarlsberg. Cover with plastic wrap and refrigerate for several hours, or overnight.

PREHEAT THE oven to 325° F.

PLACE THE bread pudding in the oven and bake for 1 hour, or until a knife inserted in the center comes out clean but moist. Remove from the oven and let it sit for 5 to 10 minutes.

TO SERVE, cut into squares or wedges and place on a heated serving platter or serve directly from the baking pan, using a large spoon.

Crustless Cheddar Quiche with Onion and Bacon Topping

Quiche originated in Lorraine, in northeastern France. The classic quiche is made without cheese and has a short pastry crust. Other variations contain Gruyère and bacon.

This recipe is more like a savory flan, with the bacon and onions adorning the top of the quiche rather than mixed with the custard as they are in the French version.

Quiche was the ultimate gourmet food in the 1960s. I suspect it was part of the Francophilia that Jackie Kennedy brought to the White House. During those days, whenever we found quiche on a menu, we knew we had located an *in* spot. There were even bumper stickers saying "Quiche me quick."

SERVES 4 TO 6

QUICHE
4 large eggs
¾ cup heavy cream
¾ cup milk
1 teaspoon Dijon mustard
½ teaspoon Worcestershire sauce
2 dashes Tabasco sauce

½ teaspoon salt
Freshly ground black pepper to taste
4 ounces sharp Cheddar, shredded (1 cup)

TOPPING
4 thick slices bacon
½ onion, thinly sliced

FOR THE Quiche, preheat oven to 375°F. Liberally butter an 8- or 9-inch ceramic or glass quiche pan or a pie pan.

PLACE THE eggs, cream, milk, mustard, Worcestershire, and Tabasco in a medium bowl or the work bowl of a food processor fitted with a steel blade. Whisk or process until blended. Add the salt, pepper, and cheese and whisk or process to blend. Pour into the pan.

PLACE THE pan in a larger shallow roasting pan and add enough boiling water to come halfway up the sides of the quiche pan. Place in the oven and bake for 40 to 45 minutes, or until a knife inserted near the center comes out clean but moist. Remove the pans from the oven, lift the quiche pan out of the water bath, and set aside to cool slightly.

MEANWHILE, MAKE the Topping: Cut the bacon crosswise into strips about ¼ inch thick. Sauté in a medium skillet over medium heat for about 5 minutes, or until crisp and brown. Remove the bacon with a slotted spoon and drain on paper towels.

ADD THE sliced onions to the bacon grease remaining in the skillet and sauté over medium heat for about 15 minutes, or until wilted and nicely browned. Drain on paper towels if necessary.

SPREAD THE onions on the quiche and sprinkle the bacon over the onions. Cut into wedges and serve warm.

Real men don't eat quiche.
–Bruce Feirstein

Rapini Frittata with Mozzarella

A frittata is a giant flat omelet that usually contains vegetables and cheese. I like to cook frittatas first in a skillet on top of the stove and then finish them under the broiler. You can also cook a frittata completely on top of the stove, by placing a large plate over the skillet when the frittata is partially cooked, inverting the skillet and the plate, and quickly sliding the frittata back into the pan to cook on the other side.

A frittata can be made with any combination of vegetables. Rapini, also known as broccoli rabe, is a dark green vegetable with an appealingly bitter flavor that tastes somewhat like a mixture of broccoli and turnip greens. It is great in frittatas because it has a lot of flavor. If you can't find rapini at your local market, substitute broccoli, spinach, artichokes, or asparagus.

My Italian friend Enrico Bartolucci likes to make frittatas with leftover spaghetti. He calls them spaghetti omelets.

SERVES 6

Salt	5 large eggs
1 bunch rapini (broccoli rabe) (1 pound)	¼ cup water
2 tablespoons olive oil	¼ to ½ teaspoon Tabasco sauce
½ small onion, finely chopped (¼ cup)	8 ounces fresh mozzarella, thinly sliced
2 cloves garlic, minced	Freshly ground pepper to taste
½ teaspoon red pepper flakes	

CUT OFF and discard the bottom 1½ inches of stems before you open the rapini bunch. Wash the rapini and shake dry. Coarsely chop into 1½- to 2-inch lengths. (There will be about 6 cups packed chopped rapini.)

BRING A large pot of water to a boil and add 2 teaspoons salt. Add the rapini and boil for 5 minutes. Drain in a colander, rinse with cool water, shake, and squeeze out the excess moisture.

HEAT THE olive oil in a broiler-proof 12-inch nonstick skillet over medium-high heat. Add the onion, garlic, and red pepper flakes and sauté briefly, until the vegetables begin to soften. Add the rapini and stir-fry the vegetables, turning and tossing, until tender, about 5 minutes. Remove from the heat, season with salt and pepper, and set the skillet aside.

PREHEAT THE broiler. Adjust the rack to accommodate the skillet 3 inches below the heat source.

CRACK THE eggs into a medium bowl and add the water and Tabasco. Beat with a fork until well combined for about 15 to 20 seconds. Return the skillet to medium heat and add the eggs. Cook, without stirring, until the bottom browns and the eggs are just beginning to set on top. Remove from the heat.

ARRANGE THE mozzarella slices over the top of the frittata. Place the skillet under the broiler and cook until the cheese is melted, browned, and bubbling. Remove from the heat and set on a rack to cool for 5 minutes.

LIBERALLY SPRINKLE the top of the frittata with black pepper. Cut into 6 wedges and serve.

VARIATION

Asparagus, Tomato, and Mozzarella Frittata

Substitute 1 pound of asparagus, trimmed and cut into 1-inch pieces, for the rapini. When you cover the top of the frittata with the cheese, add 1 tomato, cut into thin slices on top of the cheese. Finish as above.

The Ultimate Cheese Omelet

An omelet is one of the easiest breakfast or brunch dishes, and it can be made in just a matter of moments. The thing I love most about cheese omelets is the way the cheese melts from the heat of the eggs and gets soft and oozy. Then the cheese is the perfect consistency for me and its flavor melds well with the soft eggs. And I think a grilled tomato slice is the best accompaniment because of the tomato's sweetness coupled with its acidity.

I always think of Julia Child and omelets together. The first time she appeared on television was on a book review program in Boston in the early 1960s. She had been invited to talk about her new cookbook, *Mastering the Art of French Cooking.* She decided to take along her skillet and made an omelet during the broadcast. She was an instant hit, and thus began her illustrious career as a cookbook author, television cooking teacher, and bon vivant.

SERVES 1

2 large eggs

1 tablespoon water

1 dash Tabasco sauce (optional)

1 teaspoon unsalted butter

Salt and freshly ground black pepper to taste

½ ounce Cheddar, Swiss, or any melting cheese of your choice, shredded (2 tablespoons)

1 teaspoon minced fresh flat-leaf parsley, plus optional parsley sprig, for garnish

1 grilled tomato, for garnish (optional)

HEAT A serving plate in a low oven.

CRACK THE eggs into a small bowl. Add the water and Tabasco, if using, and quickly beat with a fork until well incorporated, about 15 to 20 seconds. Place the butter in an 8-inch nonstick skillet over medium-high heat. Heat until the butter is melted and just beginning to brown. Tilt the pan so that the butter coats the bottom and sides. Pour in the eggs and immediately tilt and gently swirl the pan so that they spread out over the bottom. Cook until the eggs begin to set around the edges. Lift the cooked edges of the eggs and tilt the pan so that the uncooked eggs run underneath and to the edges. Sprinkle the eggs with salt and black pepper and continue to cook for 1 minute, or until they are almost set. (The eggs will continue to cook slightly when they are removed from the heat, so they need not be completely done.) Quickly spread the cheese over half of the omelet and sprinkle with the parsley.

IMMEDIATELY SLIDE the omelet onto the heated plate, folding the omelet in half on top of itself as it slides out of the pan. Garnish with parsley and a grilled tomato slice if desired. Serve immediately.

VARIATION

Herbed Boursin and Smoked Salmon Omelet

When the eggs are almost set, crumble 1 ounce herbed Boursin onto the omelet and cover with 1 slice smoked salmon. Slide immediately onto a heated plate, folding as described above.

> What happens to the hole when the cheese is gone?
>
> **–Bertolt Brecht**

Ricotta Pancakes with Banana-Pecan Syrup

Pancakes made with ricotta are a Sunday morning treat at our house. The ricotta keeps them moist and makes them puff up and rise as they cook.

The bananas and pecans in the syrup remind me of the bananas Foster that are served at Brennan's in New Orleans. Their breakfasts are the most decadent of all.

Sometimes, when I don't want the pancakes to be so rich, I just top them with strawberry preserves or orange marmalade.

MAKES ABOUT 2 CUPS SYRUP
MAKES 16 (3-INCH) PANCAKES
SERVES 4 TO 6

BANANA-PECAN SYRUP

2 tablespoons unsalted butter

½ cup chopped pecans

2 small bananas, thinly sliced (¾ cup)

1 cup cane or maple syrup

RICOTTA PANCAKES

2 cups unbleached all-purpose flour

2 teaspoons baking powder

½ teaspoon baking soda

1 tablespoon sugar

½ teaspoon salt

2 large eggs, separated

2 cups milk

4 ounces ricotta, homemade (page 70) or store-bought, well drained (½ cup)

FOR THE Banana-Pecan Syrup, melt the butter in a medium skillet over medium heat. Add the nuts and sauté for about 1 minute, or until fragrant. Add the bananas and cook, stirring, for about 2 minutes. Add the syrup and cook for about 1 to 2 minutes, or until the syrup is hot and slightly thickened. Remove from the heat and set aside in a warm place.

FOR THE Ricotta Pancakes, sift the flour, baking powder, baking soda, sugar, and salt together onto waxed paper or a plate. Beat the egg whites in a medium bowl with an electric mixer or whisk until stiff but not dry. Beat the egg yolks, milk, and ricotta together in a large bowl until well blended and smooth. Add the dry ingredients and mix gently with a large spoon. Stir a spoonful of the egg whites into the batter to lighten it, then fold in the remaining egg whites with a rubber spatula.

WARM A serving platter in a 200°F. oven.

HEAT A nonstick flat griddle or large nonstick skillet over medium heat until hot. Grease with butter or vegetable oil. Pour ¼ to ⅓ cup batter per pancake onto the pan and cook for about 2 minutes, or until bubbles form on the surface, then flip the pancakes over using a large wide spatula. Cook on the other side for 2 minutes, or until golden brown. Transfer the pancakes to the warm platter.

SERVE IMMEDIATELY or hold in the oven while you cook the rest of the pancakes. Serve the pancakes on heated plates topped with the syrup.

> Betimes I was stirred by invalid longings for something to eat that did not come under the caption of "grub." I had visions of the maternal pantry "deep as first love, and wild with all regret," and then I asked:
> "Judd, can you make pancakes?"
>
> **–O. Henry**

Orange–Cream Cheese French Toast with Raspberry Coulis

French toast is a perfect brunch dish. In this unique recipe, orange-flavored cream cheese is spread between two thin slices of bread before they are dipped in egg and fried. It gives the French toast a surprising orange flavor and a creamy richness. Another twist is the addition of baking powder to the batter, which causes it to be a little bit puffier than usual.

MAKES ABOUT ¾ CUP COULIS
SERVES 4

RASPBERRY COULIS
½ pint raspberries (about 1 cup)

1 tablespoon sugar

2 tablespoons light corn syrup

FRENCH TOAST
8 thin slices soft bakery bread, such as brioche, challah, or raisin bread

3 ounces (⅓ cup) cream cheese, home-made (page 74) or store-bought, softened

1 tablespoon orange marmalade

1 teaspoon grated orange zest

2 large eggs

1 cup half-and-half

¼ cup Grand Marnier

1 tablespoon sugar

¼ teaspoon ground cinnamon

½ teaspoon baking powder

3 to 5 teaspoons unsalted butter

¼ cup confectioners' sugar, for garnish

4 sprigs fresh mint, for garnish

4 orange slices, for garnish

FOR THE Raspberry Coulis, wash the raspberries and drain in a colander. Reserve 8 raspberries for garnish. Place the remaining raspberries in a blender or the work bowl of a food processor fitted with a steel blade, add the sugar and corn syrup, and puree until completely smooth. Pour the sauce into a bowl and set aside.

FOR THE French Toast, lay the bread on a work surface and trim away the crusts if desired. Blend the cream cheese, marmalade, and zest in a small bowl with a fork or the back of a spoon. Spread evenly on 4 slices of the bread, not quite to the edges. Place the remaining bread on top of the cheese and press gently to stick the slices together to form sandwiches.

PLACE THE eggs, half-and-half, Grand Marnier, sugar, cinnamon, and baking powder in a shallow bowl or pie plate. Beat with a fork or a whisk. Dip the sandwiches into the egg mixture and allow them to soak for several minutes, then turn and soak on the second side for a few minutes.

PREHEAT THE oven to 250°F.

MELT 2 tablespoons butter on a griddle or in a large nonstick skillet over medium heat. Add 2 of the sandwiches and cook for 10 to 15 minutes, turning as necessary, until golden on both sides. Transfer the French toast to a baking pan and place it in the oven to keep warm until ready to serve. Add more butter to the griddle if necessary, and cook the remaining sandwiches.

TO SERVE, spoon 3 tablespoons of the coulis onto each of four heated serving plates. Tilt and swirl to spread it evenly. Place the French toast atop the coulis and dust with the confectioners' sugar, using a sieve. Garnish with the mint sprigs, orange slices, and the reserved raspberries.

Poets have been mysteriously silent on the subject of cheese.

–G. K. Chesterton

Cottage Cheese Blintzes with Strawberry Preserves

Blintzes are Eastern European pancakes that are usually filled with fruit and cheese. Pastries made with fresh white cheese are among my favorites because usually they are not as sweet and sugary as others. The common characteristic of cheeses used for pastries such as these is that they are always of a nonmelting variety. They just get soft when heated and do not melt and ooze. Pot cheese, queso blanco, cottage cheese, ricotta, and farmer cheese are all similar in this regard.

The ricotta in these blintzes makes them puff up when they bake.

MAKES ABOUT 1½ CUPS SAUCE
MAKES 12 BLINTZES
SERVES 4

STRAWBERRY SAUCE

1 pint strawberries (2 cups), washed, hulled, and quartered

1 teaspoon freshly squeezed lemon juice

3 tablespoons sugar

BLINTZES

8 ounces (1 cup) full-fat, small-curd cottage cheese, homemade (page 72) or store-bought

4 ounces ricotta, homemade (page 70) or store-bought, well drained (½ cup)

2 tablespoons sugar

1 large egg yolk

12 Crepes (page 82)

¼ cup strawberry preserves

2 tablespoons unsalted butter, melted

2 tablespoons confectioners' sugar, for garnish

Fresh mint leaves, for garnish

FOR THE Strawberry Sauce, place the strawberries in a bowl, sprinkle with the lemon juice and sugar, and mix gently. Set aside at room temperature to macerate for at least 30 minutes.

TRANSFER HALF the strawberries and their juice to a blender or the work bowl of a food processor fitted with a steel blade and puree. Add the remaining strawberries and pulse several times to crush them into a chunky sauce. Cover and set aside.

FOR THE Blintzes, put the cottage cheese in a strainer set over a bowl and allow the excess liquid to drain away.

BLEND THE cottage cheese, ricotta, and sugar in the work bowl of a food processor fitted with a steel blade until smooth. Be careful not to overprocess, or the filling will be too runny. Add the egg yolk and process for 10 seconds. Transfer to a medium bowl and set aside.

PREHEAT THE oven to 325°F. Butter a nonstick baking pan, about 15 x 10 inches, and set aside.

LAY 1 crepe on a work surface and spread a thin layer of the strawberry preserves over the bottom third of the crepe. Mound 1 heaping tablespoon of the cheese mixture on the preserves. Fold the sides of the crepe over the cheese mixture and then fold over the top and bottom to enclose the filling and form a square package. Place smooth side up in the baking pan and repeat with the remaining crepes, preserves, and cheese mixture. Brush the tops of the blintzes with the melted butter. Place the pan in the oven and bake for 10 to 15 minutes, or until the blinzes have puffed up.

TO SERVE, place 3 blintzes on each heated serving plate. Lightly dust with the confectioners' sugar, using a sieve. Spoon some of the sauce over part of the blintzes and make a pool of the sauce to the side. Garnish with mint leaves and serve warm.

Little Miss Muffett
Sat on her tuffet,
Eating her curds and whey.
Along came a spider
And sat down beside her
And frightened Miss Muffett
    away.

–Nursery rhyme

Goat Cheese Strudel

Each fall I look forward to visiting Helmut's little food stand at the Texas State Fair. Unlikely as it may seem, in the midst of the corny dogs, chili, and beer, there is always a long line waiting to buy the rich, warm apple strudel that Helmut has been making for years and years.

The simplest and easiest way to make strudel is to use phyllo dough. I like it because it is so crisp and flaky when it's baked. Serve it warm and drizzled with honey, like baklava.

SERVES 4

8 ounces (1 cup) fresh goat cheese

1 large egg

2 tablespoons unbleached all-purpose flour

¼ cup chopped toasted pecans

1 teaspoon ground cinnamon

¼ cup sugar

¼ cup currants or raisins, soaked in rum or brandy for 30 minutes and drained

4 sheets frozen phyllo dough, thawed

2 tablespoons unsalted butter, melted

1 teaspoon sugar

2 tablespoons honey, for garnish

PREHEAT THE oven to 375°F. Line a baking sheet with parchment paper and set aside.

COMBINE THE goat cheese, egg, and flour in a small bowl and mix well. Set aside. Set the pecans, cinnamon, sugar, and currants within easy reach.

LAY A sheet of phyllo dough out on a dry work surface. Brush the dough lightly and quickly with some of the melted butter. Place a second sheet of phyllo dough on top of the first sheet and brush with butter. Repeat with the remaining 2 sheets dough. Cover with a damp towel, until ready to fill.

CRUMBLE THE goat cheese mixture lengthwise down the center of the phyllo dough in a 3-inch-wide band, leaving a border at each end. Sprinkle the pecans, cinnamon, sugar, and currants over the goat cheese. Fold one long side of the dough up over the filling. Fold the ends over inward. Carefully fold the top portion of the dough over the filling, creating a long flat roll.

BRUSH AN area on the parchment paper the same size as the strudel with butter. Using two spatulas, transfer the strudel to the baking sheet, placing it seam side down on the buttered area; be careful not to break the strudel. Brush the entire strudel with butter and sprinkle the top with the sugar. Cut 3 small diagonal slits in the top of the strudel with a sharp knife to let the steam escape while cooking.

PLACE IN the oven and bake for 25 to 30 minutes, or until the pastry is a light golden brown. Remove from the oven and place on a rack to cool for about 5 minutes.

AT SERVING time, place the strudel on a serving platter and drizzle it with honey. To serve, cut into 1- to 2-inch pieces with a serrated or bread knife. Serve warm or at room temperature.

O eagle, I wish to chew acorns from a
   gentle oak,
I wish to swallow deer cheese and wild
   goat's milk.

–Kostas Krystallis

Lunch

Pizza Margherita

Pizza Margherita is named for Margherita, a queen of Italy in the late nineteenth century. Legend has it that a famous Neapolitan *pizzaiolo* created and named this pizza for her. She is said to have loved it because the red, white, and green of its ingredients resembled the Italian flag.

It's best to line your oven with quarry tiles or cook the pizza on a pizza stone. If that's not possible, cook the pizza on a preheated baking sheet. You might also try grilling your pizza on a preheated charcoal grill: Cook the dough first on one side, turn it over, add the toppings, and return it to the fire, just as Johanne Killeen and George Germon do at their wonderful restaurant Al Forno in Providence, Rhode Island.

Depending on your preference, you can roll out the dough thick or thin. The only secret is to have the oven very hot and to cook the pizza quickly.

PIZZA DOUGH MAKES ENOUGH FOR 1 THICK-CRUST PIZZA
OR 2 THIN-CRUST PIZZAS
PIZZA MARGHERITA SERVES 4

PIZZA DOUGH

½ cup plus 2 tablespoons warm water (110°F.)

1½ teaspoons active dry yeast

2 cups unbleached all-purpose flour

1 teaspoon salt

3 tablespoons extra virgin olive oil

1 teaspoon cornmeal

TOPPING

2 cups Paula's Tomato Sauce (page 84), cooked for an additional 30 minutes to thicken and reduce the sauce to about 1 cup, or store-bought

8 ounces fresh mozzarella, thinly sliced

Salt and freshly ground pepper to taste

½ teaspoon dried oregano or 8 to 10 leaves fresh basil

FOR THE Pizza Dough, put the 2 tablespoons warm water in a small bowl or measuring cup, sprinkle the yeast over the water, and blend with a small whisk or fork. Set aside to proof. (If the yeast is active it will become foamy within 5 minutes.)

PUT THE flour, salt, 2 tablespoons oil, proofed yeast, and the remaining ½ cup warm water in the work bowl of a food processor fitted with the steel blade. Process until a smooth ball forms on the blade and cleans the side of the bowl. Turn the dough out onto a floured board or work surface and knead for 1 minute to create a smooth ball. (The dough can also be made by hand: Mound the flour on a work surface. Make a well in the center of the flour, add the salt, oil, proofed yeast, and water, and combine with a fork and then by hand. Knead for 10 minutes.)

OIL A large bowl, with the remaining 1 tablespoon oil, place the dough in the bowl, and turn it to grease all surfaces. Cover the bowl with a towel or plastic wrap and set aside in a warm, draft-free location to rise for about 45 minutes, until doubled in size.

REMOVE THE dough from the bowl and place on a floured board or work surface. Punch the dough down and knead for 3 to 5 minutes. Return the dough to the bowl, cover, and allow to rise for 20 minutes.

FOR THE Pizza Margherita, line the oven with quarry tiles or place a pizza stone in it. Preheat the oven to 450°F. Wait until the oven has preheated to construct the pizzas, so that the tiles or stone has an additional 10 to 15 minutes to heat.

ON A floured surface, roll out the dough to a 12- to 14-inch round, leaving the edges slightly thicker. Sprinkle ½ teaspoon of the cornmeal on a smooth slick surface such as a baker's peel or a bread board. Place the dough on top.

SPREAD ½ to 1 cup of the tomato sauce over the dough—depending on the amount of sauce you like on your pizza—leaving a ½-inch border all around. Arrange the slices of mozzarella on top of the sauce.

SPRINKLE THE remaining ½ teaspoon of cornmeal on the tiles or pizza stone in the oven. Slide the pizza onto the tiles or stone. Bake for 15 minutes, or until the edges of the pizza are golden brown and the cheese is completely melted, bubbly all over, and turning golden brown. Remove the pizza from the oven. Sprinkle with salt and pepper and oregano.

SERVE HOT, cut into wedges.

VARIATIONS

Grilled Shrimp and Smoked Mozzarella Pizza

Briefly grill 10 unshelled large shrimp on a hot charcoal or gas grill—do not fully cook, as they will cook further on the pizza. Alternatively, cook them in a dry skillet over medium heat. Shell the shrimp. Substitute smoked mozzarella for the plain mozzarella. Arrange the cheese on the tomato sauce and top the cheese with the shrimp. Bake the pizza as directed above. Remove the pizza from the oven and sprinkle with 1 tablespoon drained capers and 5 leaves fresh basil, snipped, as well as salt and pepper if desired.

Italian Sausage and Pepper Jack Pizza

Grill or sauté 8 ounces sweet Italian sausage links. When cooked, slice the sausage into rounds. Substitute pepper Jack for the mozzarella. Arrange the cheese on the tomato sauce and top with the slices of sausage. Bake the pizza as directed above. Remove the pizza from the oven, scatter thinly sliced raw onion rings on top, and sprinkle with oregano, as well as salt and pepper if desired.

Calzone

Roll out the dough to a 12- to 14-inch round. Spread ½ cup tomato sauce over half of the dough, leaving a ½-inch border. Top the sauce with 4 ounces mozzarella, sliced, 2 thin slices prosciutto, 4 ounces ricotta, well drained and crumbled, 2 tablespoons pitted and chopped Calamata olives, and a sprinkling of dried oregano. Drizzle 2 tablespoons more tomato sauce over the top.

Lightly moisten the edges of the dough with water. Fold the unsauced half of the dough over the filled half to form a half-moon pie. Press and crimp the edges together. Brush the top lightly with extra virgin olive oil. Make a few slits in the top for the steam to escape while cooking. Bake the calzone until the crust is dark golden brown.

Pizza Bianca

There is a great little restaurant in downtown Phoenix called Pizzeria Bianco. The genius in front of the wood-burning pizza oven is Chris Bianco. He is a master pizza maker, widely recognized as making some of the best pizzas in the USA. His secret is to use the finest ingredients available, from the flour to the tomatoes and cheese.

The pizzeria is a small place and very homey. Everyone who comes in seems to know Chris and stops to say hello and visit. Vendors arrive with their produce in hand, friends stop by for a glass of wine, and music softly plays in the background as the fabulous pizzas are cooked in the oven. The restaurant is simply furnished with wooden tables and chairs. Its antique brick walls are hung with paintings done by Chris's father. It's a charming and friendly spot.

Pizza bianca means "white pizza" in Italian. It is so named because all its toppings are white—it does not have any tomato sauce. The Green and White Pizza is similar to one that Chris Bianco serves. Wolfgang Puck, of Spago in Los Angeles, was the inspiration for the Smoked Salmon and Goat Cheese Pizza.

SERVES 4

2 tablespoons extra virgin olive oil

2 large onions, sliced into thin rings

1 recipe Pizza Dough (page 199)

1 teaspoon cornmeal

8 ounces Brie, rind removed, if desired, and cut into thin slices

2 (2-inch) sprigs fresh rosemary, leaves removed and finely chopped

Salt and freshly ground pepper to taste

LINE THE oven with quarry tiles or place a pizza stone in it. Preheat the oven to 450°F. Wait until the oven has preheated to construct the pizzas, so that the tiles or stone has an additional 10 to 15 minutes to heat.

HEAT THE olive oil in a large skillet over medium heat. Add the onions and sauté slowly until caramelized and golden brown. Remove from the heat and set aside to cool.

ON A floured surface, roll out the dough to a 12- to 14-inch round, leaving the edges slightly thicker. Sprinkle ½ teaspoon of the cornmeal on a smooth slick surface such as a baker's peel or a bread board. Place the dough on top.

SPREAD THE onions over the dough, leaving a ½-inch border all around. Distribute the Brie evenly over the onions. Sprinkle the rosemary over the pizza.

SPRINKLE THE remaining ½ teaspoon of the cornmeal onto the tiles or pizza stone in the oven. Slide the pizza onto the tiles or pizza stone and bake for about 15 minutes, or until the cheese is melted, bubbly all over, and beginning to brown on the top and the crust is browned. Remove from the oven and sprinkle with salt and pepper.

SERVE HOT, cut into wedges.

VARIATIONS

Green and White Pizza

Top the dough with 8 ounces ricotta, well drained and crumbled (1 cup), and ½ ounce (2 tablespoons) freshly grated Parmigiano-Reggiano. When baked, completely cover the top of the pizza with 1 ounce whole arugula leaves, so that none of the crust or cheese is visible. Drizzle with extra virgin olive oil and sprinkle with salt and freshly ground black pepper.

Smoked Salmon and Goat Cheese Pizza

Sprinkle the dough with ½ ounce (2 tablespoons) freshly grated Parmigiano and bake until golden brown. Remove from the oven and spread with 4 ounces (½ cup) fresh goat cheese, mixed with ¼ teaspoon grated lemon zest. Completely cover the top of the pizza with 2 ounces thinly sliced smoked salmon, so that none of the cheese or crust is visible. Return to the oven very briefly, just to warm. Garnish with a few sprigs of fresh dill.

Swiss Cheese Soufflé

One of my mother's few culinary specialties was cheese soufflé. It is actually surprisingly simple to make and is always sure to impress. I love the wonderful dark golden brown crust that forms on the top and the soft and airy light texture of its interior.

My friend Zanne Stewart, food editor of *Gourmet,* suggested that I pair this soufflé with an acidic sauce to accentuate its subtle flavor, so I have listed ingredients for a simple ratatouille or a feisty pico de gallo to accompany it. Choose whichever fits your mood, or feel free to serve it alone.

Any cheese or combination of cheeses (weighing 6 to 8 ounces) can be substituted for the Gruyère.

SERVES 4 TO 6

6 tablespoons (¾ stick) unsalted butter

6 tablespoons unbleached all-purpose flour

1½ cups milk, heated

6 large eggs, separated

1 teaspoon salt, plus a pinch

½ teaspoon paprika

Dash of cayenne pepper

6 ounces Gruyère, shredded (1½ cups)

Ratatouille or Pico de Gallo (optional) (see Accompaniments, on opposite page)

PREHEAT THE oven to 400°F. Butter a 2-quart soufflé dish. Cut a piece of wax paper or aluminum foil long enough to wrap around the soufflé dish and fold it in half. Butter the part of the paper that will extend above the soufflé dish and wrap the paper around the dish to form a collar. Secure with kitchen string or a toothpick. (This will contain the soufflé when it rises up over the sides while baking.)

MELT THE butter in a large heavy saucepan. Stir in the flour when the foam subsides and cook over low heat, stirring constantly, for several minutes. Slowly add the milk and cook over medium heat, stirring constantly, for 3 to 4 minutes. Remove from the heat.

BEAT THE egg yolks in a small bowl using a whisk, then add them to the sauce little by little, beating well after each addition. Add the 1 teaspoon salt, the paprika, and cayenne. Return to low heat and cook, stirring constantly, for 1 minute. Remove from the heat and stir in the cheese.

USING A whisk or an electric mixer beat the egg whites with the pinch of salt in a clean bowl until soft peaks form. Stir a few tablespoons of the egg whites into the sauce to lighten it. Gently fold in the remaining egg whites with a rubber spatula.

POUR THE mixture into the soufflé dish. Place in the oven and bake for 35 to 40 minutes, or until puffed and golden brown on top.

SERVE THE soufflé immediately, alone or with ratatouille or pico de gallo, if desired.

ACCOMPANIMENTS

Ratatouille

SAUTÉ A combination of chopped vegetables—1 bell pepper, ½ onion, 1 clove garlic, 1 eggplant, 2 tomatoes, and 1 zucchini—in olive oil until softened. Season with salt, freshly ground black pepper, and dried thyme. Serve warm or at room temperature.

Pico de Gallo

CHOP 2 tomatoes, ½ onion, and 1 jalapeño chile. Add ½ cup minced fresh cilantro and season with salt, freshly ground black pepper, and 1 tablespoon freshly squeezed lime juice. Serve chilled or at room temperature.

Never try to eat the holes in Swiss Cheese.

–Robert Campbell

Herbed Goat Cheese Tart

Alice Waters, of Chez Panisse in Berkeley, is known at the mother of New American Cooking. She initiated the trend of cooking with fresh, regional ingredients in the early 1970s. She is also a champion of organic farming and was the first chef to use fresh American goat cheese—which she bought from Laura Chenel—in her cooking, in the very early 1980s.

This is a simple recipe that I created years ago. I've taught it in cooking classes many times and it has always been a big hit. You can use any combination of fresh herbs in any proportion, such as basil, parsley, tarragon, thyme, oregano, marjoram, rosemary, or whatever you find in your garden or the supermarket produce case.

If you're not fond of goat cheese, try the variation that uses cream cheese instead.

SERVES 6

1 (9-inch) thawed frozen or refrigerated pie crust or homemade Tart Crust, (page 208)

½ cup mixed fresh herb leaves (such as ¼ cup flat-leaf parsley, 2 tablespoons basil, and 2 tablespoons rosemary)

1 clove garlic, minced

12 ounces (1½ cups) fresh goat cheese, softened

4 ounces ricotta, homemade (page 70) or store-bought, well drained (½ cup)

4 tablespoons (½ stick) unsalted butter, softened

½ cup (4 ounces) crème fraîche, homemade (page 68) or store-bought, or sour cream

2 large eggs, at room temperature

2 tablespoons unbleached all-purpose flour

Salt and freshly ground pepper to taste

3 ounces oil-packed sun-dried tomatoes, drained and cut into strips (1 cup) (optional)

PREHEAT THE oven to 375°F. (if using the tart crust, preheat while the tart shell chills).

ROLL THE dough out on a floured board or work surface into a circle about 3 inches larger than the pan. Transfer it to a 10- to 12-inch tart pan with a removable bottom by folding it into quarters or rolling it up over the rolling pin. Press into the bottom of the pan and up the sides. Trim off any excess dough extending over the sides and crimp the edges, or fold it back on itself to make the sides thicker. Prick the shell with the tines of a fork and refrigerate for 30 minutes.

PLACE THE crust in the oven and bake until golden brown, about 7 to 10 minutes. Remove from the oven and cool on a rack. Leave the oven on.

PLACE THE herbs and garlic in the work bowl of a food processor fitted with a steel blade and pulse until finely chopped. Add the goat cheese, ricotta, butter, crème fraîche, eggs, flour, and salt and pepper. Process for 30 seconds, or until the mixture is smooth. Pour this mixture into the prebaked piecrust. If desired, decorate the top of the tart with strips of sun-dried tomatoes arranged in a design.

PLACE THE tart on a baking sheet in the oven and bake for about 30 minutes, or until the filling has puffed and the top is golden brown. Remove from the oven and set on a rack to cool slightly.

REMOVE THE outer ring of the tart pan, slip a spatula under the bottom crust to loosen it, and slide the tart onto a serving platter. Serve warm or at room temperature, cut into wedges.

VARIATION

Herbed Cream Cheese Tart

Substitute 12 ounces (1½ cups) cream cheese, softened, for the goat cheese.

Stilton and Tomato Tart

This recipe comes from my friend Weezie Mott. When I lived in Perugia and studied at the Università per Stranieri, Weezie and her husband, Howard, were my classmates. That is where our culinary adventures began. In Italy, we often had dinner together and tried new restaurants, and that tradition has continued for the past thirty years no matter where we may meet, from New York to Seattle to Florence. Since we met, Weezie has founded a cooking school in Alameda, California, near San Francisco, and she and Howard also take food lovers on fabulous tours around Europe. Their business is appropriately called Motoring with the Motts.

This tart is somewhat like a quiche. There's something very special about the combination of the acidic tomatoes and the rich and creamy Stilton.

SERVES 6 TO 8

TART CRUST

8 tablespoons (1 stick) unsalted butter

1½ cups unbleached all-purpose flour

½ teaspoon salt

1 large egg yolk

1 teaspoon freshly squeezed lemon juice, plus enough cold water to measure ¼ cup

1 large egg, beaten with 1 tablespoon water for the egg wash

FILLING

2 tablespoons minced shallots

6 dry-packed sun-dried tomatoes, cut into ⅛-inch julienne strips

2 large ripe tomatoes, thinly sliced

8 ounces Stilton, crumbled (1½ cups)

3 large eggs

⅔ cup heavy cream

⅛ teaspoon ground nutmeg

¼ teaspoon salt

Freshly ground black pepper to taste

FOR THE Tart Crust, place the butter, flour, and salt in the work bowl of a food processor fitted with a steel blade. Pulse until the mixture resembles cornmeal. Mix the egg yolk with the lemon water. With the motor running, pour this mixture through the feed tube. Pulse until all the liquid is mixed into the flour and a rough ball begins to form on the blade; do not overmix. Remove the dough, place on a piece of plastic wrap, and form into a disk about ½ inch thick. Wrap in the plastic wrap and refrigerate for at least 20 minutes.

ON A lightly floured surface, roll out the dough to a 13-inch circle, if using a quiche pan, or if using a tart pan, a circle 3 inches larger than the pan. Fold the dough into quarters or loosely roll it up over the rolling pin and gently place it into a 10-inch quiche pan or a 12-inch tart pan with a removable bottom (with sides at least 1½ inches high). Gently fit the dough into the pan, trim off the excess dough extending over the sides, and crimp the edges. Prick the bottom of the crust with a fork. Refrigerate for 30 minutes.

PREHEAT THE oven to 425°F.

LINE THE pastry crust with waxed paper or parchment paper and fill with rice or dried beans to weight it down. Place the crust in the oven and bake for about 10 minutes. Remove from the oven and carefully lift out the paper with the rice or beans. Return to the oven and continue baking for 10 to 15 minutes, or until lightly browned. Remove from the oven. Brush the egg wash onto the crust. Return to the oven to bake for 2 minutes. Remove and set aside on a rack to cool.

RESET THE oven to 375°F.

FOR THE filling, sprinkle the shallots over the bottom of the baked crust. Sprinkle with the sun-dried tomatoes. Arrange the fresh tomatoes on top. Sprinkle the Stilton over the tomatoes. Mix the eggs, cream, nutmeg, salt, and pepper in a small bowl until well blended. Pour over the tomatoes and cheese.

PLACE THE tart on a baking sheet, place in the oven, and bake for 30 minutes, or until the top is golden and the custard has just set. Remove and place on a rack to cool.

IF USING a tart pan with a removable bottom, remove the ring, loosen the tart from the bottom of the pan with a spatula, and slide the tart onto a serving platter. Serve warm or at room temperature, cut into wedges.

Brie, Ham, and Asparagus Crêpes with Mornay Sauce

Crêpes are a great party food because they can be made and assembled ahead of time, then popped into the oven to heat while you entertain your guests. They are light and a good choice for lunch or brunch.

Crêpes remind me of the wonderful old-fashioned Southern food that is served at the Dallas Woman's Club. Luncheons there are a step back into the past, with the elegant surroundings and the delicious tearoom-type foods that are served. Sunlight streams into the pastel-colored rooms overlooking lush gardens. The tables are always beautifully set. The ladies are beautifully dressed, with many wearing hats, and there seems to be lots of time for gracious visiting. The elegance, simplicity, and richness of these crêpes fit right in with this Old South atmosphere.

You could substitute fresh pasta for the crêpes and make cannelloni just as easily.

MAKES ABOUT 1 ½ CUPS SAUCE
MAKES 8 CREPES
SERVES 4 TO 8

MORNAY SAUCE

2 tablespoons unsalted butter

2 tablespoons unbleached all-purpose flour

½ cup chicken broth, homemade (page 81) or store-bought, heated

½ cup cream, heated

½ onion

1 large egg yolk, slightly beaten

2 tablespoons Dijon mustard

½ teaspoon salt

1 ounce Gruyère, shredded (¼ cup)

½ ounce Parmigiano-Reggiano, grated (2 tablespoons)

FILLING

2 tablespoons unsalted butter

1 tablespoon minced shallots

3 cloves garlic, peeled

1 tablespoon water

1 pound slender asparagus spears, tough ends removed

Salt and freshly ground pepper to taste

1 teaspoon freshly squeezed lemon juice

1 tablespoon minced fresh dill or tarragon

8 Crêpes (page 82)

5 ounces Black Forest ham, cut into 8 thin slices

8 ounces Brie, rind removed and cut into 8 slices

½ ounce Parmigiano-Reggiano, grated (2 tablespoons)

1 teaspoon paprika

4 sprigs fresh dill or tarragon, for garnish

FOR THE Mornay Sauce, melt the butter in a small saucepan over low heat. Stir in the flour when the foam has subsided and cook for several minutes. Slowly pour in the broth and cream, whisking constantly to prevent lumps. Add the onion half and cook over medium heat, stirring constantly, for about 5 minutes, or until thickened and smooth. Strain the sauce into a double boiler or a metal bowl set over a pan of simmering water. Whisk in the egg yolk, then the mustard, salt, and cheeses. When the cheese is melted and the sauce is thickened and smooth, remove from the heat and set aside.

FOR THE Filling, melt the butter in a 12-inch skillet. Add the shallots and garlic cloves and sauté briefly, until soft. Add the water and asparagus and cook over medium heat for about 5 minutes, shaking the pan as necessary to prevent scorching. When the water has evaporated and the asparagus is tender and beginning to brown, remove from the heat. Season the asparagus with salt and pepper, the lemon juice, and the dill. Remove the garlic cloves and discard. Set the asparagus aside.

PREHEAT THE oven to 400°F. Butter a 12 x 8-inch baking pan, or one just large enough to hold the crepes in one layer.

LAY 1 crêpe on a work surface. Place a slice of ham in the center, place a slice of Brie on top, and spread 1 tablespoon of Mornay sauce on top of the cheese. Divide the asparagus into 8 portions and place a portion on top of the crêpe. Roll up the crêpe around the filling into a tube and place seam side down in the pan. Repeat with the remaining crêpes and filling ingredients. Pour the remaining Mornay sauce over and spread it around the crêpes. Sprinkle with the Parmigiano and paprika.

PLACE THE crêpes in the oven and bake for 15 to 20 minutes, or until the sauce is bubbling and the top is starting to brown.

SERVE 2 crêpes to each person on heated plates, garnished with the herbs.

Ricotta and Goat Cheese Crespelle

My inspiration for this recipe came from Giuliano Bugialli's wonderful cookbook *Foods of Italy*. When it was first published, my friend Kate Willis and I used to spend hours and hours poring over the gorgeous photographs, which elicited fond memories of my years in Italy and her travels there. After great deliberation, we would decide upon our menu, shop, and then cook an Italian feast for our husbands.

Inspired by Giuliano's recipe for *crespelle* with ricotta and Parmigiano, I created this recipe using ricotta, fresh goat cheese, and herbs. I also added a tomato sauce, which I feel gives another dimension to the dish.

Crespelle are little cheese-filled crêpes. This dish is visually appealing and unusual because the crespelle are cut into short lengths that are stood on end and then baked.

SERVES 6

FILLING

2 large eggs

1½ pounds ricotta, homemade (page 70) or store-bought, well drained (3 cups)

1 ounce Parmigiano-Reggiano, grated (¼ cup)

8 ounces (1 cup) fresh goat cheese

1 tablespoon minced fresh herbs (any combination, such as basil, thyme, rosemary, mint, and/or tarragon)

Salt and freshly ground black pepper to taste

3 tablespoons unsalted butter, melted

16 Crêpes (page 82)

1 ounce Parmigiano-Reggiano, grated (¼ cup)

3 cups Paula's Tomato Sauce (page 84) or store-bought, heated

6 leaves fresh basil, cut into thin strips

FOR THE Filling, combine the eggs, ricotta, Parmigiano, goat cheese, and herbs in the work bowl of a food processor and pulse just to mix together well. Season with salt and pepper. Cover and refrigerate if not using immediately.

PREHEAT THE oven to 375°F. Grease an 11 x 7-inch or 10-inch square shallow baking dish with 1½ tablespoons of the butter.

LAY ONE crêpe on a work surface. Place 3 to 4 tablespoons of the filling down the center of the crêpe, mounding it evenly and extending it to both sides. Roll up the crêpe into a tube shape. Repeat until all the crêpes are filled.

CUT THE crêpes into thirds using a sharp knife. Stand the pieces on end, crowded one next to the other, in the baking dish. Sprinkle with the Parmigiano and drizzle with the remaining 1½ tablespoons butter.

PLACE IN the oven and bake for 30 to 45 minutes, or until the edges of the crespelle are browned.

TO SERVE, remove the crespelle from the baking dish with a spatula and place 8 crespelle pieces on each heated serving plate. Spoon the tomato sauce over several of the crespelle on each plate and into a pool to the side. Sprinkle with the basil. Serve immediately.

Italian cheeses have as many moods as Italian literature and we can thus choose our luncheon reading to match them exactly.

–Edward and Lorna Bunyard

Uptown Get-Down Macaroni and Cheese

We live in a part of Dallas called Uptown. It's a mixture of older structures, some of them historic, and new town houses, high-rise apartments, restaurants, and shops. The spine of Uptown is McKinney Avenue, where vintage trolleys roll past modern bistros, art galleries, and antique shops. It's a diverse and spirited neighborhood.

My macaroni and cheese recipe is just like Uptown, a rich mixture of ingredients that blend together to create something familiar with a new modern twist.

SERVES 4 TO 6

BÉCHAMEL SAUCE

3 tablespoons unsalted butter

3 tablespoons unbleached all-purpose flour

1½ cups milk or half-and-half, heated

½ teaspoon salt

¼ teaspoon freshly ground black pepper

¼ teaspoon Tabasco sauce

4½ ounces Parmigiano-Reggiano, grated (1 generous cup)

1 teaspoon salt

1 pound elbow macaroni

2 tablespoons unsalted butter, softened

⅛ teaspoon minced garlic

8 ounces sharp Cheddar, shredded (2 cups)

8 ounces Velveeta or processed American cheese, cut into ½-inch cubes

¼ cup fresh bread crumbs

½ ounce Parmigiano-Reggiano, grated (2 tablespoons)

½ teaspoon Seasoning Salt (page 79) or store-bought

FOR THE Béchamel Sauce, melt the butter in a heavy medium saucepan. When the foam subsides, stir in the flour and cook over low heat, stirring constantly, for several minutes. Slowly add the heated milk and cook over medium heat, stirring constantly, for 3 to 4 minutes. Reduce the heat and simmer for 3 to 4 minutes, stirring to prevent scorching. Remove from the heat and add the salt, pepper, Tabasco, and the Parmigiano, stirring well to melt the cheese. Cover and set aside.

PREHEAT THE oven to 350°F. Butter a 3-quart glass or ceramic baking dish.

FILL A large pot with water and bring to a boil over high heat. Add the salt. Pour the macaroni into the rapidly boiling water, stir vigorously, and cook for approximately 5 minutes, until slightly undercooked and very al dente. Drain the macaroni, return it to the pot, and immediately toss with the butter and garlic. Add the sauce and toss again. Set aside.

MIX THE Cheddar and processed cheese together. Place one-third of the macaroni in the baking dish. Sprinkle with one-third of the cheese. Top with another one-third of the macaroni and one-third of the cheese. Repeat with the remaining macaroni and cheese. Mix the bread crumbs, Parmigiano, and seasoning salt together on a piece of waxed paper. Sprinkle over the top of the macaroni and cheese.

PLACE IN the oven and bake for 30 to 45 minutes, or until bubbling and the top is beginning to brown. Remove from the oven and let sit for 5 minutes before serving.

VARIATIONS

Individual Macaroni and Cheese

Bake the macaroni and cheese in a shallow baking dish. Using a large round cutter or a tuna fish can with both ends removed, cut the macaroni and cheese into round discs. Serve as individual servings.

Macaroni ai Quattro Formaggi

Quattro formaggi means four cheeses. Use a combination of Parmigiano, Cheddar, Fontina, and Gruyère, or any four cheeses of your choice, totaling 1 pound, for the cheese layers.

Savory Genovese Easter Torta

Easter is a very special time in Italy. Families gather to cook traditional dishes for grand feasts that are enjoyed at long tables, lined with several generations of family members. Each region has its own particular specialties. This recipe comes from Genoa, a port city located on the Mediterranean coast of northern Italy.

This dish is also good served for brunch, since it is made with lots of eggs. Sliced into wedges, it reveals an attractive pattern, with the eggs baked on top of a spinach filling The torta can also be served as an appetizer or as a luncheon entrée. And it's great for buffet dinners too.

SERVES 4 TO 6

CRUST

2 cups unbleached all-purpose flour, sifted

1 tablespoon extra virgin olive oil

½ cup plus 1 tablespoon warm water

¼ teaspoon salt

FILLING

1 bunch spinach (about 12 ounces)

½ teaspoon salt

1½ tablespoons plus 2 teaspoons unsalted butter

1 clove garlic, minced

1 (14-ounce can) artichoke hearts, drained, rinsed, and coarsely chopped

2 teaspoons minced fresh flat-leaf parsley

8 ounces ricotta, homemade (page 70) or store-bought well drained (1 cup)

1½ ounces Parmigiano-Reggiano, grated (¼ cup plus 2 tablespoons)

6 large eggs

¼ teaspoon dried marjoram

1 tablespoon unbleached all-purpose flour

Salt

Freshly ground black pepper to taste

1 large egg white, beaten

1 tablespoon extra virgin olive oil, for brushing the crust

FOR THE Crust, place the flour, olive oil, water, and salt in the work bowl of a food processor fitted with a steel blade. Pulse until the dough forms a ball that rides on top of the blade, then process for 30 seconds longer. Transfer the dough to a floured board or work surface and knead for several minutes. It should be soft, the texture of pasta dough. If it seems too stiff, return the dough to the work bowl, add 1 to 2 additional tablespoons warm water, and pulse to knead the dough again; return to the floured board. Knead for 2 to 4 minutes, or until the dough is smooth and elastic. Set aside covered with a damp cloth or a small bowl inverted over the dough to keep it from drying out.

FOR THE Filling, trim the stems of the spinach before you untie the bunch. Wash the spinach and shake dry. Place in a large saucepan and add ½ cup water and the salt. Cook the spinach for about 5 minutes, or until wilted. Drain the spinach in a colander and let cool, then press out the excess moisture with the back of a spoon. Coarsely chop the spinach.

MELT THE butter in a 12-inch sauté pan, add the garlic and artichokes, and sauté over medium heat for about 4 minutes, or until the garlic begins to soften and become fragrant. Add the spinach and sauté briefly. Remove from the heat, stir in the parsley, and set aside to cool.

PROCESS THE spinach mixture in a food processor until finely chopped. Transfer to a large bowl. Place the ricotta, ¼ cup of the Parmigiano, 2 of the eggs, the marjoram, the flour, ¾ teaspoon salt, and pepper to taste in the work bowl. Process to a smooth consistency. Add to the spinach mixture and stir to mix well. Adjust the seasonings if necessary.

PREHEAT THE oven to 375°F. Butter an 8 x 2½-inch springform pan.

DIVIDE THE dough into two pieces, one twice as large as the other. Lightly flour a board or work surface and roll the larger piece into a 14-inch round. Fit into the springform pan letting the excess dough extend over the sides. Pour the spinach filling into the pan. Make 4 equally spaced indentations in the filling, near the edges, with the back of a large spoon. Crack open the remaining 4 eggs and pour one into each indentation. Sprinkle salt, pepper, and the remaining 2 tablespoons Parmigiano over the eggs. Dot each egg with ½ teaspoon of butter.

DIVIDE THE remaining piece of dough in half. Roll one piece into a 9-inch round. Brush the edges of the bottom crust with the egg white and place the top crust on top of the eggs. Crimp the edges of the crusts together and flute the edges. Roll out the remaining piece of dough, sculpt into leaves and vines as you like, and place on top of the crust as decoration. Brush the crust and the leaf design with olive oil. Make a few vent holes in the top, being careful not to puncture the egg yolks.

PLACE THE springform pan on a baking sheet, place in the oven, and bake for 1 hour, or until golden brown. Remove from the oven and let cool on a rack for 1 hour before serving. While the torte is still warm, brush the top lightly with olive oil and run a knife around the edge of the pan to loosen the torte.

SERVE THE torte slightly warm or at room temperature. To serve, remove the springform ring and cut the torte into wedges.

Summer Vegetable Strudel

Ig Vella is a retired county commissioner and great raconteur who has taken the helm of a generations-old cheese factory called Vella Cheese, located in a small stone building not far from the town square in Sonoma, California. He makes a wonderful Dry Sonoma Jack that he ages under a coating of cocoa and coffee. His cheese is quite famous and has even won awards in Europe. Next time you are in the charming town of Sonoma, stop by Ig's or David Viviani's Sonoma Cheese Factory, located on the square, to buy some cheese. At the Sonoma Cheese Factory, you can actually watch the cheese being made.

This strudel is delicious with Dry Sonoma Jack, aged Gouda, or a similar firm cheese. Besides the long traditional strudel form it can be wrapped like little packages for individual servings (see Variation).

SERVES 6

FILLING

2 tablespoons unsalted butter

¼ cup finely chopped red onion

1 clove garlic, minced

½ teaspoon grated fresh ginger

¼ cup matchstick julienne of carrot

¼ cup matchstick julienne of red bell pepper

¼ cup matchstick julienne of green bell pepper

¼ cup matchstick julienne of zucchini

¼ cup matchstick julienne of yellow squash

¼ cup chopped fresh cilantro

4 ounces Dry Sonoma Jack or aged Gouda, shredded (1 cup)

Salt and freshly ground black pepper to taste

4 sheets frozen phyllo dough, thawed

2 tablespoons unsalted butter, melted

4 sprigs fresh cilantro, for garnish

FOR THE Filling, melt the butter in a large sauté pan. Add the onion, garlic, and ginger and sauté over medium heat for about 2 minutes, or until the onion begins to become translucent. Add the carrot and the bell pepper and sauté for 2 minutes. Finally add the zucchini and yellow squash and sauté for 2 minutes longer. Remove the pan from the heat and set aside to cool.

PREHEAT THE oven to 400° F. Line a baking sheet with parchment paper.

STIR THE cilantro and shredded cheese into the cooled filling. Season with salt and pepper.

LAY A sheet of phyllo dough out on a dry work surface. Brush the dough lightly and quickly with some of the melted butter. Place a second sheet of phyllo dough on top of the first sheet and brush with butter. Repeat with the remaining 2 sheets dough. Cover with a damp towel until ready to fill.

DISTRIBUTE THE vegetable filling lengthwise down the center of the phyllo dough in a 3-inch-wide band, leaving a border at each end. Fold one long side of the dough up over the vegetables. Fold the ends over inward. Carefully fold the top portion of the dough over the filling, creating a long cylindrical roll.

BRUSH AN area on the parchment paper the same size as the strudel with butter. Using 2 spatulas, transfer the strudel to the baking pan, placing it seam side down on the buttered area; be careful not to break the strudel. Brush the entire strudel with butter. Cut 3 small diagonal slits in the top of the strudel with a sharp knife to let the steam escape while cooking.

PLACE IN the oven and bake for 25 to 30 minutes, or until the pastry is a light golden brown. Remove from the oven and place on a rack to cool for about 5 minutes.

TO SERVE, cut the warm strudel into 2-inch slices with a serrated or bread knife. Garnish with the cilantro sprigs.

VARIATION

Vegetable Strudel Packets

MAKES 12 PACKETS

After brushing the phyllo dough with butter and stacking it, cut the dough into twelve 4-inch squares. Divide the vegetable filling among the squares and fold over the sides and then the top and bottom of each square to make a packet. Place seam side down on a baking sheet lined with buttered parchment paper, brush with butter, and bake for 15 to 20 minutes, or until the pastry is light golden brown.

Grilled Muffaletta with Provolone

The muffaletta is said to have originated in New Orleans at the Central Grocery Company on Decatur Street, near the farmer's market in the French Quarter. When I was growing up, we took a family trip to New Orleans each summer. It was always hot and steamy, but somehow or other it seemed a little cooler down in the French Quarter. I vividly remember the dark, cool recesses of the Central Grocery, where we always stopped to buy muffalettas. The store was full of wonderfully exotic smells that we didn't have at home in Fort Worth. It seemed very foreign and wondrous!

The muffaletta is a round hero-type sandwich with an olive salad dressing. It is usually served at room temperature, but I find it even more delicious when the sandwich is flattened and grilled.

MAKES ABOUT 1¼ CUPS SALAD
SERVES 4 TO 6

OLIVE SALAD

½ cup chopped, pitted green olives

¼ cup chopped pimientos

2 tablespoons chopped bottled cherry peppers or fresh Anaheim chiles

2 tablespoons chopped cauliflower

2 tablespoons minced celery

1 tablespoon minced onion

½ teaspoon minced garlic

3 tablespoons finely chopped capers

½ to 1 teaspoon crushed dried oregano

3 tablespoons extra virgin olive oil

1½ tablespoons red wine vinegar

¼ teaspoon freshly ground black pepper

MUFFALETTA

1 (6- to 8-inch) round loaf soft-crusted Italian bread, or a long oval loaf

2 to 4 ounces Genoa salami, thinly sliced

4 ounces deli-style baked ham, thinly sliced

4 ounces provolone, thinly sliced

1 tablespoon extra virgin olive oil

FOR THE Olive Salad, mix the olives, pimientos, peppers, cauliflower, celery, onion, garlic, capers, and oregano together in a small bowl. Add the olive oil and vinegar and toss to mix. (This can be done in the work bowl of a food processor fitted with a steel blade, but be careful not to chop the mixture too fine.) Season with the pepper. Let the salad marinate at room temperature for at least 30 minutes, or cover and refrigerate for up to 1 week; bring to room temperature before proceeding.

FOR THE Muffaletta, slice the bread horizontally in half. Spread the cut sides lightly with olive salad. Layer the salami, more olive salad, the provolone, more olive salad, and then the ham on the bottom. Place the other half of the bread on top to form a giant sandwich.

HEAT A cast-iron skillet or a ridged griddle pan over medium heat. Brush both sides of the sandwich with the oil. Place the sandwich in the skillet and weight it down with another skillet or heavy pan. Cook over medium-low heat until the bottom of the bread is nicely toasted brown. Turn the sandwich over using a spatula, place the heavy weight back on top, and grill until the second side is toasted. Check to see if the cheese in the center of the sandwich has melted. If not, turn the heat to low and continue to toast the sandwich, turning frequently, until the cheese begins to melt.

REMOVE THE sandwich and cut it into 4 to 6 wedges. Serve warm.

Cheese is probably the friendliest of foods. It endears itself to everything and never tires of showing off to great advantage.

–James Beard

Portobello Mushrooms Stuffed with Crabmeat and Fontina on Field Greens

Wonderful lump crabmeat is found all along the Gulf Coast. Years ago, we used to go crabbing down in southern Louisiana. We would drop strings with bacon tied to the ends off low bridges down into the murky waters of the bayou. Soon a giant crab would come along and grab onto the bacon, and then we'd quickly hoist it up and put it in a big crab pot. Once we had enough crabs for a feast we'd go back to the house, boil them, spread out newspapers on the tables, crack the crabs open with hammers, and pick out the delicious sweet meat. It's much easier to just buy lump crabmeat, but not nearly so much fun.

I'm crazy about portobello mushrooms. They have great woodsy flavor and a great dense texture. Because their caps are so big, they are fabulous for stuffing.

SERVES 4

4 large portobello mushrooms

½ cup extra virgin olive oil, or more if needed *[handwritten: DOUBLE SEPARATELY]*

1 tablespoon red wine vinegar *[handwritten: 2ND BATCH IS DRESSING FOR GREENS]*

~~2~~ 1 clove garlic, minced

~~2~~ 1 tablespoon minced shallots

CRABMEAT FILLING

~~7~~ ~~8~~ 6 ounces lump crabmeat *[handwritten: (2½–3C IF DOUBLING)]*

6 tablespoons heavy cream

Grated zest of ½ lemon

¼ teaspoon freshly squeezed lemon juice

Salt and freshly ground pepper to taste

2 to 3 tablespoons minced fresh chives

4 ounces Italian Fontina, thinly sliced *[handwritten: 12 LONG SLICES FOR 8 SHROOMS]*

Paprika, for garnish

4 ounces mixed field greens, washed and dried (about 4 cups)

4 lemon wedges, for garnish (optional)

[handwritten: BRUSH MUSHROOMS]

REMOVE THE stems from the mushrooms. ~~With the back of a knife or a spoon, scrape the dark gills from the mushrooms. Quickly rinse the mushroom caps under cold running water and drain on paper towels.~~

[handwritten: IMMERSION BLENDER JOR –]

MIX THE olive oil, vinegar, garlic, and shallots in a ~~small bowl~~. Place the mushrooms in a shallow dish and spoon or brush on the marinade. Set aside to marinate for 15 minutes.

PREHEAT THE broiler or a grill to high. Adjust the rack so that it is 3 inches from the heat source.

REMOVE THE mushrooms from the dressing with a slotted spoon or tongs and reserve the remaining dressing for the salad.

BROIL OR grill the caps, gill side down, for 2 minutes. Turn and cook for 2 minutes longer, or until beads of liquid appear and the mushrooms are limp. Remove and set aside.

FOR THE Crabmeat Filling, pick over the crab to separate it into chunks and to check for any remaining shell or cartilage. Place the cream, lemon zest, and juice in a small saucepan. Heat to a boil over medium heat and reduce the cream by half. Remove from the heat and cool. (IN FRIDGE)   `AROUND 10-12 MINUTES`

TOSS THE crabmeat in the cooled lemon cream. Season with salt and pepper and the chives.

PREHEAT THE oven to 350°F. Lightly butter a small baking dish that will hold the mushroom caps in 1 layer.

PLACE THE mushroom caps upside down in the baking dish. Divide the filling among the mushroom caps. Top with the Fontina. Place in the oven and bake for 15 minutes, or just long enough to heat the filling and melt the cheese. Remove and sprinkle with paprika. *ANY LEFTOVERS*
MIX UP 2ND BOTTLE OF OLIVE OIL, VINEGAR, GARLIC + SHALLOT FOR DRESSING - ADD FROM BROILING
TOSS THE field greens with the remaining mushroom marinade, adding a little more oil if necessary.

TO SERVE, divide the salad among four serving plates. Place a warm mushroom on the side of each salad. Garnish with the lemon wedges, if desired.

Steve's Famous Asiago–Angel Hair Crab Cakes

Steve Bugiarelli is a very creative chef who lives in Dallas. He is famous for these crab cakes, and rightly so. He binds them with angel hair pasta and cheese rather than the traditional bread crumbs and cream. They are rich and delicious, and the sautéed pasta is wonderfully crunchy on the edges.

These can be formed into tiny silver-dollar–sized cakes or made larger. They make a great lunch or dinner accompanied by a green salad.

MAKES ¾ CUP AÏOLI
MAKES 10 (3-INCH) CRAB CAKES
SERVES 3 TO 4

SUN-DRIED TOMATO AÏOLI

5 cloves garlic

½ teaspoon salt, or to taste

6 dry-packed sun-dried tomato halves, plumped in hot water for 10 minutes and drained

3 very fresh large egg yolks

¾ cup extra virgin olive oil

5 teaspoons freshly squeezed lemon juice

CRAB CAKES

Salt

¼ pound fresh angel hair pasta

1 teaspoon extra virgin olive oil

2 tablespoons minced garlic or shallots

2 eggs, lightly beaten

¼ cup Dijon mustard

¼ cup thinly sliced scallions

Freshly ground black pepper to taste

8 ounces Asiago or Parmigiano-Reggiano, grated (2 cups)

1 tablespoon unbleached all-purpose flour

⅓ cup diced red bell pepper

8 ounces lump crabmeat, picked through for shells and cartilage

About ½ cup olive or vegetable oil

FOR THE Sun-dried Tomato Aïoli: The aïoli can be made by hand in the traditional way using a mortar and pestle or it can be made in a blender.

TO MAKE the aïoli by hand, place the garlic and salt in a mortar and, using the pestle, mash them to a paste. Add the tomatoes one by one, continuing to mash the ingredients with the pestle. Add the egg yolks one at a time, mashing until well incorporated after each addition. Drizzle in the oil drop by drop until the mixture begins to thicken. Transfer the mixture into a small bowl, switch from the pestle to a whisk, and gradually whisk in the remaining olive oil. Finally, whisk in the lemon juice and adjust the seasonings to taste.

TO MAKE the aïoli in a blender, place the garlic and salt in the blender container and finely chop the garlic. Add the tomatoes and blend to a paste. Add the egg yolks one by one, blending well after each addition. With the motor running, add the oil very slowly through the opening in the top. As the oil is absorbed the sauce will become thick and emulsified. Continue until all the oil is added, scraping down the sides as necessary. Drizzle in the lemon juice and blend to incorporate. Adjust the seasonings.

SERVE AT room temperature, within a short period of time. (The aïoli can be stored in the refrigerator only for a couple of days.)

FOR THE Crab Cakes, fill a large pot with water and bring to a boil over high heat. Add 1 teaspoon salt. Add the pasta to the rapidly boiling water, stir vigorously, and cook for 2 to 3 minutes or until slightly undercooked and very al dente. Drain the pasta; do not rinse the pasta or toss it with oil, as the starch on the pasta acts as the binder for the crab cakes. Place the pasta in a large bowl.

WHILE THE pasta is cooking, heat the olive oil in a very small skillet and sauté the garlic over medium heat for 1 to 2 minutes, or until soft.

PLACE THE garlic, eggs, mustard, scallions, and salt and pepper to taste in a small bowl and whisk to blend. Pour over the pasta. Add the cheese, flour, red pepper, and crabmeat. Mix to evenly combine all the ingredients. Clean hands are the best mixing utensils for this step; if using a spoon, look carefully to see that the crabmeat is distributed.

PLACE A large nonstick skillet over medium heat and heat ¼ cup of the oil. Scoop out a heaping ¼ cup of the pasta/crabmeat mixture and place in the skillet. Using a spatula, shape it into a round cake about 2½ to 3 inches in diameter and about ½ inch high. Push any loose strands of pasta into the crab cake with a spatula and smooth the top and sides. Add 1 or 2 more crab cakes to the pan, depending on the size of the skillet. Cook for 3 minutes on one side, or until crisp and golden brown. Turn the crab cakes and cook for an additional 2 to 3 minutes, or until lightly browned on both sides. Remove the crab cakes as they are cooked and drain on paper towels. Finish cooking the crab cakes, adding more oil as necessary.

SERVE HOT, accompanied by the aïoli.

NOTE: It's generally safe to use raw eggs in your recipes, as long as they are very fresh, grade A or AA, and have been properly refrigerated. There is, however, a slight risk of *Salmonella enteritidis* and other illnesses related to the consumption of raw eggs. I have made this recipe many, many times without any problem, but if you want to be absolutely safe you can either cook the egg yolks over a hot water bath or in a double boiler to a temperature of 145°F. or substitute pasteurized eggs (sold in the grocer's refrigerated dairy case) for the raw eggs in this recipe. As a precaution, pregnant women, babies, young children, the elderly, and all those whose health is compromised should always avoid raw eggs.

Light Feta Tacos

The markets in Mexico are, for me, the heart of the country, with all the wonderful women who come in from the countryside in their colorful attire to sell foods they have painstakingly prepared at home—giant tamales cooked in banana leaves, handmade tortillas, and all manner of fruit and vegetable dishes. The tacos, usually found at stands arranged like little open-air cafés complete with brightly painted tables and chairs, are always fresh and cooked to order.

My version contains feta and chipotle chiles, which are smoked jalapeños. They have heat and a smoky flavor. They are available dried and canned. When they are canned, they are packed in a red chile sauce called *adobo*. You can easily find them in the Mexican section of your supermarket.

SERVES 4

8 ounces mushrooms (portobello, shiitake, oyster, or a mixture), trimmed (stems removed if using shiitakes)

2 tablespoons chile-flavored oil or olive oil

2 poblano chiles

½ medium white onion, thinly sliced

8 lettuce leaves, washed and dried

2 ripe tomatoes, cut into 16 thin slices

1 avocado, peeled, pitted, and cut into 16 thin slices

8 ounces feta, cut into 8 slices

8 (6-inch) corn tortillas

Salt to taste

2 chipotle chiles in adobo, cut into thin strips, for garnish (optional)

4 sprigs fresh cilantro, for garnish

HEAT A gas or charcoal grill or the broiler.

BRUSH THE mushrooms with the oil and grill or broil, turning once, until browned on both sides. Remove, cut into thin slices, and set aside on a plate.

PLACE THE poblano chiles on the grill or under the broiler and roast, turning, until the skins blacken on all sides. Place in a bowl, cover with plastic wrap, and allow to steam until cool. Remove the skins, stems, and seeds and discard. Cut into thin strips and set aside on the plate with the mushrooms.

PLACE THE sliced onion in a colander, rinse under cold water, and shake well to drain. Place on paper towels and pat dry, then place on the plate with the mushrooms. Place the lettuce leaves, tomatoes, avocado, and feta in piles on another plate close by.

HEAT A medium skillet or griddle over medium heat. One at a time, place the tortillas in the dry skillet and warm on each side until they become pliable. Transfer to a work surface.

Place a lettuce leaf on each tortilla and top it with 2 tomato slices, a few strips of mushrooms and poblano, a few onion slices, 2 avocado slices, and a slice of cheese. Sprinkle with salt and roll up into a tube. Secure with a toothpick if necessary.

TO SERVE, place 2 tacos on each serving plate. Garnish with the chipotle chiles, if using, and sprigs of cilantro. Serve immediately.

It's not the fault of the mouse, but of the one who offers him the cheese.

–Mexican proverb

Ricotta-Potato Tacos with Charred Tomato Salsa

We often have potluck luncheon banquets at the cheese factory. We put tables together, cover them with flowered oilcloth tablecloths, and surround the table with chairs. Then we put all the food out boardinghouse-style on brightly colored platters. Because we are busy making cheese, we have to wait for just the right moment when we can leave the cheese and dash in for lunch. We play the radio, eat all the wonderful foods that everyone has brought, and have a grand time.

My idea for these tacos came from Octavia Flores, who is not only an expert cheesemaker but also a great cook. The tacos are perfect for a light supper. Made in miniature sizes, they are an unusual hors d'oeuvre.

MAKES 2 CUPS SALSA
SERVES 4

CHARRED TOMATO SALSA
3 tomatoes

1 jalapeño chile (for a mild salsa) or 2 jalapeños (for a hot salsa)

1 medium onion, unpeeled

¼ teaspoon salt, or to taste

½ to 2 teaspoons freshly squeezed lime juice

1 tablespoon coarsely chopped fresh cilantro

TACOS
2 tablespoons plus 1½ cups vegetable oil

2 large potatoes, boiled, peeled, and cut into ½-inch cubes (about 3 cups)

8 ounces ricotta, homemade (page 70) or store-bought, well drained (1 cup)

2 teaspoons fresh chopped epazote (see Note)

½ teaspoon salt, or to taste

Freshly ground black pepper to taste

12 (6-inch) corn tortillas

Toothpicks

4 sprigs fresh cilantro, for garnish

FOR THE Charred Tomato Salsa, preheat the broiler.

Place the tomatoes, jalapeño, and onion on a rimmed baking sheet and broil, turning as the vegetables blacken, until they are charred on all sides. Remove, place in a small bowl, and cover with plastic wrap.

ONCE THE vegetables have cooled, peel off the blackened skins and discard. Remove the core from the tomatoes, halve them, and squeeze out the juice. Stem and seed the jalapeño.

Place the onion and jalapeño in the work bowl of a food processor fitted with a steel blade and pulse until coarsely chopped. Add the tomatoes and pulse to the desired consistency, chunky or smooth. Pour into a small serving dish and stir in the salt, lime juice, and cilantro. Adjust the seasonings and set aside.

FOR THE Tacos, heat 2 tablespoons of the oil in a large nonstick skillet over medium-high heat. Add the potatoes and sauté until browned on all sides. Remove from the heat, transfer to a bowl, and allow to cool.

ADD THE ricotta, epazote, salt, and pepper to the potatoes. Adjust the seasonings if necessary.

POUR THE remaining 1½ cups vegetable oil into a large skillet and heat until hot but not smoking, about 350°F. One by one, using tongs, quickly dip the tortillas into the hot oil to soften them. Place on paper towels to drain. Remove the oil from the heat and set aside for later use.

PAT THE tortillas with paper towels to remove the excess oil. Lay 1 tortilla on a work surface and fill with a little less than ¼ cup of the potato/ricotta mixture. Fold the tortilla in half to form a half moon and secure with toothpicks to enclose the filling. Repeat with the remaining tortillas and filling.

RETURN THE skillet of oil to medium-high heat and heat until the oil is hot but not smoking, about 350°F. Fry the tacos in batches, turning with tongs, for about 3 minutes on each side, or until crispy and browned. Remove and place on paper towels to drain.

SERVE THE tacos 3 per plate, with a pool of salsa on the side. (Leftover salsa can be stored in the refrigerator for several days.) Garnish with the cilantro.

Note: Epazote is a Mexican herb with a pungent, somewhat medicinal flavor. Its dark green leaves are deeply serrated. If fresh epazote is not available, substitute 2 teaspoons chopped fresh oregano.

VARIATION

Taquitos

To make in a miniature size, cut about 24 tortillas into 3-inch rounds, using a cookie cutter. Fill each with 2 to 3 teaspoons of the potato mixture. Roll them into cigar shapes or fold into half moons, secure with toothpicks, and fry according to the above instructions.

Mushroom and Goat Cheese Enchiladas with Red Chile Salsa

Mexican food has really changed in Texas in recent years. When I was growing up in Fort Worth, we always had dinner at The Original, a.k.a. The Mexican Eats, on Thursdays. They served things like cheese enchiladas, tacos, rice and beans . . . dishes now referred to as Tex-Mex or Border Food. In college, I discovered there was another style of Mexican food in Austin, still Tex-Mex but Austin-style. And my eyes were really opened when I first visited Mexico City in the early 1960s. There the food was completely different and had much more of a European influence.

Today we have all these types of Mexican food in Texas, plus more modern Mexican food in which high-quality ingredients are combined to create Nuevo Tex-Mex and Mexican cuisine. I would definitely classify these enchiladas as *nuevo*.

MAKES 2 CUPS SALSA
SERVES 4

RED CHILE SALSA

1 dried árbol chile

1 dried chipotle chile

1 dried ancho chile

1 clove garlic, minced

1 small onion, finely chopped (½ cup)

1 (14.5-ounce) can peeled whole tomatoes, with their juice

1 teaspoon dried oregano, preferably Mexican

¼ cup chopped fresh cilantro

2 tablespoons vegetable oil

Chicken broth, homemade (page 81) or store-bought (optional)

Salt and freshly ground black pepper to taste

ENCHILADAS

1 ounce dried wild mushrooms

2 tablespoons vegetable oil

1 clove garlic, minced

1 pint (8 ounces) cremini mushrooms, trimmed and sliced

Salt and freshly ground pepper to taste

8 (6-inch) corn tortillas

8 ounces (1 cup) fresh goat cheese

1 cup (8 ounces) crème fraîche, homemade (page 68) or store-bought, Mexican crema, or sour cream

FOR THE Red Chile Salsa, place the chiles in a dry skillet and toast quickly over medium heat until aromatic and slightly toasted, shaking the pan constantly and turning them so they do not burn. Place in a colander and rinse under cold running water. Place in a medium bowl, cover with hot water, cover with plastic wrap, and set aside to soak and rehydrate for 20 minutes.

DRAIN THE chiles. Remove the stems and seeds from the chiles and discard. Place the chiles in the work bowl of a food processor fitted with a steel blade, add the garlic, onion, tomatoes with their liquid, oregano, and cilantro. Pulse to a puree.

HEAT THE oil in a large skillet. Add the chile/tomato puree and cook over medium heat for 15 to 20 minutes, until slightly thickened. If the salsa becomes too dry, add a little chicken broth or water. Remove from the heat, add salt and pepper, and set aside.

MEANWHILE, FOR the Enchiladas, place the dried mushrooms in a small bowl, cover with hot water, and stir to clean them fully. Lift the mushrooms out of the water with a slotted spoon and discard the water. Replace the mushrooms in the bowl, cover with hot water again, cover with plastic wrap, and soak for 30 minutes.

REMOVE THE mushrooms from the soaking liquid with a slotted spoon, discard the liquid, and cut the mushrooms into strips. (There will be about 1 cup sliced mushrooms.) Set aside.

HEAT THE oil in a large sauté pan over medium-high heat. Add the garlic and fresh mushrooms and cook, stirring constantly, for about 7 minutes, or until the liquid has evaporated and the mushrooms are limp. Add the wild mushrooms and remove from heat. Season with salt and pepper. Set aside.

PREHEAT THE oven to 350°F. Grease a shallow 11 x 7-inch baking dish with vegetable oil.

TO ASSEMBLE the enchiladas, place the salsa in a skillet over low heat. Combine the goat cheese and ½ cup of the crème fraîche in a small bowl. Once the salsa simmers, quickly dip a tortilla completely into the salsa to moisten and soften it. Lay the tortilla on a work surface and place one-eighth of the mushrooms across the center. Crumble one-eighth of the goat cheese mixture on top. Roll up the tortilla into a tube shape and place seam side down in the baking pan. Repeat with the remaining tortillas, placing the enchiladas close together to keep them rolled. Drizzle the remaining salsa over the top of the enchiladas, then drizzle the remaining ½ cup crème fraîche over the top.

PLACE THE enchiladas in the oven and bake for 15 to 20 minutes, or until beginning to brown. Remove from the oven and serve immediately.

Stacked Enchiladas

You can stack the enchiladas instead of rolling them. Place a salsa-dipped tortilla on an oiled baking pan. Top with one-eighth of the mushrooms, then one-eighth of the goat cheese and some salsa. Repeat the layers, making a total of 4 layers. Make a second stack with the remaining ingredients. To finish, drizzle the stacks with the remaining salsa and then the remaining ½ cup crème fraîche. Bake as above. Cut each stack into 4 wedges, and serve 2 wedges per person. Serve immediately.

Asadero Enchiladas with Ancho-Allspice Salsa

Make the salsa as described above, adding 1 more ancho chile and seasoning the salsa with ½ teaspoon ground allspice. Shred 12 ounces Asadero, Chihuahua, Caciotta, or Monterey Jack (3 cups) and fill the moistened tortillas with it, reserving about ¼ cup of the cheese to sprinkle on the top. Roll into enchiladas and place in the baking dish. Drizzle with the remaining salsa and sprinkle with the reserved cheese. Bake as above. Remove from the oven, sprinkle with ½ cup minced onions, and garnish with avocado slices. Serve immediately.

To test salsa, drop some on the tablecloth. If it fails to burn a hole in the cloth, it is not a good sauce.
–South Texas kitchen saying

Cheese Fondue

In French, *fondue* means "melted sauce." As a dish, it is served in a deep little pot placed over a heat source to keep the cheese molten. Bread cubes are dipped into the communal pot using long-handled forks. Tradition has it that if you drop your bread into the dish, you must either buy the next bottle of wine or kiss your partner. This makes eating fondue lots of fun!

There are all sorts of secrets for a perfect fondue: Adding a touch of lemon juice keeps the cheese from being too stringy. Dredging the cheese in flour or cornstarch before it is added to the wine helps keep the cheese in the fondue emulsified. If you like, the garlic clove may be left in the pot. You can also add a dash or so of dry mustard to perk it up.

As for the dipping medium, bread cubes are traditional. I like to use French baguettes, but pumpernickel and rye are also good, as are steamed vegetables.

SERVES 6 AS A MAIN COURSE

1 clove garlic, cut in half

2 cups dry white wine, such as Alsatian Riesling or Gewürztraminer

1 pound Gruyère, shredded (4 cups)

1 pound Emmentaler, shredded (4 cups)

4 teaspoons cornstarch

2 to 3 tablespoons kirsch

1 teaspoon freshly squeezed lemon juice

Freshly grated nutmeg to taste

Freshly grated black pepper to taste

Bread cubes and/or steamed cut-up vegetables, such as carrots, broccoli, and cauliflower

RUB THE interior of the fondue pot or a flameproof ceramic pot with garlic, and leave it in the pot, if you like. Place the pot over medium heat and add the wine. Heat until it is almost but not quite boiling. In the meantime, toss the cheeses together with the cornstarch. Gradually add the cheese to the wine, one handful at a time, stirring vigorously after each addition until the cheese melts. Add the kirsch and lemon juice and stir well. Add the nutmeg and pepper to the fondue.

REMOVE THE fondue pot from the stove and place on its stand over a heat source at the table. The heat source should keep the fondue quite hot, almost simmering. Serve with cubed bread and/or steamed vegetables, with long-handled forks for dipping.

VARIATION

A combination of 8 ounces Gruyère and 8 ounces Appenzell can be used instead of the pound of Gruyère. Combine and add the first two cheeses, then add the Emmentaler.

Blue Cheese Quesadillas with Mango Salsa

The combination of tangy blue cheese and sweet mangoes is extraordinary! The rich, salty blue cheese complements the spicy, fruity, acidic flavors of the salsa. Each ingredient takes the other to new heights. If there is any salsa left over, it is great with charcoal-grilled chicken.

This dish typifies the New Texas Cuisine that Stephan Pyles and other Southwestern chefs have pioneered in recent years. Stephan is a master at combining flavors, and he often served dishes with ingredients such as these at his popular, well-known, and much lauded restaurants, Star Canyon in Dallas, Las Vegas, and Austin.

MAKES ABOUT 1½ CUPS SALSA
SERVES 4

MANGO SALSA

1 mango, peeled, pitted, and finely chopped

2 tablespoons finely chopped red onion

2 tablespoons finely chopped jicama or apple

2 tablespoons finely chopped red bell pepper

1 teaspoon (for a mild salsa) to
1 tablespoon (for a hot salsa) minced jalapeño chile

2 tablespoons minced fresh cilantro

2 tablespoons freshly squeezed lime juice

¼ teaspoon salt

QUESADILLAS

4 ounces Roquefort, crumbled (¾ cup)

4 ounces Monterey Jack or Caciotta, shredded (1 cup)

8 (8-inch) flour tortillas

4 sprigs fresh cilantro, leaves only

3 to 4 tablespoons vegetable oil

4 sprigs fresh cilantro, for garnish

¼ cup diced red bell pepper, for garnish

FOR THE Mango Salsa, place the mango in a medium bowl. Add the onion, jicama, bell pepper, jalapeño, cilantro, lime juice, and salt. Mix briefly to combine and set aside.

FOR THE Quesadillas, combine the blue cheese and Jack cheese. Lay 4 tortillas out on a work surface. Sprinkle an equal amount of cheese on each tortilla, spreading it to within ½ inch of the edges. Place one-fourth of the minced cilantro on top of each. Place the remaining tortillas on top to form quesadillas.

PREHEAT THE oven to 250°F.

HEAT AN 8- to 10-inch nonstick skillet over medium heat. Brush both sides of the quesadillas with oil, using about 2 tablespoons in all. Brush the pan with some of the remaining oil. Place 1 quesadilla in the pan and cook until golden brown on both sides, turning once. Remove to a baking sheet. Continue with the remaining quesadillas. Place quesadillas in the oven and heat for 5 to 10 minutes, until the cheese is melted and oozy.

TO SERVE, remove the quesadillas from the oven and cut each into quarters. Place 4 overlapping wedges on each individual heated serving plate. Top with 2 tablespoons of salsa. Garnish each with a sprig of cilantro and a sprinkling of bell pepper. Serve warm.

Majestic Roqueforts looking down with princely contempt upon the others, through the glass of their crystal covers.

—Émile Zola

Chiles Rellenos

The first time I had *chiles rellenos,* or Mexican stuffed peppers, was during my college years in Austin at El Rancho, a popular Tex-Mex restaurant. I loved them immediately because of the puffy fried exterior batter and the melted cheese inside. Since then I have tried many versions, from those filled with ground meat and raisins at Mia's in Dallas to even more elaborate and glorious versions, at wonderful restaurants such as Star Canyon in Dallas and Frontera Grill in Chicago. My favorites are still the plain and simple cheese-filled ones, like those served at Rosa Mexicano in New York City.

This recipe is similar to the version I learned to make from Concha Sanchez in Dallas. She taught me to patiently and continually splash the hot oil from the frying pan onto the top and sides of the egg white–coated chiles as they cook, the way a fried egg is basted sunny side up.

SERVES 4

Vegetable oil, for frying	¼ teaspoon ground allspice
4 small poblano chiles	4 large eggs, separated
4 large dried ancho chiles	Seasoning Salt (page 79) or store-bought
8 ounces Caciotta, Chihuahua, or Monterey Jack, cut into long strips about 2 inches by ½ inch	1 cup Paula's Tomato Sauce (page 84) or store-bought
8 ounces (1 cup) fresh goat cheese	⅓ cup coarsely chopped pitted green olives
½ cup unbleached all-purpose flour	Toothpicks

HEAT ABOUT 1½ inches of vegetable oil in a large skillet over medium heat. Meanwhile, make a small lengthwise slit about 2 inches long in the side of each poblano. Fry in the hot oil turning as necessary, until the chiles are beige all over. Remove with a slotted spoon or tongs and place on paper towels to drain. Set the skillet aside.

PEEL THE skin off the chiles when they are cool enough to handle. Carefully remove the seeds through the slits, leaving the stems intact. Set aside.

MAKE A similar small slit in the anchos. Place the chiles in a dry skillet and toast quickly over medium heat until aromatic and slightly toasted, shaking the pan and turning them so they do not burn. Place in a medium bowl, cover with hot water, then cover with plastic wrap, and set aside to soak and rehydrate for 20 minutes. Drain the chiles. Remove the seeds through the small slits, but leave the stems intact.

DIVIDE THE Caciotta into 4 parts. Place one-fourth inside each poblano chile, cutting to fit if necessary. Close the slits and secure with 1 or 2 toothpicks. Divide the goat cheese into 4 parts. Place one-fourth inside each of the anchos. Close the slits and secure with 1 or 2 toothpicks.

COMBINE THE flour and allspice on a plate or waxed paper. Using a whisk, beat the egg yolks with the seasoning salt in a medium bowl. Using an electric mixer or whisk, beat the egg whites in a clean bowl until stiff. Stir a spoonful of whites into the yolks to lighten them, then fold in the remaining whites using a rubber spatula.

HEAT THE reserved oil over medium heat until hot but not smoking, about 350°F. Test the temperature by dropping some of the egg mixture into the oil. It should sizzle and begin to brown. Dredge the chiles in the flour and pat to remove the excess. Dip 1 chile into the egg mixture, turning to coat it liberally on all sides, and carefully place in the hot oil. Repeat with the remaining chiles, but be careful not to crowd the pan: Cook the chiles in batches if necessary. If there's any left, spoon a little of the remaining egg batter on top of the chiles as soon as they are placed in the oil. Use a metal spatula to carefully splash hot oil onto the tops of the chiles while they are cooking, and carefully turn the chiles until all sides are golden brown. Remove the chiles and drain on paper towels.

WHILE THE chiles are cooking, heat the tomato sauce and add the olives.

TO SERVE, spoon 2 or 3 tablespoons of the sauce onto each heated serving plate. Place one of each type of chile relleno on the sauce. Serve immediately, accompanied by the remaining sauce.

Vegetables

Bell Peppers Stuffed with Rice, Ricotta, and Jarlsberg

Ever since I had my first apartment in Fort Worth with its postage stamp–sized garden in the back, I have grown vegetables and herbs. If you have ever had a garden, you know what it's like to have an overabundance of vegetables. That's what prompted me to come up with these stuffed peppers, which not only make a wonderful vegetable accompaniment to a meal but are also just perfect for a lunch or a light dinner.

SERVES 4

2 bell peppers, any color

1 tablespoon extra virgin olive oil

½ medium onion, chopped (½ cup)

1 clove garlic, minced

2 cups cooked rice

1 tablespoon drained capers

4 ounces ricotta, homemade (page 70) or store-bought, well drained (½ cup)

1 large egg, lightly beaten

Salt and freshly ground black pepper to taste

2 ounces Jarlsberg or Gruyère, shredded (½ cup)

PREHEAT THE oven to 375°F. Lightly oil a shallow 8-inch square baking pan.

CUT THE bell peppers crosswise in half. Scrape out the seeds and excess membranes, using a paring knife or a spoon, and discard. Cut off the stems and discard.

HEAT THE oil in a skillet over medium heat and sauté the onion and garlic for 5 minutes, or until soft. Remove from the heat. Add the rice, capers, ricotta, and egg, stir to mix, and season with salt and pepper.

USING A large spoon, stuff each of the pepper halves with one-fourth of the rice mixture, mounding it on top and patting it smooth. Place the stuffed peppers in the baking pan, one next to the other. Pour ½ cup of water around the peppers. Sprinkle the Jarlsberg over the top. Place in the oven and bake for 30 minutes, or until the peppers are cooked through and the Jarlsberg is beginning to brown. Remove from the oven.

SERVE HOT or at room temperature.

Roman Stuffed Artichokes

Castroville, on the Monterey Peninsula in California, is the world's capital of artichokes. As incredible as it may seem, more than three-fourths of all the world's artichokes are grown there. The climate is perfect and the growing conditions are optimum. From Castroville, artichokes are sent around the world.

When I visited Castroville, I saw a huge container being packed full of cases of artichokes and then filled with crushed ice. I was told that, once sealed, it would be sent on a ship across the Pacific Ocean to Japan, where it would arrive a month later with some of the ice still frozen. Doesn't it make you wonder about the age of some of the artichokes in your grocery store?

Artichokes are also grown abundantly in Italy. And they often figure as part of Roman cuisine squashed flat and fried, stuffed, roasted, boiled, grilled and served in countless other ways.

SERVES 4

1 lemon

4 artichokes

1 cup toasted fresh bread crumbs (or dry bread crumbs)

4 ounces Pecorino Romano, grated (1 cup)

1 tablespoon chopped fresh flat-leaf parsley

1 tablespoon chopped fresh cilantro

1 teaspoon dried oregano

2 tablespoons minced shallots

¼ teaspoon salt

¼ teaspoon freshly ground black pepper

¼ cup extra virgin olive oil

GRATE THE zest from the lemon and set aside. Halve and juice the lemon. Fill a large bowl with cold water and add the lemon juice plus the juiced lemon halves.

FIT A large saucepan with a steamer and add water to come to just below the steamer rack.

CUT THE stem off each artichoke and then cut 1 inch off the top. With kitchen scissors, trim the tips of the remaining leaves, placing each artichoke in the lemon water as it is trimmed. Transfer the artichokes and lemon halves to the steamer, place the pan over high heat, and bring to a boil. Reduce the heat, cover, and simmer for 30 minutes, or until the artichokes are just beginning to become tender. Remove from the heat and run cold water over the artichokes to cool them. Set the lemon halves aside.

REMOVE THE small leaves and the fuzzy choke in the center of each artichoke, using a sharp knife, a teaspoon, or a grapefruit spoon. As each artichoke is finished, place it upside down in a colander to drain.

PREHEAT THE oven to 375°F. Grease an 8-inch or 10-inch square baking pan with olive oil.

COMBINE THE bread crumbs, Pecorino, parsley, cilantro, oregano, shallots, ⅛ teaspoon of the salt, the pepper, and the lemon zest in a medium bowl. Open the leaves of the artichokes and spread the center of each artichoke apart. Fill each artichoke with one-fourth of the stuffing, allowing some of the mixture to fall between the leaves. Place the stuffed artichokes close together in the baking pan. Drizzle 1 tablespoon of olive oil over each artichoke. Add 1 cup water, the remaining ⅛ teaspoon salt, and the reserved lemon halves to the baking pan. Tightly cover the pan with aluminum foil and place on a baking sheet.

PLACE THE pan in the oven and bake for 30 to 45 minutes, or until the artichoke leaves are easily removed and the centers are tender when pierced with a knife. Remove from the oven.

SERVE THE artichokes warm. The leaves of the artichokes should be pulled out of the choke, one by one, and the tender flesh scraped off with your teeth. The fibrous tough leaves should be discarded and the bread crumb stuffing and the artichoke hearts should be eaten using a fork. It's messy, but delicious.

Carrot-Ricotta Pudding

When I began the Mozzarella Company, I arranged for a cheese professor to come from Italy to give us a crash course in cheesemaking. First we learned to make mozzarella, and next ricotta. The interesting thing about ricotta is that it is traditionally a by-product of mozzarella because it is made from the whey of the mozzarella curds. The cheese professor told us that ricotta contains all the noble properties of the milk—the vitamins and minerals and few of the fats and calories.

If you can find ricotta that is made in the traditional way, from whey, you should always buy it rather than ricotta made from whole or skim milk. Because ricotta made the this way is drained in baskets, it is drier and doesn't need to be drained before it is used, as does the kind sold in tubs.

This savory pudding is similar in texture to a fluffy custard. It is a wonderful accompaniment to roasted and grilled meats.

SERVES 4 TO 6

4 tablespoons (½ stick) unsalted butter

1 pound carrots, shredded or grated
(3 cups)

1 small onion, finely chopped (1 cup)

¼ teaspoon grated orange zest

2 tablespoons unbleached all-purpose
flour

1 cup milk, heated

½ cup heavy cream

2 large eggs

8 ounces ricotta, homemade (page 70) or
store-bought, well drained (1 cup)

¼ teaspoon ground nutmeg

Salt and white pepper to taste

PREHEAT THE oven to 375°F. Butter a deep round 1½- to 2-quart baking dish, about 6 to 8 inches in diameter.

MELT 2 tablespoons of the butter in a large skillet over medium heat. Add the carrots and onion and sauté for several minutes, or until soft. Add the orange zest and remove from the heat.

MELT THE remaining 2 tablespoons butter in a heavy medium saucepan over low heat. When the foam subsides, stir in the flour and cook over low heat for 3 minutes, stirring constantly. Add the milk and cook over medium heat for 3 to 4 minutes, stirring constantly. Stir in the cream and cook for 3 minutes, stirring constantly. Remove from the heat.

BEAT THE eggs in a small bowl with the ricotta, nutmeg, and salt and white pepper. Slowly add to the sauce, stirring constantly. Add the carrots and onion and stir to combine. Adjust the seasoning if necessary.

POUR THE carrot mixture into the baking dish. Set the dish in a large shallow baking pan and pour boiling water to come halfway up the sides of the baking dish. Place the pan in the oven and bake for 45 minutes to 1 hour, or until the pudding is puffed and golden brown on top. Remove the pudding from the oven.

SERVE IMMEDIATELY.

To recognize good cheese:
Not at all like Helen,
Nor weeping, like Magdalene.
Not Argus, but completely blind,
And heavy, like a buffalo.
Let it rebel against the thumb,
And have an old moth-eaten coat.
Without eyes, without tears, not at all
  white,
Moth-eaten, rebellious, of good weight.
—*Le Ménagier de Paris* (c. 1400)

Eggplant Parmigiana Towers

In this Eggplant Parmigiana, the eggplant is stacked into individual mini-towers rather than being layered in a baking dish. Also, the eggplant is broiled rather than fried, so it is much faster to make and less greasy than the classic recipe.

Eggplant is a very Mediterranean vegetable. It's found in dishes from Spain to France, Italy, and Greece. The secret to cooking eggplant is to sprinkle it with salt, to draw out all the bitter juices before it is cooked.

SERVES 6

1 large eggplant

Salt to taste

About ¼ cup extra virgin olive oil

1 pound fresh mozzarella, thinly sliced

1½ to 2 cups Paula's Tomato Sauce (page 84) or store-bought

18 leaves fresh basil

1 ounce Parmigiano-Reggiano, grated (¼ cup)

CUT THE eggplant crosswise into slices about ¼ inch thick; you will need a total of 18 slices. Sprinkle with salt on both sides. Place in a colander in the sink or over a bowl to drain for 30 minutes.

PREHEAT THE broiler or a grill to high. Adjust the rack so that it is 3 inches from the heat source.

RINSE THE eggplant slices with cold water, place on paper towels to drain, and pat dry. Brush or spray on one side with olive oil. To broil, place on a baking sheet in a single layer, oiled side up, and broil for about 5 minutes, or until the slices are limp and golden brown. Turn over, brush or spray the other side with oil, and continue to cook until golden brown. Or, if grilling, start with the oiled side down, and brush the slices with oil before turning over. Place the eggplant slices on a plate.

PREHEAT THE oven to 350°F. Lightly oil a shallow baking pan.

TO MAKE the individual stacks, place 1 slice of eggplant in the pan. Top with 1 slice of mozzarella, 1 tablespoon of tomato sauce, and 1 basil leaf. Repeat the layering, leaving the basil off the top layer. Repeat the process to make 5 more stacks.

PLACE THE pan in the oven and bake for 10 to 15 minutes, or until the eggplant is tender and the cheese is just beginning to melt. Remove from the oven and sprinkle with the Parmigiano.

PREHEAT THE broiler to high and place the pan under the broiler. Broil for 3 minutes, or until the Parmigiano is golden brown and bubbling. Remove and let stand for 5 minutes. Reheat the remaining sauce to serve on the side, if desired.

TO SERVE, place 1 stack on each serving plate. Top each with a basil leaf. Serve warm or at room temperature, with the additional sauce on the side, if desired.

In baiting a mouse trap with cheese,
always leave room for the mouse,

–Saki

Baked Fennel Parmigiano

Fennel is very popular in Italy, but I had never heard of it until I lived there. I was crazy about it the first time I tried it; I loved its anise flavor.

Soon after I first tasted fennel, I decided to buy some for a salad. I vaguely remembered that the fennel was mixed with onions in the salad I had enjoyed. Although I didn't know the Italian word for onion, I looked for some at the market. Once back in my apartment, I prepared the salad with the fresh tiny bulbs of the green onions I had found and the fennel and dressed it with olive oil and lemon juice. I couldn't wait to try it, but when I tasted the salad, it seemed much stronger than I remembered. That evening, an Italian friend whom I had invited for dinner told me that I had bought fresh garlic rather than onions and that the salad was completely inedible!

I've learned a lot since then, and I'm sure you'll enjoy this fennel recipe much more.

SERVES 4 TO 6

BÉCHAMEL SAUCE
3 tablespoons unsalted butter

3 tablespoons unbleached all-purpose flour

1½ cups milk, heated

1 clove garlic, peeled

½ teaspoon salt

¼ teaspoon freshly ground black pepper

½ teaspoon ground nutmeg

4 fennel bulbs

½ teaspoon salt

2 ounces Parmigiano-Reggiano, grated (½ cup)

2 tablespoons unsalted butter

FOR THE Béchamel Sauce, melt the butter in a small saucepan over medium heat. When the foam begins to subside, stir in the flour and cook for 2 minutes. Slowly add the milk, stirring constantly. Add the garlic, reduce the heat to low, and simmer for 5 minutes, stirring to prevent scorching. Remove the garlic clove and discard. Stir in the salt, pepper, and nutmeg. Cover and set aside.

PREHEAT THE oven to 350°F. Butter a 10-inch gratin pan or 11 x 7-inch baking pan.

PEEL AWAY the distressed outer layer of the fennel bulb, cut off green stalks, and discard. Cut the fennel bulb lengthwise into ½-inch-thick slices.

PLACE A medium saucepan of water over high heat and bring to a rapid boil. Add the salt and parboil the fennel for 3 minutes. Drain the fennel in a colander and rinse briefly with cold water to stop the cooking.

SPREAD A thin layer of sauce in the bottom of the prepared pan. Place half of the fennel in an overlapping layer on top of the sauce. Cover with a thin layer of sauce, sprinkle with ¼ cup of the Parmigiano, and dot with butter. Repeat with the remaining fennel, sauce, Parmigiano, and butter.

PLACE IN the oven and bake for 30 to 45 minutes, or until bubbling and golden brown on top.

SERVE HOT.

A corpse is meat gone bad. Well and what's cheese? Corpse of milk.

–James Joyce

Green Beans with Boursin

Boursin, the rich creamy cheese flavored with garlic and herbs, makes a quick and easy sauce for green beans or any other vegetable.

SERVES 4

1 pound green beans

¼ teaspoon salt

2 tablespoons extra virgin olive oil

1 small onion, thinly sliced

1 (5-ounce) package Boursin

2 tablespoons pimientos, cut into thin strips

2 thick slices bacon, cooked until crisp and chopped (optional)

REMOVE THE ends and any strings from the beans if necessary. Cut the larger beans into 2-inch lengths; leave the small beans whole.

PLACE THE beans in a medium saucepan, sprinkle with the salt, and barely cover with water. Place over high heat, bring to a boil, reduce the heat, and cook the beans until tender, about 7 to 12 minutes, depending on the size. Drain the beans in a colander. (If holding the beans for a period of time before finishing the dish, rinse them with cold water to stop the cooking and retain the green color.)

IN THE meantime, heat the olive oil in a large skillet over medium heat. Add the onion and sauté until tender and translucent, about 5 minutes.

ADD THE beans to the skillet. Add the Boursin and stir to melt the cheese. Add the pimientos and stir to distribute them.

TO SERVE, arrange in a serving dish and sprinkle the chopped bacon over the top, if desired. Serve warm.

VARIATION

Green Beans with Goat Cheese

Substitute an equal amount of fresh goat cheese for the Boursin.

Baked Vidalia Onions Smothered with Smoked Gouda

When Jim and I first married, we lived in Athens, Georgia. It was there that I was introduced to a wonderful sweet onion variety grown in the town of Vidalia in southern Georgia. The onions are so mild and sweet they can be eaten like an apple. Later I found that similar onions called Sweet 1015s are grown in Texas. Sweet Walla Walla onions are grown Washington, and sweet OSO onions come from Chile.

The inspiration for this recipe came from Agnes Albritton and Marguerite Perry, Jim's sisters, who live in Georgia. The onions are served whole, one to a person, for maximum effect. Gruyère or Jarlsberg can be substituted for the Gouda.

SERVES 4

4 large Vidalia onions or other sweet onions

4 chicken bouillon cubes

2 teaspoons freshly ground black pepper

2 teaspoons extra virgin olive oil

4 ounces smoked Gouda, cut into 4 slices

PREHEAT THE oven to 350°F. Lightly grease a small baking pan, about 8 inches square, with butter.

SLICE OFF ¼ inch from the top and bottom of each onion. Using a sharp paring knife, remove and discard the center core of each onion, forming a cavity about ½ inch wide but leaving the bottom intact. Place the onions in the baking pan; they should be touching each other. Place a bouillon cube, ½ teaspoon pepper, and ½ teaspoon olive oil in each onion. Cover the baking pan tightly with aluminum foil and place on a baking sheet.

PLACE IN the oven and bake for 1½ hours, or until the onions almost collapse and are very tender when tested with the tip of a knife. Remove the pan and remove the foil.

PREHEAT THE broiler to high. Adjust the rack so that the onions will be 3 inches below the heat source.

TOP EACH onion with a slice of Gouda. Place the pan under the heat and broil for 3 minutes, or until the cheese is bubbly and beginning to brown. Remove from the broiler.

SERVE IMMEDIATELY.

Garlicky Goat Cheese Potatoes

In Italy, potatoes are often cooked and served with olive oil rather than butter. At first I thought this was rather peculiar, but I have grown to love the flavor combination. Here, I have combined olive oil with roasted garlic and goat cheese to flavor mashed potatoes. The amount of goat cheese will depend on how flavorful the cheese that you use is as well as on how pronounced you want the goat cheese flavor to be.

It is very important to keep the potatoes warm until they are whipped with the milk and cheese, or they will become pasty. If you intend to serve these potatoes to company and don't want to be in the kitchen whipping the potatoes at the last moment, you can prepare them ahead of time and then bake them in a large shallow ceramic dish at 400°F. for about 20 to 30 minutes just before serving. They brown beautifully and come out of the oven puffy, airy, and light, with the most marvelous crust on top.

SERVES 4 TO 6

3 heads garlic cloves, separated but not peeled

½ cup extra virgin olive oil

2½ pounds Yukon Gold or new potatoes

Salt

¾ cup milk, plus extra if needed

4 to 6 ounces (½ to ¾ cup) fresh goat cheese, softened (see introduction to recipe)

Freshly ground black pepper to taste

PREHEAT THE oven to 350°F.

PLACE THE unpeeled garlic cloves in a small ovenproof container and cover with the olive oil. Cover with a lid or aluminum foil. Place in the oven and roast for 20 minutes, or until the cloves are tender when tested with the tip of a knife. Remove the garlic cloves and place on a plate to cool. Strain the olive oil and set aside for later use. Squeeze the roasted garlic out of the skins when cool enough to handle. Puree the garlic by chopping and smashing it with the blade and side of a knife, or with a mortar and pestle.

MEANWHILE, PEEL the potatoes and cut them into 2-inch pieces. (There will be about 8 cups of potatoes.) Place them in a large saucepan. Add enough water to cover the potatoes by 1 inch. Sprinkle with 1 teaspoon salt, place the pan over high heat, and bring to a boil. Reduce the heat, cover the saucepan with a lid placed slightly ajar, and simmer the potatoes for 20 to 30 minutes, or until tender when pierced with the tip of a knife.

COMBINE THE milk and goat cheese in a small saucepan and heat to a simmer, stirring until there are no lumps.

WHEN THE potatoes are cooked, drain them, return them to the pan, and place in the still-warm oven, uncovered, to dry out for 10 minutes.

REMOVE THE POTATOES from the oven and pass them, along with the garlic, through a potato ricer or a food mill fitted with the fine disk. Alternatively, the potatoes can be whipped using an electric mixer. Add the reserved garlic oil and the goat cheese–milk mixture and whip the potatoes with a mixer or by hand, adding additional milk if too dry. Reheat, covered, over very low heat if necessary.

SERVE HOT.

A cheese may disappoint. It may be dull, it may be naïve, it may be oversophisticated. Yet it remains cheese, milk's leap toward immortality.

–Clifton Fadiman

Potatoes au Gratin with Brie and Chervil

Debbie Ryan and I have been friends all our lives. When my family moved to Spanish Trail in Fort Worth in 1949, she lived across the street, and we met the very day I moved in. We went all through school together, shared an apartment after college, and were bridesmaids in each other's weddings. Today we both live in Dallas, where Debbie, a wonderful cook, often invites friends over for dinner. These potatoes fit right in with her style of cooking, and are perfect for entertaining.

SERVES 6

2 pounds Yukon Gold or russet potatoes

Salt

12 ounces Brie

¼ cup chopped fresh chervil

Freshly ground black pepper to taste

½ cup chicken broth, homemade (page 81) or store-bought, plus extra if needed

1 teaspoon unsalted butter

PREHEAT THE oven to 400°F. Butter a shallow 2-quart baking dish.

PEEL THE potatoes and cut them into ½-inch cubes. (You will have about 5 cups.) Place in a large saucepan and cover with cold water by 1 inch. Add 1 teaspoon salt. Place the pan over high heat and bring to a boil. Reduce the heat and simmer for 5 minutes. Drain the potatoes in a colander.

MEANWHILE, CUT the rind off the Brie and discard. Cut the cheese into ¼-inch-thick slices. Set aside.

PUT THE potatoes in the baking dish, add the chervil, and season with salt and pepper. Toss the potatoes with the seasonings and spread out in the dish. Place the cheese on top of the potatoes. Pour the chicken broth over the potatoes.

PLACE THE baking dish in the oven and bake for 20 minutes. Check the liquid surrounding the potatoes and add additional broth if the potatoes look too dry. Reduce the heat to 350°F. and bake for 40 minutes longer, or until the top is golden brown and the potatoes are soft. Remove from the oven and let rest for 5 minutes before serving.

Peas with Minted Mascarpone

Peas are the perfect springtime vegetable. At the Farmers' Market in Dallas, there are stands where you can have your peas shelled while you wait. This is a luxury to which I readily succumb and gladly pay extra for the privilege.

In Italy, peas are often served with pasta. One of my favorite dishes is fettuccine with peas and prosciutto. You could easily serve these peas over pasta, and even add prosciutto if that suits your fancy.

SERVES 4

2 cups freshly shelled peas or
1 (10-ounce) package frozen peas

¼ cup chicken broth, homemade
(page 81) or store-bought

1 clove garlic, peeled (optional)

Salt and freshly ground black pepper to
taste

4 ounces (½ cup) mascarpone, homemade (page 73) or store-bought

2 tablespoons chopped fresh mint

PLACE THE peas in a small saucepan and add the chicken broth and garlic if using. Place over high heat, bring to a boil, reduce the heat, and simmer for 3 to 5 minutes, or until the peas are tender. The liquid should be reduced to about 1 tablespoon; if not, increase the heat and reduce the broth accordingly. Remove the pan from the heat, discard the garlic clove, if you used it, season with salt and pepper, and stir in the mascarpone and mint.

AS SOON as the cheese has melted, serve the peas.

Scalloped Sweet Potatoes with Leeks and Blue Cheese

After my father died, Jim, my mother, and I began a tradition of spending Thanksgiving with our friends Peggy and Wayne Dear and their family. As the years have passed, we have spent Thanksgivings with them across the state: in Houston, Dallas, and on their ranch near Cleburne. Peggy prepares the turkey and most of the desserts herself. Guests often bring vegetable dishes and salads. It is truly a feast!

These sweet potatoes are perfect with turkey for Thanksgiving, with roasted and grilled meats, and even alone. They can be served directly from the baking dish if you use a pretty casserole, or cut into squares or diamond shapes and served on a platter.

SERVES 6

3 large sweet potatoes (2 pounds)

3 large leeks

4 tablespoons (½ stick) unsalted butter, cut into small pieces

Salt and freshly ground black pepper to taste

2 teaspoons minced fresh tarragon or 1 teaspoon dried tarragon

8 ounces Danish Blue cheese, crumbled (1½ cups)

1 cup milk

PEEL THE potatoes and slice about ⅛ inch thick, using a knife or a mandoline. Set aside.

CUT THE green tops off the leeks on a diagonal, to expose more of the interior white part, and discard. Cut the white part of the leeks diagonally into slices about ⅛ inch thick, discarding the root end. Plunge the leeks into a bowl of cold water. Lift the leeks from water with your hands, shake to remove excess water, and place in a colander to drain. Repeat several times to remove all the sand and grit. (There should be about 3½ cups leeks.)

PREHEAT THE oven to 325°F. Liberally butter a large shallow rectangular baking dish, about 11 x 7 x 2 inches.

OVERLAP ONE-THIRD of the potato slices in a layer over the bottom of the dish. Sprinkle with salt and pepper. Cover the potatoes with a layer of leeks, using half of them. Dot with butter and sprinkle on half of the tarragon. Distribute one-third of the blue cheese over the leeks. Add another layer of potatoes, top with the remaining leeks, and sprinkle with salt and pepper and the remaining tarragon. Dot with butter and crumble another one-third of the cheese on top. Finish with the remaining potatoes and cheese. Pour the milk over the potatoes and dot the top with the remaining butter.

PLACE THE dish in the oven and bake for 1 hour and 15 minutes, or until the cheese on top is golden brown. Remove from the oven and place on a rack to cool for 15 minutes.

SERVE HOT.

VARIATION

Scalloped White Potatoes with Leeks and Blue Cheese

Substitute russet or Yukon Gold potatoes for the sweet potatoes. Increase the baking time to 1½ hours.

Cheese is a mystery to most people, sort of like North Korea or automobile transmissions.

–Willie Gluckstern

Baked Manchego Tomatoes Provençal

At her house in Provence, Patricia Wells has a huge spreading tree in her backyard that over-looks the vineyards and Mont Ventoux. She often spreads brightly colored tablecloths on a long table under the tree, pulls up antique white iron chairs, places flowers from her garden and twin-kling candles on the table, and voilà, a perfect outdoor dining room! Her husband, Walter, has il-luminated the tree with lights hidden up among the branches, so that light filters down through the leaves onto the table, just like moonlight. It's an idyllic spot.

This dish is similar to the tomatoes that Patricia cooks in her outdoor brick oven. Since they are cooked for such a long time, they take on a very intense tomato flavor that is sweet, yet acidic at same time from the balsamic vinegar. Don't become alarmed that it takes so long to brown and caramelize the tomatoes in the skillet. Be patient. At first the juices come out of the tomatoes, then they cook away, and finally the tomatoes begin to brown.

SERVES 8

4 large vine-ripe tomatoes	Freshly ground black pepper to taste
2 tablespoons extra virgin olive oil	2 tablespoons balsamic vinegar
1 clove garlic, minced	2 tablespoons water
1 teaspoon dried herbes de Provence	2 ounces Manchego, grated (½ cup)
½ teaspoon salt	

CUT THE tomatoes crosswise into halves. Heat the olive oil in a large nonstick skillet over medium heat. Sprinkle the garlic into the pan and place the tomatoes cut side down on the garlic. Do not crowd the tomatoes. This step may be done in batches if necessary. Cook the tomatoes, shaking the pan occasionally so they do not stick, for 20 to 30 minutes, or until they are caramelized and browned on the cut side. Peek gently at the cut sides of the tomatoes with a spatula to monitor the color change.

MEANWHILE, PREHEAT the oven to 350°F.

REMOVE THE cooked tomatoes and place them, browned side up, in a shallow ceramic, terra-cotta, or glass baking dish just large enough to hold them snugly in one layer. Sprinkle with the herbes de Provence, salt, and pepper. Pour the balsamic vinegar and water into the sauté pan and cook for several minutes over low heat, scraping up any browned bits. Reduce the liquid by half. Drizzle the liquid over the tomatoes.

PLACE THE tomatoes in the oven and bake for 45 minutes. Remove from the oven and sprinkle the Manchego over the tomatoes. Return to the oven and bake for 15 minutes longer, or until the cheese begins to brown. Remove from oven.

SERVE WARM or at room temperature.

Caseus ille bonus quem dat avara manus.

(That cheese is good which is served with a sparing hand.)
–School of Salerno (c. 1000)

Layered Vegetable Gratin Provençal

This dish was inspired by the flavors of Provence, that magical part of France. It's a sun-kissed land full of rustic cooking, accented with fragrant herbs. The Provençal markets are legendary—brimming with fabulous produce, cheeses, herbs, flowers, fabrics, and more. Farmers come to town with homegrown vegetables that they set out to sell on wooden tables under brightly colored umbrellas. The markets tumble down the hilly village streets.

Each of the vegetables used in this dish figures strongly in the gastronomic landscape of Provence. Traditionally they come together in ratatouille, that quintessentially Provençal dish. In this gratin, they are layered instead as a terrine. The Gruyère not only binds the dish but gives it depth and dimension.

This intense and rich dish could easily be a vegetarian entrée. It can be served warm or at room temperature.

SERVES 6

2 large red bell peppers

2 large green bell peppers

½ cup plus 2 tablespoons extra virgin olive oil

1 eggplant, cut lengthwise into ¼-inch-thick slices

2 large zucchini, cut lengthwise into ¼-inch-thick slices

1 large onion, thinly sliced crosswise

2 cloves garlic, thinly sliced

Salt and freshly ground black pepper to taste

8 ounces Gruyère, shredded (2 cups)

20 leaves fresh basil

¼ heaping teaspoon dried herbes de Provence

PREHEAT THE broiler to high. Adjust the rack so that the vegetables will be 3 inches below the heat source.

PLACE THE bell peppers on a baking sheet and roast them under the broiler, turning, with tongs, until all sides, including the tops and bottoms, are blackened. Transfer to a bowl, cover tightly with plastic wrap, and let steam for 15 minutes. Remove the peppers from the bowl, cut lengthwise in half, and place on a plate to cool.

REMOVE THE blackened skins, seeds, and stems when the peppers are cool and discard. Cut the peppers lengthwise in half again so they are in quarters. Set aside.

MEANWHILE, POUR the ½ cup olive oil into a small bowl. Place the eggplant slices on a baking sheet. Using a pastry brush, brush both sides of the eggplant with oil. Place under the broiler and brown on both sides, turning as necessary. Remove from the broiler and set aside to cool.

REPEAT THE process with the zucchini.

HEAT THE remaining 2 tablespoons olive oil in a large skillet over medium-low heat. Add the onion, breaking the slices apart into rings, and sauté for 4 minutes. Add the garlic and sauté for about 15 minutes, or until the onions are caramelized and golden brown. Remove from the heat and set aside.

PREHEAT THE oven to 375°F. Oil an 11 x 7-inch ceramic or glass baking dish or a 10-inch square baking dish.

LIGHTLY SPRINKLE all of the vegetables with salt and pepper. Place all of the eggplant in a layer on the bottom of the baking dish. Sprinkle with a generous ⅓ cup of the Gruyère and 4 or 5 basil leaves torn into small pieces. Follow with a layer of the green bell peppers and sprinkle with another one-fifth of the Gruyère and 4 or 5 torn basil leaves. Continue in this fashion for the next layer of the zucchini, Gruyère, and basil, followed by the onions, Gruyère, and basil. Top with the red bell peppers and the remaining Gruyère. Sprinkle the herbes de Provence on top.

COVER THE dish tightly with foil and bake for 15 minutes. Uncover the dish and bake for another 15 minutes. Remove the gratin from the oven and allow to cool on a rack for 15 minutes.

TO SERVE, cut the gratin into slices. (The gratin can be chilled overnight and cut while cold. Bring back to room temperature or reheat before serving.)

SERVE WARM or at room temperature.

Bacon, Egg, and Cheddar Scones (page 287)

Sun-Dried Tomato and Basil Pesto Mascarpone Torta (page 108)

Portobello–Goat Cheese Napoleons (page 120)

**Ancho Chicken
Broth with
Goat Cheese-
Stuffed Squash
Blossoms**
(page 146)

**Frico Salad
with Fennel
and Orange**
(page 134)

Grilled Swordfish Steaks Stuffed with Pepper Jack (page 262)

Rack of Lamb

with Goat Cheese Crust (page 267)

Cornish Game Hens on Gorgonzola Polenta with Caramelized Onions (page 270)

Asiago-Stuffed Veal Roll (page 274)

Grilled Shrimp and Smoked Mozzarella Pizza (foreground) (page 200) and **Italian Sausage and Pepper Jack Pizza (background)** (page 201)

Light Feta Tacos (page 226)

Savory Herbed Cheesecake (page 96)

Apple Pie with Cheddar Crust (page 336)

Lace Cookies with Orange-Mascarpone Filling and Raspberries (page 322)

Cannoli Filled with Pistachio Ricotta (page 330)

Stilton and Tomato Tart (page 208)

Fish, Poultry, and Meat

Quick and Easy Chicken Breasts with Fresh Mozzarella

I have taught this recipe countless times in cooking classes. Students often tell me that they go straight home and cook it for dinner that evening. And years later, they will tell me that they use this recipe all the time and it is one of their family's favorites. I hope you'll like it just as much. The secret is to barely melt the mozzarella, until it is soft but not completely melted.

SERVES 4

4 large skinless, boneless chicken breasts (1½ pounds total)

Salt and freshly ground black pepper to taste

2 tablespoons unsalted butter

1 clove garlic

½ cup dry white wine

8 ounces fresh mozzarella, cut into 8 slices

4 sprigs fresh tarragon

WASH THE chicken and pat dry. Season the chicken breasts with salt and pepper. Melt the butter in a large skillet over medium heat. Add the garlic and chicken breasts and sauté for 6 to 10 minutes, or until the chicken is golden brown on both sides and almost cooked through, turning as necessary. Transfer to a plate and keep warm.

ADD THE wine to the pan, scraping to loosen any browned bits on the bottom, and simmer briefly to reduce to half its original volume. Return the chicken to the skillet and cook for 1 minute. Place 2 slices of fresh mozzarella and 1 sprig of tarragon on top of each chicken breast. Cover the pan, remove it from the heat, and set aside in a warm place for a few minutes to let the mozzarella soften and begin to melt. Sprinkle the chicken with additional salt or pepper as desired. Remove the garlic and discard.

TO SERVE, transfer the chicken to heated serving plates and spoon some of the sauce over it.

SERVE IMMEDIATELY.

Grilled Swordfish Steaks Stuffed with Pepper Jack

The swordfish in this dish is served with a zesty herb sauce that goes with everything from other fish to chicken to beef. Mixed with olive oil and vinegar, it makes a flavorful salad dressing, and it's even good stirred into mayonnaise as a dressing for vegetables.

The first time I tasted a sauce similar to this was one that Joyce Goldstein prepared many years ago at a wine festival in the Napa Valley. She told me it was Moroccan and that it was called *charmoula*.

In Italy, it's a big no-no to combine seafood and cheese, but this recipe proves the Italians wrong! The pepper Jack keeps the swordfish moist and tender, and the smooth, spicy cheese complements the fish.

MAKES ABOUT 1 CUP SAUCE
SERVES 4

HERB SAUCE

4 cloves garlic

½ cup tightly packed fresh flat-leaf parsley leaves

½ cup tightly packed fresh cilantro leaves

¼ cup freshly squeezed lemon juice

1 to 2 teaspoons ground cumin

¼ to ½ teaspoon cayenne pepper

Salt to taste

½ cup extra virgin olive oil

Freshly ground black pepper to taste

SWORDFISH

4 swordfish steaks, each 1 inch thick (2 pounds total)

8 ounces pepper Jack or Ancho Chile Caciotta (see Note), shredded (2 cups)

4 sprigs fresh cilantro, leaves only, plus 4 whole sprigs for garnish

2 tablespoons extra virgin olive oil

Seasoning Salt (page 79), or salt and freshly ground black pepper to taste

Toothpicks

FOR THE Herb Sauce, with the motor running, drop the garlic through the feed tube into the work bowl of a food processor fitted with a steel blade. Add the parsley and cilantro and pulse to finely chop the herbs. Add the lemon juice, cumin, cayenne, and salt and process to blend. With the motor running, drizzle the oil through the feed tube, and process until thickened and emulsified. Taste and adjust the seasonings. Set aside. (Refrigerate if the sauce will not be served within an hour or so; bring to room temperature before serving.)

FOR THE Swordfish, preheat a gas grill to high or build a hot fire with hardwood charcoal, charcoal briquettes, or wood and allow it to burn until the coals are covered in gray ash. Adjust the rack so that it is 3 to 4 inches from the heat source.

RINSE THE fish and pat dry. Cut a horizontal slit in the side of each steak to form a pocket. Stuff each steak with one-fourth of the cheese and one-fourth of the cilantro leaves. Secure the openings with toothpicks. Rub with oil on all sides and season liberally with the seasoning salt.

PLACE THE steaks on the grill, cover, and cook for about 3 minutes on each side. When done, the flesh of the fish should be opaque but not dry; it should flake when the tip of a knife is inserted and the cheese should be soft and beginning to melt. Spoon 2 tablespoons of the sauce onto each steak, spreading it out, cover, and cook for 1 minute.

TO SERVE, transfer the swordfish to a serving platter. Garnish with the sprigs of cilantro. Pass the remaining sauce in a bowl on the side.

Note: Ancho Chile Caciotta is available from the Mozzarella Company (see Sources, page 373).

Poached Salmon
with Feta Mayonnaise

The dining room of La Rosetta Hotel in Perugia was one of the best in town. It was no-nonsense: The decor was simple, the tables were covered with white cloths, the lights were bright, and it was always full. On Sundays, the Rosetta served poached fish, beautifully displayed on a huge platter and decorated with lemon slices. When the waiters served it, they would deftly debone it tableside using a spoon and fork. It was always served with a mayonnaise made with olive oil and lemon juice.

Their fish was the inspiration for my poached salmon. I've added the feta and capers to the mayonnaise just for fun.

MAKES ABOUT 1½ CUPS MAYONNAISE
SERVES 4

FETA MAYONNAISE

3 very fresh large egg yolks

1½ teaspoons Dijon mustard

3 tablespoons freshly squeezed lemon juice

2 cloves garlic, minced

½ teaspoon salt

1 cup extra virgin olive oil

4 ounces feta, crumbled (¾ cup)

2 tablespoons chopped capers

POACHED SALMON

4 salmon steaks, each 1 inch thick (2 pounds total)

4 cups water

½ cup dry white wine

1 whole clove

1 onion, cut into quarters

1 carrot, coarsely chopped

1 rib celery, coarsely chopped

8 whole black peppercorns

Juice from 1 lemon (lemon halves reserved)

1 bay leaf

1 teaspoon dried thyme

2 teaspoons salt

4 sprigs flat-leaf parsley, for garnish

4 slices lemon, for garnish

FOR THE Feta Mayonnaise, place the egg yolks in the container of a blender. Add the mustard, lemon juice, garlic, and salt and blend well. With the blender running, slowly drizzle in the oil through the opening in the lid (check from time to time to make sure the oil is being absorbed and emulsifying before adding more) and blend until the mayonnaise is very thick and homogeneous. Transfer the mayonnaise to a bowl. Fold in the feta and capers using a rubber spatula. Cover and refrigerate until serving time. (If there is leftover mayonnaise, be sure to use it within a couple of days, because of the raw egg yolks. See Note.)

FOR THE Poached Salmon, rinse the salmon steaks. Check the fish for any pin bones and remove them with needle-nose pliers or tweezers. Secure the two tips of each steak together with a toothpick.

SELECT A fish poacher with a rack or use a large deep skillet or saucepan that will hold the fish in one layer; if using a saucepan, fit it with a rack or line it with a thick layer of cheesecloth to assist in lifting the fish out of the liquid when it is cooked. Pour the water and wine into the pan. Stick the clove into one of the onion quarters and add the onion, carrot, celery, peppercorns, lemon juice and squeezed lemon halves, bay leaf, thyme, and salt to the pan. Bring to a boil over high heat, reduce the heat to low, and simmer for 20 minutes, loosely covered.

GENTLY PLACE the salmon in the simmering liquid and cook the fish for 10 minutes, or until just opaque throughout; it should flake when the tip of a knife is inserted. Transfer the fish to a platter, cover loosely with aluminum foil, and set aside to cool for about 30 minutes. Reserve some of the poaching liquid and brush it on the top of the fish a few times to keep it moist as it cools.

TO SERVE, place the fish on serving plates and top each with 1 heaping tablespoon of the mayonnaise. Garnish with the parsley and lemon slices. Serve barely warm or at room temperature. Pass the remaining mayonnaise.

NOTE: It's generally safe to use raw eggs in your recipes, as long as they are very fresh, grade A or AA, and have been properly refrigerated. There is, however, a slight risk of *Salmonella enteritidis* and other illnesses related to the consumption of raw eggs. I have made this recipe many, many times without any problem, but if you want to be absolutely safe, you can either cook the egg yolks over a hot water bath or in a double boiler to a temperature of 145°F. or substitute pasteurized eggs (found in the grocer's refrigerated dairy case) for the raw eggs in this recipe. As a precaution, pregnant women, babies, young children, the elderly, and all those whose health is compromised should always avoid raw eggs.

Parmigiano-Crusted Chicken

Parmigiano-Reggiano is known as the King of Cheeses. Its history goes back for centuries. In fact, it is mentioned in Boccaccio's *Decameron,* which was written in 1353. Italian law dictates that it can be produced only in a designated geographic area near Parma and that it must be aged for at least two years. The name Parmigiano is even trademarked. If I could have only one cheese in all the world, I would choose Parmigiano-Reggiano because it is so versatile—good for cooking, good for eating, good with wine—and so very tasty!

This dish is a wonderful alternative to fried chicken. The bread crumbs and Parmigiano create a crunchy coating on the chicken. The grated lemon zest and the freshly ground black pepper give it a special zip. At room temperature, it's perfect for picnics and al fresco dinners.   SERVES 4

4 large skinless, boneless chicken breasts (1½ pounds total)

Salt and freshly ground black pepper to taste

¼ cup unbleached all-purpose flour

2 large eggs

1 cup fresh bread crumbs made from dense home-style bread (about 3 slices)

4 ounces Parmigiano-Reggiano, grated (1 cup)

2 teaspoons minced fresh thyme

½ teaspoon grated lemon zest

2 to 4 tablespoons extra virgin olive oil

8 sprigs fresh thyme, for garnish

1 lemon, thinly sliced, for garnish

PREHEAT THE oven to 350°F. Lightly oil a baking pan large enough to hold the chicken in one layer.

WASH THE chicken and pat dry with paper towels. Season the chicken well with salt and pepper. Place the flour on a plate or waxed paper. Beat the eggs in a shallow bowl. Combine the bread crumbs, Parmigiano, thyme, and lemon zest on a plate or waxed paper. Dredge each chicken breast in the flour, shaking off any excess, then dip in the egg, and finally into the bread crumb mixture. Be sure to evenly coat the chicken at each step. Place in the baking pan. Divide any remaining crumbs equally among the breasts, patting them onto the chicken.

PLACE IN the oven and bake for 15 minutes. Brush the olive oil onto the bread-crumb crust. Return the chicken to the oven and cook for 15 to 25 minutes, or until the breasts are golden brown and cooked through. Remove from the oven and allow the breasts to rest for a few minutes.

TO SERVE, place on a serving platter and garnish with the thyme sprigs and lemon slices. Serve warm or at room temperature.

Rack of Lamb with Goat Cheese Crust

Whenever we go to Santa Fe to visit our friends Linda and Mike Waterman, we cook a glorious meal of charcoal-grilled leg of lamb seasoned with rosemary and accompanied by roasted potatoes. We've been enjoying this same meal together as long as I can remember.

The flavors of lamb and goat cheese combine brilliantly, and rosemary and garlic bring out the gamy juices of the succulent rack of lamb. In honor of the Watermans, I created this goat cheese crust that dresses up a rack of lamb while keeping it moist and tender.

SERVES 4

GOAT CHEESE CRUST

4 ounces (½ cup) fresh goat cheese, softened

¼ cup fresh bread crumbs

1 tablespoon minced garlic

1 tablespoon minced fresh rosemary

1 large egg yolk, lightly beaten

¼ teaspoon salt

Generous ½ ounce Pecorino Romano, grated (2 heaping tablespoons)

1 teaspoon freshly ground black pepper

LAMB

2 tablespoons extra virgin olive oil

One 8-chop rack of lamb, trimmed and frenched (have the butcher do this) (2 pounds)

Seasoning Salt (page 79) or salt and freshly ground black pepper to taste

4 sprigs fresh rosemary, for garnish

PREHEAT THE oven to 500°F.

FOR THE Goat Cheese Crust, place the goat cheese, 1 tablespoon of the bread crumbs, the garlic, rosemary, egg yolk, and salt together in a small bowl and blend. Combine the remaining 3 tablespoons bread crumbs, the Pecorino, and pepper in another small bowl. Set aside.

RUB THE oil over the meat and season with the seasoning salt. Place the lamb on a rack in a shallow baking pan and roast for 20 minutes, or until a meat thermometer inserted into the thickest part of the meat reads 110°F. Remove from the oven and reduce the oven temperature to 450°F. Coat the top side of the rack of lamb with the goat cheese mixture. Pat the bread crumb mixture over this, pressing slightly so it adheres. Return to the oven and cook for 20 minutes, or until medium-rare. The internal temperature should be 125°–130°F. and the cheese crust should be golden brown. If a more browned crust is desired, place it 3 inches from the heat under the hot broiler for the last few minutes before the lamb reaches 125°–130°F. Remove from the oven and let rest for 3 to 5 minutes.

TO SERVE, cut the rack into chops, being careful to keep the crust with each chop. Serve 2 chops to each person, garnished with the rosemary.

Roasted Chicken Stuffed with Ricotta

My friend Margaret Anne Cullum has always said that the mark of a good restaurant kitchen is its roasted chicken. In fact, she orders it everywhere she goes and is a great judge of roasted chicken.

This is a quick and easy way to make a roasted chicken extra special, because the ricotta puffs up under the skin. It's almost like a soufflé, and it keeps the chicken moist and tender.

SERVES 4

1 broiler-fryer chicken (2½ to 3½ pounds)

Salt and freshly ground black pepper to taste

2 tablespoons dried herbes de Provence

1 lemon, quartered

1 small onion, quartered

8 ounces ricotta, homemade (page 70) or store-bought, well drained (1 cup)

3 leaves fresh sage, minced

3 large leaves fresh basil, minced

3 sprigs fresh thyme, leaves only, minced

1 teaspoon minced fresh rosemary

1 tablespoon extra virgin olive oil

Seasoning Salt (page 79) or salt and freshly ground black pepper to taste

¼ cup dry white wine or water

Kitchen string

PREHEAT THE oven to 400°F.

WASH THE chicken well and remove any visible excess fat. Pat dry with paper towels. Season the cavity with salt and pepper and 1 tablespoon of the herbes de Provence. Place the lemon and onion in the cavity. Set the chicken aside.

COMBINE THE ricotta, sage, basil, thyme, and rosemary in a small bowl and mix well. Separate the chicken skin from the breast, thigh, and leg meat by gently slipping your fingers and hand between the skin and the meat; take care not to rip the skin with your fingernails. Spread the ricotta mixture under the loosened skin and smooth the top of the skin with your fingers, to distribute the cheese in an even layer. Tie the legs of the chicken together with kitchen string and tuck the wing tips under. Rub the chicken with the oil and sprinkle abundantly with the seasoning salt and the remaining 1 tablespoon herbes de Provence. Set the chicken on a rack in a roasting pan just large enough to hold it.

PLACE IN the oven and roast for 15 minutes. Reduce the heat to 350°F. and roast for 45 minutes to 1 hour longer, basting with the pan juices every 15 minutes, until the juices run clear when chicken is pierced with the tip of a knife near the thigh. Remove the chicken from the oven and place on a cutting board or platter, covered loosely with foil, and let stand for 5 minutes before carving.

DRAIN THE pan drippings into a cup and remove the fat that rises to the top. Add the white wine to the pan, scraping up any browned bits from the bottom, then pour in the pan juices. Cook for 1 to 2 minutes over medium heat, or until the sauce has thickened.

TO SERVE, carve or quarter the chicken and drizzle with the pan juices.

To Make an Excellent Winter Cheese—
To a cheese of 2 gallons of new milke, take 10 quarts of stroakings and 2 quarts of cream, put it to 4 spoonfuls of rennit, set it together as hot as ye can from ye cow.

–Martha Washington

Cornish Game Hens on Gorgonzola Polenta with Caramelized Onions

My husband, Jim, loves to hunt doves, so I often prepare this dish with those little game birds. Squab is a good substitute because they are similar to doves; both are small, dark-meated birds with a gamy taste. If you substitute squab, you'll only need one per person, but if you use doves, you should count on at least two birds per person. Cornish game hens are just the right size to serve as an individual portion.

The polenta is cooked first with water, then with milk to make it richer. It's finally flavored with Gorgonzola. If you can't find Gorgonzola, any blue cheese can be substituted. The perfect accompaniment for this dish is sautéed spinach.

MAKES ABOUT 5 CUPS POLENTA
SERVES 4

CORNISH HENS

4 Cornish game hens (each 1¼ pounds)

Salt and freshly ground black pepper to taste

6 cloves garlic, peeled, 4 left whole and 2 thinly sliced

4 sprigs fresh rosemary plus 2 (4-inch long) sprigs fresh rosemary

Kitchen string

¼ cup extra virgin olive oiil

CARAMELIZED ONIONS

2 tablespoons extra virgin olive oiil

2 onions, thinly sliced

3 tablespoons balsamic vinegar

Salt to taste

GORGONZOLA POLENTA

6 cups water

2 teaspoons salt

2 cups fine stone-ground cornmeal

2 cups milk, or more as needed

8 ounces Gorgonzola, crumbled into ½-inch pieces (about 1½ cups)

Freshly ground black pepper to taste

4 sprigs fresh rosemary, for garnish

FOR THE Cornish Hens, preheat the oven to 375°F.

WASH THE hens and pat dry. Season with salt and pepper inside and out. Place a clove of garlic and a sprig of rosemary in each hen's cavity. Tie the legs together with kitchen string and tuck the wing tips under.

HEAT 2 tablespoons of the olive oil in a large skillet over medium heat. Add the hens, sliced garlic, and rosemary sprigs and sauté until the hens' skin begins to brown, about 20 minutes, turning as necessary. (Cook the hens in 2 batches if necessary.) Be careful not to break the skin when turning the hens.

WHEN THE hens are browned, arrange them breast side up in a roasting pan just large enough to hold them and place in the oven. Roast the hens for 30 to 45 minutes, basting every 15 minutes, or until cooked through. Test the hens by piercing them near the thigh: The juices should run clear. Leave the oven on. When the hens are done, if you would like a crisper skin, preheat the broiler. Place the hens on the rack at least 4 inches under heat source and broil for 5 minutes, or until nicely browned. Transfer the hens to a heated platter and discard the garlic cloves and rosemary. Set the hens aside, loosely covered with foil, while you prepare the onions. About 5 minutes before serving, return the hens to the oven to reheat.

FOR THE Caramelized Onions, add the oil to the drippings in the skillet in which the hens were cooked and place over medium heat. Stir well to release any browned bits on the bottom of the pan. Add the onions, stir well, and sauté for about 20 minutes, or until they are browned and beginning to caramelize. Reduce the heat to low, add the vinegar, and cook slowly, stirring as necessary, until the vinegar is almost absorbed. Remove from the heat, lightly salt the onions, and set aside.

MEANWHILE, FOR the Polenta, pour the water into a large heavy saucepan, place over high heat, and bring to a boil. Add the salt. Slowly add the cornmeal, releasing a steady stream with one hand while whisking constantly with the other hand. Once all of the cornmeal has been added, switch to a long-handled wooden spoon, reduce the heat to low, and cook, stirring, as the polenta begins to thicken. Add the milk, in small amounts, as necessary to keep the polenta moist and soupy. If any lumps develop, break them up against the sides of the pan with the back of the spoon. Cook, stirring and adding milk as necessary, for about 30 minutes, or until the polenta is completely cooked and most of the liquid has been absorbed. It should be somewhat soupy and runny. Remove from the heat. Add the Gongonzola and stir vigorously to blend it into the polenta. Season with salt and pepper. Serve immediately.

TO SERVE, pour the polenta onto a shallow heated serving platter, top with the onions, and arrange the hens on top of the onions. Garnish with the sprigs of rosemary.

Lamb Osso Buco
with Manchego Mashed Potatoes

Bob and Pat Long are longtime friends who live in the Napa Valley. Bob makes wonderful wine and is a fantastic cook. Their home is located in an idyllic spot in the midst of their vineyards on a hill overlooking Lake Hennessey. We have spent many a glorious evening there, in the summers out under the pergola and in the winters inside in front of a big roaring fire. I love all of Bob's wines, but I would choose Long Vineyards Sangiovese for this osso buco because the meat is rich and the wine is somewhat lean, like a Chianti.

SERVES 4

LAMB OSSO BUCO

4 meaty bone-in lamb shanks, each 2 inches thick (3 to 4 pounds total)

Seasoning Salt (page 79) or salt and freshly ground black pepper to taste

½ cup unbleached all-purpose flour

3 tablespoons plus ¼ cup extra virgin olive oil

4 ounces thinly sliced prosciutto, cut into thin strips (¾ cup)

2 large onions, chopped (3 cups)

2 cloves garlic, minced

3 carrots, chopped (1½ cups)

2 cups dry red wine

2 tablespoons tomato paste

½ teaspoon dried sage

½ teaspoon dried rosemary

½ teaspoon dried thyme

About 2 cups chicken broth, homemade (page 81) or store-bought

2 ounces Manchego, grated (½ cup)

MANCHEGO MASHED POTATOES

1½ pounds Yukon Gold potatoes, peeled and cut into 1-inch cubes

Salt

2 tablespoons unsalted butter

½ cup heavy cream, heated

Freshly ground black pepper to taste

4 ounces Manchego, grated (1 cup)

GREMOLADA

2 teaspoons grated lemon zest

1 clove garlic, minced

¼ cup minced fresh flat-leaf parsley

1 anchovy fillet, minced (optional)

½ ounce Manchego, grated (2 tablespoons)

FOR THE Lamb Osso Buco, liberally sprinkle the seasoning salt over the lamb shanks and rub it in. Dust with the flour and shake off the excess. Set aside.

HEAT 3 tablespoons of the olive oil in a large heavy skillet over medium heat. Add the prosciutto, onions, garlic, and carrots and sauté until golden brown. Remove the mixture and set aside.

ADD THE remaining ¼ cup olive oil to the pan and increase the heat to medium-high. Add the lamb shanks and brown them on all sides, turning as necessary using tongs. Add the wine, tomato paste, sage, rosemary, and thyme and mix well. Scrape the browned bits on the bottom of the pan into the sauce. Return the vegetables to the pan. Cover and slowly braise the meat over low heat for 1½ hours, or until the meat is very tender and almost ready to fall off the bone. (Or use an ovenproof skillet and braise in a 350°F. oven.) Add ½ cup of the chicken broth after 15 minutes. Turn the meat occasionally and add additional chicken broth whenever there is less than an inch of liquid in the pan.

MEANWHILE, MAKE the Manchego Mashed Potatoes: Place the potatoes in a saucepan and cover with water by 1 inch. Place over medium-high heat, bring to a boil, and add ½ teaspoon salt. Reduce the heat, partially cover, and simmer the potatoes for 20 to 30 minutes, or until tender when tested with a fork. Drain the potatoes, return to the pan, add the butter, cover, and set aside for 5 minutes to melt the butter. Mash the potatoes in the pan with a potato masher, or pass them through a potato ricer or a food mill fitted with the fine disk back into the pan. Add the cream and beat the potatoes with a handheld electric mixer or whisk. Season with salt and pepper. Stir in the Manchego until it is melted. Cover the pan and set aside in a warm place or in a very low oven to keep warm.

FOR THE Gremolada, mix the zest, garlic, parsley, anchovy (if using), and Manchego in a small bowl. Set aside.

WHEN THE lamb is cooked, transfer the shanks to a plate. Place the skillet over medium heat and cook the sauce, scraping up and dissolving any browned bits on the bottom of the pan, until slightly reduced. Just before serving, blend in the Manchego, stirring until it is melted. Return the shanks to the pan.

TO SERVE, place a portion of the mashed potatoes on each heated plate or shallow serving bowl. Top with the lamb shanks, spoon the sauce over and around the meat, and sprinkle the meat with the gremolada.

Asiago-Stuffed Veal Roll

In Italy, meat rolls with fillings are quite popular. They are not difficult to make. All you do is pound veal scaloppine thin, arrange it to form a large sheet, spread on the filling, and then roll it up and tie it. All the work is done ahead of time so that you are free while it's merrily cooking away in the oven.

This one, with roasted garlic, spinach, and Asiago, can be served either warm or at room temperature.

SERVES 6

1 bunch spinach, stems removed and washed (about 12 ounces)

12 cloves garlic, unpeeled

1 tablespoon extra virgin olive oil

2 pounds veal scaloppine

1½ teaspoons Seasoning Salt (page 79) or salt and freshly ground black pepper to taste

½ cup fresh bread crumbs

1 ounce Asiago, grated (¼ cup)

3 tablespoons drained capers

1 teaspoon dried oregano

1 teaspoon freshly ground black pepper or to taste

Kitchen string

2 tablespoons extra virgin olive oil

3 cups Paula's Tomato Sauce (page 84) or store-bought

6 sprigs fresh basil, for garnish

PREHEAT THE oven to 350°F.

PLACE THE spinach in a large skillet, add 1 tablespoon water, cover, and bring to a boil over high heat. Reduce the heat and steam for 3 minutes. Remove from the heat, remove the cover, and set aside to cool.

PLACE THE garlic in a small ovenproof dish and drizzle with the olive oil. Cover with aluminum foil. Place in the oven and roast for 20 minutes, or until soft. Remove from oven, uncover, and set aside to cool. Leave the oven on.

LAY A sheet of plastic wrap on a work surface, place a piece of veal on the plastic, and cover with another sheet of plastic wrap. With a meat pounder or other flat utensil, pound to a thickness of ¼ inch. Repeat with the remaining pieces.

ARRANGE THE scallopine on a clean sheet of plastic wrap, with the grain all going the same way, slightly overlapping each other so that they form a rectangle of about 16 x 12 inches, with a long side facing you. Sprinkle the meat with ½ teaspoon of the seasoning salt. Spread the spinach leaves out flat on top of the meat, completely covering it. Top the spinach with the bread crumbs and Asiago, distributing them evenly. Sprinkle the capers, oregano, and pepper on top.

REMOVE THE garlic from the oil and squeeze it out of its skin. Smash and flatten with the flat side of a knife. Distribute on top of the veal. Roll up the meat fairly tightly, starting with the long bottom edge, to enclose all of the stuffing. Push anything that pops out back into the roll, and do not worry about any small separations on the inside. Place the roll on a cutting board and cut in half crosswise using a sharp knife, so that you have 2 rolls about 8 x 3 inches. Tie each roll with kitchen string, wrapping the string around the roll at 1-inch intervals, and then tie lengthwise to contain the filling. Rub the veal with the remaining 1 teaspoon seasoning salt. (The meat can be prepared to this point and refrigerated for up to 24 hours; increase the cooking time by 15 minutes.)

HEAT THE olive oil in a 12-inch skillet over medium-high heat. Add the veal rolls and sear on all sides, turning as necessary using tongs. Place the veal in a baking dish about 13 x 9 inches. Pour the tomato sauce over and around the veal.

PLACE IT in the oven and roast for 45 minutes, or until the meat is golden brown and registers 155°F. on a meat thermometer. Remove from the oven, snip and remove the string, and set aside, loosely covered with foil, for 15 minutes. Serve warm.

TO SERVE, slice the rolls into 1-inch slices. Place 2 slices on each heated serving plate and spoon sauce over the edges of the slices. Garnish with the basil. Pass the remaining sauce.

Veal Suitcases Perugina

When I lived in Perugia, there was a little restaurant called Falchetto located on a narrow medieval street just behind the Duomo. Its small front windows were always beautifully decorated with wild game, seasonal produce, homemade pasta, and local cheeses. Inside, the tables were covered with pink tablecloths trimmed in white. It was a typical rustic restaurant, with vaulted brick ceilings that dated back to medieval times.

One memorable lunch there was with the Gordons, friends of my parents who were passing through Perugia to bring greetings from home. We all enjoyed my favorite dish, *valigette,* which translates as "little suitcases," because the veal is stuffed with prosciutto and cheese and then folded to form a package. After lunch, I pointed them on their way to Rome and they drove away with their real suitcases packed as tightly as the little suitcases they had enjoyed at lunch.

SERVES 4

8 veal scaloppine, about 3 ounces each (have the butcher pound them to ⅛ inch thick, if you like)

8 very thin slices prosciutto (about 4 ounces)

8 ounces fresh mozzarella, cut into 8 slices

Salt and freshly ground black pepper to taste

¼ cup unbleached all-purpose flour

2 tablespoons unsalted butter

2 tablespoons extra virgin olive oil

½ cup dry Marsala

1 tablespoon freshly squeezed lemon juice

2 tablespoons minced fresh flat-leaf parsley

LAY A sheet of plastic wrap out on a work surface, place a piece of veal on the plastic, and cover with another sheet of plastic. Pound the meat with a meat pounder or other flat utensil until it is uniformly ⅛ inch thick. Repeat with the remaining pieces. (The butcher could also do this step.)

LAY THE veal out on the work surface. Top each piece with a slice of prosciutto and then a slice of cheese. Fold the veal over to completely enclose the prosciutto and cheese and secure with toothpicks. You should have nice little flat packages about 3 x 2 inches. Sprinkle both sides of the veal with salt and pepper. Place the flour on a small plate and dredge the veal packages in the flour, shaking off any excess.

HEAT THE butter and oil in a large skillet over medium-high heat. When the butter foam subsides, add the meat and brown on both sides, turning as necessary. Reduce the heat if necessary to keep the veal from burning. When the packages are golden brown, transfer them to a heated plate.

ADD THE Marsala to the pan juices and stir well to release the browned bits on the bottom of the pan. Reduce the heat to low, return the veal to the pan, and simmer for 2 to 3 minutes, with a lid slightly ajar, until the meat is tender and cooked through. Return the veal to the heated plate. Add the lemon juice and parsley to the pan, increase the heat, and cook for a minute, or until the sauce has thickened.

TO SERVE, remove the toothpicks and serve 2 little suitcases, drizzled with the sauce, per person. Serve immediately.

Chile-Rubbed Beef Tenderloin with Mascarpone-Poblano Sauce

Robert Del Grande of Cafe Annie in Houston is a master of meats and chiles. He's also a man who loves mascarpone, so I created this recipe in his honor. Robert is one of the chefs who pioneered and developed Southwestern cuisine. Along with Dean Fearing, he is a member of the musical group The Barbed Wires. They sing and play at the drop of a chile. They are good musicians, but if they give up their day jobs, it will be a loss for all of us!

MAKES ABOUT 1½ CUPS SAUCE
SERVES 6 TO 8

MASCARPONE-POBLANO SAUCE

1 poblano chile

2 cloves garlic, unpeeled

1 tablespoon extra virgin olive oiil

8 ounces (1 cup) mascarpone, home-made (page 73) or store-bought

3 tablespoons minced fresh cilantro

1 teaspoon ground cumin

1 teaspoon pure chile powder

½ teaspoon salt

CHILE-RUBBED BEEF

2 tablespoons extra virgin olive oil

1 whole beef tenderloin, trimmed (4 to 5 pounds)

¼ cup pure chile powder

2 tablespoons ground cumin

3 tablespoons Seasoning Salt (page 79) or store-bought

1 tablespoon freshly ground black pepper or to taste

FOR THE Mascarpone-Poblano Sauce, preheat the broiler to high. Adjust the rack so that it is 3 inches under the heat source.

LAY THE poblano on a small baking sheet, place under the broiler, and roast, turning with tongs, until the skin is blackened on all sides. (Alternatively, hold the chile over an open flame using a long-handled fork.) Place the chile in a bowl, cover with plastic wrap, and steam for 15 minutes. Remove from the bowl and let cool.

PEEL OFF the charred skin from the chile. Remove the stem and seeds and discard. Cut into julienne strips ¼ inch wide and 1 inch long. Set aside.

IN THE meantime, preheat the oven to 350° F.

PLACE THE garlic cloves in a small flameproof dish, drizzle with the olive oil, and cover with aluminum foil. Place in the oven and roast for 20 minutes, or until soft. Remove, remove the foil, and let cool. Squeeze the garlic out of the skins and chop, then mash to a paste with the flat side of a knife. Place in a small bowl. Add the mascarpone, cilantro, cumin, chile powder, and salt and mix well. Stir in the poblano. Set aside at room temperature.

FOR THE Chili-Rubbed Beef, massage the oil into the meat. Mix the chile powder, cumin, seasoning salt, and pepper together in a small bowl. Rub this mixture all over the beef.

PLACE THE tenderloin on a rack in a shallow roasting pan. Place in the oven and roast for 25 to 35 minutes for rare; the internal temperature, when tested with a meat thermometer, should read 120°–125°F. Or cook longer if more well-done meat is desired. (Remember that the roast will continue to cook after it is removed from the oven.) Remove the meat from the oven.

TRANSFER THE beef to a heated serving platter. Spread the sauce over the beef and cover loosely with aluminum foil. Let it stand for 10 minutes before serving—the sauce will melt over the meat.

TO SERVE, slice the meat about ½ inch thick. Serve the slices with some of the melted sauce.

VARIATION

Chipotle-Mascarpone Sauce

Stir 2 tablespoons minced chipotle chiles in adobo into the mascarpone instead of the roasted poblano chile.

Sophisticated Chili

Chili is just a meat stew with a sauce flavored with chile powder. It is said to have originated in Texas around the campfires during the Longhorn cattle trail drives. Nowadays there are as many chili recipes and theories as there are stars in the Texas sky! Some believe chili should never contain tomatoes, others decree that it shouldn't contain beans, and still others swear that the secret ingredient of chili is armadillo! There are chili cookoffs around Texas and around the nation. Chili is serious stuff!

This recipe is loosely based on one I saw Dean Fearing, chef of the Mansion on Turtle Creek, prepare on his television cooking show. It involves making a true chile sauce from dried chiles and then combining it with sautéed sirloin steak.

If you have time, keep the chili in the refrigerator for a day or two before serving it to give the flavors a chance to meld.

SERVES 4

ANCHO SAUCE
6 dried ancho chiles

1 dried chipotle chile

2 tablespoons extra virgin olive oil

3 cloves garlic, minced

1 small onion, diced (½ cup)

½ jalapeño chile, stem and seeds removed, minced

1½ cups chicken broth, homemade (page 81) or store-bought

2 (6-inch) corn tortillas, torn into pieces

¼ cup minced fresh cilantro

1 teaspoon dried oregano

½ teaspoon cumin seeds

CHILI
3 tablespoons extra virgin olive oil

1½ pounds boneless sirloin steak, cut into 1-inch cubes

Seasoning Salt (page 79), or salt and freshly ground black pepper to taste

1 cup coarsely chopped onions

1 cup beer

Salt and freshly ground black pepper to taste

4 ounces pepper Jack or Ancho Chile Caciotta (see Note), shredded (1 cup)

4 ounces (½ cup) fresh goat cheese, crumbled

ACCOMPANIMENTS, AS DESIRED
Chopped avocados

Chopped onions

Chopped tomatoes

Crushed tortilla chips

Minced fresh cilantro

FOR THE Ancho Sauce, slit the ancho and chipotle chiles open using a knife. Remove the stems and seeds and discard. Rinse under running water and set aside.

HEAT THE oil in a medium saucepan over medium heat. Add the garlic, onion, and jalapeño and sauté for about 10 minutes, or until the onion is browned. Pour in the chicken broth and stir to mix. Add the chiles, tortillas, cilantro, oregano, and cumin. Bring to a boil, reduce the heat to medium-low, and cook for 20 to 30 minutes. Transfer everything to a blender and puree until smooth. Remove and set aside.

FOR THE Chili, heat the oil in a large heavy skillet over high heat. Season the meat with the seasoning salt, add the meat, and sear, stirring and tossing as necessary until well browned. Add the onions and sauté until dark brown, about 10 minutes. Add the beer and stir to dissolve the browned particles on the bottom of the pan. Add the sauce and stir to combine. Cook over low heat for 30 to 45 minutes, or until the meat is tender. Season with salt and pepper, to taste.

TO SERVE, spoon the chili into large heated shallow bowls. Garnish each generously with a sprinkling of pepper Jack and a dollop of goat cheese. Pass the accompaniments so that the diners can add to their bowls as desired.

Note: Ancho Chile Caciotta is available from the Mozzarella Company (see page 373).

Sirloin Steak with Blue Cheese Butter

Years ago, when I was looking for a location to lease for the Mozzarella Company, I wandered into a famous old meat market near downtown Dallas called Rudolph's. I had often shopped there for steaks. The meat market was run by Cyrill Pokladnik, who had come to Dallas around 1920, when he was ten years old. He found a job working at the meat market, the job stuck, and Cyrill went on to buy the market and eventually the entire block. He owned the little building on the corner and he agreed to rent it to me. The Mozzarella Company has been there ever since.

Today Cyrill's grandchildren run the meat market. They still hang their beef to age it; few places go to this trouble, and this is one of the secrets of their great steaks. I am convinced that the butchers at Rudolph's cut the very best steaks in all of Dallas, and I should know, because I have had so many of them through the years.

Red meat and blue cheese are a classic combination. This recipe is one of the easiest and most delicious ways to combine the two. And both just beg for a big red wine like Carolyn Wente's Cabernet Sauvignon from the Charles Wetmore Vineyard in California's Livermore Valley.

MAKES 1 CUP BUTTER
SERVES 4

BLUE CHEESE BUTTER

4 tablespoons (½ stick) unsalted butter, softened

8 ounces Danish Blue cheese, at room temperature

SIRLOIN STEAK

1 sirloin steak, 1¼ to 1½ inches thick (bone-in, 3 to 3½ pounds; boneless, 2½ to 3 pounds)

Salt and freshly ground black pepper to taste

¼ cup extra virgin olive oil

4 sprigs fresh rosemary, plus extra for garnish

FOR THE Blue Cheese Butter, place the butter and blue cheese in a small bowl. Mash into a smooth paste using a fork. Place the mixture on a sheet of waxed paper or plastic wrap. Roll up the butter in the paper or plastic and shape it into a cylinder about 1½ inches in diameter. Twist the ends of the paper or plastic together to close it and smooth the roll with your hands. Refrigerate until firm.

PREHEAT A gas grill to high or build a fire with hardwood charcoal, charcoal briquettes, or wood and allow it to burn until the coals are covered in gray ash. Adjust the rack so that it is 3 to 4 inches from the heat source.

SEASON THE steak liberally with salt and pepper. Place the steak on the grill and baste it with the oil, using 1 of the rosemary sprigs as a brush. Throw 3 rosemary sprigs onto the coals in an area not directly under the steak. Cook the steak on the first side for about 6 to 8 minutes. Turn the steak over and cook, continuing to baste with oil, for an additional 6 minutes or until medium-rare.

REMOVE THE steak from the heat and place it on a heated platter.

CUT THE blue cheese butter into ¼-inch rounds and place on top of the hot steak—the butter will melt over the meat. Allow the meat to rest for 5 minutes.

JUST BEFORE serving, cut the steak against the grain into slices about ¾ inch thick. Garnish with sprigs of rosemary.

When is it done?

You can test the steaks you cook using the following method:
- For rare, when you press down on the meat, it will be soft
- For medium-rare, there will be some resistance
- For well-done, the steak will be fairly firm

Roasted Pork Loin with Dried Fruit Stuffing and Roquefort Sauce

Susan and Ed Auler, who own Fall Creek Vineyards, have pioneered the growth of Texas vineyards and have won awards far and wide for their great wines. Their winery is a lovely, state-of-the art facility located on the banks of Lake Buchanan, in the Texas Hill Country outside Austin. They are among my favorite friends. No doubt the combination of wine and cheese has something to do with it!

The dried fruits in this stuffing are sweet and pair well with the rich Gorgonzola sauce, and plumping the fruit in red wine keeps the stuffing moist. A wonderful meat dish like this just cries out for a great red wine, and Ed's Fall Creek Meritus would be the perfect choice.

When selecting the meat, be sure to choose a wide piece of loin, about 5 inches across, to allow enough room for the stuffing.

MAKES 1¼ CUPS SAUCE
SERVES 6 TO 8

DRIED FRUIT STUFFING

¼ cup chopped pitted prunes

¼ cup chopped dried cranberries or dried cherries

¼ cup chopped dried apples

¼ cup chopped dried apricots

1 cup dry red wine

2 tablespoons extra virgin olive oil

¼ cup chopped walnuts

1 tablespoon minced shallots

½ cup fresh bread crumbs

¼ teaspoon rubbed sage

¼ teaspoon dried thyme

Pinch of ground allspice

¼ teaspoon Seasoning Salt (page 79), or salt and freshly ground black pepper to taste

Salt and freshly ground black pepper to taste

PORK LOIN

1 boneless center-cut pork loin roast, not tied (4 pounds) (see introduction to recipe)

2 tablespoons extra virgin olive oil

2 teaspoons rubbed sage

2 teaspoons dried thyme

2 teaspoons Seasoning Salt (page 79), or salt and freshly ground black pepper to taste

Kitchen string

ROQUEFORT SAUCE

1 cup heavy cream

4 ounces Roquefort, crumbled (¾ cup)

FOR THE Dried Fruit Stuffing, plump the dried fruits in the red wine for 30 minutes.

MEANWHILE, LAY the meat on a work surface and, using a sharp knife, cut a wide pocket horizontally in the center of the meat; be careful not to cut through to the exterior. (You can also ask your butcher to do this for you.) Rub the meat all over with the oil. Season the outside of the meat and the pocket with the sage, thyme, and seasoning salt. Set aside.

PREHEAT THE oven to 500°F.

HEAT THE oil in a medium skillet over medium heat and sauté the walnuts for 5 minutes, or until browned and aromatic. Add the shallots and cook briefly, or until softened. Remove from the heat.

DRAIN THE fruit, reserving the wine, and add to the skillet. Add the bread crumbs, sage, thyme, allspice, and salt and pepper to the skillet and mix together. Taste the stuffing and adjust the seasonings if necessary.

FILL THE pocket in the pork loin with the stuffing, taking care to spread it in an even layer throughout. Use toothpicks or skewers to hold the stuffing in place while you tie the roast at 1-inch intervals with kitchen string, closing the pocket; remove the toothpicks. (The meat can be prepared to this point and refrigerated for up to 12 hours; increase the cooking time by 15 to 30 minutes.)

PLACE THE roast in a shallow baking pan just large enough to hold it, so the pan drippings will not burn. Add ½ cup water to the pan, place in the oven, and roast for 30 minutes. Reduce the oven temperature to 325°F. and roast the meat for 1½ hours longer, or until a meat thermometer inserted in the thickest part of the meat (not in the stuffing) reads 155°F. Transfer the roast to a serving platter and snip and remove the string. Cover loosely with foil and set aside.

FOR THE Roquefort Sauce, remove any excess fat from the baking pan and discard. Pour the reserved wine into the pan, scraping up and dissolving any browned particles on the bottom. Transfer the liquid to a small saucepan, place over medium heat, and reduce the wine by half. Add the cream and reduce by half. Remove from the heat, add the Roquefort and stir until most of the Roquefort has melted but some chunks remain.

TO SERVE, cut the meat into ½-inch slices and arrange on a heated serving platter. Drizzle some of the sauce over the meat. Pass the remaining sauce. Serve hot.

Breads

Bacon, Egg, and Cheddar Scones

Scones, which originated in England, are similar to biscuits, but they are much richer. They are made from a short pastry, with lots of butter and cream incorporated into the dough. They are very flaky and tender. They are usually cut into large triangles.

Once on a morning walk I passed an elegant coffee bar in downtown Seattle. There on the counter were the most gorgeous scones, labeled Bacon and Egg Scones. I had never heard of this variation before, but I thought it was a great idea, combining all the ingredients for a complete breakfast into a handheld meal.

MAKES 6 SCONES

2 cups unbleached all-purpose flour

4 teaspoons baking powder

1 teaspoon salt

5 tablespoons unsalted butter, cold

3 large eggs

¾ cup heavy cream

2 ounces Cheddar, shredded (½ cup)

2 large eggs, lightly scrambled and broken up into pieces about 1 inch square

3 strips bacon, partially cooked and cut into ½-inch-wide strips

PREHEAT THE oven to 450°F. Lightly butter a baking sheet or line it with parchment paper.

SIFT THE flour, baking powder, and salt together. Place in either a medium bowl or the work bowl of a food processor fitted with a steel blade. Cut the butter into the flour so that it is completely incorporated, using two knives, a pastry blender, or your hands, or process until incorporated. Beat 2 of the raw eggs and the cream together and add to the dry ingredients. Mix or process just to incorporate the eggs into the flour and butter; do not overmix. If using the processor, transfer to a bowl. Fold the cheese, scrambled eggs, and bacon into the flour mixture. It will be sticky and chunky. Stir and knead the dough as little as possible while distributing the cheese, scrambled eggs, and bacon throughout.

TRANSFER THE dough to a well-floured work surface. Pat the dough into a rectangle about 12 x 4 x ¾ inch high. Cut the dough into three 4-inch squares. Cut the squares on the diagonal to form triangles.

PLACE THE scones at least 1 inch apart on the baking sheet. Beat the remaining 1 egg with 2 tablespoons water and use this wash to brush the tops of the scones.

BAKE FOR 10 to 12 minutes, or until golden brown. Remove and serve warm.

Black Pepper and Brie Biscuits

When I was growing up in Fort Worth, dinnertime meant biscuits on the table, and my father liked them browned and crisp on the outside. I remember watching our cook melting shortening in the baking pan, and then tilting it on the counter so that she could dip both sides of the biscuits into the grease before scooting them to the upper part of the pan. Afterward, she would spread them far apart in the baking pan so that the sides could brown and the biscuits would get crispy all over.

I'm sure that every household in the South has its own favorite biscuit recipe. Shirley Corriher, from Atlanta, makes the most heavenly biscuits I've ever tasted, full of butter and cream. She says the secret is to barely mix the dough, leaving the butter in gigantic clumps. When she makes her biscuits, the dough is very wet and sticky. She advocates scooping the biscuit dough up by hand in globs and placing the biscuits close together in the baking pan. Shirley says that when the biscuits are baked one up against the other, they are more moist.

Here are two different baking methods. Choose the one that suits you.

MAKES 12 TO 16 (2-INCH) BISCUITS

1 tablespoon unsalted butter, melted

2 cups unbleached all-purpose flour

1 tablespoon baking powder

½ teaspoon salt

5⅓ tablespoons (⅓ cup) shortening or unsalted butter

¾ cup buttermilk

4 ounces Brie, some rind removed and cut into ½-inch cubes

1 teaspoon freshly ground black pepper

PREHEAT THE oven to 450°F. Line a baking sheet or a 9-inch round cake pan with parchment paper or lightly butter with about 1 teaspoon of the melted butter. (The biscuits can be set about ½ inch apart on a baking sheet for a crispy exterior; if you want moister, fluffier biscuits place them close together in one cake pan.)

COMBINE THE flour, baking powder, and salt in a bowl. Add the shortening and cut it into the dry ingredients, using two knives, a pastry blender, or your hands, until it is reduced to pea-sized pieces. Add the buttermilk and mix briefly, just to incorporate it. It is very important not to overwork the dough, or the biscuits will not be delicate and light. Gently mix in the Brie and pepper. The dough will be fairly sticky.

TRANSFER DOUGH to a well-floured work surface and pat it out with your hands to about ¾ inch thick. Cut out the biscuits using a 2-inch-diameter glass or a round cookie cutter. Dip the cutter into flour between cuts to keep from sticking. Place the biscuits on or in the prepared pan—using one baking sheet for crispy biscuits or one cake pan for moister biscuits. The remaining dough can be gently gathered together and patted out again for more biscuits. Brush the tops of the biscuits with the remaining melted butter.

PLACE IN the oven and bake for about 10 minutes, or until the tops are golden brown. (If baking the biscuits close together in one pan, bake for 15 to 20 minutes, until golden brown on top.) Remove from the oven and serve warm.

VARIATION

Asiago and Basil Biscuits

Substitute 3 ounces Asiago, shredded (¾ cup), for the Brie and 2 tablespoons chopped fresh basil for the black pepper.

Southwestern Chile-Cheese Corn Bread

Corn bread like this is so substantial that it can be served as a side dish with a meal. It's great with grilled foods. You'll like the texture and taste of the fresh kernels of corn, the chiles, and the cheese. If you cook it in a round skillet, cut it into wedges like a pie.

This is truly campfire food, easily cooked in a cast-iron skillet atop embers. Jim and I used to take canoe trips with our friends the Works and the Henrys. We would pile into the Works' Suburban, with our canoes strapped on top and camping gear piled high, and strike off for the wild rivers in Oklahoma and Arkansas for a weekend of wilderness adventure. We made some wonderfully creative and delicious meals over the campfire, and dishes like this corn bread were often part of the menu.

SERVES 6 TO 8

5 tablespoons extra virgin olive oil

1 small onion, finely chopped (½ cup)

½ teaspoon minced garlic

½ cup finely chopped red bell peppers

1 jalapeño chile, seeded, stemmed, and minced

2 ears fresh corn, husked and kernels cut off the cob (1½ to 2 cups)

1 cup unbleached all-purpose flour

1 cup cornmeal

1 tablespoon baking powder

1 teaspoon salt

1½ cups buttermilk

3 large eggs, well beaten

4 ounces pepper Jack or Ancho Chile Caciotta (see Note), shredded (1 cup)

4 ounces Longhorn or Cheddar, shredded (1 cup)

PREHEAT THE oven to 375°F.

HEAT 2 tablespoons of the olive oil in a medium skillet. Add the onion, garlic, bell peppers, and jalapeño and sauté for about 4 minutes, or until the vegetables are beginning to soften. Add the corn and sauté for several minutes. Remove the pan from the heat and set aside.

SIFT THE flour, cornmeal, baking powder, and salt together into a large bowl and set aside. Mix the buttermilk with 2 tablespoons of the olive oil and the eggs in a medium bowl. Add the liquid to the dry ingredients and stir briefly to combine. Add the sautéed corn mixture and the cheeses and stir again to combine.

HEAT A 10-inch cast-iron skillet over low heat and pour in the remaining 1 tablespoon olive oil. Swirl the skillet around so that the oil completely coats the bottom and sides. If a cast-iron skillet is not available, grease an 8-inch square or 11 x 7-inch glass baking dish well with the olive oil. Pour the corn bread batter into the pan.

PLACE IN the oven and bake for 40 minutes to 1 hour, or until a toothpick inserted into the middle comes out clean and the top is golden brown. (The bread will bake more quickly in a baking dish than in a cast-iron skillet, so begin checking after 40 minutes.) Remove the corn bread and let cool slightly in the pan on a rack before cutting and serving.

TO SERVE, cut into wedges or squares. Serve warm.

NOTE: Ancho Chile Caciotta is available from the Mozzarella Company (see Sources, page 373).

This place certainly reeks of hospitality and good cheer, or maybe it's this cheese.

–Jean Harlow, in *Red Dust*

Lori's Lavosh with Blue Cheese

Back in the early 1980s, a French restaurant called The Riviera opened in Dallas. Its food reflected that glorious region of France. Two young chefs, Lori Finkelman and David Holben, manned the kitchen and their food was magical. The restaurant is still popular today and is known as one of the best restaurants in Dallas. Lori and David have gone their separate ways, but their creative genius still shines at the Riviera.

This is Lori's recipe for lavosh. It is as thin as paper and very crispy. It's as good alone as it is with cheese.

SERVES 15 TO 20

2⅓ cups all-purpose unbleached flour

2 tablespoons sugar

½ teaspoon baking powder

½ teaspoon salt

6 tablespoons (¾ stick) unsalted butter, softened

¾ cup buttermilk

Coarse sea salt to taste

¼ cup sesame seeds

4 ounces Roquefort, crumbled (¾ cup)

PLACE THE flour, sugar, baking powder, and salt in a large bowl. Cut the butter into the flour, using two knives, a pastry blender, or your hands, so that it is completely incorporated. Add the buttermilk and mix well. Cover and set aside to rest for 30 minutes. (The dough can also be wrapped in plastic and refrigerated for 2 to 3 days.)

PREHEAT THE oven to 350°F. Line a large baking sheet with parchment paper.

ROLL OUT one-fourth of the dough on a well-floured work surface until very thin. Sprinkle the top with ¼ to ½ teaspoon coarse salt and 1 tablespoon of the sesame seeds. Press the salt and seeds into the dough by rolling over them gently with the rolling pin. Roll the thin dough up around the rolling pin, transfer, and unroll on the baking sheet.

PLACE IN the oven and bake until golden brown and crisp, about 15 to 20 minutes. Remove from the oven and place on a rack to cool. (Leave the oven on.)

REPEAT THE rolling and baking process with the remaining dough.

WHEN COOL, break the lavosh into large pieces, place them on several baking sheets, and sprinkle the crumbled Roquefort over the top. Place in the oven just long enough to heat and soften the cheese, about 1 to 2 minutes.

SERVE WARM or at room temperature. The plain lavosh, without the cheese, can be stored in an airtight container and kept for one week.

Lavosh Pizza with Goat Cheese and Pesto

Roll a piece of dough about the size of a golf ball into a round approximately 10 inches in diameter and bake as directed. Once cooled, spread with a thin layer of Basil Pesto (page 80) and top with 1 ounce (2 tablespoons) fresh goat cheese, crumbled. Return to the oven to heat to soften the cheese.

A raven sat upon a tree,
And not a word he spoke, for
His beak contained a piece of Brie,
Or, maybe, it was Roquefort?
We'll make it any kind you please—
At all events, it was a cheese.

—**Guy Welmore Carryl**

Dilly Bread

When I was a young schoolteacher in Fort Worth, I used to make loaf after loaf of this bread to give away for Christmas. It is a great bread to serve with soups and stews, it is delicious for sandwiches, and it's even good toasted.

I like to make my dilly bread in free-form round loaves; however, it can be made into larger traditional loaves and baked in loaf pans, or even formed into rolls. If you prefer to keep the extra loaves, once they are cooled, they can be wrapped tightly with plastic wrap and frozen.

MAKES 6 TO 8 SMALL LOAVES OR ABOUT 36 [2-INCH] ROLLS

½ cup warm water (about 110°F.)

2 (¼-ounce) packages active dry yeast

½ teaspoon plus ¼ cup sugar

2 tablespoons unsalted butter

2 teaspoons salt

1 tablespoon dill seeds

1 tablespoon dried dillweed

1 tablespoon minced onion

1 pound (2 cups) full-fat, small-curd cottage cheese, homemade (page 72) or store-bought

3 ounces Cheddar, shredded (¾ cup)

2 large eggs

½ teaspoon baking soda

5 cups unbleached all-purpose flour

2 tablespoons unsalted butter, softened

PLACE THE warm water in a small bowl and sprinkle the yeast over the water. Add the ½ teaspoon sugar and stir to moisten the yeast. Set aside to proof; if the mixture bubbles and has foam on the surface, the yeast is active.

WHILE THE yeast is proofing, melt the butter in a small saucepan over medium heat. Add the remaining ¼ cup sugar, the salt, dill seeds, dillweed, minced onion, and cottage cheese. Heat to lukewarm. Remove from the heat and pour into a warm bowl. Add the Cheddar, eggs, baking soda, and proofed yeast. Gradually stir in the flour. When all the flour is absorbed, cover and let rise until doubled in bulk, about 1 hour.

GREASE ONE or two baking sheets with butter, or line with parchment paper. Punch down the dough. Divide it into 6 to 8 equal parts for small loaves of bread. (The dough may also be divided into smaller pieces about the size of a golf ball to make buns.) Form into balls. Place the dough balls, seam side down, about 4 inches apart on the baking sheet(s). Rub the tops of the loaves with 1 tablespoon of the softened butter. Cover and let rise until doubled in size, about 45 minutes to 1 hour.

PREHEAT THE oven to 350°F.

PLACE THE loaves in the oven and bake for 25 to 30 minutes for loaves (or 18 to 20 minutes for buns). Remove from the oven and rub with remaining 1 tablespoon softened butter while still warm. Place on racks to cool.

SERVE WARM or at room temperature.

Fromage et pain
Est médecin au sain.

(Bread and cheese, medicine for the healthy.)

–French proverb

Maria Vittoria's Umbrian Cheese Bread

While living in Perugia, I became friends with an Italian girl who was studying biology at the University of Perugia. Maria Vittoria Pelliccioli was from a nearby Umbrian town called Viterbo. One Easter, she invited me home to spend the holiday with her family. It was a wonderful feast and the whole family was present, including her grandparents, who served a delicious sweet Moscato wine made in their nearby vineyard. This is the recipe for the cheese bread that Maria Vittoria's family served that day.

MAKES 1 (10-INCH) LARGE LOAF (ALMOST 3 POUNDS)
OR 2 SMALLER ONES (ABOUT 1 ½ POUNDS EACH)

STARTER SPONGE

1 cup warm water (about 110°F.)

1 (¼-ounce) package active dry yeast

½ teaspoon sugar

1¼ cups unbleached all-purpose flour

CHEESE BREAD

¼ cup warm water (about 110°F.)

2 teaspoons active dry yeast

Pinch of sugar

5 large eggs

2 tablespoons extra virgin olive oil

6 ounces Parmigiano-Reggiano, grated (1½ cups)

4 tablespoons (½ stick) unsalted butter, softened

1½ teaspoons salt

3¼ cups unbleached all-purpose flour, or more if needed

2 ounces Gruyère, cut into ½-inch cubes

1 large egg yolk

FOR THE Starter Sponge, place the warm water in a small bowl and sprinkle the yeast over the water. Add the sugar and stir to moisten the yeast. Set aside to proof; if the mixture bubbles and has foam on the surface, the yeast is active. Place the flour in a large bowl, add the proofed yeast, and stir to combine. Cover and set aside in a warm place to rise until doubled in volume, about 2 hours.

FOR THE Cheese Bread, place the warm water in a small bowl, sprinkle the yeast over the water, add the pinch of sugar, and stir to moisten the yeast. Set aside to proof; if the mixture bubbles and has foam on the surface it is active.

BEAT THE eggs with the olive oil, Parmigiano, butter, and salt in a small bowl. Add the proofed yeast and mix well. Stir this mixture into the starter sponge. Add the flour and mix well. Mix in the cubed Gruyère. Turn the dough out onto a floured work surface and knead for 10 to 15 minutes, adding flour if necessary. Shape the dough into a smooth flattened ball.

BUTTER AND flour a 9 x 2-inch round pan (at least 2 quarts) and place the dough in the pan. Or divide the dough in half, shape it, and place it in two 8 x 2-inch round pans or 9 x 5-inch loaf pans. The pans should be no more than half-full. Cover and set aside to rise until doubled in volume, about 2 hours.

PREHEAT THE oven to 400°F.

BEAT THE egg yolk with a fork and brush on the top of the dough. Place the pan in the oven and bake for 20 minutes, then turn the temperature down to 325°F. and continue to bake for 40 to 50 minutes longer, or until the bread has risen high above the sides of the pan(s) and the crust is a deep golden brown. Do not open the oven door during the first hour of baking. Or, if using two smaller pans, bake at 400°F. for 15 minutes, then at 325°F. for about 30 minutes. Remove the bread from the oven and set on a rack to cool for 10 minutes. Remove the bread from the pan(s) to finish cooling.

VARIATION

Cheese and Prosciutto Bread

When you add the Gruyère, add 2 to 3 ounces of thinly sliced prosciutto cut into ½-inch strips.

Salami-and-Provolone-Stuffed Bread

Years ago, when the cheese factory was young, there was a man in Dallas who made long, skinny loaves of pepperoni bread. Back then we had a lot of extra time, and we used to make sandwiches by cutting his loaves in half and melting our mozzarella on top, which we then sold to neighbors. More recently, I came across a similar bread from a bakery near Aspen, with various meats and large amounts of cheese and herbs baked inside. Both inspired me to create this stuffed loaf.

The amount of dough in this recipe will make 2 loaves or 24 to 30 bread sticks, or *grissini* in Italian. You could also make 1 loaf of bread with half the dough and bread sticks with the other half.

MAKES 2 LOAVES

DOUGH

1⅓ cups warm water (about 110°F.)

1 (¼-ounce) package active dry yeast

2 teaspoons sugar

3½ to 4 cups unbleached all-purpose flour

2 teaspoons salt

FILLING

12 dry-packed sun-dried tomatoes halves, plumped in hot water for 15 minutes, drained, and cut into julienne strips

4 ounces Genoa salami, thinly sliced

12 ounces provolone, thinly sliced

1 teaspoon dried oregano

1 large egg white, beaten with ¼ cup water for the egg wash

FOR THE Dough, place ⅓ cup of the warm water in a large bowl. Sprinkle the yeast over the water. Add the sugar and stir to moisten the yeast. Set aside to proof; if the mixture bubbles and has foam on the surface, the yeast is active.

MIX THE 3½ cups flour and the salt together on a piece of waxed paper. When the yeast has proofed, add the flour to the yeast mixture in the bowl, 1 cup at a time, alternately with the remaining 1 cup warm water. Turn the dough out onto a lightly floured work surface and knead for about 10 minutes, adding more flour if necessary so that it is not sticky, until it has an elastic consistency.

LIGHTLY GREASE a large bowl and transfer the dough to the bowl; turn to coat it. Set aside, covered, in a warm place to rise until doubled, about 1 to 1½ hours.

WHEN THE dough has risen, punch it down and transfer it to a lightly floured work surface. Knead the dough for about 5 minutes. Divide the dough in half. Press or roll into a rectangle about 12 x 4 inches.

FOR THE Filling, divide the salami evenly between the two pieces of dough, laying it lengthwise down the center of each rectangle and leaving the edges bare. Place the provolone, sun-dried tomatoes, and oregano on top of the salami. Beginning on a long side, roll each piece of dough into a long loaf; pinch the ends together and fold them under so that the cheese won't run out during baking, Place the loaves seam side down on a nonstick baking sheet. leaving several inches between the loaves so that there is space to rise. Slash the tops of the loaves diagonally with a sharp knife. Set aside in a warm place, loosely covered, to rise until doubled in size, 45 minutes to 1 hour.

PLACE A shallow pan of boiling water on the lowest rack in the oven to create steam while the bread is baking. Preheat the oven to 425°F.

BRUSH THE egg wash onto the loaves, to create a crusty exterior. Place the loaves in the oven and bake for 10 to 15 minutes. Reduce the heat to 350°F. and continue baking for 15 to 20 minutes longer, or until the loaves are golden brown. Remove the bread from the oven and place the loaves on a rack to cool briefly.

SERVE THE bread warm, sliced diagonally into ½-inch slices.

VARIATION

Parmigiano Grissini (Bread Sticks)

MAKES 24 TO 30 BREAD STICKS

Omit the filling. After the dough has risen once, punch it down and knead it. Pinch pieces of the dough off in balls about the size of a Ping-Pong ball. With your hands, roll out each small ball on a floured surface to form a snake of dough about 10 inches long. Then hold one end in place while twisting the other end; place the bread sticks 2 inches apart on two nonstick baking sheets. Let rise until doubled in size, about 45 minutes.

Brush the bread sticks with the egg wash. Sprinkle liberally with 4 ounces Parmigiano, grated (1 cup). Or spread out the cheese on waxed paper, dip the bread sticks one at a time into the grated cheese, and return to the baking sheet. Bake at 425°F. for 10 to 15 minutes, or until crispy and golden brown.

Desserts

Patricia's Cherry and Goat Cheese Gratin

This recipe comes from Patricia Wells, one of America's gifts to France. Patricia is a restaurant critic for the *International Herald Tribune,* as well as the author of numerous cookbooks celebrating French food and *The Food Lover's Guide to Paris.* Patricia and her husband, Walter, have a charming farmhouse in Provence, where Patricia shops at the local markets in Vaison and Saint-Rémy for cherries and other seasonal fruits.

This dish, somewhat like a clafouti, was created by Patricia one day while she was stuck at home waiting for a delivery man to arrive. She meant to make the recipe using cream, but she had none, so she substituted fresh goat cheese. If goat cheese is not your favorite, use yogurt or cream cheese in its place. If cherries are not available, substitute peaches, berries, or even seeded grapes.

SERVES 4 TO 6

1½ pounds cherries, pitted

4 ounces (½ cup) fresh goat cheese

⅓ cup sugar

2 large eggs

½ cup finely ground blanched almonds

Pinch of salt

½ teaspoon pure vanilla extract

½ teaspoon almond extract

1 tablespoon confectioners' sugar, for garnish

PREHEAT THE oven to 375°F. Butter a 12-inch round ceramic baking dish.

ARRANGE THE cherries in one layer in the bottom of the baking dish. Beat the goat cheese, sugar, eggs, almonds, salt, vanilla, and almond extract together in a medium bowl or in the work bowl of a food processor fitted with a steel blade until well blended. Pour over the cherries.

PLACE THE dish on the middle rack of the oven and bake for 30 minutes, or until the top is a deep golden brown. Remove from the oven and let cool on a rack.

TO SERVE, dust with confectioners' sugar and cut into wedges.

SERVE AT room temperature.

Stilton Soufflé
with Pears Poached in Port

When I lived in Perugia, I met a girl from England, Jenny Bayly Franks, who was also studying Italian. We became fast friends. I visited her several times in Malta, where her father commanded the NATO troops. For the past thirty years, Jim and I have been visiting Jenny and her family in England, where they now live. From those heady days in Malta when we watched the American astronauts land on the moon to New Year's Eve celebrations in the English countryside, we have always enjoyed meals that ended with that most delicious of all English cheeses—Stilton.

Stilton and port are a perfect pair; add pears and the trio is heavenly. This soufflé is a twist on the classic British ending to a fine meal. I suggest serving it with a glass of port.

Sweet dessert soufflés are always a special treat. They are not that difficult to do, because everything can be prepared ahead up to a point. Then, at the last moment, all you need to do is whip the egg whites and fold them into the base. It's easy to accomplish this before sitting down to dinner. The soufflé can cook during your meal.

MAKES ABOUT 1½ CUPS SYRUP
SERVES 6

POACHED PEARS

3 cups port

¾ cup sugar

2 pieces lemon zest (2 inches by ½ inch)

2 whole cloves

6 ripe but firm Bosc pears

6 leaves fresh mint

SOUFFLÉ

2 tablespoons unsalted butter

2 tablespoons unbleached all-purpose flour

2 cups milk, heated

2 tablespoons sugar

⅛ teaspoon salt

5 large eggs, separated

6 ounces Stilton, crumbled (about 1 cup)

1 large egg white

FOR THE Poached Pears, pour the port into a deep saucepan just large enough to hold the 6 pears (on their sides). Add the sugar and stir until dissolved. Add the lemon zest and cloves. One at a time, peel the pears, leaving the stems attached, and trim a thin slice off the bottoms so that they will stand up. As you prepare each one, immediately place it in the port and spoon the port over it to keep it from discoloring. Place the pan over medium heat and bring the port to a simmer. Cook the pears for 10 to 15 minutes, turning them carefully and spooning the port over them so that the wine colors all sides, or until tender but not mushy. Test the pears with the tip of a knife inserted near the bottom; they should be firm yet tender. Transfer to a plate to cool.

REDUCE THE port by boiling it vigorously to half its volume, about 20 minutes, stirring as necessary. Set aside and let cool. (The port sauce will become thicker as it cools.)

FOR THE Soufflé, preheat the oven to 400°F. Butter and flour a 7 x 3-inch soufflé dish. Make a foil collar by folding a piece of aluminum foil that is approximately 25 inches long lengthwise in half. Butter and flour the part of the collar that will extend above the soufflé dish. Wrap the foil around the dish and secure it with toothpicks or kitchen twine.

MELT THE butter in a saucepan over low heat. When the foam subsides, stir in the flour and cook for 1 minute, stirring continuously. Add the milk, whisking constantly, and cook over medium heat for 3 to 4 minutes, or until thickened. Add the sugar and salt. Remove from the heat and add the Stilton. Return to low heat and continue to stir until the cheese is completely melted. Add the egg yolks one by one, stirring constantly. Pour into a large mixing bowl and let cool slightly. (The soufflé base can be prepared several hours ahead and refrigerated. Remove from the refrigerator about 30 minutes before ready to bake.)

BEAT THE egg whites to stiff peaks in a clean bowl. Stir a few tablespoons of the beaten whites into the soufflé mixture and then gently fold in the remaining whites using a rubber spatula. Pour into the prepared soufflé dish.

PLACE IN the oven and bake for 35 to 40 minutes, or until the soufflé has risen and is golden brown on top; do not open the oven door. Keep an eye on the soufflé through the glass in the oven door, if possible. If the top begins to get too brown, reduce the heat to 375°F.

WHILE THE soufflé is baking, place each of the pears standing up straight on a serving plate. Drizzle the port sauce over the pears liberally, so that it forms a pool on the plate. Garnish each pear with a mint leaf inserted at the stem end.

WHEN THE soufflé is cooked, immediately remove it from the oven.

TO SERVE, spoon a portion of the soufflé onto each serving plate next to the pear. Serve immediately.

> Stilton and port remains one of the
> great marriages in all gastronomy.
> **–Jonathan Reynolds**

Apple Spice Cake with Cream Cheese Icing

Apples remind me of fall. And in Texas, fall invariably arrives around Halloween. We have a family tradition of spending Halloween with our godchildren, Winston, Hannah, and Virginia Cutshall. After they leave dressed up in their crazy costumes to go trick-or-treating, we usually enjoy a piece of cake and a cup of coffee with their parents.

This is the perfect fall cake. The spices, apples, nuts, and raisins in this cake all are complemented by the smooth cream cheese icing. It's actually like a rich buttercream but it is made with cream cheese instead of butter. Decorate the cake simply with walnut or pecan halves or festively with edible flowers. Serve it with coffee or a glass of sweet dessert wine such as a late-harvest Riesling.

SERVES 8

APPLE SPICE CAKE

8 tablespoons (1 stick) unsalted butter, softened

½ cup packed dark brown sugar

¾ cup molasses

4 large eggs

2½ cups unbleached all-purpose flour

2 teaspoons baking powder

1 teaspoon baking soda

2 teaspoons ground ginger

½ teaspoon ground cloves

½ teaspoon ground cinnamon

½ teaspoon ground nutmeg

½ teaspoon ground allspice

½ teaspoon salt

1 cup buttermilk

1 medium apple, peeled, cored, and finely chopped (1 cup)

½ cup chopped toasted pecans or walnuts

½ cup raisins

CREAM CHEESE ICING

8 ounces (1 cup) cream cheese, home-made (page 74) or store-bought, softened

2 cups confectioners' sugar

2 tablespoons heavy cream

2 teaspoons pure vanilla extract

12 toasted pecan or walnut halves, for garnish (optional)

Edible flowers, for garnish (optional)

PREHEAT THE oven to 350°F. Butter two 9-inch round cake pans. Place a piece of waxed paper in the bottom of each pan and then butter the paper. Dust with flour.

CREAM TOGETHER the butter and brown sugar in a large bowl, using an electric mixer. Beat in the molasses. Beat in the eggs one at a time, scraping the sides of the bowl as necessary.

SIFT TOGETHER the flour, baking powder, baking soda, ginger, cloves, cinnamon, nutmeg, allspice, and salt. Slowly add the dry ingredients to the butter mixture, alternating with the buttermilk, beating on low speed until well combined. Fold in the apple, nuts, and raisins. Pour batter into the cake pans.

PLACE IN the oven and bake for 30 to 45 minutes, or until brown on top and a toothpick inserted in the center comes out moist but clean. The cake should spring back when gently touched in the center.

REMOVE THE cake from the oven and let cool in the pans on a wire rack for about 10 minutes. Invert the layers onto a rack, remove the pans, and let cool completely.

FOR THE Cream Cheese Icing, cream together the cream cheese, confectioners' sugar, and cream in a medium bowl, using an electric mixer. Add the vanilla and beat to combine.

ONCE THE cake has cooled, remove the waxed paper and place one layer upside down on a serving platter. Spread one-third of the icing on top. Place the second layer on top, right side up, and frost the entire cake with the icing. Make swirls and designs in the icing with the tines of a fork. Decorate the top of the cake with toasted nut halves and edible flowers, if desired.

TO SERVE, cut into slices.

On Limburger:
I cannot think why this cheese was not thrown from the aeroplanes during the war to spread panic amongst enemy troops. It would have proved far more efficacious than those nasty deadly gases that kill people permanently.
–Eric Weir

Chocolate Cream Cheese Brownies

Baking the cream cheese on top of these brownies creates the illusion of a layer of white frosting. They are incredibly rich and moist.

MAKES 24 (2-INCH) BROWNIES

BROWNIES

3 ounces (3 squares) unsweetened chocolate, coarsely chopped

4 ounces bittersweet chocolate, coarsely chopped

½ pound (2 sticks) unsalted butter, cut into pieces

8 large eggs

1 cup granulated sugar

1 cup packed light brown sugar

2 teaspoons pure vanilla extract

1½ cups unbleached all-purpose flour

CREAM CHEESE TOPPING

8 ounces (1 cup) cream cheese, home-made (page 74) or store-bought, softened

4 cups (1 pound) confectioners' sugar

½ cup bittersweet chocolate chunks or chips (3 ounces)

2 tablespoons confectioners' sugar, for garnish (optional)

PREHEAT THE oven to 350°F. Butter a 13 x 9 x 2-inch glass baking dish, dust with flour, and set aside.

PLACE THE unsweetened and bittersweet chocolate and the butter in a microwave-safe bowl or in the top of a double boiler over simmering water. If using the microwave, heat for 1-minute intervals, checking and stirring the chocolate before heating again, until melted. Or stir constantly over the simmering water until smooth and glossy. Remove from the heat and pour chocolate into a large bowl. One at a time, add 6 of the eggs, beating with a wooden spoon after each addition. Stir in the granulated and brown sugars. Stir in the vanilla. Add the flour and blend until no white shows. Pour the mixture into the baking dish and smooth the top with a rubber spatula. Set aside.

FOR THE Cream Cheese Topping, place the cream cheese and confectioners' sugar in a large bowl. Beat until just combined, using an electric mixer at low speed or a wooden spoon. Add the remaining 2 eggs and continue to beat for several minutes at medium speed. Scrape the sides of the bowl as necessary. Pour over the chocolate mixture in the pan. Sprinkle the chocolate chunks over the top.

PLACE THE pan in the oven and bake for 35 to 45 minutes, or until the top is set and golden brown. Remove and place on a rack to cool.

TO SERVE, dust the top with confectioners' sugar, using a sieve, if desired. Cut into 2-inch squares, remove from dish, and place on a platter.

Dallas Cheesecake

About the time I started the Mozzarella Company, Lyn Dunsavage, who published the *Downtown Dallas News,* decided to give up the newspaper career and move to New York, Texas, a sleepy little town in East Texas. Lyn and her husband had decided they wanted to move down to the country to get away from the mad rush of Dallas. Once there, Lyn began producing the most decadently rich and dense cheesecakes, which she sold far and wide. She called them New York–Texas cheesecakes. As her business grew, she was baking cheesecakes around the clock. So much for getting away from the mad rush! This recipe is even richer than Lyn's, so I call it Dallas cheesecake.

There are two schools of thought regarding how a cheesecake should be baked. I prefer my method because it results in a cheesecake that is dense yet relatively light textured; however, the top may crack slightly. If you want to have a cheesecake that is denser and does not crack, wrap the bottom and sides of the springform pan with heavy-duty aluminum foil and place it in a larger pan filled with 1 inch of boiling water. Bake for 45 minutes, then turn off the oven and leave the cake in the oven with the door closed for 1 hour. Remove the cake and water bath from the oven, place the cake on a rack (the center will still be very jiggly and quivery), and allow to cool for 1 hour. Cover with plastic wrap and refrigerate for at least 4 hours, or overnight, before serving.

SERVES 12

CRUST

1½ cups crushed graham crackers

¼ cup sugar

6 tablespoons (¾ stick) unsalted butter, melted

1 teaspoon ground cinnamon

FILLING

2 pounds (4 cups) cream cheese, home-made (page 74) or store-bought, softened

1 cup (8 ounces) crème fraîche, home-made (page 68) or store-bought, or sour cream

2 teaspoons pure vanilla extract

1 cup sugar

4 large eggs

Grated zest of 1 orange

Grated zest of 1 lemon

8 ounces (1 cup) mascarpone, home-made (page 73) or store-bought

FOR THE Crust, lightly butter the sides of a 10 x 3-inch springform pan.

COMBINE THE graham cracker crumbs, sugar, butter, and cinnamon in a small bowl and mix well. Transfer to the pan and press evenly onto the bottom of the pan, about ¼ inch thick, and as far up the sides as possible. Refrigerate for 30 minutes.

PREHEAT THE oven to 325°F. Line a baking sheet with aluminum foil.

FOR THE Filling, place the cream cheese and crème fraîche in the large bowl of an electric mixer and beat at medium speed until soft and fluffy. Add the vanilla, then gradually beat in the sugar. Increase the speed to high and beat for 4 minutes, scraping the sides as necessary. Add the eggs one at a time, beating well after each addition. Add the orange and lemon zests and mascarpone, beating just to incorporate them. Pour the batter into the springform pan. Tap the pan gently on a flat surface to remove any air bubbles.

PLACE THE springform pan on the baking sheet, place in the oven, and bake for 1 hour to 1 hour and 15 minutes. The cheesecake should be slightly risen and still a little liquid in the center. Turn off the oven and prop the oven door open with a wooden spoon to allow the heat to escape. Leave the cake undisturbed in the oven for 1 hour. It will finish cooking in the turned-off oven. (See introduction to recipe if you prefer a dense-textured cheesecake.)

REMOVE THE cake from the oven and place on a rack to cool for 1 hour. Cover and refrigerate for at least 4 hours before serving.

TO SERVE, slice the cheesecake with a sharp thin knife dipped in warm water and dried before each slice. Serve chilled.

VARIATIONS

Walnut-Crusted Stilton Cheesecake with Caramelized Apple Topping

Replace 1 cup of the graham crackers in the crust with 1 cup chopped walnuts. Replace the mascarpone with 8 ounces Stilton, crumbled, and omit the lemon and orange zest. Bake and cool as directed. Refrigerate for at least 4 hours before serving.

For the topping, peel and core 3 apples. Cut across each apple to make rounds approximately ¼ inch thick. Sauté the apples in 3 tablespoons butter in a large nonstick skillet over medium heat until soft, turning once or twice. Be careful not to break the rings when turning. Add 1 cup packed light brown sugar and 2 tablespoons apple brandy or Calvados and continue sautéing until the juices are thick and syrupy. Cool to room temperature, about 30 minutes. Pour the topping onto the chilled cheesecake just before serving.

Lemon-Ricotta Cheesecake with Blueberry Topping

Replace the graham crackers in the crust with vanilla wafers. Replace the cream cheese with 1 pound ricotta, well drained. Omit the orange zest and use the zest from 6 lemons. Add ¼ cup freshly squeezed lemon juice with the vanilla. Bake and cool as directed. Refrigerate for at least 4 hours before serving.

For the topping, melt 1 cup apple jelly in a medium saucepan over low heat. Remove from the heat and add 1 pint (2 cups) blueberries. Stir carefully to coat the blueberries with jelly, but be careful not to crush them; let cool. Spoon the cooled topping over the chilled cheesecake.

Melt ½ cup apple jelly with 1 teaspoon freshly squeezed lemon juice in a small saucepan and cook until it thickens and large bubbles form. While warm, brush this glaze over the blueberries. Cover loosely and refrigerate until ready to serve.

Mocha Cheesecake with Chocolate Crust

Substitute crushed chocolate wafers for the graham crackers in the crust.

Stir ¼ cup instant coffee granules into the sour cream. Omit the orange and lemon zests. Melt 4 ounces bittersweet chocolate in a double boiler over low heat or in a microwave. Let cool. Make the cheesecake batter and transfer 1 cup of the batter to a small bowl. Add the chocolate to the 1 cup of the batter. Pour half the plain batter into the springform pan, then spoon the chocolate batter on top in pools. Pour on the remaining plain batter. Using the handle of a wooden spoon, swirl the chocolate batter to create a marbleized effect. Bake and cool as directed. Refrigerate for at least 4 hours before serving.

For the topping, just before serving, place 2 ounces bittersweet chocolate, chopped, in a small heavy-duty plastic bag and melt in the microwave. Snip off a corner of the bag and drizzle the melted chocolate in a swirling design on the top of the cheesecake.

Amaretto Cheesecake with Peach Topping

Replace 1 cup of the graham crackers in the crust with 1 cup finely chopped blanched almonds. Add ½ cup amaretto liqueur to the cake batter after the eggs. Bake and cool as directed. Refrigerate for 4 hours before serving.

For the topping, melt 1 cup peach preserves in a medium saucepan over low heat. Remove from the heat and gently stir in 2 peaches that have been peeled, pitted, and sliced. Set aside to cool. Spoon over the chilled cheesecake just before serving.

Forgotten Torte
with Mascarpone Sorbet and Berries

This recipe originated in the Deep South, where it was passed between friends and from generation to generation. I learned about it from my friend Margaret Anne Cullum, who served it to me as a birthday cake ages ago. It is like a giant soft meringue cooked in an angel food cake pan. It is light as a feather and irresistibly sweet. It's called a forgotten torte because you can leave it in the oven and forget about it for hours.

Once, when the Mansion on Turtle Creek invited me to be Chef of the Day, this is the dessert recipe I gave them to serve. It can be served with any summer fruit. If you don't have time to make the mascarpone sorbet, you can substitute whipped crème fraîche. (See the Variation.)

SERVES 12

6 large egg whites

¼ teaspoon salt

½ teaspoon cream of tartar

1½ cups sugar

1 teaspoon pure vanilla extract

1 pint (2 cups) strawberries, washed and hulled, for garnish

1 pint (2 cups) blueberries or black-berries, washed and hulled, for garnish

Minted Mascarpone Sorbet (page 328)

PREHEAT THE oven to 450°F. Butter only the bottom of a 9-inch angel food cake pan or 12-cup Bundt pan.

BEAT THE egg whites with the salt and cream of tartar in a large bowl, using an electric mixer, until almost stiff. Beat in the sugar 2 tablespoons at a time, beating until you have a stiff and shiny meringue. Beat in the vanilla. Pour the batter into the pan. Tap the pan on the counter several times to eliminate any large air pockets.

PLACE THE torte in the oven and immediately turn off the heat. Forget the torte and leave it in the oven for several hours or overnight, or until the cake has cooled completely.

LOOSEN THE edges of the torte from the sides of the pan using a knife, invert the cake pan, and turn the torte out onto a plate. Refrigerate until serving time.

TO SERVE, decorate the torte with the strawberries and blueberries. Cut into slices and serve with the sorbet.

Forgotten Torte with Whipped Crème Fraîche and Berries

Whip 1 cup (8 ounces) crème fraîche, homemade (page 68) or store-bought, and substitute for the Mascarpone sorbet. Serve with strawberries and blueberries as directed.

Cheese, that the table's closing rites
  denies,
And bids me with the unwilling
  chaplain rise.

–John Gay

Chocolate Layer Cake
with Strawberries and Mascarpone

I love the chocolates called *Baci,* which means "kisses" in Italian, that come from Perugia. Each chocolate and hazelnut candy comes wrapped with a romantic quotation on a tiny piece of paper. The quotations are translated into four languages, Italian, French, English, and German, so you can practice saying loving and romantic phrases in all four languages as you enjoy the chocolates.

When you decorate this cake with Baci as well as strawberries, you'll have a chance to read lots of those romantic quotations.

SERVES 8

CHOCOLATE LAYER CAKE

4 ounces unsweetened chocolate

8 tablespoons (1 stick) unsalted butter, softened

1 cup sugar

3 large eggs, separated

1 cup milk

1 teaspoon pure vanilla extract

2 cups unbleached all-purpose flour

1 teaspoon ground cinnamon

1 tablespoon baking powder

½ teaspoon baking soda

¼ teaspoon salt

FILLING

½ cup confectioners' sugar

1 pound (2 cups) mascarpone, home-made (page 73) or store-bought

½ cup heavy cream, whipped just to stiff peaks

1 pint strawberries, washed, hulled, and sliced ¼ inch thick (2 cups)

8 Baci (optional)

Fresh mint leaves, for garnish (optional)

FOR THE Chocolate Cake, preheat the oven to 350°F. Butter two 9-inch round or 8-inch square cake pans. Place a piece of waxed paper in the bottom of each cake pan. Butter the waxed paper and the sides of the pans and dust the inside of the pan with cocoa powder, shaking off the excess.

PLACE THE chocolate in a double boiler and melt over low heat, stirring until smooth. Alternatively, melt it in the microwave. Remove from the heat and set aside to let cool.

PLACE THE butter and sugar in a large bowl and cream together, using an electric mixer. Beat in the egg yolks one at a time, scraping the sides of the bowl as necessary. Add the melted chocolate and then the milk. Beat on low speed until well combined. Add the vanilla and mix well.

SIFT TOGETHER the flour, cinnamon, baking powder, baking soda, and salt two times. Slowly add to the chocolate mixture, beating on low speed.

IN A clean bowl, beat the egg whites to stiff peaks. Blend a spoonful of the whites into the chocolate mixture, then gently fold in the remaining whites using a rubber spatua.

DIVIDE THE batter between the two prepared pans. Place in the oven and bake for 20 to 25 minutes, or until a toothpick inserted near the center comes out clean but moist. The cake should spring back when gently touched in the center.

REMOVE FROM the oven and allow to cool in the pan on a cake rack for about 10 minutes. Invert the layers onto a cake rack, remove the pans, and let cool completely. Once cooled, remove the waxed paper.

FOR THE Filling, stir the confectioners' sugar into the mascarpone in a small bowl. Fold in the whipped cream.

PLACE ONE cake layer upside down on a serving platter. Spread about half of the mascarpone filling on the layer. Place half the strawberries on top in a single layer. Place the second cake layer on top, right side up. Cover the top with the remaining mascarpone filling. Arrange the remaining strawberries and the Baci, if using, on top of the mascarpone. Cover with plastic wrap and refrigerate for at least 1 hour and up to 4 to 6 hours.

TO SERVE, garnish with mint leaves, if desired, and cut into wedges. Served chilled.

Nick's Sweet Ricotta Cheesecake

Nick Malgieri is a fabulous pastry chef and cookbook author. He has written many cookbooks, including one of recipes for Italian desserts. He is truly a master, so when he offered to give me a recipe for his ricotta cheesecake, I jumped with glee! He is also a wonderful teacher. Not only does he teach at the James Beard House and Peter Kump's Cooking School in New York, he often travels across the country giving classes. If he ever comes to a cooking school near you, sign up for a class!

With its candied orange peel and cinnamon, this cheesecake's ricotta filling showcases Sicilian and Neapolitan flavors. It looks very Italian too, with its latticed top pastry crust.

SERVES 12

PASTRY CRUST

8 tablespoons (1 stick) unsalted butter

2 cups unbleached all-purpose flour

⅓ cup sugar

Pinch of salt

½ teaspoon baking powder

2 large eggs

RICOTTA FILLING

1½ pounds ricotta, homemade (page 70) or store-bought, well drained (3 cups)

½ cup sugar

4 large eggs

1 teaspoon pure vanilla extract

1 tablespoon anisette

3 tablespoons chopped candied orange peel or citron (optional)

1 teaspoon ground cinnamon

1 egg, beaten with a pinch of salt, for the egg wash

FOR THE Pastry Crust, place the butter, flour, sugar, and salt in the work bowl of a food processor fitted with a steel blade. Pulse until the mixture resembles cornmeal. Pour the eggs through the feed tube with the motor running. Continue to pulse until a rough ball of dough forms on the blade. Do not overmix. Remove the dough, place on a piece of plastic wrap, and form into a disk. Wrap in plastic wrap and refrigerate for 30 minutes, or until firm.

PREHEAT THE oven to 350°F. Butter a 9 x 2-inch round cake pan or 10-inch pie pan or quiche pan.

FOR THE Ricotta Filling, place the ricotta in a medium bowl and beat with a wooden spoon until smooth. Beat in the sugar, then beat in the eggs one at a time. Stir in the vanilla, anisette, candied orange peel, if using, and ½ teaspoon of the cinnamon.

CUT OFF one-third of the pastry crust and set it aside. Roll the rest of the dough into a 14-inch disk on a lightly floured work surface. Transfer the dough to the pan by folding it in quarters or by rolling it up over the rolling pin. Fit the dough snugly into the pan. Cut the excess dough off even with the top of the pan using a sharp knife. Pour in the ricotta filling. Sprinkle with the remaining ½ teaspoon cinnamon.

ROLL THE remaining dough into a 10-inch square and cut it into ten 1-inch-wide strips. Brush the strips with the egg wash. Arrange the strips on top of the filling, with 5 laid in each direction, weaving them to form a lattice-work pattern. Trim the strips so that the ends extend over the edges about ½ inch. Loosen the dough at the top of the pan with the back of a small knife and ease the ends of the lattice strips down between the dough and the sides of the pan. Crimp the crust.

PLACE IN the oven and bake for 45 minutes, until the filling is set and the pastry crust is a deep golden color. Remove, place on a rack, and let cool in the pan.

TO SERVE, cut into wedges. Serve at room temperature.

Take cheese and pound it till smooth and pasty; put cheese in a brazen sieve; add honey and spring wheat flour. Heat in one mass, cool, and serve.

–Athenaeus, giving the first cheesecake recipe, A.D. 230

Cream Cheese Pound Cake

Pound cakes are so versatile; they are wonderful alone or with ice cream and macerated fresh fruit. They stay moist and fresh for days, and they even taste good toasted for breakfast. They can be ultra-sophisticated at a dinner party, or tarted up for a festive occasion. For years my husband, Jim, has made a wonderful cake for my birthday by layering pound cake, ice cream, blueberries, and fresh peaches. He invites all our friends and their children to come over and have a big slice to celebrate with us.

It's very old-fashioned to flavor pound cakes with mace, and I've heard that the custom originated in New England with the early colonists. Like me, you may have wondered where mace comes from—the mace tree? Well, it's the coating or skin of the nutmeg seed. It has a slightly different taste than nutmeg, but in a pinch you can substitute one for the other. **SERVES 12 TO 16**

8 ounces (1 cup) cream cheese, home-made (page 74) or store-bought, softened

¾ pound (3 sticks) unsalted butter, softened

3 cups sugar

6 large eggs

1 teaspoon pure vanilla extract

3 cups cake flour

1 teaspoon ground mace or nutmeg

½ teaspoon salt

3 tablespoons confectioners' sugar

PREHEAT THE oven to 325°F. Butter and flour two 9 x 5-inch loaf pans or a 12-cup Bundt pan.

CREAM THE cream cheese, butter, and sugar together in a large bowl, using an electric mixer on high speed, until light and fluffy. Beat in the eggs one at a time, scraping the sides of the bowl as necessary. Beat in the vanilla.

SIFT THE flour, mace, and salt together two times. Slowly add to the butter mixture, beating on low speed until well combined. Beat for 3 to 4 minutes. Pour the batter into the pan(s).

PLACE IN the oven and bake until the top is golden brown and a toothpick inserted in the center comes out clean but moist, 65 to 70 minutes if using loaf pans, 1 hour and 30 minutes to 1 hour and 45 minutes if using a Bundt pan. The top crust may be cracked. Remove the cake(s) from the oven and let cool in the pan(s) on a cake rack for 10 minutes. Invert the cake(s) onto a rack, remove the pan(s), and let cool completely.

TO SERVE, sift confectioners' sugar over the top and cut into slices. Serve at room temperature.

David's Cinnamon-Ricotta Sorbet

David Brawley, a Dallas pastry chef, created this wonderfully refreshing sorbet. David has been a friend since we first met when he was the pastry chef at Baby Routh Restaurant in Dallas in the 1980s. Whenever I delivered cheese to him in those days, he would open up the freezer and pull out some wonderful creation that he would insist I try. Needless to say, I looked forward to those deliveries!

MAKES ABOUT 2½ CUPS
SERVES 4

SIMPLE SYRUP
1 cup water

1 cup sugar

1½ tablespoons light corn syrup

2 cinnamon sticks

CINNAMON-RICOTTA SORBET
12 ounces ricotta, homemade (page 70) or store-bought, well drained (1½ cups)

½ cup heavy cream

1⅓ cups Simple Syrup

FOR THE Simple Syrup, combine the water, sugar, and corn syrup in a saucepan. Stir the mixture and place over medium heat. Bring to a boil, stirring occasionally, then lower the heat and stir until the sugar dissolves completely. Remove from heat and add the cinnamon sticks. Set aside to cool. Remove and discard the cinnamon sticks just before using.

FOR THE Cinnamon-Ricotta Sorbet, combine the ricotta and cream in the work bowl of a food processor fitted with a steel blade and process until very smooth. Add the 1⅓ cups syrup and pulse to combine. Strain the mixture through a fine-mesh sieve or a strainer lined with several thicknesses of cheesecloth into a bowl and refrigerate until very cold.

POUR THE mixture into an ice cream machine and freeze according to the manufacturer's directions until the sorbet reaches a "soft-serve" consistency. Transfer the sorbet to a metal or other freezer container, place in the freezer, and let harden for at least 2 hours.

VARIATION

Steep other strongly flavored herbs or spices in the hot syrup to make an infusion of flavors; strain before adding to the pureed ricotta.

Fred's Ricotta Fig Fool

We used to have prune whip as a dessert when I was growing up. I loved it because it was so smooth, so light, and so airy. Mother always served it in parfait glasses and we ate it with iced-tea spoons. A fool is rather like a whip; it's made with pureed fruit, whipped cream, and egg whites.

Fred Penn is a great friend. He gave me the idea for this fig fool, no fool he, so I have named it for him.

MAKES ABOUT 2¾ CUPS
SERVES 4

12 dried figs

½ cup pear liqueur (poire or pear William) or rum or brandy

8 ounces ricotta, homemade (page 70) or store-bought, well drained (1 cup)

¼ cup sugar

¾ cup (6 ounces) crème fraîche, home-made (page 68) or store-bought, or heavy cream

2 large egg whites

Fresh mint leaves, for garnish

PLACE THE figs in a small bowl and cover with the pear liqueur. Marinate them for 1 hour.

DRAIN THE figs, set aside 2 for the garnish, and place the remaining figs in the work bowl of a food processor fitted with a steel blade. Process to a puree. Add the ricotta and sugar and continue to process until perfectly smooth. Transfer to a large bowl.

IN A clean bowl, whip the egg whites until stiff, using a whisk or an electric mixer. Stir several tablespoons of the whites into the figs, then gently fold in the remaining whites, using a rubber spatula. In the bowl you used for the egg whites beat the crème fraîche, with the mixer or a whisk, until fairly stiff. Fold the whipped cream into the fig mixture, using a rubber spatula.

CUT THE reserved figs into strips. Spoon the fool into parfait glasses and refrigerate until cold.

SERVE CHILLED, garnished with the fig strips and mint leaves.

NOTE: It's generally safe to use raw eggs in your recipes, as long as they are fresh, grade A or AA, and have been properly refrigerated. There is, however, a slight risk of *Salmonella enteritidis* and other illnesses related to the consumption of raw eggs. I have made this recipe many, many times without any problem, but to be absolutely safe, pregnant women, babies, young children, the elderly, and all those whose health is compromised should always avoid raw eggs.

Roquefort Pears

This is a great finish to a dinner. It combines three ingredients that are made to go together—pears, blue cheese, and nuts. It's fresh and not too heavy or too rich. It looks very elegant when it is served with the pears standing up tall.

My French friend Patrick Esquerre, the founder of La Madeleine Cafés, says that all successful endeavors contain a moment of surprise. Guests are always surprised when they find the cheese in the center. Obviously, Patrick loves this dessert.

SERVES 4

4 ounces Roquefort , crumbled (¾ cup)

4 ounces (½ cup) cream cheese, home-made (page 74) or store-bought, or mascarpone, homemade (page 73) or store-bought, softened

Juice of 1 lemon

4 large pears

1 cup pecans or walnuts, finely chopped

4 leaves fresh mint, for garnish

MIX THE Roquefort and cream cheese together in a small bowl until smooth, using the back of a spoon or a fork. Combine the lemon juice with ½ cup water in a small bowl. Peel the pears, leaving the stems attached, and trim a ¼-inch slice off the bottom of the pears so that they will stand upright. Cut each pear lengthwise in half, remove the core, and scoop out a cavity inside each pear half. Place each pear into the lemon water as soon as it is prepared to prevent discoloring.

DIVIDE THE cheese into eighths and place the nuts on a piece of waxed paper. Remove pears from lemon water, fill the cavities of the pears, and press the two halves of each pear together so that they are whole pears again. Smooth and remove any cheese that shows between the two halves. Roll the pears in the nuts. Place the pears on a plate or tray standing upright, cover loosely with plastic wrap, and refrigerate for at least 1 hour before serving.

JUST BEFORE serving, garnish each pear by inserting a mint leaf near the stem. To serve, place the pears, standing upright, on dessert plates. Serve chilled.

Mascarpone Tart Topped with Fresh Fruit

There is a famous little pastry shop and café on the main street of Perugia called Pasticceria Sandri, where I often enjoyed dessert and an espresso after lunch in my student days. Their windows are always filled with gorgeous, tempting, mouth-watering pastries and tarts topped with fresh fruit, just like this one. Whenever I return to Perugia, I visit Sandri's and even now, more than thirty years later, the same employees man the cash register and espresso machine, and they always smile in their friendly way and say, "Welcome back, Signorina."

This is an elegant dessert, yet it's simple to make. I serve it in the summertime, topped with fresh strawberries and blueberries, but you can use different varieties of sliced fruit and serve it year-round. You can bake the tart crust the day before, if you need a head start; however, it's best to assemble the tart on the day you will serve it, so that the crust will be crisp.

SERVES 8

SWEET PASTRY CRUST
7 tablespoons unsalted butter

⅔ cup sugar

½ teaspoon grated lemon zest

3 large egg yolks

1½ cups unbleached all-purpose flour

Pinch of salt

FILLING
1 pound (2 cups) mascarpone, home-made (page 73) or store-bought, cold

¼ cup sugar

3 tablespoons Grand Marnier or other fruit-based liqueur

1 pint (2 cups) blueberries

1 pint (2 cups) strawberries

¼ cup apple jelly

FOR THE Sweet Pastry Crust, place the butter, sugar, and lemon zest in the work bowl of food processor fitted with a steel blade. Pulse until the ingredients are well mixed. Add the egg yolks and pulse to mix well. Add the flour and salt and pulse briefly until the flour is mixed in. Be careful not to overwork the dough; it will be very crumbly. Remove the dough from the work bowl, press it into a disk, and wrap in plastic wrap. Refrigerate for at least 30 minutes.

BUTTER AND flour a 10- to 12-inch tart pan with a removable bottom.

PLACE THE dough on a lightly floured piece of waxed paper on a work surface. Roll the dough out to a round 1 to 2 inches larger than the tart pan. Pick up the dough and the waxed paper, place the dough waxed paper side up in the tart pan, and peel off the paper. Carefully fit the dough in the pan; if any of the dough tears, just patch it together with your fingers. Roll a rolling pin over the top of the tart pan to trim the edges. Pierce the bottom of the tart shell with the tines of a fork. Refrigerate for 30 minutes.

PREHEAT THE oven to 375°F.

PLACE THE tart shell in the oven and bake for 20 to 25 minutes, or until light golden brown. Remove to a rack to cool.

FOR THE filling, mix the mascarpone with the sugar and 2 tablespoons of the Grand Marnier in a small bowl. Spread the mascarpone mixture into the cooled crust using a rubber spatula. Refrigerate.

REMOVE ANY stems from the blueberries, and wash and dry the berries. Wash and hull the strawberries. If the strawberries are large, cut them into slices, halves, or quarters. Arrange the berries over the filling in an attractive pattern.

PLACE THE jelly and the remaining 1 tablespoon Grand Marnier in a small saucepan and simmer over low heat, stirring constantly, until it thickens and large bubbles form. Remove from the heat. Use a pastry brush to paint the glaze over the fruit.

REMOVE THE sides of the tart pan and loosen the tart from the bottom of the pan using a spatula. Slide off the pan and place the tart on a serving platter. Refrigerate for at least 30 minutes, and up to 4 hours.

TO SERVE, cut into wedges. Serve chilled.

Lace Cookies with Orange-Mascarpone Filling and Raspberries

Lace cookies are flat, very crisp, dark brown cookies that have little openings that make them resemble lace. They are very thin and brittle, so it's best to leave them on the aluminum foil or parchment paper after they are baked, then peel them off once cooled.

You can also be creative and shape the lace cookies into cups or other shapes while they are warm. Stephan Pyles, the genius behind Star Canyon, who is also an accomplished pastry chef, shapes his lace cookies to resemble taco shells and then fills them with whipped cream and berries. I have more of an Italian bent, so I stack my lace cookies like a short leaning Tower of Pisa!

MAKES 24 TO 30 COOKIES ABOUT 2½ TO 3 INCHES IN DIAMETER
MAKES ABOUT 1½ CUPS FILLING
SERVES 8

LACE COOKIES

½ cup pecans

½ cup sugar

4 tablespoons (½ stick) unsalted butter, softened

1 tablespoon unbleached all-purpose flour

1½ teaspoons molasses

1 tablespoon heavy cream

⅛ teaspoon pure vanilla extract

ORANGE-MASCARPONE FILLING

½ cup heavy cream, chilled

4 ounces (½ cup) mascarpone, home-made (page 73) or store-bought, at room temperature

1 tablespoon Grand Marnier

1 teaspoon sugar

½ teaspoon finely grated orange zest (preferably mandarin orange)

2 half-pints raspberries, rinsed and dried (2 cups)

Fresh mint leaves, for garnish

FOR THE Lace Cookies, preheat oven to 350°F. Line an 18 x 12-inch baking sheet with aluminum foil.

PLACE THE pecans and sugar in the work bowl of a food processor fitted with a steel blade and process until the nuts are coarsely chopped. Add the butter, flour, molasses, cream, and vanilla and process until well mixed and the nuts are finely chopped. Transfer the dough to a bowl.

PLACE HEAPING teaspoonfuls of the dough on the foil-lined baking sheet, spacing the cookies far apart and leaving lots of room to expand—make only 6 cookies at a time.

PLACE IN the oven and bake for 10 minutes, or until bubbly all over and golden brown. Watch the cookies carefully, as they turn from brown to burned very quickly; the baking time may need to be adjusted according to your oven. Remove from the oven and place, still on the foil, on a cake rack to cool completely. Continue to bake the cookies in batches until all the dough is used. (Make extra cookies, as they are very fragile and break easily.) Once they are cooled, very carefully peel the foil away from the back of the lace cookies; it is very easy to break the cookies. If holding the cookies for any length of time, place in an airtight container.

FOR THE Orange Mascarpone Filling, place the cream in a small bowl and whip by hand or with an electric mixer until fairly stiff. Using a whisk, stir in the mascarpone, Grand Marnier, sugar, and orange zest until the mixture is smooth. Be careful not to overmix, because the mascarpone might separate. Use immediately, or set aside and refrigerate for up to 3 hours.

TO ASSEMBLE, place 1 lace cookie on a dessert plate. Spread 1 tablespoon of the filling gently over the cookie, or pipe, using a pastry bag. Place 4 raspberries, equally spaced, on the filling. Repeat the layers. Place a third cookie on top of the raspberries and top with 1 tablespoon of the filling.

GARNISH EACH dessert with 3 or 4 raspberries and a mint sprig. Serve immediately.

This is your wine and cheese crowd, and nothing ever goes wrong at such events.

–Richard Messener,
New York City police officer

Ginger-Lime Mascarpone Mousse with Dried Fruit Compote

While this dessert is a modern creation, the spices that flavor it were originally brought to Europe in the Middle Ages by caravans from the Far East, and dried fruit compotes were a popular way to use them then. The mousse is very easy to put together, but its complex combination of a light and fluffy texture with a dark, spicy flavor is very impressive. Its refreshing and delicate undertones of lime and ginger evoke thoughts of the Orient.

I like to spoon the compote over the mousse when I serve it, but another lovely presentation is to create a parfait, with the compote in the bottom of a glass and the mousse spooned on top.

MAKES ABOUT 2 CUPS COMPOTE
SERVES 8

GINGER-LIME MASCARPONE MOUSSE

¼ cup cold water

1 (¼-ounce) package unflavored gelatin

1½ cups apple juice

½ cup sugar

1 (1-inch) knob fresh ginger, peeled and sliced

Grated zest of 2 limes

Juice of 2 limes

2 tablespoons Cantoni (ginger-flavored liqueur), Grand Marnier, or other fruit liqueur

1 pound (2 cups) mascarpone, homemade (page 73) or store-bought, cold

2 cups (1 pound) heavy cream or crème fraîche, homemade (page 68) or store-bought, whipped to soft peaks

DRIED FRUIT COMPOTE

1 cinnamon stick, broken into pieces

1 teaspoon whole allspice

2 tablespoons sugar

1½ cups red wine (about ½ bottle)

¼ cup dried apples, coarsely chopped

¼ cup dried apricots, coarsely chopped

¼ cup dried cranberries or dried cherries, coarsely chopped

¼ cup prunes, coarsely chopped

½ cup slivered blanched almonds

1 teaspoon freshly squeezed lime juice

Small square of cheesecloth and kitchen string

8 leaves fresh basil, for garnish (optional)

FOR THE Ginger-Lime Mascarpone Mousse, place the water in a medium saucepan and sprinkle the gelatin over the top. Let stand for 5 minutes to soften.

ADD THE apple juice, sugar, ginger, lime zest, and lime juice to the gelatin and bring to a boil, stirring constantly. Immediately remove from the heat and cool to room temperature over a bowl of ice water. Stir in the liqueur. Continue stirring until chilled. Strain through a

fine-mesh sieve or a strainer lined with cheesecloth into a large bowl. (Discard the solids in the sieve.) Slowly and gently whisk the mascarpone into the apple juice mixture until blended. (Do not beat with an electric mixer, because the mascarpone might separate and turn to butter.) Fold in the whipped cream using a rubber spatula. Pour the mousse into a large glass bowl and refrigerate for at least 4 hours.

MEANWHILE, MAKE the Dried Fruit Compote: wrap the cinnamon and allspice in a piece of cheesecloth and tie it with a string to make a bag. Place the sugar and the bag in a saucepan. Add the wine and heat over medium heat, stirring to dissolve the sugar. Add the apples, apricots, cranberries, prunes, and almonds. Reduce the heat and simmer for 30 minutes, or until the compote is thick and the liquid is somewhat syrupy. Remove from the heat. Stir in the lime juice. Set aside to let cool to room temperature, then remove the spice bag and squeeze its juice back into the compote.

TO SERVE, spoon the mousse onto dessert plates and top each with 1 to 2 tablespoons of compote. Serve chilled. Garnish with the basil leaves, if desired.

It is a bit of a mystery why so many aspiring American hosts—gourmet and otherwise—came to think of mass quantities of cheese *before* dinner as an appropriate hors d'oeuvre; but cheese was strictly for the sophisticated set.

–Jane and Michael Stern

Tiramisù

This must be the most popular Italian dessert of all, at least in America! In Italy, the oft-repeated anecdote is that *tiramisù,* which means "lift me up," was a favorite of university students who were studying for exams. They got energy to continue studying late into the night from it since it contained cream, eggs, coffee, and chocolate. Italians always seem to have the right idea about such things—tiramisù is much more nutritive than No-Doz and much more delicious!

When we first began making cheese, I wanted to make mascarpone. I was convinced it would be very popular. In the mid-1980s when I took it around to show my customers, few had heard of mascarpone, much less tiramisù. Nowadays, there's scarcely a restaurant in the United States that doesn't offer some form of tiramisù for dessert.

SERVES 12

24 ladyfingers, amaretti cookies, or savoiardi (dry ladyfingers)

1½ cups strong espresso (or 1¼ cups espresso mixed with ¼ cup rum or brandy)

6 large eggs, separated

½ cup granulated sugar

1 pound (2 cups) mascarpone, homemade (page 73) or store-bought, cold

6 ounces bittersweet chocolate, coarsely grated or shaved

12 sprigs fresh mint or cocoa powder, for garnish (optional)

SELECT A 2-quart or larger glass bowl. Briefly dip 16 of the ladyfingers into the coffee and arrange them in a single layer on the bottom and around the sides of the bowl. Try not to let the cookies get too soggy with coffee.

IN A large bowl, whisk the egg yolks with the sugar until the mixture is light in color and fluffy in texture. Add the mascarpone to the yolk mixture and mix until smooth. Be careful not to overbeat, or the mascarpone might separate and curdle. In another large bowl, beat the egg whites until stiff. Stir a heaping tablespoon of the whites into the yolk mixture to lighten it, then fold the remaining beaten whites into the yolk mixture with a rubber spatula.

PLACE HALF of this mixture on top of the ladyfingers in the bowl. Sprinkle one-third of the grated or shaved chocolate over the mascarpone mixture. Dip 4 more ladyfingers into the coffee and arrange them on top of the chocolate. Top with half of the remaining mascarpone mixture. Sprinkle with another one-third of the chocolate. Make another layer of the remaining 4 coffee-dipped ladyfingers and top with the remaining mascarpone mixture and

the rest of the chocolate. Cover the tiramisù with plastic wrap and refrigerate for at least 1 hour before serving. (The tirasmisù can be made up to 24 hours in advance.)

TO SERVE, cut through all of the layers, using a large spoon, and place a portion on each dessert plate. Serve chilled. Garnish with a sprig of mint or dust with cocoa powder, if desired.

NOTE: It's generally safe to use raw eggs in your recipes, as long as they are very fresh, grade A or AA, and have been properly refrigerated. There is, however, a slight risk of *Salmonella enteritidis* and other illnesses related to the consumption of raw eggs. I have made this recipe many, many times without any problem, but to be absolutely safe, pregnant women, babies, young children, the elderly, and all those whose health is compromised should always avoid raw eggs.

Sweet cheese is the *trompe l'oeil* of food. It will try to trick you; it supplies both the illusion of lightness and the satisfaction of having eaten something really, really sinful.

–Molly O'Neill

Minted Mascarpone Sorbet

Nothing is as refreshing as mint. A mint dessert is a perfect ending to a meal. This mascarpone sorbet is flavored with lemon and mint and accompanied by fresh fruit.

You can serve this in many ways. Try the fruit in the bottom of the bowl with the sorbet on top. Or vice versa. Garnish the dishes with more fresh mint and lemon slices if desired. You could also make an ice-cream sandwich using sugar cookies.

MAKES ABOUT 1 QUART
SERVES 4 TO 6

¾ cup sugar

1½ cups water

6 (3-inch) sprigs fresh mint

12 ounces (1½ cups) plain yogurt

8 ounces (1 cup) mascarpone, home-made (page 73) or store-bought, cold

2 tablespoons freshly squeezed lemon juice

Macerated Fresh Fruit (recipe follows) (optional)

Fresh mint leaves, for garnish

PLACE THE sugar and water in a saucepan and bring to a boil over medium heat, stirring to dissolve the sugar. Reduce the heat slightly and boil for 10 minutes. Remove from the heat and add the mint leaves to the syrup to steep. Poke the leaves down with a wooden spoon and bruise them so they will give up more flavor. Let cool completely, then remove and discard the mint.

COMBINE THE yogurt and mascarpone in a bowl. Add the lemon juice and cooled syrup. Mix well, but be careful not to overbeat, or the mascarpone might separate. Refrigerate for at least 1 hour, or until cold.

FREEZE IN an ice cream maker (that holds at least 1 quart) according to the manufacturer's instructions. Transfer to a metal or other freezer container, place in the freezer, and let harden for at least 2 hours.

TO SERVE, scoop the sorbet into shallow bowls. Serve alone or accompanied by the macerated fruit, garnished with mint leaves.

Macerated Fresh Fruit

MIX 2 cups (total) strawberries, melon, and kiwi—cut into ½-inch pieces—with ¼ cup sugar and ¼ cup freshly squeezed lemon juice in a bowl. Macerate for 45 minutes at room temperature before serving.

As between mice and men, man is easily the more devoted to cheese, and always has been. The mouse, scientists have found, will content himself with cheese for want of something better, but his real passion is for gumdrops.

–Vivienne Marquis and Patricia Haskell

Cannoli Filled with Pistachio Ricotta

While they are now available all over Italy, cannoli are traditionally a Sicilian dessert in which ricotta is mixed with candied fruits, nuts, or chocolate to fill crispy pastry shells. Cannoli shells are easy to make yourself, but they can also be found in Italian grocery stores or gourmet shops, in both regular and mini sizes.

Because Sicily is an island in the middle of the Mediterranean, over the ages many different people colonized it. You'll find Greek, Arab, Roman, and even Norman influences. So while toasted pistachio nuts and dried cranberries may not be a traditional cannoli filling, they still have a Sicilian feel. Not to mention an Italian color scheme—green, white, and red.

If you are game, you can easily make cannoli shells using egg roll wrappers. The hard part will be finding something to use as a mold. I use aluminum tubing that was cut to the proper length at a hardware store, but some specialty gourmet shops do carry cannoli molds.

MAKES 8 LARGE OR 12 MINI CANNOLI
SERVES 4 TO 6

¼ cup dried cranberries or dried cherries, chopped

2 tablespoons amaretto liqueur

8 ounces ricotta, homemade (page 70) or store-bought, well drained (1 cup)

¼ cup sugar

2 ounces (¼ cup) mascarpone, homemade (page 73) or store-bought, cold

¼ cup toasted pistachio nuts, chopped

8 large or 12 mini cannoli shells, homemade (recipe follows) or store-bought

¼ cup confectioners' sugar, for garnish

SOAK THE dried cranberries in the amaretto in a small bowl for 30 minutes.

COMBINE THE ricotta and sugar in a small bowl and whip until smooth. Add the mascarpone and stir to incorporate. Be careful not to overmix, or the mascarpone might separate. Fold in the pistachios and dried cranberries with their soaking liquid.

TRANSFER TO a pastry bag fitted with a plain tip and pipe the mixture into the cannoli shells. If you don't have a pastry bag, put the filling into a plastic bag, snip off one corner, and squeeze the filling out into the pastry shells. (Do this close to serving time so the shells won't lose their crispness.) Refrigerate until serving time.

TO SERVE, dust with confectioners' sugar, using a sieve. Serve chilled.

Canolli Shells

12 egg roll wrappers   **1 cup vegetable oil**

CUT THE egg roll wrappers into circles 4 inches in diameter. Roll the wrappers around molds or pieces of aluminum tubing that are 1 inch in diameter and 4½ to 5 inches in length. Moisten the overlapped flap of dough with water to seal each wrapper.

HEAT THE oil in a large skillet until hot but not smoking, about 350°F. Add the shells, still on the tubing, and fry, turning with tongs as necessary, until golden brown and crispy on all sides. Remove immediately, using tongs, and stand the tubing on end on paper towels to drain. When cool, slip the cannoli shells off the tubing.

VARIATION

Cassata

SERVES 8

Rather than using the cannoli shells, slice a 2-pound pound cake, about 8½ x 4½ x 2½ inches, into 3 horizontal layers. Place the cake layers on a flat surface. Drizzle each layer with amaretto liqueur. Spread the ricotta filling on all the layers and reassemble the cake. Cover tightly with plastic wrap and refrigerate. To serve, garnish the top of the cake with the dried cranberries and toasted pistachios pressed down into the ricotta. Cut the cake into 1-inch slices. Serve chilled.

Orange-Ricotta Almond Tart

I adore the combination of oranges and almonds. They remind me of the heavy sweet floral fragrance of the air in Seville.

This is a crustless tart that is somewhat reminiscent of flan but not so sweet. You'll find it quite Mediterranean with its topping of slightly bitter candied orange peels.

SERVES 8 TO 12

TART

6 ounces (1½ cups) slivered blanched almonds

6 large eggs

1½ pounds ricotta, homemade (page 70) or store-bought, well drained (3 cups)

½ cup sugar

Grated zest of 2 large oranges

¼ cup Grand Marnier or another orange liqueur

1 teaspoon pure vanilla extract

½ teaspoon ground nutmeg

TOPPING

3 large oranges

1 cup water

1 cup sugar

1 cinnamon stick

3 tablespoons sugar

½ cup (4 ounces) crème fraîche, homemade (page 68) or store-bought, or sour cream

Fresh mint leaves, for garnish

FOR THE Tart, preheat oven to 350°F. Liberally butter a 9-or 10-inch quiche dish or glass or ceramic pie plate. (You could also use a 12-inch tart pan with a removable bottom, placed on a baking sheet.)

SPREAD THE almonds on a cookie sheet and bake until light brown. Remove and set the pan on a rack to cool. Reduce the oven temperature to 325°F. When the almonds are cool, grind them into a fine meal in the work bowl of a food processor fitted with a steel blade. Add the eggs, ricotta, sugar, orange zest, orange liqueur, vanilla, and nutmeg. Process until well mixed, smooth, and fluffy.

POUR THE batter into the baking dish, almost filling it, and place in the oven. Bake for 1 hour, or until puffed up. Remove and place on a rack to cool for 1 hour, then refrigerate for at least 1 hour.

FOR THE Topping, remove the zest from the oranges in long, very thin strips by peeling around the oranges to form spirals. Be careful to remove only the zest and not the bitter white pith underneath. Then cut the orange zest into julienne strips. (Or use a zester if you have one.)

COMBINE THE water and sugar in a small saucepan. Bring to a simmer over low heat, stirring to dissolve the sugar. Add the orange zest and cook slowly for 1 hour. If the syrup becomes too thick, add a little more water. Remove from the heat, add the cinnamon stick, and set aside to cool.

JUST BEFORE serving time, remove the tart from the refrigerator. Place the sugar on a piece of waxed paper. Remove the candied orange zest from the syrup (reserve the syrup), shake off the excess syrup, place the zest on the sugar, and toss well to coat. Distribute the orange zest evenly over the tart.

TO SERVE, cut the tart into wedges. Place on serving plates, top each with a dollop of crème fraîche, and drizzle with a teaspoon of the reserved syrup. Garnish with fresh mint leaves. Serve chilled.

It might be the early bird who gets the worm, but it's the second mouse who gets the cheese.

–Robert

Darren's Lemon Goat Cheese Tart

Darren DeVille is a traveling pastry chef in Dallas. This means that every day he travels from restaurant to restaurant making desserts. He also sells his desserts to catering companies.

This dessert is one of my favorites. It is a very thin little tart, not more than an inch high. The lemon curd on top is wonderfully tart, the thin creamy goat cheese filling is rich and smooth, and the crust is buttery and crisp.

SERVES 6 TO 8

TART CRUST

1¼ cups unbleached all-purpose flour

¼ cup confectioners' sugar

10 tablespoons (1¼ sticks) unsalted butter

GOAT CHEESE FILLING

4 ounces (½ cup) goat cheese

½ cup (4 ounces) crème fraîche, homemade (page 68) or store-bought, or sour cream

¼ cup sugar

1 large egg

2½ teaspoons unbleached all-purpose flour

LEMON CURD

6 large egg yolks

½ cup freshly squeezed lemon juice

1 cup sugar

4 tablespoons (½ stick) unsalted butter

¼ cup sugar, for garnish (optional)

FOR THE Tart Crust, combine the flour, confectioners' sugar, and butter in the work bowl of a food processor fitted with a steel blade. Pulse until a soft ball begins to form on the blade. Be careful not to overprocess. Remove the dough and press into the bottom and up the sides of an 11-inch tart pan with a removable bottom. Prick the dough with a fork and refrigerate for 30 minutes.

PREHEAT THE oven to 350°F.

PLACE THE tart shell in the oven and bake for 15 to 20 minutes, or until golden brown. Remove and set aside to cool. Leave the oven on.

FOR THE Goat Cheese Filling, mix the goat cheese, crème fraîche, sugar, egg, and flour together in a small bowl. Pour this mixture into the tart crust.

PLACE IN the oven and bake for 20 to 25 minutes, or until the filling is just set. Set aside on a cake rack to cool.

FOR THE Lemon Curd, combine the egg yolks, lemon juice, and sugar in the top of a double boiler. Place over simmering water and cook over medium-low heat, stirring constantly, until the mixture coats the back of a spoon, about 10 minutes; do not boil. When the mixture thickens and wisps of steam start to rise from it, remove from the heat and stir in the butter until it melts. Set aside to cool for 15 minutes.

POUR THE lemon curd over the baked tart when slightly cooled. Refrigerate for at least 1 hour and up to 12 hours before serving.

JUST BEFORE serving, if desired, sprinkle the chilled tart with the sugar, making an even layer. Holding a household propane torch 4 to 5 inches away, heat the sugar until it turns golden brown and caramelizes. Alternatively, place the tart 3 inches under the broiler, preheated on high.

TO SERVE, slice into wedges. Serve chilled.

Each sort of cheese reveals a pasture of
a different green, under a different sky.
–Italo Calvino

Apple Pie with Cheddar Crust

When I was growing up, my father always liked a slice of Cheddar cheese with his apple pie. I really don't know where this tradition originated, but I do know that its popularity is widespread. Some people reheat slices of apple pie and melt the cheese on top before serving. Other times the slice of cheese is just placed on the dish alongside the pie. The sweetness of the apple pie and the salty sharpness of the Cheddar make a popular combination. Here I incorporate the cheese straight into the crust.

SERVES 6 TO 8

CHEDDAR CRUST

12 tablespoons (1½ sticks) unsalted butter

4 ounces sharp Cheddar, shredded (1 cup)

2 cups unbleached all-purpose flour

⅛ teaspoon salt

3 to 5 tablespoons ice water

FILLING

6 Golden Delicious apples, peeled, cored, and sliced into thin wedges

2 Granny Smith apples, peeled, cored, and sliced into thin wedges

½ cup sugar

2 tablespoons cornstarch

1 teaspoon ground cinnamon

½ teaspoon ground nutmeg

¼ cup raisins (optional)

¼ cup chopped toasted pecans or walnuts (optional)

Juice of 1 lemon

FOR THE Cheddar Crust, cream the butter and cheddar together in a medium bowl with a wooden spoon. Combine the flour and salt in another bowl and stir. Cut the butter mixture into the flour, using two knives, a pastry blender, or your hands. Sprinkle 3 tablespoons of the water onto the dough and stir with a wooden spoon or a fork to incorporate the water into the dough, adding more water if needed; do not overmix.

TURN THE dough out onto a lightly floured work surface and form into a ball. Remove one-third of the dough, form into a ball, flatten into a disk about ½ inch thick, and wrap with plastic wrap. Flatten the other piece of dough similarly into a ½-inch-thick disk and wrap. Refrigerate both disks for at least 30 minutes.

PREHEAT THE oven to 375°F. Lightly grease a 9- to 10-inch pie pan and set aside.

REMOVE THE larger disk of dough from the refrigerator and place it on a lightly floured work surface. Roll out the dough into a 12- to 13-inch circle. Roll the dough up over the rolling pin and transfer it to the pie pan. Press the dough into the pan and cut off the excess. Refrigerate for 15 minutes.

FOR THE Filling, remove the pie pan from the refrigerator and layer about half of the apples, using both kinds, in concentric circles in the pie shell. Mix the sugar, cornstarch, cinnamon, and nutmeg together in a small bowl. Sprinkle half the sugar mixture over the apples. Top with half the raisins and half the nuts, if using. Layer the remaining apples in the pan and top with the remaining sugar, raisins, and nuts. Drizzle with lemon juice.

REMOVE THE smaller disk of dough from the refrigerator and roll out on a floured work surface to a round slightly larger than the top of the pie. Cut the dough into strips about ⅓ inch wide using a knife or a pastry cutter. Weave the strips to form a latticework pattern on top of the pie. Trim the ends of the strips if necessary. Crimp the edges of the bottom crust and the lattice together by pinching the dough.

PLACE THE pie pan on a baking sheet, place in the oven, and bake for 40 to 50 minutes, or until the apples are bubbling and the crust is golden brown. Remove from the oven and let cool on a cake rack.

TO SERVE, cut the pie into wedges. Serve warm or at room temperature.

An apple pie without some cheese
Is like a kiss without a squeeze
–American proverb

The Cheese Course

THE FRENCH GASTRONOME BRILLAT-SAVARIN WROTE that "a dinner that ends without cheese is like a beautiful woman with only one eye." I agree with him completely. Cheese is a gracious way to end a meal. It's a wonderful way to finish a bottle of red wine or begin a bottle of dessert wine. It invites conversation. It slows things down and urges you to savor each taste of cheese and sip of wine.

The cheese course originated in Europe. During the eighteenth century, the French widely believed that cheese aided digestion when served at the end of the meal. In France, it is still served after the main course, before dessert. In England, cheese is served following dessert, accompanied by a glass of port.

The cheese course is now gaining popularity in the United States and is served in select restaurants from coast to coast. Some restaurants serve the cheese course from a trolley, others use a tray, and some serve the cheeses already cut and arranged on serving plates. Max McCalman, the man behind the extensive selection of cheese served at Picholine in New York City, proclaims that "the cheese course has arrived in the United States." He distinctly draws a line and insists that the cheese course is not "coming back," because it was never here before!

It's so easy to serve a cheese course. It takes only a moment to organize and does not require any slaving over a hot stove. It's entirely personal and creative. There are no set rules as to how the cheese course should be served. The cheeses can be placed on a marble slab or on a silver platter just as easily as they can be placed on a willow tray or a wooden kitchen cutting board.

Cheese choices can range from one perfect and magnificent cheese to a glorious array of cheeses from around the world. They can be similar or diverse. They can all be local cheeses from your own culinary neighborhood or cheeses from France or Italy. If you're energetic and enterprising, one of the cheeses can even be your own creation, a fresh one that you made in your own kitchen. (See Making Cheese at Home, page 63.)

The choices are endless. There are no hard-and-fast rules, and there are no limits. The best rule of thumb is to choose cheeses that you like. The cheeses can mirror the theme of your dinner or contrast with it. They can be similar or diverse in flavor and texture. They can have different shapes, sizes, and colors.

The best advice is to buy the best-quality cheeses that you can find and to buy them as close to when you plan to serve them as you can. And don't buy more than you need.

First decide how much cheese you'll need to buy. For a cheese course that follows a meal, I usually suggest a total of about one to two ounces per person. This should be a sufficient amount for just a taste of each cheese, a flavorful morsel of each.

Next, go to a reputable cheese shop so that you can choose from a good array of cheeses in optimum condition. Look carefully at the selection available. Then talk to the people in the cheese department and ask what is particularly good that day, just as you would ask the man behind the fish counter what is good that day. Now you are ready to make some decisions. (See Buying Cheese, page 45.)

DECIDE ON THE CHEESES

- **How Many Cheeses to Serve on a Cheese Board?** Usually three to five cheeses make a nice choice and a nice display. More than that is too many cheeses to taste and think about.

- **How Much to Buy?** Remember that you need to buy only about one to two ounces per person. You can always exceed this amount, especially when you see how little that amount of cheese is. One ounce is roughly equal to a one-inch-square cube of cheese. You'll probably want to buy more, especially if you want to have an abundant arrangement and attractive presentation. But remember that your guests won't eat much, particularly if you are serving the cheese as an interlude before dessert. They'll just serve themselves a smidgen of one or two cheeses.

- **How to Store Cheese Once You Get it Home.** If you will be serving the cheeses within a few hours, leave them out at room temperature if the ambient temperature is 60° to 70°F. If it will be longer or if the room is warmer, refrigerate the fragile, very soft cheeses. If the cheeses will be served on another day, refrigerate all of them in the wrappers you bought them in. After you have served the cheeses, the leftovers should be individually rewrapped tightly and snugly in fresh, clean plastic wrap and refrigerated.

- **How to Serve the Cheese.** Serve the cheeses at room temperature, around 70°F. Remove them from the refrigerator and unwrap them at least one hour before serving. Arrange the cheeses on a tray or wooden board. It is nice to cover the tray first with grape leaves, fresh or paper. Space the cheeses apart so that they have room to breathe. Place a small knife next to each cheese. Loosely cover the tray with a barely moist dish towel and set it aside until serving time.

DECIDE ON THE ACCOMPANIMENTS

You will need to serve bread with the cheese course. In England, butter is always served too, but not in France. Decide which you prefer. There is no need to serve more than one or two additional accompaniments. Here are a few suggestions:

- **Bread and crackers:** Serve a basket of fresh sliced bread. Thinly slice a baguette or another loaf of white or wheat bread and toast several of the slices ahead of time. Fruit and nut breads are wonderful with cheese and can be served thinly sliced, toasted or untoasted. You can also serve plain unflavored crackers.

- **Fruits:** Choose ripe seasonal fruits or dried fruits such as dates, raisins, or figs.

- **Nuts:** Toasted walnuts, hazelnuts, pecans, and almonds go well with cheese.

- **Other accompaniments:** Fruit chutneys and fruit pastes such as *membrillo* from Spain, wildflower honey, candied nuts, brandied fruit compotes, and dense and intense plum and fig cakes all go particularly well with cheese.

- **Wine:** Serve cheeses that will complement the wine you are drinking with your dinner. The cheeses you select should not call for a lighter wine than your dinner wine. Plan to move from that wine on to another, perhaps a sweet dessert wine such as a late-harvest wine or port.

ENJOY THE CHEESES

- Eat the cheeses in the order of their strength, moving from mild to robust to very strong.

- Eat cheese slowly, savor it, and allow it to melt in your mouth.

- Soft, semi-soft, and blue cheeses are best tasted by pressing them against your palate with your tongue. Harder and sharper cheeses are tasted best with the tip of the tongue.

- Accentuate the flavors of the cheese with a glass of wine or a piece of fruit.

SOME CHEESE BOARDS

Here are some suggestions for cheese boards, and the reasons I chose them. It is best if the cheeses contrast with each other in flavor, intensity, texture, milk type, and appearance. You can choose any number of cheeses from these lists and then use them alone or as a starting point for your own selections. Nothing is written in stone. The final decisions should be made at your cheese shop, once you know what they have and which cheeses are at the peak of perfection on the day you shop. Remember, ask for tastes. *Then* make your choices.

Cheese Board	Why Chosen/Type of Milk
Classic Cheese Board	
Vermont or English Cheddar	Mellow and traditional/cow
Roquefort or Stilton	Sharp and blue/sheep or cow
Chèvre	Fresh, mild, and tangy/goat
Camembert or Brie	Rich, creamy, and smooth/cow
Sbrinz or Parmigiano-Reggiano	Robust and firm/cow
Blue Cheese Board	
Maytag Blue	Sharp and American/cow
Stilton	Intense and English/cow
Roquefort	Tangy and French/sheep
Cambozola	Creamy and soft-ripened/cow
Westfield Farms Blue Log	Goaty with blue rind/goat

Goat Cheese Board	Why Chosen/Type of Milk
Fresh Chèvre	Mild and creamy/goat
Crottin de Chavignol	Earthy and flinty/goat
Goat Milk Gouda or Cheddar	Mellow and nutty/goat
Goat Milk Camembert	Creamy, rich, and tangy/goat
Cabrales or Blue Goat	Sharp and blue/goat

American Cheese Board	
Vermont Cheddar	Mellow and sharp/cow
Sonoma Dry Jack	Nutty and robust/cow
Maytag Blue	Tangy and blue/cow
Peluso Teleme	Creamy and smooth/cow
Chèvre	Mild, fresh, and goaty/goat

Italian Cheese Board	
Parmigiano-Reggiano	Robust and nutty/cow
Pecorino Toscano	Rustic and mellow/sheep
Gorgonzola	Smooth and blue/cow
Smoked Buffalo Mozzarella	Fresh, milky, and smoky/water buffalo
Mascarpone Torta with Basil	Rich and herby/cow

French Cheese Board	
Brie or Camembert	Mild and creamy/cow
Saint-André or Explorateur	Rich and buttery/cow
Morbier or Tomme de Savoie	Mellow and flavorful/cow
Crottin de Chavignol	Tangy and chalky/goat
Pont l'Evêque	Woodsy and pungent/cow

English Cheese Board	Why Chosen/Type of Milk
Stilton	Rich and blue/cow
Cheddar	Savory and sharp/cow
Caerphilly	Salty and lemony/cow
Cheshire	Mild and tangy/cow
Lancashire	Mellow and slightly sour/cow

Artisanal American Cheese Board	
Coach Farms Green Peppercorn Goat Cheese	Mellow chèvre loaf studded with green peppercorns with bloomy rind/goat
Capriole Crocodile Tear	Assertive chèvre shaped like a teardrop with moldy exterior/goat
Cypress Grove Humboldt Fog	Assertive chèvre with a layer of ash/goat
Mozzarella Company Basil Mascarpone Torta	Rich and buttery with layers of basil pesto/cow
Shelburne Farms Farmhouse Cheddar	Mellow, fruity, and nutty/cow
Old Chatham Sheepherding Company Sheep's Milk Camembert	Rich and creamy with a bloomy rind/sheep

Pairing Wine and Cheese

CHEESE AND WINE SHARE A great deal of history because they have been enjoyed together since ancient times. Both are products of fermentation. Both may be consumed while fresh, simple, and young as well as later in life, in their magnificent aged and more complex forms. They were made for each other.

There are no hard-and-fast rules as to which wines should be served with which cheeses. There is an old adage that you should drink red wine with hard cheeses and white wine with soft cheeses. But, like red wine with fish, there's always an exception. Just as one bottle of wine is not always like another, neither is one cheese like another. Both are living and constantly changing.

There are so many cheeses and so many wines. First you must decide which will take priority—the wine or the cheese—and then match to that. Harmony should exist between the wine and the cheese. The flavor of the cheese and wine should be similar in intensity so that one doesn't overpower the other. Always make sure that there is balance. Strong and powerful cheeses should be paired with similar wines, while delicate cheeses should be paired with lighter wines. Your choices should set off the best characteristics of both the wine and the cheese. A great cheese will elevate an average wine, but a mediocre cheese will deflate a good wine. An old saying for the port trade was "buy on apples and sell on cheese," because cheese brings out the best flavors of the wine, while the tartness of the apple shows the faults of the wine.

GENERAL PAIRING GUIDELINES

Taste is a personal preference. You may prefer one cheese with a particular wine while someone else may like an entirely different pairing. There are, however, some guidelines that you can follow:

- Young milky cheeses go with delicate wines that are light, young, and fruity, both red and white, like Sauvignon Blanc and Pinot Noir.
- Assertive, strong-flavored cheeses go well with young robust red wines like Chianti and Shiraz.
- Aged mellow cheeses go best with older, more robust wines such as Cabernet Sauvignon and Zinfandel.
- Strong pungent cheeses require young full-bodied wines or sweet dessert wines such as Merlot or late-harvest Riesling and Sauternes.
- Soft-ripened cheeses like Brie and Camembert are best with full-flavored Chardonnays.
- Older fine wines need a soft, rich cheese whose flavor and taste are not overpowering.
- Sweet dessert wines like port or Sauternes are fabulous with intense and complex blue cheeses.

REGIONAL CLASSIC PAIRINGS

One rule of thumb is to select a wine or beverage that comes from the same region as the cheese. There are many classic matchings:

- Pouilly Fumé and Sancerre with the goat cheeses from Touraine
- Rich, old Chardonnays with Camembert

- Champagne with Brie

- Amontillado sherry with Manchego

- Chianti with Pecorino Toscano

- Spanish Rioja with Cabrales

- Sauternes with Roquefort

- Champagne with rich triple-crème cheeses such as Brillat-Savarin or Explorateur

MORE FABULOUS PAIRINGS

There are many other wonderful combinations of wine and cheese:

- Gewürtztraminer with Gruyère

- Late-harvest botrytised wine with Gorgonzola

- Port with Stilton

- Beaujolais with Tomme de Savoie

- Barolo with aged Provolone

- Australian Shiraz with aged Gouda

- Claret with Gruyère

- Beaujolais with Banon

- Cabernet with young chèvre

Cheese coats the palate. The proteins in cheese react with the tannins in red wine to soften them and smooth them out on your palate. Therefore, a young tannic red goes well with most cheeses, while high-acid cheeses go with high-acid wines. When in doubt, remember that the acidity in a cheese will explode with the sweetness of a dessert wine.

Tangy, stronger goat cheeses do well with Burgundies—and there are those who enjoy Scotch, Bourbon, or Calvados with big, earthy cheeses such as Pont l'Évêque or Livarot. The list goes on and on—the pairing possibilities are endless.

The best recommendation is for you to be in a mood for experimentation and enjoyment. Choose several cheeses and several wines. One pairing will be best for you and another for someone else. You can't go wrong. It will create conversation. It will be interesting. And always fun!

Cheese Tables

MOST OF US DO OUR everyday shopping in supermarkets rather than specialized cheese shops. Although the variety of cheeses found in supermakets has expanded dramatically within the past few years, the selection is limited compared to the cheeses available in a great cheese shop. With this in mind, I have tried to choose the most commonly found cheeses for my various recipes. If it wasn't available at my local supermarket, I didn't use the cheese in a recipe.

I have organized these tables with cooking in mind. My primary desire is to indicate which cheeses can easily be substituted for each other. By consulting these tables, you can decide whether or not to use the most easily and commonly found cheese in a recipe or to substitute something rarer and more exotic, if you happen to find it or just happen to have some in your refrigerator.

Here's my rule: As long as the textures and flavors are somewhat similar, you can use one cheese in place of another. I urge you to try something new and to be adventuresome with my recipes. One thing I know: The recipes will be good any way they are cooked because cheese makes everything more delicious.

I also hope that my cheese tables will encourage you to experiment with new cheeses. By reading the descriptions of the flavors, you will find that certain cheeses you don't know and haven't tried are actually very similar to ones that you know and love. The tables should also help you choose cheeses for cheese boards by showing the relationships among different cheese textures, families, and countries of origin, as well as milk types and flavor characteristics.

All of this should aid you in creating delicious cheese combinations while expanding your horizons. If the cheeses in these tables are not available where you live, please turn to the Sources section on page 373 to order them.

TABLE 1. Cheeses by Texture

Texture / Family	Cheese Name	Type of Milk	Country of Origin
Extra-hard	Grana Padano	cow	Italy
Extra-hard	Parmigiano-Reggiano	cow	Italy
Extra-hard	Sbrinz	cow	Switzerland
Hard	Asiago	cow	Italy
Hard	Beaufort	cow	France
Hard	Cheddar	cow	England/USA
Hard	Cheshire	cow	England
Hard	Colby	cow	USA
Hard	Dry Jack	cow	USA
Hard	Gloucester	cow	England
Hard	Gruyère	cow	Switzerland
Hard	Jarlsberg	cow	Norway
Hard	Lancashire	cow	England
Hard	Manchego	sheep	Spain
Hard	Sapsago	cow	Switzerland
Hard/pasta filata	Caciocavallo	cow	Italy
Hard/pasta filata	Kasseri	sheep	Greece
Hard/pasta filata	Provolone	cow	Italy

TABLE 1. **Cheeses by Texture** *(continued)*

Texture / Family	Cheese Name	Type of Milk	Country of Origin
Hard/smoked	Idiazábal	sheep	Spain
Hard/washed rind	Appenzell	cow	Switzerland
Hard/whey cheese	Gjetost	cow and goat	Norway
Semi-firm to Extra-hard	Pecorino Romano	sheep	Italy
Semi-firm to Hard	Crottin de Chavignol	goat	France
Semi-firm to Hard	Edam	cow	Holland
Semi-firm to Hard	Emmental	cow	Switzerland
Semi-firm to Hard	Mahón	cow	Spain
Semi-firm	Caerphilly	cow	Wales
Semi-firm	Cantal	cow	France
Semi-firm	Comté	cow	France
Semi-firm	Fontina	cow	Italy
Semi-firm	Montasio	cow	Italy
Semi-firm	Raclette	cow	Switzerland
Semi-firm	Tête de Moine	cow	Switzerland
Semi-firm	Ubriaco	cow	Italy
Semi-firm/bloomy rind	Chabichou	goat	France
Semi-firm/blue	Cashel Blue	cow	Ireland
Semi-firm/blue	Danish Blue (Danblu)	cow	Denmark
Semi-firm/blue	Maytag Blue	cow	USA
Semi-firm/blue	Roquefort	sheep	France
Semi-firm/blue	Shropshire Blue	cow	England
Semi-firm/blue	Stilton	cow	England
Semi-firm/blue/wrapped in leaves	Cabrales	cow, goat, and sheep	Spain
Semi-soft to Semi-firm	Gouda	cow	Holland
Semi-soft to Semi-firm	Morbier	cow	France
Semi-soft to Semi-firm	Pecorino Toscano	sheep or sheep and cow	Italy
Semi-soft to Semi-firm	Pepato	sheep	Italy
Semi-soft to Semi-firm	Tomme de Savoie	cow	France
Semi-soft to Semi-firm/brined	Feta	sheep, goat, or cow and mixed	Greece
Semi-soft to Semi-firm/pasta filata	Scamorza	cow	Italy

TABLE 1. **Cheeses by Texture** *(continued)*

Texture / Family	Cheese Name	Type of Milk	Country of Origin
Semi-soft	Caciotta	cow	Italy
Semi-soft	Monterey Jack	cow	USA
Semi-soft/blue	Bleu d'Auvergne	cow	France
Semi-soft/blue	Forme d'Ambert	cow	France
Semi-soft/blue/washed rind	Gorgonzola	cow	Italy
Semi-soft/washed rind	Bel Paese	cow	Italy
Semi-soft/washed rind	Brick	cow	USA
Semi-soft/washed rind	Havarti	cow	Denmark
Semi-soft/washed rind	Limburger	cow	Germany
Semi-soft/washed rind	Livarot	cow	France
Semi-soft/washed rind	Maroilles	cow	France
Semi-soft/washed rind	Munster	cow	France
Semi-soft/washed rind	Port Salut	cow	France
Semi-soft/washed rind	Tilsit	cow	Germany
Soft to Semi-firm/bloomy rind	Sainte-Maure	goat	France
Soft to Semi-firm/bloomy rind	Valençay	goat	France
Soft to Semi-firm/fresh	Farmer Cheese	cow	USA
Soft to Semi-firm/moldy rind/ herb-coated	Brin d'Amour	sheep or goat	France/Corsica
Soft to Semi-soft/blue/bloomy rind	Cambozola	cow	Germany
Soft to Semi-soft/washed rind	Taleggio	cow	Italy
Soft/bloomy rind	Brie	cow	France
Soft/bloomy rind	Bûcheron	goat	France
Soft/bloomy rind	Camembert	cow	France
Soft/bloomy rind	Coulommiers	cow	France
Soft/bloomy rind/flavored	Gaperon	cow	France
Soft/bloomy rind/triple-crème	Brillat-Savarin	cow with cream	France
Soft/bloomy rind/triple-crème	Explorateur	cow with cream	France
Soft/bloomy rind/triple-crème	Saint André	cow with cream	France
Soft/fresh	Cottage Cheese	cow	USA
Soft/fresh	Cream Cheese	cow	USA

TABLE 1. Cheeses by Texture *(continued)*

Texture / Family	Cheese Name	Type of Milk	Country of Origin
Soft/fresh	Crescenza/Stracchino	cow	Italy
Soft/fresh	Fromage Blanc/ Fromage Frais	cow or goat	France
Soft/fresh	Montrachet/Chèvre	goat	France/USA
Soft/fresh	Quark	cow	Germany
Soft/fresh	Robiola	cow or sheep	Italy
Soft/fresh/pasta filata	Mozzarella	cow or water buffalo	Italy
Soft/fresh/triple-crème	Mascarpone	cow with cream	Italy
Soft/fresh/triple-crème/flavored	Boursin	cow with cream	France
Soft/moldy rind/wrapped in leaves	Saint-Marcellin	cow or cow and goat	France
Soft/ripened	Teleme	cow	USA
Soft/washed rind	Epoisse	cow	France
Soft/washed rind	Gubbeen	cow	Ireland
Soft/washed rind	Liederkranz	cow	USA
Soft/washed rind	Milleens	cow	Ireland
Soft/washed rind	Pont l'Evêque	cow	France
Soft/washed rind	Reblochon	cow	France
Soft/washed rind	Vacherin Mont d'Or	cow	Switzerland
Soft/whey cheese	Manouri	sheep	Greece
Soft/whey cheese	Mizithra	sheep or cow	Greece
Soft/whey cheese	Ricotta	cow, sheep, or goat	Italy
Soft/wrapped in leaves	Banon	goat, sheep, or cow	France

TABLE 2. Cheeses by Flavor/Taste

Flavor/Taste	Texture/Family	Type of Milk	Cheese Name	Country of Origin
Mild and buttery to rich, spicy, sharp, salty and piquant with age	Hard/pasta filata	cow	Provolone	Italy
Mild and buttery to savory with age	Semi-soft to Semi-firm/pasta filata	cow	Scamorza	Italy
Mild, buttery, and rich	Soft/fresh/triple-crème	cow	Mascarpone	Italy
Mild, buttery, and fruity to medium with age	Semi-soft/washed rind	cow	Bel Paese	Italy
Mild, buttery, fruity, nutty, and flowery with a pungent aroma	Soft/washed rind	cow	Reblochon	France
Mild, buttery, mushroomy, earthy, and nutty	Soft/washed rind	cow	Gubbeen	Ireland
Mild, buttery, and rich to sharp and strong with age	Soft/bloomy rind/triple-crème	cow with cream	Explorateur	France
Mild, buttery, rich, tangy, velvety, and moussey	Soft/bloomy rind/triple-crème	cow with cream	Saint André	France
Mild, buttery, and sometimes flavored with herbs and spices	Semi-soft/washed rind	cow	Havarti	Denmark
Mild, buttery, and sweet to mellow and savory with age	Semi-soft	cow	Caciotta	Italy
Mild, clean, acidic, and salty to mellow, nutty, tangy, and sharper with age	Hard	cow	Cheshire	England
Mild, clean, and slightly acidic	Soft/fresh	cow	Quark	Germany
Mild, clean, gently tart, and yogurty to fruity with age	Soft/fresh	cow	Crescenza/Stracchino	Italy
Mild, clean, lightly spicy, and slightly salty and acidic to stronger with age	Semi-firm to Hard	cow	Edam	Holland
Mild, clean, milky, bland, salty, and lemony	Soft to Semi-firm/fresh	cow	Farmer Cheese	USA
Mild, creamy, buttery, and slightly moldy	Soft to Semi-soft/blue/bloomy rind	cow	Cambozola	Germany
Mild, creamy, and fresh	Soft/fresh	cow	Cream Cheese	USA
Mild, creamy, fresh, and clean	Semi-soft	cow	Monterey Jack	USA

TABLE 2. **Cheeses by Flavor/Taste** (continued)

Flavor/Taste	Texture/Family	Cheese Name	Type of Milk	Country of Origin
Mild, creamy, fruity, earthy, grassy, and mushroomy to tangy, hearty, and complex with age	Soft/bloomy rind	Camembert	cow	France
Mild, creamy, fruity, and mushroomy to nutty, tangy, and stronger with age	Soft/bloomy rind	Coulommiers	cow	France
Mild, creamy, lemony, rich, and slightly sour	Soft/bloomy rind/triple-crème	Brillat-Savarin	cow with cream	France
Mild, creamy, milky, nutty, and flowery to stronger with age	Semi-firm	Cantal	cow	France
Mild, creamy, rich, and flavored with garlic and herbs	Soft/fresh/triple-crème/flavored	Boursin	cow with cream	France
Mild, creamy, and tangy to stronger with age	Soft/ripened	Teleme	cow	USA
Mild, delicate, and spicy to sharp and piquant with age	Semi-soft/washed rind	Tilsit	cow	Germany
Mild, delicate, subtle, slightly bland, buttermilky, lemony, salty, and tangy	Semi-firm	Caerphilly	cow	Wales
Mild, fruity, sweet, buttery, and nutty to sharper and piquant with age	Hard	Cheddar	cow	England, USA
Mild, delicately goaty, lemony, nutty, and mildly sharp to musty and stronger with age	Soft to Semi-firm/bloomy rind	Valençay	goat	France
Mild, goaty, and tangy to assertively goaty and stronger with age	Soft/bloomy rind	Bûcheron	goat	France
Mild, goaty, and tangy to more goaty and piquant with age	Semi-firm/bloomy rind	Chabichou	goat	France
Mild, goaty, tangy, slightly tart, and zippy	Soft/fresh	Montrachet/Chèvre	goat	France/USA
Mild, herby, sheepy, and slightly sour to nutty, earthy, and tangy	Soft to Semi-firm/moldy rind/herb-coated	Brin d'Amour	sheep or goat	France/Corsica
Mild, milky, and bland	Soft/fresh	Cottage Cheese	cow	USA
Mild, milky, fresh, and faintly soured	Soft/fresh/pasta filata	Mozzarella	cow or water buffalo	Italy

TABLE 2. Cheeses by Flavor/Taste (continued)

Flavor/Taste	Texture/Family	Type of Milk	Cheese Name	Country of Origin
Mild, milky, and slightly acidic	Soft/fresh	cow or goat	Fromage Blanc / Fromage Frais	France
Mild, milky, lemony, and delicately spicy to more piquant with age	Soft/fresh	cow or sheep	Robiola	Italy
Mild, milky, and meadowy to earthy, foresty, fruity, and honey-like to nutty and mellow with age	Semi-firm	cow	Fontina	Italy
Mild, milky, piquant, and salty to sharp with age	Semi-soft to Semi-firm/brined	sheep, goat, or cow and mixed	Feta	Greece
Mild, milky, sweet, and bland	Soft/whey cheese	cow, sheep, or goat	Ricotta	Italy
Mild, milky, sweet, citrusy, and salty	Soft/whey cheese	sheep	Manouri	Greece
Mild, nutty, earthy, and slightly sour	Soft/wrapped in leaves	goat, sheep, or cow	Banon	France
Mild, nutty, fruity, very buttery, mushroomy, and savory with a slightly barnyard aroma	Soft/bloomy rind	cow	Brie	France
Mild, nutty, and salty to sharp and yeasty with age	Soft/moldy rind/wrapped in leaves	cow or cow and goat	Saint-Marcellin	France
Mild, nutty, slightly lemony, fruity, and tangy to sharp and piquant with age	Hard	cow	Asiago	Italy
Mild, sweet, citrusy, savory, earthy, and nutty	Semi-soft to Semi-firm	cow	Tomme de Savoie	France
Mild, faintly sweet, fruity, tangy, slightly acidic, woodsy, and full-bodied with a pungent aroma	Soft/washed rind	cow	Pont l'Evêque	France
Mild, sweet, and nutty to pungent and tangy with age	Semi-soft/washed rind	cow	Brick	USA
Mild, sweet, nutty, butterscotchy, and slightly salty to slightly tangy to robust with age	Hard	sheep	Manchego	Spain
Mild, sweet, olivey, and nutty to mellow with age	Semi-soft to Semi-firm	sheep or sheep and cow	Pecorino Toscano	Italy

TABLE 2. Cheeses by Flavor/Taste (continued)

Flavor/Taste	Texture/Family	Type of Milk	Cheese Name	Country of Origin
Mild, sweet, and similar to Cheddar but lighter	Hard	cow	Colby	USA
Mild to mellow and piquant with age	Hard/pasta filata	cow	Caciocavallo	Italy
Mild to sharper and salty with age	Soft/whey cheese	sheep or cow	Mizithra	Greece
Mild to spicy and tangy to very strong, robust, and meaty with age and with a very pungent aroma	Semi-soft/washed rind	cow	Munster	France
Mellow, buttery, fruity, sweet, and yeasty with a pungent aroma	Semi-soft to Semi-firm	cow	Morbier	France
Mellow, buttery, grassy, fruity, tangy, and acidic	Hard	cow	Lancashire	England
Mellow, caramely, very sweet, pasty, and fudgelike	Hard/whey cheese	cow and goat	Gjetost	Norway
Mellow, creamy, savory, earthy, and nutty	Semi-soft/washed rind	cow	Port Salut	France
Mellow, fruity, buttery, robust, nutty, caramely, and hazelnutty	Hard	cow	Beaufort	France
Mellow, fruity, caramely, salty, robust, slightly sweet, and nutty with a fragrant aroma	Extra-hard	cow	Parmigiano-Reggiano	Italy
Mellow, fruity, hazelnutty, woody, and savory to strong with age	Semi-firm to Hard	cow	Emmental	Switzerland
Mellow, nutty, sweet, and slightly sour	Hard	cow	Jarlsberg	Norway
Mellow, rich, buttery, fruity, butterscotchy, and spicy	Extra-hard	cow	Sbrinz	Switzerland
Mellow, rich, nutty, and raisiny with lemony acidity. Single: softer and milder; double: mellow, creamy, and strong	Hard	cow	Gloucester	England
Mellow, sweet, fruity, honey-like, walnutty, and farmyardy	Hard	cow	Gruyère	Switzerland
Mellow, sweet, spicy, and nutty to sharper and slightly salty with age	Extra-hard	cow	Grana Padano	Italy
Medium, buttery, fruity, hazelnutty, fudgy, toffee, and salty	Semi-firm	cow	Comté	France

TABLE 2. Cheeses by Flavor/Taste *(continued)*

Flavor/Taste	Texture/Family	Type of Milk	Cheese Name	Country of Origin
Medium, buttery, fruity, nutty, butterscotchy, and Cognacky to robust, tangy, salty, sharp with age	Semi-soft to Semi-firm	cow	Gouda	Holland
Medium, buttery, rich, and lightly piquant to more piquant with age	Semi-soft/blue	cow	Bleu d'Auvergne	France
Medium, buttery, and sour to tangy, nutty, fudgy, strong, and salty with age	Semi-firm to Hard	cow	Mahón	Spain
Medium, creamy, fruity, nutty, and tangy to strong, rich, and assertive with age	Semi-soft/blue	cow	Forme d'Ambert	France
Medium, creamy, fruity, and tangy to piquant with age	Semi-firm	cow	Montasio	Italy
Medium, creamy, rich, sweet, and floral with farmyard aroma	Soft/washed rind	cow	Milleens	Ireland
Medium, creamy, sheepy, peppery, and spicy	Semi-soft to Semi-firm	sheep	Pepato	Italy
Medium, flinty, chalky, earthy, and nutty to very sharp, piquant, salty, and spicy with age	Semi-firm to Hard	goat	Crottin de Chavignol	France
Medium, fruity, and earthy to strong, nutty gutsy, and meaty with age	Soft to Semi-soft/washed rind	cow	Taleggio	Italy
Medium, fruity, and flavored by herb, spice, and wine wash	Hard/washed rind	cow	Appenzell	Switzerland
Medium, grassy, barnyardy, and resiny	Soft/washed rind	cow	Vacherin Mont d'Or	Switzerland
Medium, herby, smoky, farmyardy, and tangy	Hard/smoked	sheep	Idiazábal	Spain
Medium, nutty, tangy, winey, and peppery to sharp with age	Semi-firm	cow	Ubriaco	Italy
Medium, olivey, salty, and pungent	Hard/pasta filata	sheep	Kasseri	Greece
Medium, sweet, buttery, and nutty to robust and savory with age	Hard	cow	Dry Jack	USA
Medium, sweet, musty, walnutty, and tangy	Semi-firm	cow	Tête de Moine	Switzerland
Medium, sweet, woody, and spicy to strong, savory, earthy, tangy, piquant, and slightly pungent with age	Semi-soft/blue/washed rind	cow	Gorgonzola	Italy

TABLE 2. Cheeses by Flavor/Taste *(continued)*

Flavor/Taste	Texture/Family	Type of Milk	Cheese Name	Country of Origin
Medium, tangy, and salty with a pungent aroma	Soft/washed rind	cow	Liederkranz	USA
Medium, woody, walnutty, and lemony to sharp, spicy, sheepy, tangy, and peppery with age	Semi-firm to Extra-hard	sheep	Pecorino Romano	Italy
Robust, bold, intense, salty, tangy, subtle, piquant, a little sweet, and strong	Semi-firm/blue	sheep	Roquefort	France
Robust and distinctively goaty to sharp with age	Soft to Semi-firm/bloomy rind	goat	Sainte-Maure	France
Robust, herby, moldy, tangy, sharp, and salty to stronger and piquant with age	Semi-firm/blue	cow	Cashel Blue	Ireland
Robust, rich, buttery, nutty, woody, tangy, spicy, earthy, leathery, molassesy, and salty	Semi-firm/blue	cow	Stilton	England
Sharp, assertive, sour, and winey tang	Semi-firm/blue	cow	Shropshire Blue	England
Sharp, creamy, nutty, lemony, and tangy to peppery and piquant with age	Semi-firm/blue	cow	Maytag Blue	USA
Medium-strong and tangy with pungent aroma to stronger and more pungent with age	Semi-soft/washed rind	cow	Maroilles	France
Strong, and assertive with a pungent aroma to stronger with age	Semi-soft/washed rind	cow	Livarot	France
Strong, fruity, tangy, and barnyardy	Semi-firm	cow	Raclette	Switzerland
Strong, pungent, and flavored with garlic and peppercorns	Soft/bloomy rind/flavored	cow	Gaperon	France
Strong, sharp, and herby	Hard	cow	Sapsago	Switzerland
Strong, sharp, earthy, rustic, nutty, spicy, tangy, and peppery with a piquant aroma	Semi-firm/blue/wrapped in leaves	cow, goat, and sheep	Cabrales	Spain
Strong, sharp, pungent, spicy, and salty	Semi-soft/washed rind	cow	Limburger	Germany
Strong, sharp, tangy, piquant, salty, and bitter	Semi-firm/blue	cow	Danish Blue (Danblu)	Denmark
Strong, tangy, spicy, and barnyardy, and very pungent	Soft/washed rind	cow	Epoisses	France

TABLE 3. **Cheeses by Country of Origin**

Country of Origin	Cheese Name	Texture/Family	Type of Milk
Denmark	Danish Blue (Danblu)	Semi-firm/blue	cow
Denmark	Havarti	Semi-soft/washed rind	cow
England, USA	Cheddar	Hard	cow
England	Cheshire	Hard	cow
England	Gloucester	Hard	cow
England	Lancashire	Hard	cow
England	Shropshire Blue	Semi-firm/blue	cow
England	Stilton	Semi-firm/blue	cow
France	Beaufort	Hard	cow
France	Crottin de Chavignol	Semi-firm to Hard	goat
France	Cantal	Semi-firm	cow
France	Comté	Semi-firm	cow
France	Chabichou	Semi-firm/bloomy rind	goat
France	Roquefort	Semi-firm/blue	sheep
France	Morbier	Semi-soft to Semi-firm	cow
France	Tomme de Savoie	Semi-soft to Semi-firm	cow
France	Bleu d'Auvergne	Semi-soft/blue	cow
France	Forme d'Ambert	Semi-soft/blue	cow
France	Livarot	Semi-soft/washed rind	cow
France	Maroilles	Semi-soft/washed rind	cow
France	Munster	Semi-soft/washed rind	cow
France	Port Salut	Semi-soft/washed rind	cow
France	Sainte-Maure	Soft to Semi-firm/bloomy rind	goat
France	Valençay	Soft to Semi-firm/bloomy rind	goat
France/Corsica	Brin d'Amour	Soft to Semi-firm/moldy rind/ herb-coated	sheep or goat
France	Brie	Soft/bloomy rind	cow
France	Camembert	Soft/bloomy rind	cow
France	Coulommiers	Soft/bloomy rind	cow

TABLE 3. **Cheeses by Country of Origin** *(continued)*

Country of Origin	Cheese Name	Texture/Family	Type of Milk
France	Bûcheron	Soft/bloomy rind	goat
France	Brillat-Savarin	Soft/bloomy rind/triple-crème	cow with cream
France	Explorateur	Soft/bloomy rind/triple-crème	cow with cream
France	Saint André	Soft/bloomy rind/triple-crème	cow with cream
France	Gaperon	Soft/bloomy rind/flavored	cow
France	Fromage Blanc/ Fromage Frais	Soft/fresh	cow or goat
France, USA	Montrachet/Chèvre	Soft/fresh	goat
France	Boursin	Soft/fresh/triple-crème/flavored	cow with cream
France	Saint-Marcellin	Soft/moldy rind/wrapped in leaves	cow or cow and goat mixed
France	Epoisse	Soft/washed rind	cow
France	Pont l'Evêque	Soft/washed rind	cow
France	Reblochon	Soft/washed rind	cow
France	Banon	Soft/wrapped in leaves	goat, sheep or cow
Germany	Limburger	Semi-soft/washed rind	cow
Germany	Tilsit	Semi-soft/washed rind	cow
Germany	Cambozola	Soft to Semi-soft/blue/ bloomy rind	cow
Germany	Quark	Soft/fresh	cow
Greece	Kasseri	Hard/pasta filata	sheep
Greece	Feta	Semi-soft to Semi-firm/brined	sheep, goat, cow and mixed
Greece	Manouri	Soft/whey cheese	sheep
Greece	Mizithra	Soft/whey cheese	sheep or cow
Holland	Edam	Semi-firm to Hard	cow
Holland	Gouda	Semi-soft to Semi-firm	cow
Ireland	Cashel Blue	Semi-firm/blue	cow
Ireland	Gubbeen	Soft/washed rind	cow

TABLE 3. **Cheeses by Country of Origin** *(continued)*

Country of Origin	Cheese Name	Texture/Family	Type of Milk
Ireland	Milleens	Soft/washed rind	cow
Italy	Grana Padano	Extra-hard	cow
Italy	Parmigiano-Reggiano	Extra-hard	cow
Italy	Asiago	Hard	cow
Italy	Caciocavallo	Hard/pasta filata	cow
Italy	Provolone	Hard/pasta filata	cow
Italy	Pecorino Romano	Semi-firm to Extra-hard	sheep
Italy	Fontina	Semi-firm	cow
Italy	Montasio	Semi-firm	cow
Italy	Ubriaco	Semi-firm	cow
Italy	Pecorino Toscano	Semi-soft to Semi-firm	sheep or sheep and cow mixed
Italy	Pepato	Semi-soft to Semi-firm	sheep
Italy	Scamorza	Semi-soft to Semi-firm/ pasta filata	cow
Italy	Caciotta	Semi-soft	cow
Italy	Gorgonzola	Semi-soft/blue/washed rind	cow
Italy	Bel Paese	Semi-soft/washed rind	cow
Italy	Taleggio	Soft to Semi-soft/washed rind	cow
Italy	Crescenza/Stracchino	Soft/fresh	cow
Italy	Robiola	Soft/fresh	cow or sheep
Italy	Mozzarella	Soft/fresh/pasta filata	cow or water buffalo
Italy	Mascarpone	Soft/fresh/triple-crème	cow with cream
Italy	Ricotta	Soft/whey cheese	cow, sheep, or goat
Norway	Jarlsberg	Hard	cow
Norway	Gjetost	Hard/whey cheese	cow and goat
Spain	Manchego	Hard	sheep

TABLE 3. **Cheeses by Country of Origin** *(continued)*

Country of Origin	Cheese Name	Texture/Family	Type of Milk
Spain	Idiazábal	Hard/smoked	sheep
Spain	Mahón	Semi-firm to Hard	cow
Spain	Cabrales	Semi-firm/blue/wrapped in leaves	cow, goat, and sheep/mixed milks
Switzerland	Sbrinz	Extra-hard	cow
Switzerland	Gruyère	Hard	cow
Switzerland	Sapsago	Hard	cow
Switzerland	Appenzell	Hard/washed rind	cow
Switzerland	Emmental	Semi-firm to Hard	cow
Switzerland	Raclette	Semi-firm	cow
Switzerland	Tête de Moine	Semi-firm	cow
Switzerland	Vacherin Mont d'Or	Soft/washed rind	cow
USA	Colby	Hard	cow
USA	Dry Jack	Hard	cow
USA	Maytag Blue	Semi-firm/blue	cow
USA	Monterey Jack	Semi-soft	cow
USA	Brick	Semi-soft/washed rind	cow
USA	Cream Cheese	Soft/fresh	cow
USA	Farmer Cheese	Soft to Semi-firm/fresh	cow
USA	Cottage Cheese	Soft/fresh	cow
USA	Teleme	Soft/ripened	cow
USA	Liederkranz	Soft/washed rind	cow
Wales	Caerphilly	Semi-firm	cow

Acidity   Delicate sourness or tartness.

Affinage   Aging, finishing, and curing of cheese.

Aged cheese   Cheese that is ripened before it is sold.

Annatto   Natural yellow/red vegetable extract used to color cheeses such as Cheddar.

Artisanal cheese   Cheese made by hand in small batches at small cheese factories.

Bloomy rind   Thin coating of delicate white mold growing on the surface of a cheese.

Blue veining   Blue, green, or black striations and pockets of mold throughout a cheese.

Brined cheese   Cheese ripened in a salt-and-water solution.

Clabber   To sour milk and cause it to thicken and curdle.

Coagulation   Process by which milk is transformed from a liquid to a gelatinous solid state.

Cooked curds   Curds heated and cooked during the cheesemaking process.

Cultures/Starter   Selected bacteria used to encourage lactic development in cheesemaking.

Curdling   Separation of milk into liquid and solid components.

Curds   Semi-solid portion of coagulated milk.

Enzymes   Proteins that cause biochemical transformations such as coagulation.

Eyes   Holes of varying sizes produced by gas formation in the body of a cheese.

Farmhouse/Farmstead cheese   Cheese made at a farm with milk that comes from that particular farm.

Fresh cheeses   Unripened cheeses that are sold as soon as they are made.

Homogenization   Mechanical process that breaks the fat globules in milk into tiny particles so that they are evenly distributed throughout and the cream no longer separates and rises to the top.

Lactic acid   Acid produced when milk sours.

Lactose   Natural sugar found in milk.

Mold   Spores or fungi that grow in or on cheeses and contribute to flavor development.

Mold-ripened cheese   Cheese that matures as a result of surface and/or interior molds.

Natural rind   Dry outer layer that develops on cheese while air-drying during aging.

Paste   Interior portion of cheese.

Pasteurization   Process of heating milk to destroy unwanted and dangerous bacteria.

Penicillium candidum   White mold used on soft-ripened cheeses such as Brie.

Penicillium roqueforti   Blue mold used to develop blue-veined cheeses such as Roquefort.

Pressing   Process of applying pressure to encourage drainage of whey to produce a drier and firmer cheese.

Raw-milk cheese   Cheese made from raw milk that is not pasteurized.

Rennet   Substance, either animal or vegetable, used to coagulate milk.

Rind   Outer covering of cheese.

Ripening   Process of aging cheese for flavor development.

Specialty cheeses   Cheeses made in limited quantities in small cheese factories.

Spun curd   Curds of pasta filata cheeses that are processed by stretching and stringing in hot water.

Surface-ripened cheese   Cheese that ripens from the exterior inwards by means of surface mold, yeast, or bacteria.

Table Cheeses   Cheeses that are good for cooking and eating as snacks and in sandwiches.

Turophile   A person who loves cheese.

Washed rind   Exterior coating produced by bathing and/or wiping the exterior of cheese during maturation.

Wax   Paraffin coating used to protect the exterior of the cheese during aging.

Whey   Watery yellow liquid drained from coagulated curds.

Bibliography

Aidells, Bruce, and Dennis Kelly. *The Complete Meat Cookbook*. New York: Houghton Mifflin Company, 1998.

Anderson, Pam. *The Perfect Recipe*. New York: Houghton Mifflin Company, 1998.

Battistotti, Bruno, et al. *Cheese: A Guide to the World of Cheese and Cheesemaking*. New York: Facts on File, 1983.

Beard, James. *James Beard's American Cookery*. Boston: Little, Brown and Company, 1972.

———. *Beard on Bread*. New York: Alfred A. Knopf, 1974.

Beranbaum, Rose Levy. "Smooth, Creamy Cheesecake." *Fine Cooking,* November 1999, pp. 64–69.

Bettoja, Jo, and Anna Maria Cornetto. *Italian Cooking in the Grand Tradition*. New York: Dial Press, 1982.

Bittman, Mark. *How to Cook Everything*. New York: Macmillan, 1998.

Boni, Ada. *Italian Regional Cooking*. New York: Bonanza Books, 1969.

Brody, Jane. *Jane Brody's Nutrition Book*. New York: W. W. Norton, 1981.

Bugialli, Giuliano. *The Fine Art of Italian Cooking*. New York: Quadrangle/The New York Times Book Company, 1977.

———. *Giuliano Bugialli's Foods of Italy*. New York: Stewart, Tabori & Chang, 1984.

Carr, Sandy. *Simon & Schuster Pocket Guide to Cheese*. New York: Simon & Schuster, 1981.

Cheese Facts. Washington, DC: National Cheese Institute, 1998.

Chenel, Laura, and Linda Siegfried. *Chevre! The Goat Cheese Cookbook*. Santa Rosa, CA: Peaks Pike Publishing Company, 1983.

Corriher, Shirley. *Cookwise*. New York: William Morrow and Company, 1997.

———. "Cheesecake 101." *Fine Cooking*. November 1999, p. 74.

The Dallas Junior League Cookbook. Dallas: Dallas Junior League, 1976.

Duyff, Roberta Larson. *The American Dietetic Association's Complete Food and Nutrition Guide*. Minneapolis: Chronimed Publishing, 1996.

Edelman, Edward, and Susan Grodnick. *The Ideal Cheese Book*. New York: Harper & Row Publishers, 1986.

Ensrud, Barbara. *The Pocket Guide to Cheese*. New York: Perigee Books, 1981.

———. *Wine with Food.* New York: Fireside, 1991.

Forgione, Larry. *An American Place.* New York: William Morrow and Company, 1996.

Freeman, Sarah. *The Real Cheese Companion.* London: Little, Brown and Company, 1998.

Gayler, Paul. *A Passion for Cheese.* New York: St. Martin's Press, 1997.

Greenspan, Dorie. *Baking with Julia.* New York: Willam Morrow and Company, 1996.

Harbutt, Juliet. *Cheeses of the World.* New York: Lorenz Press, 1999.

Herbst, Sharon Tyler. *Food Lover's Companion.* 2nd ed. Hauppauge, NY: Barron's, 1995.

Jamison, Cheryl Alters, and Bill Jamison. *The Border Cookbook.* Boston: Harvard Common Press, 1995.

———. *The Rancho de Chimayo Cookbook.* Boston: Harvard Common Press, 1991.

———. *Texas Home Cooking.* Boston: Harvard Common Press, 1993.

Jenkins, Steven. *Cheese Primer.* New York: Workman Publishing, 1996.

Jones, Evan. *The World of Cheese.* New York: Alfred A. Knopf, 1984.

Labensky, Steven, et al. *Webster's New World Dictionary of Culinary Arts.* Upper Saddle River, NJ: Prentice Hall, 1997.

Madison, Deborah. *The Savory Way.* New York: Bantam Books, 1990.

———. *Vegetarian Cooking for Everyone.* New York: Broadway Books, 1997.

Mariani, John. *The Dictionary of American Food and Drink.* New York: Hearst Books, 1994.

———. *The Dictionary of Italian Food and Drink.* New York: Broadway Books, 1998.

Marshall, Lydie. *A Passion for Potatoes.* New York: Harper Perennial, 1992.

Masui, Kazuka, and Tomoko Yamada. *French Cheeses.* New York: DK Publishing, 1996.

Martinez, Zarela. *Food from My Heart.* New York: Macmillan, 1992.

McGee, Harold. *On Food and Cooking.* New York: Scribner, 1984.

McNair, James. *Cheese.* San Francisco: Chronicle Books, 1986.

Nantet, Bernard. *Cheeses of the World.* New York: Rizzoli International Publications, 1992.

Ogden, Bradley. *Bradley Ogden's Breakfast, Lunch, and Dinner.* New York: Random House, 1991.

Peel, Mark, and Nancy Silverton. *The Food of Campanile.* New York: Villard Books, 1997.

Pyles, Stephan. *The New Texas Cuisine.* New York: Doubleday, 1993.

Ridgway, Judy. *The Cheese Companion.* Philadelphia: Running Press, 1999.

Robinson, R. K., and R. A. Wilbey. *Cheesemaking Practice.* 3rd. ed. R. Scott, 1st ed. Gaithersburg, MD: Aspen Publishers, 1998.

Rombauer, Irma S., and Marion R. Becker. *Joy of Cooking.* Indianapolis: Bobbs-Merrill Company, 1975.

Rosso, Julee, and Sheila Lukins. *The Silver Palate Cookbook.* New York: Workman Publishing, 1982.

Saveur Cooks Authentic American. Editors of *Saveur* magazine. San Francisco: Chronicle Books, 1998.

Sax, Richard. *Classic Home Desserts.* Shelburne, VT: Chapters Publishing, 1994.

Suavez, F. L., D. A. Savaiano, and M. D. Levitt. "A Comparison of Symptoms After the Consumption of Milk or Lactose-Hydrolyzed Milk by People with Self-Reported Severe Lactose Intolerance." *New England Journal of Medicine* 333(1):1–4.

Sunset Books. *Cheese, How to Choose, Serve, and Enjoy.* Menlo Park, CA: Lane Publishing Company, 1986.

Sustaining Members of the Fort Worth Junior League. *Menu Cookbook.* Fort Worth: Fort Worth Junior League.

Teubner, Christian. *The Cheese Bible.* New York: Penguin Studio, 1998.

Timperley, Carol, and Cecilia Norman. *A Gourmet's Guide to Cheese.* Los Angeles: HP Books, 1989.

U.S. Department of Agriculture. *Cheeses of the World.* New York: Dover Publications, 1972.

Weir, Joanne. *You Say Tomato.* New York: Broadway Books, 1998.

Wells, Patricia. *Patricia Wells' Trattoria.* New York: William Morrow and Company, 1993.

Widcome, Richard. *The Cheese Book*. Secaucus, NJ: Chartwell Books, 1978.

Willinger, Faith. *Red, White & Greens*. New York: HarperCollins Publishers, 1996.

Wisconsin Cheesecyclopedia: Cheese at Foodservice. Madison Wisconsin Milk Marketing Board, 1995.

Zaslavsky, Nancy. *Meatless Mexican Home Cooking*. New York: St. Martin's Press, 1997.

Mail-Order Cheese Suppliers

Balducci's
New York, NY
Phone: (800) 225-3822
www.balducci.com

The Cheese Store of Beverly Hills
Beverly Hills, CA
Phone: (800) 547-1515
www.cheesestorebh.com

Dean & Deluca
New York, NY
Phone: (800) 221-7714
www.dean-and-deluca.com

Formaggio Kitchen
Boston, MA
Phone: (617) 354-4750

Fromages.com
www.fromages.com

Ideal Cheese Shop
New York, NY
Phone: (800) 382-0109
www.idealcheese.com

International Gourmet (Gourmet)
Phone: (877) 446-8763
www.igourmet.com

Marty's
Dallas, TX
Phone: (214) 526-4070
www.martysdfw.com

Murray's Cheese Shop
New York, NY
Phone: (212) 243-3289
(888) 692-4339
www.murraycheese.com

Say Cheese–La Grande Pantrie
Simsbury, CT
Phone: (888) 243-3373
www.saycheese-lgp.com

Specialty Cheese Company
Lowell, WI
Phone: (800) 367-1711
www.specialcheese.com

Zingerman's
Ann Arbor, MI
Phone: (888)636-8162
www.zingermans.com

*Small American Cheese Factories
with Mail-Order Service*

BelGioioso Cheese Inc.
Denmark, WI
Phone: (920)863-2123
www.belgioioso.com
Italian varieties, including
Gorgonzola and mascarpone

Bellwether Farms
Petaluma, CA
Phone: (707) 763-0993
www.bellwethercheese.com
Sheep milk cheeses

Brewster Dairy, Inc.
Brewster, OH
Phone: (800)874-8874
www.brewstercheese.com
Amish cheeses, Colby, Swiss,
Monterey Jack, farmer cheese, and
yogurt

Brier Run Chèvre
Birch River, WV
Phone: (304)649-2975
Goat cheeses

Cabot Creamery
Cabot, VT
Phone: (802)563-2231
www.cabotcheese.com
Cheddar

Capriole
Greenville, IN
Phone: (812)923-9408
Goat cheeses, including Old
Kentucky Tomme and Crocodile
Tears

Coach Farms
Pine Plains, NY
Phone: (518)398-5325
Goat cheeses

Cypress Grove
McKinleyville, CA
Phone: (707)839-3168
www.cypressgrovechevre.com
Goat cheeses, including Humboldt
Fog

Grafton Village Cheese Company
Grafton, VT
Phone: (800)472-3866
www.graftonvillagecheese.com
Cheddar

Hilmar Cheese Company
Hilmar, CA
Phone: (800)577-5772
www.hilmarcheese.com
Cheddar and Monterey Jack

Laura Chenel's Cheese
Sonoma, CA
Phone: (707)996-4477
Goat cheeses

Loleta Cheese Company
Loleta, CA
Phone: (707)733-5470
(800)995-0453
Fax: (707)733-1872

Marin French Cheese Company
Petaluma, CA
Phone: (800)292-6001
sfweb.sfnet.net/cheesefactory
Camembert, Brie, Breakfast
Cheese, and Schloss

Maytag Dairy Farms
Newton, IA
Phone: (800)247-2458
Maytag Blue cheese

Mozzarella Company
Dallas, TX
Phone: (214)741-4072
(800)798-2954
www.mozzco.com
Many varieties of mozzarella, mascarpone, Caciotta, ricotta, queso fresco, Scamorza, and goat cheeses

Old Chatham Sheepherding Company
Old Chatham, NY
Phone: (888)743-3760
www.oldsheepinn.com
Sheep milk cheeses

Park Cheese Company
Brownsville, WI
Phone: (920)583-3401
Pepato

Prima Käse
Monticello, WI
Phone: (608)938-4227
www.primakase.com
Old World cheese varieties

Redwood Hill
Sebastopol, CA
Phone: (707)823-8250
www.redwoodhill.com
Goat cheeses and yogurt

Rumiano Cheese Company
Crescent City, CA
Phone: (707)465-1535
Dry, Jack, Monterey Jack, and Cheddar

Sea Stars Goat Cheese
Santa Cruz, CA
Phone: (408)423-7200
Goat cheeses

Shelburne Farms
Shelburne, VT
Phone: (802)985-8686
www.shelburnefarms.org
Cheddar

Smith's Country Cheese
Winchendon, MA
Phone: (800)700-9974
www.verygouda.com
Gouda

Sonoma Cheese Factory
Sonoma, CA
Phone: (800)535-2855
www.sonomacheese.com
Cheddar, Jack, and Teleme cheeses

State of Maine Cheese Company
Rockport, ME
Phone: (800)762-8895
www.cheese-me.com
Cheddar and Monterey Jack

Straus Family Creamery
Marshall, CA
Phone: (415)663-5464
www.strausmilk.com
Cheddar, Monterey Jack, cottage cheese, crème fraîche, fromage blanc

Tomales Bay Foods/Cowgirl Creamery
Point Reyes Station, CA
Phone: (415)663-9335
www.cowgirlcreamery.com
Cottage cheese

Vella Cheese Company
Sonoma, CA
Phone: (800)848-0505
www.vellacheese.com
Dry Sonoma Jack, Monterey Jack, and blue cheese

Vermont Butter and Cheese
Websterville, VT
Phone: (802)479-9371
Goat cheese and mascarpone

Vermont Shepherd
Putney, VT
Phone: (802)387-4473
www.vermontshepherd.com
Aged sheep milk cheese

Westfield Farms
Hubbardston, MA
Phone: (508)928-5510
www.chevre.com
Blue goat cheese log, fresh goat
cheese, and aged cow cheese

Widmer Cheese Cellars
Theresa, WI
Phone: (920)488-2503
www.widmerscheese.com
Brick cheese, Cheddar, and Colby

Yerba Santa Goat Dairy
Lakeport, CA
Phone: (707)263-8131
Aged goat cheese

Cheesemaking Supplies

**New England Cheesemaking
Supply Company**
Ashfield, MA
Phone: (413)628-3808
www.cheesemaking.org
Cheesemaking ingredients,
equipment, and supplies

Useful Internet Cheese Sites

American Cheese Society
www.cheesesociety.org
Provides links to many
cheesemakers

American Dairy Association
www.ilovecheese.com

**California Cheese and Butter
Association**
www.cacheeseandbutter.org

Cheese from Spain
www.cheesefromspain.com

Cheese Net
www.wgx.com/cheesenet

The Cheese Reporter
www.cheesereporter.com

The Cheese Wizard
users.cgi.forne.com/cheese.wizard/
cfmboard.html

The Great Cheeses of New England
www.newenglandcheese.com

Italian Cheeses
www.formaggio.it

Vermont Cheese Council
www.vtcheese.com

Acknowledgments

I would like to thank the following people for their many kindnesses:

Kris Ackerman, for testing the recipes
Milton Perry, Tom Nixon, and **Nicole Duncan,** for keeping the Mozzarella
Company running smoothly
Steve Bulgarelli, for inspiration
Margaret Ann Cullum, for a friendly ear
Susan Derecskey, for editing
Barb Durben, for articles on food allergies
Janice Easton, for being my wonderful editor
Martha Gooding, for food styling
Janie Hibler, for finding my agent and for moral support
Judy Lippe, for nutrional information
Nick Malgieri, for his ricotta cheesecake recipe
Greg Milano, for food photography
Stephan Pyles, for always being there
Patricia Quintana, for inspiration and friendship
Toni Rachiele, for production editing
Lisa Smith, for creative help with the recipes
Zanne Stewart, for inspiration and invaluable advice

Judith Weber, for being my agent

Amy Whitelaw, for helping at the last moment

Suzanne Bartolucci and Carole Jordan, for believing in my dream

The cheesemakers of the Mozzarella Company, for making the most wonderful cheeses of all

All the customers of the Mozzarella Company throughout the years, for their undying support

The American Cheese Society, for recognizing my efforts from the very beginning

All my friends, far and wide, who have been there for me when I needed them

Index